Search Engine Optimization

Your visual blueprint™ for effective Internet marketing, 2nd Edition

by Kristopher B. Jones

WILEY

Wiley Publishing, Inc.

Search Engine Optimization: Your visual blueprint™ for effective Internet marketing, 2nd Edition

Published by
Wiley Publishing, Inc.
10475 Crosspoint Boulevard
Indianapolis, IN 46256

www.wiley.com

Published simultaneously in Canada

Library of Congress Control Number: 2010930727

ISBN: 978-0-470-62075-5

Manufactured in the United States of America

10 9 8 7 6 5 4 3 2

Trademark Acknowledgments

Contact Us

For general information on our other products and services please contact our Customer Care Department within the U.S. at 877-762-2974, outside the U.S. at 317-572-3993 or fax 317-572-4002.

For technical support please visit www.wiley.com/techsupport.

Temple Expiatori de la Sagrada Família (Church of the Holy Family)

A work in progress since 1882, the Sagrada Familia was initially designed in a neo-Gothic style by Francisco de Paula del Villar. Construction had barely begun when modernist architect Antoni Gaudí took over the project. Gaudí made drastic design changes and revised them constantly, so that upon his death in 1926 only one of a proposed 18 towers, a single façade, the apse, and the crypt — his final resting place — had been completed. Through two world wars and the civil war of 1936, this amazing cathedral has crept steadily toward completion, anticipated between 2026 and 2041.

For more about this and other Barcelona landmarks, see *Frommer's Barcelona,* 3rd Edition (ISBN 978-0-470-38747-4), available wherever books are sold or at www.Frommers.com.

Credits

Sr. Acquisitions Editor
Stephanie McComb

Sr. Project Editor
Sarah Hellert

Technical Editor
Vince Averello

Copy Editor
Scott Tullis

Editorial Director
Robyn Siesky

Editorial Manager
Rosemarie Graham

Business Manager
Amy Knies

Sr. Marketing Manager
Sandy Smith

Vice President and Executive Group
Publisher
Richard Swadley

Vice President and Executive Publisher
Barry Pruett

Sr. Project Coordinator
Lynsey Stanford

Graphics and Production Specialists
Carrie Cesavice
Andrea Hornberger
Jennifer Mayberry

Quality Control Technician
Lindsay Littrell

Proofreader
Melissa D. Buddendeck

Indexer
Estalita Slivoskey

Screen Artists
Ana Carrillo
Jill A. Proll
Ron Terry

Illustrator
Cheryl Grubbs

About the Author

Kristopher B. Jones is considered one of the top Internet marketing experts in the world. Kris is a frequent keynote speaker, presenter, and moderator at major national and international marketing conferences, including Search Engine Strategies (SES), Affiliate Summit, and the Electronic Retailer Association. Kris is also a sought-after speaker at colleges and universities around the country and has delivered inspirational lectures to thousands of college and graduate students at schools such as Penn State University, the University of Pittsburgh, and Villanova University.

Kristopher was the former President and CEO of Pepperjam, a full-service internet marketing agency and affiliate network, which Kris founded in 1999. During Kris' tenure at Pepperjam the company was recognized for three consecutive years by *Inc.* magazine as one of the fastest growing companies in the United States, and was celebrated as one of the best places to work in the State of Pennsylvania. Pepperjam was acquired by GSI Commerce (NASDAQ – GSIC), an e-commerce solutions and marketing services provider, in September 2009.

Kristopher was recognized as an Entrepreneur of the Year by Bank of America (2005), finalist for the prestigious Ernst & Young Entrepreneur of the Year (2008), and twice as one of the "Top 20 Business Leaders" in northeastern Pennsylvania under the age of 40 (2006, 2010). Kris' first book, *Search Engine Optimization: Your visual blueprint for effective Internet marketing,* sold more than 20,000 copies in its first two years in print and was ranked on Amazon.com as the best-selling book within the search-engine marketing category in 2008 and 2009.

An avid reader, traveler, public speaker, entrepreneur, and business leader, Kristopher truly defines a spiritually motivated individual dedicated to the community in which he lives. Since selling Pepperjam in 2009 Kris has launched several successful businesses and is in the process of writing his third book. Kris is a former senior staff member to Congressman Paul E. Kanjorski (PA-11).

Kristopher has participated on numerous technology, educational, and non-profit boards of director and advisory committees, including the Misericordia University Board of Trustees, the Great Valley Technology Alliance (Co-Chair), Penn State University (WB) Department of Information Science and Technology, Albany Law School Alumni Association, Pennsylvania Keystone Innovation Grant Committee (KIG), CAN BE Business Incubator, Greater Wilkes-Barre Chamber of Commerce Strategic Planning Committee, Luzerne Foundation Millennium Circle, and the United Way, among others.

Kristopher received a Bachelor of Arts from Pennsylvania State University, a Master of Science from Villanova University, and a Juris Doctorate from Albany Law School.

Learn more about Kris on his personal blog, located at www.krisjones.com.

Follow Kris on Twitter @krisjonescom and on Facebook at www.facebook.com/krisjonescom.

Contact Kris at kris@krisjones.com.

Author's Acknowledgments

The second edition of this book is dedicated to my loving family, including my wife Robyn, children Kris Jr. and Lauren, my mother Charlotte, my father "Harvey," my brother Rick, and my sister Jennifer. I'd also like to recognize the unconditional love, friendship, and continued support I receive from my mother-in-law Terry and father-in-law "Lenny" Martin.

The completion of the second edition of this book would not have been possible without the hard work of my editorial team at Wiley Publishing, including Stephanie McComb, Sarah Hellert, Scott Tullis, and Vince Averello. The professional suggestions and expertise I received throughout the writing process helped make this book a reality and the finished product something to be proud of.

Finally, I'd like to acknowledge Matthew Blancarte and Josh Mullineaux from Unique Blog Designs who worked diligently and within a strict time frame to launch my personal blog, located at www.krisjones.com. KrisJones.com provides readers of this book with a venue to ask follow-up questions and to share your suggestions for future editions.

How to Use This Visual Blueprint Book

Who This Book Is For

This book is for advanced computer users who want to take their knowledge of this particular technology or software application to the next level.

The Conventions in This Book

❶ Steps

This book uses a step-by-step format to guide you easily through each task. Numbered steps are actions you must do; bulleted steps clarify a point, step, or optional feature; and indented steps give you the result.

❷ Notes

Notes give additional information — special conditions that may occur during an operation, a situation that you want to avoid, or a cross reference to a related area of the book.

❸ Icons and Buttons

Icons and buttons show you exactly what you need to click to perform a step.

❹ Extra or Apply It

An Extra section provides additional information about the preceding task — insider information and tips for ease and efficiency. An Apply It section takes the code from the preceding task one step further and allows you to take full advantage of it.

❺ Bold

Bold type shows text or numbers you must type.

❻ Italics

Italic type introduces and defines a new term.

❼ Courier Font

`Courier font` indicates the use of scripting language code such as statements, operators, or functions, and code such as objects, methods, or properties.

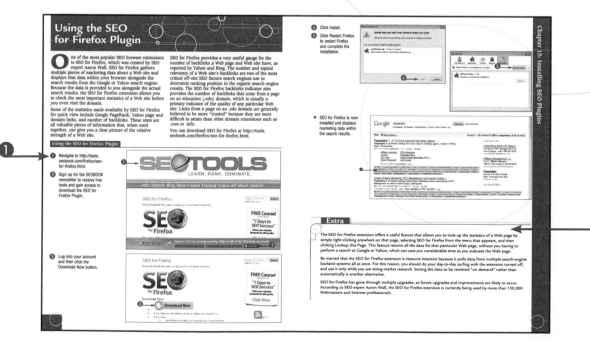

TABLE OF CONTENTS

TABLE OF CONTENTS

TABLE OF CONTENTS

THE HISTORY OF SEARCH-ENGINE OPTIMIZATION

Search-engine optimization, or *SEO*, is the process of setting up your Web site so that it ranks well for particular keywords within the organic search results of major search engines, including Google, Yahoo, and Bing. Unlike paid search marketing, which requires you to pay for every click sent to your Web site from a search engine, traffic sent to your site from a search engine's organic results is free.

In the early days of SEO, the process of gaining top ranking for keywords was much easier than it is today. In those "good old days," search-engine algorithms were easy to crack. All you had to do was include the keyword you wanted to rank for in the title tag of your Web page and sprinkle that keyword throughout the content of your page, and chances were you would rank within the top ten results of your favorite search engine. Not surprisingly, over the years search-engine algorithms have become increasingly complex, which has resulted in Web site owners either outsourcing SEO to professional firms or self-educating through books like this one.

Dating back to 1996 or so, search engines started to become a very popular tool for Web surfers looking for all sorts of information. Long before Google and Yahoo became popular, search engines such as AltaVista and InfoSeek were pioneers at providing search results to users within a fraction of a second. Search results in the early days were nowhere near as relevant as they are today. However, search-engine users in the millions began relying on Web sites like AltaVista more and more frequently to retrieve information about everything from health abnormalities to pricing on the latest gadget.

Search-engine optimization found its start in 1997 through public reports and commentary provided by search-engine experts, including Danny Sullivan and Bruce Clay, among others. Early reports about SEO looked at search-engine algorithms and how the various search engines ranked search results. Inspired entrepreneurs and Web site owners began studying these reports and testing strategies for how they could rank well within the search results. Before long the profession of search-engine optimization emerged and individuals were offering services to help rank Web sites on major search engines.

As the World Wide Web grew at a remarkable pace the popularity of AltaVista and Infoseek started to wane. Other search engines came and went, but no company has had more of an impact on search-engine marketing than Google.

Google: The Birth Child of Larry and Sergey

Google was cofounded by Larry Page and Sergey Brin while they were students at Stanford University. Although the company was officially incorporated in 1998, the idea of creating a search engine that would "organize the world's information and make it universally accessible and useful" began as part of a doctoral research project Larry and Sergey began in 1996.

The key to Google's early success was that the algorithm behind the Google search engine was different from the algorithms before it. Based on Larry and Sergey's experience with the process of academic research, they believed that Web page authority and relevance could be derived algorithmically by indexing the entire Web, and then analyzing who links to whom. This idea came from the fact that in academia authority is derived when researchers advance their own research by citing one another as part of the research process. Indeed, each piece of published scholarly work (including Larry and Sergey's dissertation) has a works-cited page at the end of each finished piece of written research, which includes a list of resources that were cited as relevant to the work being advanced.

Larry and Sergey took the process of citing in academic research, and hypothesized that Web pages with the most links to them from other highly relevant Web pages must be the most relevant pages associated with a particular search. To further bolster the concept, Larry and Sergey created PageRank (named after Larry Page), which not only counts how many links point to any given page, but also determines the quality of those links.

Although the Google algorithm is more complex than just analyzing who links to whom, the process of algorithmically analyzing links was a great idea that has separated Google from its competition. In fact, today Google is the leading search engine with more than 60 percent market share in the United States and is quickly becoming the preferred search engine in other parts of the world.

SEO: Beware of Snake Oil Salesman

Search-engine optimization is a critical component of a well-rounded Internet marketing strategy. Having a great Web site is simply not enough. Hundreds of millions of people use search engines every day to scour the Internet and find information from relevant Web sites just like yours. In order to appear alongside your competition in the search results, your Web site must be search engine friendly. Moreover, to be competitive within the search results you need to take steps that convince search engines that your Web site is an authority and that your content is relevant for particular keywords related to your business or enterprise.

If you are reading this book, you do not need convincing that SEO is integral to your online marketing success. However, the profession of SEO has taken significant criticism for being nothing more than a spammy attempt to manipulate search-engine results. Unfortunately, criticism has come primarily as a result of so-called SEO experts who sell guaranteed top ten placements and instant success formulas for achieving front page search-engine rankings. Fortunately, such unethical, get-rich-quick, snake oil salesman represent a very small percentage of SEO professionals.

The majority of SEO experts are ethical professionals who understand the complex dynamics of search-engine algorithms and offer assistance and counsel on how to maximize your placement on search engines. The truth is that there are no guarantees in SEO. In fact, if an alleged SEO professional tells you he offers guaranteed placement within Google's top ten organic rankings, you need to decline the offer. The process of SEO requires great skill and is not quick. You must have patience. In fact, you should look at SEO as an ongoing process that is necessary for you to maintain and maximize your position in the organic search results in the long term. You should set your expectations accordingly and educate other Web site owners of the process so they do not waste money based on hollow pitches from unethical SEO professionals.

Get Started

The first step to getting started with your search-engine-optimization campaign is to select a topic. If you already have a Web site covering a topic that you are satisfied with, then you may want to skip this step. However, keep in mind that you need to set realistic expectations based on your chosen topic. Increasing your Web site rankings for competitive topics is much more difficult than increasing rankings for less competitive topics.

To get the most from your SEO efforts, you must carefully consider your target audience. Your target audience includes the specific people you are trying to put your Web site in front of. Understanding who your target audience is and what they are searching for can greatly increase the effectiveness of a search-engine-optimization campaign.

Prior to beginning your SEO efforts, you should set goals, including how much money you want to dedicate to your efforts. If you are going to conduct SEO internally, you need to set a budget only around the tools you need and the amount of money you must allocate to paying your internal SEO team. If you intend to outsource your SEO, you should set aside a minimum of $3,000 to $5,000 monthly for a dedicated SEO professional.

Putting together an internal team of people to help with your SEO requires you to select one or more individuals with varying proficiency in HTML writing, knowledge of CSS, data analysis, graphical design, server administration, copywriting, link building, and blogging. Although the scope of your project dictates how many people you need to fill out your team, you can always consider outsourcing one or more components of the job.

Although writing large amounts of original content may seem like a daunting task, there are countless professional copywriters that can provide you with well-written content at a reasonable price. Moreover, online services such as Elance allow you to hire copywriters and other service providers through an auction system. The auction system allows you to post your work so that multiple service providers compete for the job. You have the option of comparing multiple vendors and ultimately choosing one or more based on skill level and past performance within the Elance network.

One of the best places to keep up-to-date with what is happening in the search-engine marketing industry is to read blogs and other online news sources. Blogs such as SearchEngineLand.com, seroundtable.com, and SEOmoz. com provide current perspectives and tips, and news Web sites including DMNews.com, ClickZ.com, and WebProNews.com provide breaking news and commentary on search-engine marketing.

Another way to increase your knowledge about the search-engine marketing space is to attend an industry conference. Leading search marketing conferences, including Search Engine Strategies (SES) (www.searchenginestrategies.com) and Search Marketing Expo (SMX) (www. searchmarketingexpo.com) offer dozens of educational sessions led by panels of search marketing experts.

Keyword Generation

Effective keyword generation is one of the most critical elements of successful search-engine optimization. All keywords are not created equal; some keywords are easier to rank for than others, and some keywords tend to be almost impossible to rank for. Broad or general keywords tend to be highly competitive and therefore should represent only a small portion of your overall SEO efforts. Specific keywords, which include those keywords that describe your specific product or service and are more than three keywords in length, are less competitive and therefore should make up the bulk of your keyword generation efforts.

For example, if you own an e-commerce Web site you stand a better chance of ranking within the top search results for product-level keywords than you do for broad keywords that generally describe your business. Although broad keywords tend to generate higher levels of search volume, product-level terms can generate significant search volume and tend to convert at higher rates than broad terms.

There are numerous useful keyword generation tools that can help you discover effective keywords for your Web site. Keyword generation tools such as Keyword Discovery, Wordtracker, and Google's Keyword Suggestion Tool allow you to carefully research, analyze, and filter potential keywords. It is not enough to just generate massive lists of keywords. Instead, your keyword lists should represent a cross section of broad and specific terms that your Web site stands a legitimate chance of ranking for. Because keyword generation is so critical to your SEO success, consider making a modest financial investment by purchasing subscriptions to tools such as Keyword Discovery, Rapid Keyword, and Wordtracker even though Google and other companies offer tools for free.

Keep in mind that despite the fact that keyword generation tools can quickly generate thousands upon thousands of keywords, each page of your Web site should be search engine optimized for only one or two keywords. Therefore, focus less on generating massive lists of keywords and more on generating keyword lists that directly relate to your Web site and give you the best shot at ranking well on search engines.

One of the most effective ways to generate target keywords beyond basic keyword generation is through competitive research. Readily available competitive research tools such as SEMRush, KeywordSpy, Compete.com, and KeyCompete provide various data about your competition, including what keywords your competitors rank for in the organic search results, as well as what keywords your competitors are using on pay-per-click search engines such as Google. Armed with competitive research information, you can compare your success to your competition and use the information to devise a plan of attack to improve your own ranking within the organic and paid search results.

Create Pages

For the purposes of search-engine optimization, keep in mind that search engines do not actually rank Web sites; instead, search engines rank individual Web pages. Therefore, in order to succeed with SEO each and every page of your Web site must be optimized for search-engine purposes. The most important element of each of your Web pages is substantial unique content. However, you can optimize numerous other important structural and technological factors on your Web pages to ensure that you position yourself to rank well within the search-engine results.

For example, optimizing technical on-site Web page factors such as adding correct filenames, title tags, meta description tags, meta keyword tags, and meta robots tags is crucial to making sure the search-engine spiders can determine the relevance of your Web site. Besides your domain name, the first things search engines discover when spidering through the pages of your Web site are your filenames. Every single page of your Web site resides in a different file. By titling your pages with search-engine optimization in mind, you have a powerful opportunity to establish relevance to a certain topic or keyword.

Each page of your Web site should contain a unique title tag that includes the target keywords you want to rank for. Search engines place great importance on the text contained within your title tag and use it as a primary indicator of what your Web page is about. Therefore, your title tag should include your target keywords and also provide a concise statement summarizing the content of your Web page.

Although search engines rarely use description and keyword tags for ranking purposes, each page of your Web site should include unique description and keyword tags. Description tags can be especially important because search engines often use them as the display text shown when a search query triggers your Web page. Therefore, your description tag should include a call-to-action marketing message so that your listing stands out among other listings and gets clicked.

Optimizing your content with header tags and other text modifiers allows you to stress the main ideas and topics that your content covers. Header tags are HTML tags used to apply significance to keywords or phrases within a Web page. Placing a selection of text within a header tag tells the search-engine spiders that the text is of a certain level of importance. Using text modifiers, you can emphasize certain blocks of text by bolding, italicizing, or underlining.

Taking care to optimize Web page images is important for those Web browsers that do not support images, and because search-engine spiders are unable to accurately read the content of an image, doing so presents an extra opportunity to add keyword-rich content to your page. Links provide the pathways that search-engine spiders need to find your Web pages. Creating links with search-engine optimization in mind is necessary for optimal results.

Throughout the process of creating Web pages you should try to adhere to the standards set forth by the W3 Consortium, which works to create standards in Web design and development that ensure Internet-wide compatibility.

Basic Web Site Structure

A well-optimized Web site design and structure helps to improve the overall performance of your Web site, making it easier for users to navigate and for search engines to find and index all of your content. You want to balance your Web site design between the needs of your users and the needs of the search engines. To be successful, your Web site should not only provide a superior user experience, but also include an optimal structure so that search engines index your content.

One way to ensure that search engines find all of your content is by submitting a sitemap. Think of your sitemap as an outline of your entire Web site. A sitemap displays the inner framework and organization of your Web site's structure to the search engines. A sitemap should reflect the entire navigational structure of your Web site so that search-engine spiders can find and index all of your content. As you add new content to your Web site, you should submit your sitemap to the search engines on a regular basis, every 24 hours or so.

To establish trust and credibility in the eyes of your visitors and search engines, your Web site should include both a company information and privacy page. A company

information page helps to strengthen your reputation in the eyes of both your Web site visitors and the search engines. Adding a company information page helps build trust with your visitors by explaining who you are and where you come from by providing company biographies, history, and staff photos.

In addition to a company information page, your Web site should also contain a page explaining your privacy policy. A privacy policy page helps to establish trust by declaring that you are committed to protecting the privacy of your visitors' personal information. Try to keep your privacy policy simple and make it easy to read, easy to understand, and easy to find on your Web site. You should consider adding a link to your privacy policy next to a link to your company information page. This way, your visitors can see that you are a trustworthy and legitimate entity.

Advanced Web Site Structuring

Once you have the basic structure of your Web site in place, you can implement several additional advanced structural considerations to optimize your site for search-engine purposes. For example, beyond setting up your Web site so that it is indexed, you may want to instruct the search engines not to index a particular page. A robots.txt file allows you to tell the spiders what they may and may not do when they arrive at your domain. Robots.txt files also provide you a means to prevent both potential copyright infringements and search-engine spiders from consuming excessive amounts of bandwidth on your server.

One primary example of advanced Web site structuring includes the use of the nofollow attribute. The nofollow attribute instructs search-engine spiders that they should not follow a particular link or view that link as anything of significance when determining ranking. Because search engines count links from your Web site to another Web site as a vote for search-engine ranking purposes, you can add nofollow if you do not want the search-engine spider to credit the link.

A second advanced Web site structural consideration is the way you structure your URLs. URLs must be structured so that they are easily spidered and organized and create a user-friendly Web site navigation system. For example, search engines as well as people prefer URLs that are simple and that include the keywords describing the page within the URL string.

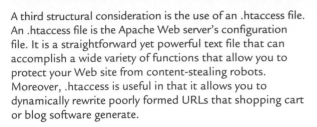

A third structural consideration is the use of an .htaccess file. An .htaccess file is the Apache Web server's configuration file. It is a straightforward yet powerful text file that can accomplish a wide variety of functions that allow you to protect your Web site from content-stealing robots. Moreover, .htaccess is useful in that it allows you to dynamically rewrite poorly formed URLs that shopping cart or blog software generate.

Other advanced Web site structural considerations include using `mod_rewrite` to rewrite URLs, redirecting non-www traffic to your www domain, and using 301 redirects whenever you change or redesign your Web site. Each advanced structuring technique provides you with procedures to ensure that search engines recognize your Web site and that each of your Web pages are correctly indexed.

Content Creation

Creating well-written, original content is absolutely critical to your long-term search-engine-optimization success. Content is what visitors use to determine value and one of the primary factors that search engines use to rank your Web site. Whether your Web site ends up on the first page or the one-hundredth page of Google largely depends on the quality and relevance of your content.

Although you should keep SEO principles in mind when you create content, the key to building long-term ranking on search engines is to write content for people, not search engines. Original and naturally flowing content provides your readers with a positive, enjoyable user experience and greatly improves your chances of top search-engine rankings. Avoid writing content solely for search-engine-optimization purposes and you can greatly increase your likelihood of long-term SEO success.

When you write content, you must avoid duplicate content. Duplicate content occurs when your Web site contains content that already exists on the World Wide Web. Duplicate content issues can have a detrimental effect on your SEO success and should be avoided at all costs. Writing original content is the most obvious way to avoid duplicate content. If you feel that you do not have the time to build large amounts of unique content, you can employ tools on your Web site, such as user reviews, that allow for user-generated content. User-generated content allows your content to remain fresh, which is one of the factors search engines use to rank one Web site over another with similar authority.

Writing original content and adding user-generated content does not entirely protect you from duplicate content issues. You must protect yourself from others stealing your content because Google cannot algorithmically detect who owns content. Fortunately, tools such as Copyscape are available that help you avoid and prevent duplicate content issues.

Although you should write content for people and not search engines, you should also use proper keyword density throughout each page of your Web site. First, you want to optimize each page of your Web site for no more than one or two target keywords, while at the same time making sure that you do not inadvertently repeat nontarget keywords. By using available tools to maximize optimal keyword density, you can incorporate a substantial number of target keywords throughout your content without compromising the naturally flowing aesthetics of the writing.

You should keep in mind a few important content creation principles as you build your Web site. First, search-engine algorithms cannot read text that is included in images. Therefore, always include important text and target keywords that appear in images in text form. You can still use images, but search engines cannot read the text contained within them. Second, when drafting your content you can use a powerful content creation principle called *latent semantic content,* which involves using keywords very similar to your target keywords to enhance the theme and relevance of your page. For example, if your target keyword is "Old Spice," you can also use words like "deodorant" and "cologne" to enhance the thematic relatedness and relevancy of your page for your target keyword "Old Spice."

Create Communities

Creating a community such as a blog or forum on your Web site is one of the most effective ways to keep your content fresh, while helping to establish your site as an authority for your given area of business. Search engines such as Google favor Web sites with fresh content over similarly authoritative Web sites that do not update content as often. Starting a community is easy and inexpensive.

A clear benefit of creating a community on your Web site is the fact that communities promote interaction and content creation among your users. User-generated content from blogs and forums is a great way to build a reputation as an authority and provides you with opportunities to gain additional, unanticipated search-engine rankings.

A *blog* is an online journal or diary that is frequently updated by an author and typically allows readers to interact by providing comments after each blog post is published. Regardless of what kind of Web site you own, having a blog is a good idea. First, a blog provides clear search-engine-optimization benefits through controlled content creation and user-generated content via user comments. Second, a blog helps to establish you as an expert. As an expert, other Web sites will link to your content, which helps to improve your search-engine ranking. Third, blogs are sticky. In other words, your users will want to join your RSS feed and come back to your Web site frequently to check for new content and learn about your products and services.

Blogs are a great tool for communicating special offers and deals to loyal readers, and they allow you to go into detail about specific products that might require detailed explanation. For example, if you are about to launch a new product that includes a new, revolutionary way of doing something, a blog allows you to make the case for the benefits and usefulness of the product versus older-generation products.

Unlike a blog, a *community forum* is a discussion board where members and forum moderators interact by posting questions and answers and discussing common problems. A forum encourages your visitors to return again and again by allowing interaction and information sharing.

Because forums are ultimately message boards where people ask and answer questions, a forum can provide a great place to refer a customer who has a question that may be shared by other members of the community. If a visitor has a question about the durability of a particular product or is unsure about one product over another, a forum provides a venue to get feedback and to generate interest in your products.

Having a forum on your Web site allows you to understand more about your visitors by reading the conversations and discussions between them. You can use this type of information to minimize demand placed on your customer service by addressing a customer concern before it spreads. Additionally, you can use a forum to ask your customers about what products they want that you do not currently have.

Regardless of whether it is good or bad, consumer feedback can be invaluable and can help you market your products or services more effectively. Keep in mind that a forum on your Web site does not solely have to be about promoting your products and services. Equally valuable is the information that you can get from your customers to improve your overall Web site initiatives.

Build Links

If creating large amounts of original, well-written content is considered King for search-engine-optimization purposes, building quality links back to your Web site might be considered the Holy Grail. You must have more than just quality content, because Google and other major search-engine algorithms evaluate the number and quality of Web sites that link to your Web pages as a primary and fundamental component of ranking your Web site over another.

Search engines conclude that Web sites with more backlinks must be more popular and authoritative than Web sites with fewer backlinks. Keep in mind that search-engine algorithms not only evaluate the number and quality of backlinks going to your Web site, but also what those links say in the form of anchor text. *Anchor text* is the text contained in front of a hyperlink from one page to another.

Building links is sort of like trying to answer the age-old question of what comes first, the chicken or the egg. Should you just build great content and wait for other Web sites to link to you, or should you proactively recruit others to link to your site?

If you are serious about search-engine optimization, you should proactively and aggressively build links. It is true that if you build original, compelling content, others are likely to link to your Web site, and over time Google might conclude that you are an authority. However, the process of gaining and maintaining search-engine ranking is very competitive, and if you want to rank well in the search results you need to have not only great content, but also quality, relevant backlinks.

All links are not created equal. Although quantity is important, focus on trying to build quality and relevant links. Relevant links come from Web sites related to your line of business and content. For example, if you have a gourmet food Web site, getting a link from *Gourmet Retailer* magazine is better than getting a link from an equally popular celebrity gossip Web site. Quality links tend to come from popular Web sites that are generally trusted sources. Two of the main measures of popularity are Google's PageRank and the Alexa ranking system.

PageRank gives you a rough idea of how authoritative Google thinks the Web site is, and Alexa provides a measure to compare the traffic volume of potential linking partners. In general, you should look for quality and relevant linking partners that have PageRank scores and Alexa rankings as good as or better than your own. A popular tool for helping you evaluate the quality of links is called Linkscape, which includes both free and paid versions.

Building links can be extremely time consuming and may even cost money if you decide to use a link broker or a pay-per-post network. One of the more time-consuming forms of link building includes requesting one-way or reciprocal links directly from other Web sites. The process usually involves reaching out to potential link partners via e-mail and asking politely for a link or suggesting a barter situation where you link to them if they link to you.

Another way of building links is through blog and forum participation. However, in many cases, search engines such as Google either devalue or do not count blog and forum comments as links toward your PageRank. Despite this, other search engines use links from blogs and forums for ranking purposes.

Sending out online press releases through companies such as PRWeb and the PR Newswire is a great way to build links. Blogs and other content providers use press release services as a source for article ideas. Typically, when other people use your release as a basis or a source for an article, they also provide a link back to your Web site. In other cases, content aggregators reproduce and distribute your content, keeping in place any anchor-text-rich links that you may have strategically inserted into the body of your press release.

The most simple and easy way to build links is to buy them through link brokers and pay-per-post networks. However, consider carefully before you use link brokers and pay-per-post networks because search engines such as Google have strict policies against the use of paid links as a way of increasing PageRank. If Google concludes that one of your links is not natural, the link is likely to be devalued for PageRank purposes. Keep in mind that despite Google's policies against buying links for purposes of boosting PageRank, purchasing links from high-quality, relevant Web sites has other benefits, including branding and traffic generation.

Google Analytics

Google Analytics is a free analytics solution that was designed to give you a complete view of every aspect of activity on your Web site. Understanding how to properly analyze and implement the numerous types of data Google Analytics provides gives you a considerable edge over your competition in the quest for top organic search rankings. Moreover, Google Analytics gives you a high-level view of your Web site traffic and user interaction, which allows you to analyze the various traffic sources coming to your Web site. You can take this information to improve your overall traffic-generation strategies, including pay-per-click, search-engine optimization, affiliate marketing, and any other traffic sources.

Google Analytics is free and easy to install. The most important detail in the installation process is making sure that your tracking code is correctly placed on every single page of your Web site. This ensures that all of your Google Analytics reports are as accurate and reliable as possible. After you have Google Analytics in place, you can analyze your traffic data in various ways. Looking through your traffic sources in Google Analytics is a simple way of finding out what keywords are sending you traffic.

Another way to use Google Analytics is to set and track goals. For example, if your Web site tracks orders through a shopping cart or leads in the form of a newsletter subscription, e-mail submit, or catalog request, goal tracking allows you to evaluate the number of transactions that occurred and the keyword that triggered the conversion. Goal tracking is especially useful when targeting keywords in your SEO efforts. Knowing ahead of time what keywords are already converting for your site and targeting those keywords until you reach the top organic positions is a very effective SEO strategy.

Google Analytics allows you to not only track traffic that is coming to your Web site, but also any traffic that may leave in the form of an external click. For example, if you are setting up any traffic trades or promoting any affiliate offers on your Web site, you will want to keep track of how many clicks you are sending to external sites.

A key benefit of Google Analytics is that you can send yourself or colleagues e-mail reports. You can also provide others with access to your Analytics account with full or restricted access. Moreover, reports can be sent and downloaded in multiple popular formats including PDF and CSV, which make it very easy to combine or compare reports across different online and offline sources.

Social Media Optimization

Social media optimization, or *SMO*, is a form of online marketing that focuses on participating on various social media Web sites to generate traffic, buzz, and links back to your Web site. Social media Web sites include social news Web sites such as Digg, Sphinn, and StumbleUpon; video-sharing Web sites such as YouTube and Revver; and social network Web sites, including Facebook, Twitter, Google Buzz, and LinkedIn. Various recognized SEO and SMO pundits have referred to SMO as "the new SEO" because SMO is often used as an effective and powerful method to quickly build large numbers of links back to your Web site, which can lead to improved organic search-engine rankings.

Leading social networks contain millions of active members. Although there is a common misconception that only teenagers use Web sites like MySpace and Facebook, millions of adults also use social networks to stay in touch with old and new friends and interact through sharing pictures, videos, and more. In fact, an increasing number of businesses are currently using Facebook and most recently Twitter as a vehicle to manage reputation, build brand recognition, promote products, and generate buzz.

Facebook has become the largest and most actively used social network with more than 400 million members. You can use Facebook to interact with current and prospective business associates while generating considerable traffic to your Web site and buzz about your business. Facebook is a service used by businesses of all sizes and people of all ages to network and communicate in real time.

In addition to a personal profile page, Facebook also allows you to create dedicated pages, commonly referred to as "fan pages," to promote your business. A dedicated Facebook fan page allows you to provide fans with your company overview, Web site(s), contact info, press releases, videos, blog RSS, Twitter updates, company news, and status. You can also interact with your fans by responding to comments they post to your fan page, as well as through other social networking tools made available through Facebook.

StumbleUpon is a peer- and social-networking technology that includes a toolbar that you install in your Web browser. The StumbleUpon toolbar allows you to discover and rate Web pages, videos, photos, and news articles. Getting your Web pages, videos, photos, and news articles submitted to StumbleUpon is an effective way to generate buzz, traffic, and build backlinks to your Web site.

Twitter is a free social networking service that allows you to micro-blog by sending short "updates" of 140 characters or less to others via a text message from your mobile phone, by typing a message from the Twitter site, or using instant messaging from Jabber or Google Talk. Twitter is a great way to build a list of followers. For business purposes, you can quickly send messages to your Twitter friends when a popular item comes back into stock or as a means to share a special offer or deal.

Twitter Search is Twitter's powerful and increasingly popular real-time search engine. Unlike major search engines like Google, Bing, and Yahoo that update their search indexes every few days or weeks, Twitter Search updates its entire database of news and personal updates, also known as *tweets*, as they occur. The most powerful way to use Twitter Search and build the amount of people who follow you on Twitter is to type keywords into Twitter Search that relate to your specific product or service. Once Twitter delivers search results, you should follow those users who mention the target keyword.

LinkedIn is a popular business-oriented social networking site that allows you to network with like-minded business professionals and build a list of contacts. By building a database of contacts with people you know and trust in business, you have access to a large network of friends with whom you can conduct business, offer jobs, and promote your business. LinkedIn is an effective network for sharing professional information and news about your business-related activities.

Video sharing Web sites such as YouTube and Revver allow users to upload, view, and share video clips. Videos are a great way to promote your business or to generate buzz and interest in your Web site. The most effective videos either tend to make people laugh or are extremely creative and unique. For example, some of the most viral videos on YouTube are homegrown videos that contain something outrageous or embarrassing. In addition, videos put a face on an otherwise faceless business pitch. Videos build trust in your users and can even result in a "celebrity" or "cult" following if people find your videos interesting.

Social news Web sites such as Digg and Sphinn allow users to submit news stories for other members to view and vote on. News stories that are most timely or interesting tend to make it to the front page of social news Web sites like Digg, which can generate thousands of unique visitors and hundreds of links back to your Web site within a few hours.

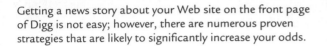

Getting a news story about your Web site on the front page of Digg is not easy; however, there are numerous proven strategies that are likely to significantly increase your odds.

Create Pay-per-Click Campaigns

With search-engine optimization (SEO), your goal is to rank for free within the organic search results for target keywords related to your Web site. In contrast, with pay-per-click (PPC) your goal is to pay for placement by competing with other advertisers for ranking within the sponsored results section of search results. There is no charge when someone clicks your organic listing, but you are charged every time someone clicks your PPC listing. PPC listings are typically designated as sponsored listings and appear above and to the right of the organic results.

Regardless of your SEO success you should also use PPC as a primary method to promote your Web site. In fact, research suggests that having both a high-sponsored and high-organic ranking greatly increases the credibility of your Web site and, therefore, increases the traffic to your Web site. If you think of the search results page as a piece of real estate, a powerful strategy is to get your Web site onto that piece of property as many times as you can.

The largest and most popular PPC advertising platform is Google AdWords, but competitive platforms are available through Yahoo Search Marketing and MSN adCenter. Before you open a PPC account on Google and start spending money, familiarize yourself with the structure of various components of an AdWords account. You should also study the various free educational resources Google provides.

All major PPC engines allow you to target your ads in various ways. The most common form of targeting is *geo-targeting*, which allows you to display your PPC ads in specific geographical regions. Geo-targeting is especially effective for regional businesses and can be used as a strategy to test various regional markets.

Another popular form of targeting is called *dayparting*, which involves showing your PPC ads only during specific times of the day or week. For example, you may find that your conversion rate slips on Mondays and Wednesdays and peaks from 9:00 a.m. to 5:00 p.m. Tuesdays and Fridays. With dayparting technology you tell the search engines what days and at what times you want to activate or pause your PPC ads.

Writing effective ad copy, using available keyword matching options, and setting effective bid strategies are important components of a successful PPC advertising campaign. Each of the major search engines allows you to draft multiple advertisements. The search engines test each of your advertisements and serve the ads with the highest click-through rates most often. Writing effective ad copy means using compelling language that separates your ads from the competition, entices people to click, and contains a high conversion rate.

Keyword matching options are important because they tell the search engine how broadly or specifically you want to advertise based on the keywords you bid on. For example, using a broad-match option on the keyword "cheese" might trigger your advertisement when a user types the popular keyword "Chuck E. Cheese" into a search engine. On the other hand, using an exact-match option on the keyword "cheese" will trigger your advertisement only when the exact word "cheese" is typed into a search engine.

Understanding basic and advanced PPC account reporting is critical to maximizing your advertising spend and analyzing your PPC advertising success. A major benefit of PPC advertising is robust, real-time, keyword-level PPC reporting. If you choose, you have the option of digging as deep as you want into the efficacy of your PPC initiatives. In addition, you can select to use conversion tracking, which allows you to set conversion goals and monitor return-on-investment, or *ROI,* at the keyword level.

Once you have spent a reasonable amount of time getting to know the inner workings of a PPC account, you are ready to deposit money and begin generating targeted Web site traffic. Keep in mind that you will be charged for all clicks in real time. Make sure you set strict budget limits at first and go slow. Your methodology and diligence will determine your ultimate success, not how many keywords and campaigns you have active at any given time.

Quality Score Optimization

Quality score optimization, or *QSO,* is a set of strategies for improving quality score. Quality score is a principal ranking factor that search engines use to determine your relative ranking and pricing for a particular keyword listing. In today's PPC advertising environment, the highest bidder does not always win. Instead, Google and other leading search engines rank Web sites based on numerous quality factors, and use your designated maximum cost per click as only one of many factors that determine whether you achieve a given keyword placement. The goal of QSO is to understand the factors that Google and others use to calculate quality score so that you can maintain PPC advertisements at the highest possible position and the lowest cost per click.

The primary factors that search engines consider for calculating quality score are click-through rate, ad group and campaign structure, ad copy, landing page quality, and keyword bid. Note that many of the quality score factors influence one another. For example, the quality of your ad copy almost certainly affects your click-through rates, and your ad group and campaign structure is likely to influence your perceived landing page quality.

Click-through rate refers to the percentage of times your ad was clicked compared to how many times it was shown. The higher your click-through rate is for any given keyword-ad combination, the higher quality the search engines are likely to rate your advertisement, and the lower the price you will have to pay for placement. One way of quickly improving your click-through rates is to remove keywords with low click-through rates from your ad groups. Another way to improve click-through rates is to write more appealing ad copy.

The structure of your ad groups and campaign can influence quality score. For example, ad groups that have large numbers of unrelated keywords are likely to have low-quality scores because the search engines conclude that your advertisements do not accurately reflect each keyword in your ad group. Similarly, the search engines might perceive campaigns that contain numerous unrelated ad groups as less relevant. Ad groups that contain keywords that are tightly related and include well-written ad copy tend to have higher-quality scores. Moreover, making sure that your campaigns are closely related is likely to improve your quality score.

Writing multiple advertisements and making sure that your ad copy is well written and appealing is one of the most effective ways to improve your quality score. As mentioned earlier, your ad copy must directly relate to the keywords in your ad group. One way of doing this is to use advanced methods that allow you to dynamically insert your target keyword into the advertisement.

Google and the other search engines allow you to test multiple advertisements. Therefore, you should submit numerous advertisements, making sure that you include enticing ad copy that contains the keywords you want to

rank for. The search engines show each of the advertisements until one or more of the ads emerge with the highest click-through rate.

Landing page quality refers to the perceived value and relevancy of the page that you send your PPC traffic to. Landing page quality is so important that a low landing page score can be disastrous to your overall PPC advertising initiatives. In fact, if you have a poor landing page score you may be required to pay as much as 10 dollars per click for placement on a keyword, whereas another advertiser deemed to have a high landing page score pays only 35 cents for the same keyword placement. Some of the factors that affect your landing page score are the relatedness of your ad copy and landing page and whether the keyword you are bidding on is included on the landing page. Google also appears to take into consideration the PageRank of your Web site, as well as how many people link to the landing page in question.

Your *keyword bid* is the maximum that you are willing to pay for a click on a particular keyword or ad group of keywords. Your quality score directly and significantly affects the amount you pay for a given click. In general, the more you are willing to pay, the more likely your ad will appear. However, as an overall ranking factor, keyword bid is much less a primary indicator of position that it was in the past. The more effective you are in increasing your quality score based on the factors mentioned earlier, the less you have to pay per click and the higher your ranking is likely to be.

This approach to QSO is not exhaustive. Quality score is a very dynamic and complex algorithm and is likely to be tweaked and changed as Google and the other search engines constantly strive to improve search quality and make more money.

Optimize for Other Engines

Internet search allows you to retrieve information at lightning speed. Although search engines such as Google, Yahoo, and Bing are the most common forms of search sites, many Web sites specialize in organizing very specific types of Web sites rather than trying to index the entire Internet. Getting your site exposure on these more-targeted search engines can send extra traffic or allow you to target a niche that may be too competitive to rank for in the major search engines.

Technorati is a popular search engine for searching blogs. If you can get your blog to rank well on Technorati, you can gain considerable exposure and traffic. Moreover, other bloggers use Technorati to look for stories to write about. In this way, getting your blog ranked on Technorati can be used as an effective link-building strategy.

Del.icio.us is a popular social bookmarking Web site that allows users to share the sites that they visit most frequently and allows other users to gauge which sites on the Internet are most popular. Many users like to browse the bookmarks of other people with similar tastes, so showing up on these lists is essential to your success. Be sure to build out your own del.icio.us profile and become part of the community.

Google Images is a popular service for searching images. Getting Google Images to index your images can potentially lead to significant traffic, especially because Google recently began to show their image results at the top of their regular organic listings.

If you sell products, chances are you can benefit from having your products listed in shopping search engines, such as Shopping.com, Shopzilla, and BizRate.com. Shopping search engines accept product feeds from online retailers and allow users to search and sort these lists by various criteria. Keep in mind that most shopping search engines require you to pay them on a cost-per-click or cost-per-action basis.

Whether potential customers find your products on auction services such as eBay and classified services such as Craigslist greatly depends on whether your listings are optimized for the eBay and Craigslist search engines. Your title and description for both services should include keywords that someone looking for your product is most likely to use. Moreover, you should include text to describe each of the images you use to promote your products.

Monetize Web Site Traffic

You may not have an e-commerce Web site that has an obvious monetization method. Instead, you may have a great Web site with unique, well-written content that generates a lot of traffic, and you may wonder how you can effectively monetize your traffic. The Internet opens up the door to making lots of money without having to actually sell anything. In fact, with revolutionary money-making models such as affiliate marketing, contextual advertising, and ad widgets, many Web site owners can make enough money to significantly supplement existing income or in some cases support lucrative full-time employment.

The most commonly used tool for making money from your Web site traffic is Google AdSense. Google AdSense is a contextual advertising technology that serves ads from the Google AdWords Content Network based on contextual relevance. All you have to do is insert a piece of code into your Web site where you want the ads to appear and Google does the rest. The most impressive thing about Google AdSense is the sophistication of the technology. Instead of having to worry that Google might serve ads unrelated to your content, Google's technology has an incredible track record of serving highly relevant advertisements, which enhances the user experience and encourages visitors to come back to your Web site in the future. Even if they leave your Web site by clicking an ad, you get paid a percentage of the amount that the advertiser pays Google to display the ad. Affiliate marketing is responsible for generating billions of dollars in e-commerce each year. Affiliate marketing allows you to monetize your Web site traffic by partnering with various merchants on a pay-for-performance basis. You get paid only when a lead or sale is referred through your Web site. Thousands of merchants, including many of the largest and most recognized brands in the United States such as Target, Apple, Dell, Amazon, and Wal-Mart, have affiliate programs. These companies pay you a percentage of any sales referred when you promote them on your Web site. In addition, a number of businesses, including many notable insurance, real estate, and dating companies, pay you a flat fee every time you refer a lead through your Web site.

Top affiliates such as Upromise, Cashbaq.com, and Brad's Deals make millions of dollars per year in commission. If you have a niche Web site or know how to effectively supplement your organic traffic with targeted pay-per-click traffic, you are likely to benefit significantly from promoting affiliate marketing offers. The big three affiliate networks are Commission Junction, LinkShare, and Performics. Other newer networks such as AZN and Pepperjam Network are using innovative approaches and technologies to help affiliates monetize Web site traffic and bank large commission checks.

SEO Plugins

SEO plugins provide you with on-demand information about various aspects of search-engine optimization. Instead of having to run a specific program every time you want to learn more about a Web site, you simply install an

SEO plugin, such as the Google Toolbar, that directly interacts with your Web browser in real time to retrieve important technical information about the Web site you are visiting. SEO plugins typically display information in the form of a toolbar or by integrating with your Web browser or e-mail client.

The Google Toolbar is a plugin that interacts with your Web browser to provide useful information about the Web pages you visit. The Google Toolbar includes a range of useful SEO features, including the PageRank of each page you visit, a tool to highlight a given keyword within a page, and an AutoFill option to cut down on the time you spend typing the same information over and over again. The Google Toolbar is free and is highly customizable based on your needs. Note that during installation you will be asked if you approve of Google collecting information about your browsing behavior. Although Google may use this information to serve more relevant advertisements and deliver a more personalized search experience, you need to consider the benefits versus legitimate privacy concerns.

The Alexa Toolbar is a useful plugin that provides information about the traffic ranking of Web sites. Note that Alexa collects information from users who have installed an Alexa Toolbar, allowing Alexa to provide statistics on Web site traffic. Because Alexa collects data only from individuals who install the Alexa Toolbar, many commentators have suggested that Alexa rankings are skewed toward the Webmaster community because a high proportion of Webmasters install the toolbar and the average person surfing the Web does not. Despite this, the Alexa Toolbar allows you to perform multiple levels of competitive analysis and community research throughout your SEO campaigns, while also offering you a shortcut to the information provided on the www.alexa.com Web site.

One of the most useful and popular SEO browser extensions is SEO for Firefox, which gathers multiple pieces of marketing data about a Web site and displays that data within your browser alongside the search results from the Google or Yahoo search engines. Some of the statistics SEO for Firefox makes available for quick view include Google PageRank, Yahoo page and domain links, and number of backlinks.

If you use WordPress to manage your blog, you can benefit from various plugins that assist the search-engine-optimization process. For example, installing a WordPress Title Tag plugin allows you to customize each title tag on your Web site. Installing a WordPress Description Tag plugin allows you to easily customize the description meta tag on each of your Web pages, and installing a WordPress Sitemap Generator makes sure that you are notifying the search engines each time content is updated on your Web site.

Choose a Topic

I f you are starting from scratch and do not have a previously developed Web site to begin working on, choosing a topic for your Web site is the first step in starting a successful search-engine-optimization plan. The topic you choose can have a dramatic effect on both the quality of the results your search-engine optimization achieves as well as the speed at which you can achieve them.

Increasing your Web site rankings for competitive topics is much more difficult than increasing rankings for less competitive topics. Examples of highly competitive topics include mortgages, debt relief, and prescription medications. Web sites concentrating on these topics can be extremely lucrative to Web site owners if they manage to generate visitors. Even one visitor to a mortgage application Web site can produce a large profit if that visitor applies and is approved for a mortgage.

If you are starting a brand-new Web site with dreams of becoming profitable quickly, you may not want to start by focusing on these highly competitive terms. Web sites ranking highly for terms like "mortgages" have likely been around for many years, contain a tremendous amount of content, and possess thousands of relevant inbound links. The importance of factors such as Web site age, quality and quantity of content, and quality and quantity of inbound links are discussed in later chapters.

Unless your Web site already possesses those factors, you should choose a less competitive topic. Optimizing for less competitive topics can provide quicker and more impressive ranking results. If you are developing a Web site about mortgages, consider focusing on a specific topic within the overall topic of "mortgages," such as "Pennsylvania mortgages" or the even more specific "Wilkes-Barre mortgages." Although less traffic exists for these more specific terms, there is also less competition and a higher likelihood of early success.

Choose a Topic

❶ Navigate to www.google.com.

❷ Search for a popular topic, such as "mortgages."

● Notice 37,800,000 results.

③ Search for "pennsylvania mortgages."

● Notice 14,700,000 results.

④ Search for "wilkes barre mortgages."

● Notice 190,000 results.

Fewer results implies less competition within a particular niche.

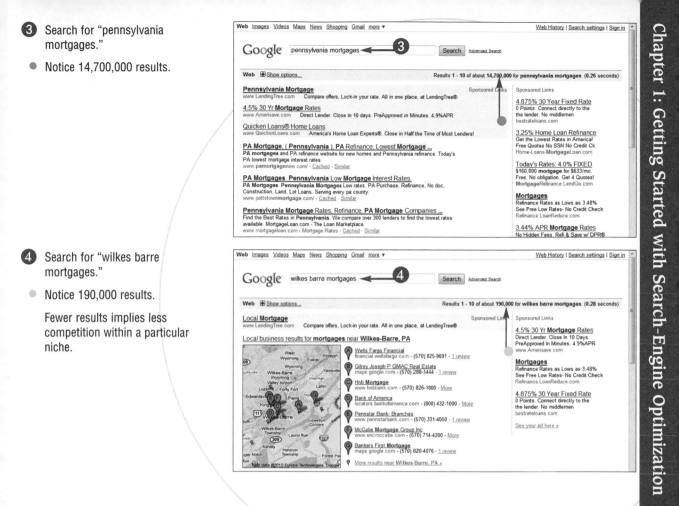

Extra

Most general terms are very competitive and extremely difficult to rank for. Keywords and phrases span from very general to very specific. An example of this progression would be pets, dogs, large dogs, Great Danes, brown Great Dane puppies.

The term "pets" is very general, and although the traffic for such a term is enormous, that traffic may not translate into a large number of sales. If you are creating a Web site or marketing a Web site about breeding Great Danes, the Web site is more likely to succeed if specific terms are targeted.

Google provides free access to its Keyword Tool at https://adwords.google.com/select/KeywordToolExternal. Type any keyword or phrase into this tool, and it generates a list of related terms, displays the amount of advertiser competition, and displays how much volume those searches received that month across the search engine. This tool is extremely useful if you are building out a pay-per-click advertising campaign, which is discussed in more detail in Chapters 11 and 12.

Find Your
Target Audience

To get the most from your search-engine-optimization efforts, you should design and optimize your Web site for your target audience. Your target audience is the group of people who you are trying to reach through your online marketing efforts. Target audiences are often defined by demographics such as age groups, nationalities, or specific interests. Understanding who your target audience is and what they are searching for can greatly increase the effectiveness of a search-engine-optimization campaign.

Make sure you are speaking your target audience's language when optimizing your Web site. If your business is an online marketing company, your main focus is to generate more traffic to your customers' Web sites. If you focus all your efforts on gathering visitors searching for the term "online marketing company," you are missing traffic from people searching for "online media buying," "pay-per-click advertising," and "search-engine optimization." Make sure you speak the same language on your Web site that your target audience

uses. More advanced keyword research and analysis is discussed in Chapter 2.

Research and analysis uncovers the key terms and phrases that Web users are searching for. This may be as simple as figuring out what terminology people are using when searching. Are people searching for "seo" or "search engine optimization"? You can use a tool like Google Trends to discover trends in the popularity of different search queries.

Knowing your target audience also provides you the opportunity to identify other online marketing opportunities. If your target audience is primarily the teenage demographic, marketing on platforms such as MySpace could be lucrative. If your target audience is mostly young college graduates, marketing on a social network like Facebook may provide benefit. The benefits of having a full understanding of your target audience cannot be overlooked. Rather than waste time trying to figure out what that audience is later, try to define your audience early in the search-engine-optimization process.

Find Your Target Audience

① Navigate to www.google.com/trends.

② Type **seo, search engine optimization**.

- Notice the traffic trend from 2004 through 2009. The term "seo" is increasing in popularity.

- Results are separated by regions of the world, cities, and languages.

3 Change All Regions to United States.

- Results are limited to traffic from the United States.

4 Click More News Results.

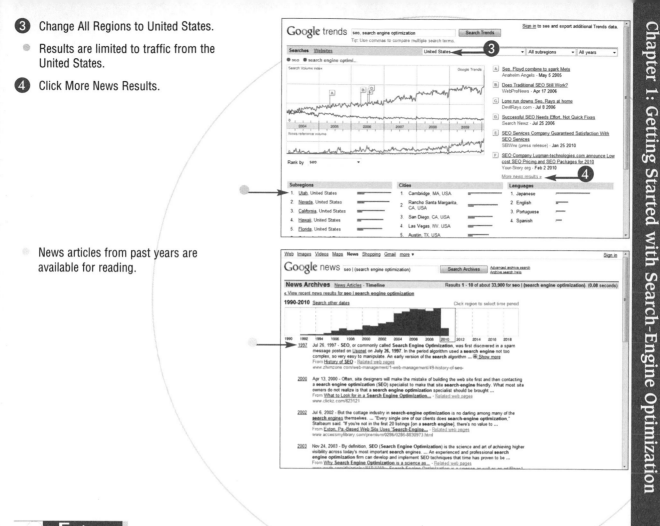

- News articles from past years are available for reading.

Extra

Optimizing for your target audience involves customizing your Web site design as much as your Web site content. If your target audience is the teenage demographic, and your Web site is designed to resemble a legal document, it may not matter how relevant your content actually is. If your Web site users are turned off by the Web site design, they may not stick around long enough to read the content anyway.

When you design your Web site, be sure to design it around the tastes of your target audience. An art school's Web site design should be different from the design of a site about the world's most demanding law schools. The target audiences for these two markets are very different despite the overall theme being the same.

Make a point to study your successful competition before you move forward with Web site design and content development. Try to stay original, but do not feel the need to reinvent the wheel. Much of the research has already been done for you. Your mission is to improve upon what products or services are already available while keeping your target audience in mind.

Set a Budget

If you decide to do your own search-engine optimization, more than just your time is required. Set aside a budget for your search-engine optimization as if it is any other form of marketing. Certain tasks are involved in a comprehensive search-engine-optimization plan that require a financial investment. You may not need to hire a company to do your search-engine optimization, but you should give yourself the best opportunity to increase your rankings, increase your traffic, and beat your competitors. To give yourself that opportunity, a budget is required.

Web Design and Development Costs

Numerous costs are involved in just getting a Web site running. Free Web hosting should be avoided; a domain name is required; and unless you are adept at Web site design, having a professional Web site developed can cost a significant amount of money. These are necessary costs that cannot be avoided. Generally, Web hosting can cost anywhere from $5 per month to hundreds of dollars per month depending on the type of hosting required. Selecting a Web host and a domain name are discussed in more detail in Chapter 4.

A domain name can be purchased for less than $10 depending on where you look, but professional Web site design can cost hundreds, thousands, or more depending on the complexity of design required. High cost does not necessary translate into great results, and there are instances where a redesign of a Web site can positively or negatively impact your search-engine rankings. Web site design can not only affect search-engine rankings, but it also can directly affect your site's *conversion rates*. The conversion rate of your site is the percentage of visitors that are converted into a sale. A difference in only a fraction of a percentage point can have an enormous impact on whether a search-engine-optimization campaign is profitable or a drain on financial resources.

Content Development Costs

Your content creation is also a consideration. You may decide to outsource content creation to skilled copywriters who write content at an hourly rate. These rates vary depending on the skill and experience of the writer. You should expect to pay between $15 and $75 per hour for content writing. As discussed in Chapter 3, a Web site's content is a very influential factor in search-engine rankings. To compete with other Web sites in competitive markets, your site has to contain a substantial amount of unique, relevant content. If you want your visitors to trust your Web site as an authority source in your field, make sure your content is well written and factually correct.

Link-building Costs

Also, be sure to have a budget for link building. If you choose to pay for links, the cost can be a few dollars per link to upwards of a few hundred dollars per link, depending on the quality of that link. As discussed in Chapter 3, both the number and quality of inbound links to your Web site are possibly the most influential factors on your search-engine rankings.

Keyword Research Costs

Other costs may arise. Quality keyword research and analysis tools can be a necessity depending on the size of the project, and these tools normally cost between $50 and $100 per month. These tools are reviewed in detail in the next chapter. A quality keyword research and analysis tool is often one of the first investments that any search-engine-optimization specialist makes.

Set Goals

Setting realistic goals for your search-engine-optimization project ensures that you stay on task and keep focused despite the many mountains and valleys you are sure to encounter. Search-engine optimization is not an exact science, and even if you follow best practices, there are no guarantees. Many search-engine-optimization companies guarantee front-page rankings or even place time frames on when success is likely to be realized, but ultimately, the search engines decide your fate. Set realistic goals for the project, and you are less likely to be disappointed and distracted throughout the process.

Progress Steadily

Search-engine optimization is much like exercise and diet. You may not notice immediate results from a single workout or cutting out a single fatty meal, but over the course of weeks, months, and years, the effects accumulate. Similarly, with search-engine optimization, you can rest assured knowing that your efforts build over time to produce results. Also, much like exercise and diet, working slowly and steadily over time is much more likely to produce results than trying to cram all the work into a few weeks or months. Spread out your search-engine-optimization work over time or risk a penalty from the search engines for trying to manipulate their ranking algorithms.

Spammers historically manipulated the search engines by programming content generators capable of building Web sites with thousands of pages of text in minutes or less. At one time, these Web sites almost immediately gained high rankings in the search engines due to their large quantity of "unique" content. Upon closer inspection though, this content was very evidently machine-generated garbage.

The same holds true in your efforts to build inbound links back to your Web site. Spammers have historically manipulated the search engines by programming link generators capable of building thousands of links back to their Web sites in a very short period of time. Most of the time, these programs target online guest books and message boards, and automatically generate entries on the guest books or posts on the message boards that include a link back to a selected Web site. In a time where quantity of links was considered much more important and easier to measure than quality of links, this practice, especially in combination with an automatic Web site generator, fed the search engines with the ingredients considered important for a high-ranking Web site.

Focus on Natural Growth

The search engines want to see a slow, steady, and natural growth of your Web site. They realize that a single person or even a group of people are unlikely to have the ability to generate hundreds of pages of content as soon as a Web site goes live. This type of growth is the fingerprint that a machine-generated Web site leaves behind. The engineers behind the search-engine ranking algorithms work hard to ensure that machine-generated content and links are penalized appropriately.

As you learn different search-engine-optimization techniques in this book, think about how they fit into your overall goals. Are you trying to build more traffic to your Web site overall? Are you trying to increase sales of a certain product? Are you trying to establish your brand? Your specific goals determine how you should approach the project. Plan out what strategies you are going to implement, how you are going to implement them, and when you plan to have the projects completed.

Put a Team Together

Not everyone is going to be an expert at every aspect of search-engine optimization. To take full advantage of what search-engine optimization has to offer your Web site, many skills are required. These skills include but are not limited to HTML writing, knowledge of CSS, data analysis, graphical design, server administration, copywriting, link building, blogging, and so on. Do not hesitate to put together a team of people skilled in these different areas to assist in the project. You do not need to hire a team of people to work at your side; you can outsource some of the work to others through popular outsourcing Web sites such as Elance.

You are sure to find that you excel at some search-engine-optimization tasks and lack the knowledge or motivation to excel in others. You may be an excellent Web designer and copywriter, but terrible at server administration and link building. In this case, you may want to consider an outsourced employee to help you take advantage of the advanced server-side search-engine-optimization techniques and someone else to assist in link building; or, you may want to pass on the Web designing and copywriting and focus solely on link building. Either way, many alternatives are out there to doing all the work yourself. How you decide to take advantage of these alternatives depends on your level of experience and ultimately your budget.

As you read through the rest of this book, you are going to encounter many techniques that you feel uncomfortable performing due to lack of knowledge or just a lack of time. Just about everything can be outsourced, so do not hesitate to explore that option if necessary.

Put a Team Together

1 Navigate to www.elance.com.

2 Enter a description of the service that you want.

3 Click Search.

● You see a list of service providers, their feedback, and the total amount of money they have earned on the Elance platform.

You can click a provider from the list to see their portfolio, feedback, and contact information.

4 Click Post Your Job and sign in with your Elance account.

⑤ Enter pertinent details about your project.

⑥ Click Continue to post your project.

Elance providers can now view your project and choose to bid.

Extra

Although Elance.com is the most popular online source for finding freelance workers to perform jobs, another fast-growing alternative may be worth trying.

oDesk, located at www.odesk.com, has more than 170,000 certified professionals waiting to bid on your projects. oDesk has an advanced and very friendly user interface. It has a unique online platform that enables you to supervise your workers and track their time worked and tasks performed. You can view and verify their time logs to create detailed bills that can be paid by credit card. Unlike Elance, you can pay by the hour, which eliminates the problem of paying a fixed fee based on a project description.

oDesk is known for its high quality of providers and its efforts to return trust to the online contracting industry. The programmers are hooked up to Web cameras, and random screenshots of their desktops are taken to make sure they are working. A reputation system is in place that lists diplomas and certifications, and, based on a programmer's reputation, oDesk can suggest a price for that programmer.

These factors combined make oDesk a worthy competitor to Elance. oDesk comes highly recommended throughout the Web community as a platform to use when looking to outsource your work.

Keep Up with Industry News

The Web is full of informative blogs and forums where industry experts freely share their knowledge and experiences in search-engine marketing. Keep up with the pulse of the Internet marketing industry by reading these blogs and forums on a daily basis. Search-engine optimization is not an exact science. The ranking algorithms are constantly changing, and though the optimization techniques generally remain the same, new tips and tricks are constantly discovered by these industry gurus.

This book provides you with a framework upon which true industry expertise can be built. Much like other industries, continuing education is a must if you plan to excel at search-engine optimization. Take advantage of every free resource that is made available to you. Unlike many other industries, search-engine marketing experts are generally not afraid to share some of their best secrets.

There are literally hundreds and possibly thousands of constantly updated resources pertaining to search-engine optimization. Respected industry blogs like Search Engine Land (www.searchengineland.com), SEOmoz (www.seomoz.org), pepperjamBlog (www.pepperjam.com/blog), and others are updated frequently, sometimes numerous times per day. Although it is impossible to keep up-to-date with every resource, it can be just as difficult to keep up with only a few blogs due to the rapid frequency of updates. To alleviate this problem, customize a free newsreader like Google's personal home pages to display the most recent entries of your favorite blogs. Each of these industry blogs uses RSS to syndicate content throughout the Internet. Google's customizable home page reads these RSS feeds and updates your personal home page with the headlines of the most recent posts of each blog whose RSS feed you subscribe to.

Keep Up with Industry News

① Navigate to www.google.com.

② Click iGoogle.

Note: *If you do not already have an iGoogle page, click Get Started and create your iGoogle page following the instructions.*

③ Click Add Stuff.

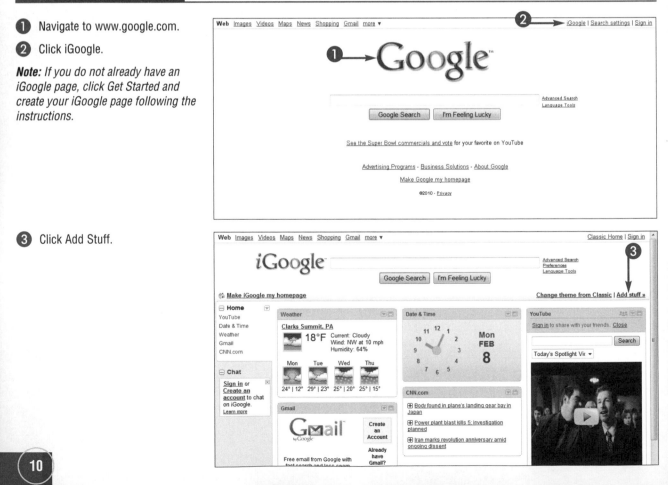

4 Click Add Feed or Gadget.

5 Enter the site address.

6 Click to close the window.

7 Click Back to iGoogle Home.

● The latest headlines from the site you chose in Step 5 are added to your personalized home page.

Attend an
Industry Conference

One of the most effective strategies for learning more about search-engine marketing and to network within the search-marketing space is to attend an industry conference. Leading search marketing conferences, including Search Engine Strategies (SES) (www.searchenginestrategies.com) and Search Marketing Expo (SMX) (www.searchmarketingexpo.com) offer dozens of educational sessions led by panels of search marketing experts. Thousands of businesspeople with varying levels of search marketing expertise attend search marketing conferences such as SES and SMX, which are held annually in the United States and around the world. The largest annual search conference is SES New York, which is held each spring in New York City.

When attending a search marketing conference, you want to select educational content based on your specific skill level, as well as the specific topic you want to learn more about. For example, both SES and SMX offer content on topics such as SEO Link Building, Optimizing Paid Search Campaigns, and Social Media Optimization Strategies, among others. Each session is designated either "beginner," "intermediate," or "advanced." In addition to topic-based educational sessions, search conferences also include keynote speakers, typically featuring provocative lectures from leading thought shapers. Search conferences are typically held over a two- or three-day period.

Business leaders of all levels of management attend search conferences. It is common for C-level executives, as well as marketing managers, IT professionals, and entrepreneurs of all ages to attend search conferences. If you want to learn more about search marketing, you should attend a search marketing conference.

Cost to attend search conferences varies based on access level. For full access to all educational sessions on all days of a given conference, individual tickets can cost in excess of $1,500. Tickets with limited access to content are typically under $1,000.

Attend an Industry Conference

1. Navigate to www.searchenginestrategies.com.

2. Click one of the upcoming industry events.

3. Click Take the First Step – Register Here.

④ Review rates and registration details

⑤ Click Register Now.

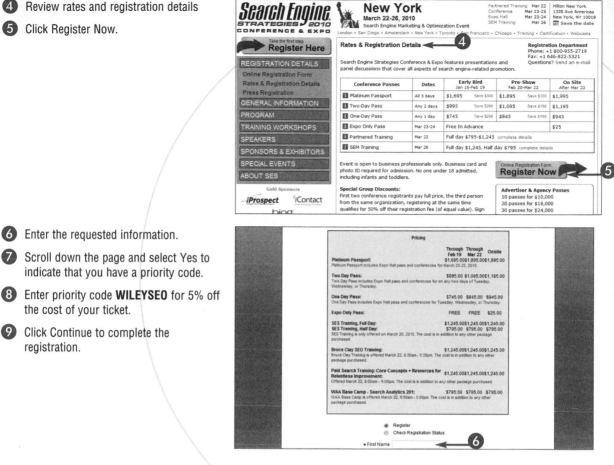

⑥ Enter the requested information.

⑦ Scroll down the page and select Yes to indicate that you have a priority code.

⑧ Enter priority code **WILEYSEO** for 5% off the cost of your ticket.

⑨ Click Continue to complete the registration.

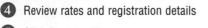

Extra

Numerous leading Internet conferences exist outside of SES and SMX, such as Affiliate Summit, Ad-Tech, and Internet Retailer, that feature search marketing content as part of broader Internet marketing educational sessions. Moreover, as search marketing continues to expand as a primary marketing channel niche, conferences in industries as diverse as food service, book publishing, and construction are covering search marketing content. For a comprehensive list of Internet marketing conferences, see www.conferencecalendar.com.

Affiliate Summit (www.affiliatesummit.com) is a leading Internet marketing conference that offers attendees access to educational sessions focused primarily on affiliate and search engine marketing. Educational sessions cover many important search-related topics, including search-engine optimization, pay-per-click, and social media tactics and strategies. Affiliate Summit is held twice per year on the East and West coasts. Tickets to Affiliate Summit range from $149 to approximately $1,250 based on access level.

In addition to serving as an educational resource, search marketing industry conferences present excellent professional networking opportunities. All of the major conferences hold networking sessions that are meant to provide attendees with social opportunities to professionally network, exchange business cards, and have fun.

An Introduction to Keyword Generation

After selecting a Web site topic, keyword generation is the first and arguably most important step of the search-engine-optimization, or *SEO*, process. The bulk of your Web site, from the directory and filenames to the title tags and page copy, is built around the words and phrases you choose during the keyword-generation phase. The process of keyword generation is very important to a successful SEO campaign and should never be rushed or taken lightly.

Initially, you want to generate a potential keyword list that is as large as possible, with the keywords organized by search volume. *Volume* refers to the number of searches performed on a unique keyword over a period of time. A large list ensures that you have a healthy mix of keyword terms. Selecting only keywords with little search volume, or keywords with rankings dominated by established authority sites, could spell disaster for your SEO efforts before they have even gotten off the ground. In this chapter, you learn about various tools that help make your keyword research and generation process highly successful. Moreover, you learn numerous tips about competitive research that can save you time and money.

Select Keywords

The first step in the keyword-generation process is to strategically select keywords that you want your Web site to rank for on the major search engines. There are two kinds of keyword terms, *head terms* and *tail terms*. Head terms refer to short keywords, usually one to two words in length that tend to have very high search volume. Tail terms are the longer keyword terms, typically three or more words that tend to have a much lower search volume than head terms. An effectively executed SEO strategy sets out to generate large amounts of quality Web site traffic by targeting a blend of head terms and tail terms.

Analyze Your Competition with Compete.com

Compete.com is a keyword research service that allows you to analyze your competition, including the keywords your competitors rank for on search engines, as well as how Web site users interact with your competitors' Web sites. This unique data is made possible through the distribution of the Compete toolbar, which collects information as a user surfs the Web. Despite being only rough estimates, the data Compete.com provides can be incredibly useful to your SEO campaigns. This tool provides a glimpse of the actual value of a keyword in terms of visitor interaction and site usage. After all, simply getting users to your Web site is only the first step. Having them interact with your Web site, digest your content, and eventually take your call to action for your monetization strategy is the ultimate goal. Knowing what keywords can send active users to your Web site can provide you with a powerful advantage during the keyword-generation process.

Keyword Research with KeyCompete

KeyCompete is a tool that allows you to see the exact keywords your competition is targeting through pay-per-click campaigns. By carefully analyzing the keywords your top competitors are bidding on, you can save considerable time and energy during the initial stages of generating relevant keywords for your Web site. KeyCompete allows you to download reports and aggregate data from multiple competitors. A comprehensive analysis of the individual keywords used by all your competition provides you with a best estimate of what keywords are likely to perform for your Web site. You can take the keywords generated through your KeyCompete analysis and combine them with many of the other tools discussed in this chapter to formulate your own optimal keyword list. This list can then be used for both SEO and pay-per-click, or *PPC*, advertising.

Keyword Research with KeywordSpy

KeywordSpy is a powerful tool that allows you to perform keyword research based on what keywords your competition is bidding for on a pay-per-click basis, as well as what keywords your competition ranks for organically on major search engines like Google, Bing, and Yahoo. KeywordSpy's real-time keyword tracking technology allows you to easily assess the effectiveness of your keyword ranking, which in turn can influence your keyword research strategy. The keyword list of your organic rankings should serve as an excellent reference source for your ongoing keyword research and generation efforts.

Analyze Your Competition with SEMRush

SEMRush is a competitive research tool that allows you to easily determine the top keywords that your competitors rank for organically on Google.com. SEMRush offers two options for accessing competitor keywords. Nonregistered users are allowed up to ten free domain searches per hour, and registered users are provided up to ten domain searches per hour. Another benefit of registration is a function called site-wide search. The site-wide search function allows you to search for the top 20 rankings for every single page of a Web site, as opposed to just searching the home page rankings. Registration is free and only requires verifying your e-mail address.

Research Keywords with Keyword Discovery

Keyword Discovery is a subscription fee-based keyword tool that allows you to examine the estimated search volume for thousands of keywords. Keyword Discovery pulls data from more than 180 search engines and has an extensive keyword database with considerable historical information dating back several years. Keyword Discovery also has several other databases beyond the major search engines, which include searches from eBay, as well as other popular shopping sites and foreign search engines. Keyword Discovery allows you to examine comparatively which engines send the majority of volume for each keyword.

Using Wordtracker's Keyword Tool

Wordtracker offers a free version of its subscription fee-based keyword tool that is ideal for doing quick keyword research. The Wordtracker tool provides you with a list of related terms to your base keyword as well as the estimated daily search volume for each individual keyword. The paid version of the tool is more robust and allows you to save keyword lists for later use and editing.

Analyze Keywords with Keyword Discovery

Keyword Discovery allows you to analyze the keywords you develop during the research phase, including the number of pages where the term occurs, as well as the *keyword effectiveness indicator*, or *KEI*. The keyword effectiveness indicator is a comparison between the search volume of keywords and the amount of sites that use those same keywords. Ideally, you want to find keywords with substantial volume and minimal competition. These terms have a low KEI number, as the Keyword Discovery research tool demonstrates.

Using the Google Keyword Suggestion Tool

Google offers a powerful no-cost keyword suggestion tool that provides you with access to historical user search behavior from the largest and most powerful search engine in the world, Google.com. The Google Keyword Suggestion Tool provides you with powerful keyword research data, including individual keyword search volume, as well as a comparative evaluation of how much competition exists for a given keyword within Google's pay-per-click product AdWords. Although the Google Keyword Suggestion Tool does not give exact numbers in terms of search volume, it does provide a useful, at-a-glance take on how competitive a given term will be in PPC advertising.

Filter Keywords with Keyword Discovery

Another feature of Keyword Discovery is a filter tool. You will find filter tools very useful when expanding on existing keyword lists. With a filter tool, you can quickly add common prefixes and suffixes to large keyword lists in seconds. You can also use a filter tool to do a mass find-and-replace with common synonyms. Filter tools are ideal for adding "buying" words like *buy*, *order*, and so on to your keyword list. Filter tools can also instantly double the size of your keyword list by swapping your main keyword with a common synonym.

Select Keywords

Selecting general and specific keywords that are relevant to the specific products, services, or content of each page of your Web site is an essential component of search-engine optimization, or SEO. General or generic keywords are one or two keywords in length and are commonly referred to as *long-tail* or *head terms*; specific keywords are three or more keywords in length and are commonly referred to as *tail terms*. For example, the keyword "cheese" could be considered a head term; the keyword "gourmet cheese gift basket" could be considered a tail term.

Head terms tend to generate substantially more traffic than tail terms, but do not necessarily lead to more sales or repeat visitors. Tail terms typically send much less traffic, but often convert at a higher rate than head terms. Therefore, you should select a blend of both head and tail terms to incorporate into each of the pages of your Web site.

Choose Between Head and Tail Terms

Regardless of whether you are optimizing an existing Web site or building a new Web site, you should select keywords that are consistent with the content of each unique Web page, as well as the overall theme of the Web site. In general, you should select tail terms when optimizing Web pages with specific content and head terms when optimizing Web pages with more general content.

Select head keywords for your home page that represent the overall theme of your Web site. For example, if your Web site is about gourmet cheese, for SEO purposes you want to select the keyword "gourmet cheese" for your home page. Typically, your home page has the highest number of backlinks (links pointed to your Web site from other Web sites) out of all the pages on your site. Home pages are also generally viewed as the most important page of a Web site and are meant to tell both readers and search-engine spiders what the overall Web site is generally about. For this reason, your home page has the highest chances of ranking for the competitive head terms, and your subpages should target less-competitive head terms, as well as tail terms.

Select Head Terms Sparingly

It is difficult to rank for head terms, especially head terms that define your particular industry or Web site category. In fact, only the top ten Web sites within any particular industry or category rank on the front page of a search engine for a general head term. Unfortunately, even if you take and apply all the suggestions in this book, there is no guarantee that you will rank for one or more competitive head terms.

In many cases, the Web sites that rank high for competitive head terms use manipulative tactics that are inconsistent with the terms and conditions of the major search engines. As a result, Web sites using shady SEO practices tend to enjoy top ranking for only a short period of time prior to being banned from the search engines for a short time or indefinitely. Although you may be tempted to use manipulative practices that may allow your Web site to be competitive for head terms in the short term, the risk associated with such practices is great. Instead, focus on building great content with an emphasis on providing your readers with a great user experience.

Select Tail Terms for Most Web Pages

Your primary SEO strategy should focus on building content that ranks well in the search engines for long tail terms. Too often the SEO efforts of Web site owners fail because of an overemphasis on ranking for head terms. Although the traffic volume for head terms is greater, you stand a much greater chance of ranking well for specific tail terms. Moreover, ranking well for just a few tail terms is much better than not ranking at all for a head term. Always keep in mind that you need to set long-term goals for SEO. Over time, as you build out content on your Web site and optimize each page for select keywords, you will notice that your Web site traffic has grown substantially.

Optimize Every Page of Your Web Site

When you select keywords to incorporate into your Web site, remember that your goal is not to optimize your Web site all at once, but to optimize each page of your Web site. You should never optimize for more than one or two target keywords per Web page because doing so dilutes your optimization in too many directions and decreases your overall effectiveness and ranking potential.

The approach you take to optimizing each page of your Web site is different depending on whether you are optimizing existing Web page content or building new content. If you are optimizing existing Web page content, you should select one or two keywords that best summarize that page. In addition, you may need to manipulate the content a bit to make sure that your target keywords are emphasized and stand out from the rest of the content. If you are building new content, you should have one or two target keywords in mind before you start writing. For example, if your target keyword is "Extra Double Aged Gouda," your Web page content should focus specifically on gaining ranking for that keyword. See Chapter 6 for more information about building optimized Web page content.

Add Target Keywords to Meta Tags

When optimizing your Web site, you should strategically place one or two target keywords in the title tag of your Web page, as well as in the description and keyword meta tags. Your selected keywords should ideally be the starting point used to generate the content for each Web page you construct. If not, you should make sure that your target keywords are strategically sprinkled throughout the page. When you are building backlinks to your pages, keep the target keywords for each page in mind. If your page is about storing gourmet cheeses, building links with the anchor text "storing gourmet cheese" produces the optimal results. See Chapter 8 for more about backlinks and anchor text.

Be realistic when you select your head terms, and evaluate the competition. Picking head terms that have established Web sites ranking for them within the top few search results is setting yourself up for failure if you are starting from scratch with a nonestablished domain. Although ranking within the top few organic results for the keyword "mortgage" could lead to significant revenue generation, a newly established Web site with no authority in the eyes of search engines stands little chance of gaining top placement for such a competitive head term. And even though you cannot immediately rank for a general head term like "mortgage," you can break down the general term "mortgage" into smaller, more specific topics, and optimize for those tail terms throughout your Web site.

Analyze Your Competition with Compete.com

Compete.com, located at www.my.compete.com, is a competitive analytics tool that provides a robust look at where your competition is generating search-engine traffic on both pay-per-click and organic searches. Compete.com also provides information on user interaction with your Web site, which is a powerful data set that other popular keyword research tools such as Wordtracker and Keyword Discovery do not provide.

Unlike other popular keyword research and suggestion tools, Compete.com does not gather data directly from the search engines. Instead, Compete.com gathers information from actual Internet users who have installed the Compete toolbar. This firsthand data collection allows Compete.com to provide significantly more information by analyzing not only how users search, but how they behave on the sites they visit after searching. This includes the time a user spends on a site, what percentage of the site's traffic comes from each individual keyword, and a relative measure of how much each keyword is worth to the competitor site.

In order to have access to user interaction data, you must create an account at Compete.com and upgrade it to a premium service level. Service levels range from $199 per month for a basic account to more than $500 per month for an enterprise account. Though on the expensive side, the amount of analytical data that you can generate from Compete.com is substantial. If you want the advantage of knowing how you are doing versus your competition or how your competition ranks against one another, you may want to consider paying for a premium Compete.com account.

Compete.com also offers free keyword research and Web site analytics services, including the ability to compare estimated traffic statistics for up to 5 domains at a time over the last 12 months. This data can be very useful to you in forecasting seasonal trends, as well as in identifying who is doing the best job of capitalizing on seasonal traffic bursts.

Analyze Your Competition with Compete.com

1. Navigate to www.my.compete.com and click Register Now.

2. Click Sign-up under MyCompete Free.

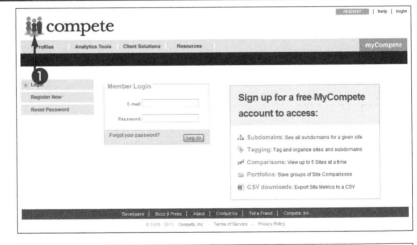

③ After signing up for MyCompete Free, navigate to http://searchanalytics.compete.com.

④ Enter the domain of your competitor into the Site field.

⑤ Click Go.

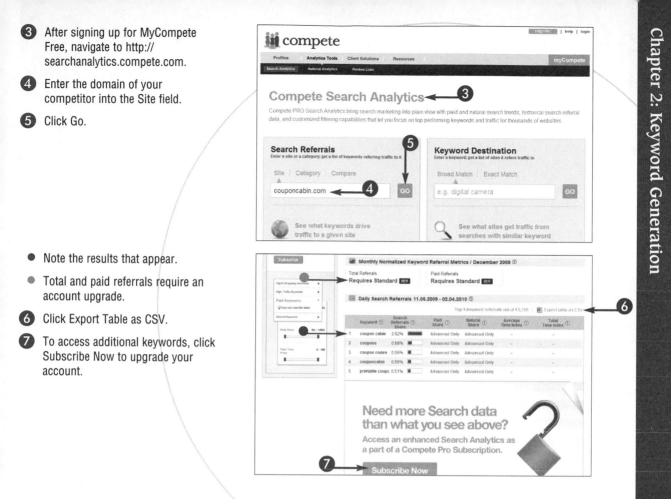

● Note the results that appear.

● Total and paid referrals require an account upgrade.

⑥ Click Export Table as CSV.

⑦ To access additional keywords, click Subscribe Now to upgrade your account.

Extra

The advanced data that Compete.com offers on a competitor's Web site is broken down into a few categories. They are as follows:

- Volume Rank refers to the rank of each keyword in terms of what keyword is sending the most volume. This gives a quick look at the top-performing keywords, ignoring everything but raw traffic levels.

- Site Share refers to the percentage of the overall search-engine traffic that comes to a Web site from each individual keyword.

- Keyword Engagement is a measure of the average amount of time a user spent on the site and can be used as a gauge of user interaction on your Web site. This is broken down to a keyword level, so you can see what keywords are sending the highest number of interested Web site users.

- Keyword Effectiveness is a combination of Volume Rank and Keyword Engagement. It is a basic measure of what keywords are the most valuable in terms of referred users who were active when they hit the Web site. Keyword Effectiveness provides an additional measure of user interaction on your Web site.

Compete.com allows you to sort the keyword list by any of these fields. This information can prove to be invaluable to your SEO research.

Keyword Research with KeyCompete

One of the most effective methods for generating keywords is to evaluate what keywords your competition is bidding for on major pay-per-click search engines such as Google AdWords and Yahoo Search Marketing. Competitive research tools such as KeyCompete.com, which typically charge a monthly or annual membership fee, enable you to see the specific keywords your competition is bidding on, while also giving you access to useful keyword-generation data.

Generating competitor keyword lists using KeyCompete can be done using four primary strategies, depending on how many keywords your competitor is bidding on and how granular you want your keyword-generation research to be.

One way KeyCompete allows you to evaluate competitors' keywords is by typing a competitor's Web site URL directly into the KeyCompete system. Using the URL method allows you to quickly access thousands of competitor keywords at any one time. However, the KeyCompete technology does not return results if your competitor is not using paid search. If your competitor is bidding on a very large list of keywords, you should request keywords in groups, instead of all at once. This procedure requires you to type multiple KeyCompete commands.

To search for competitor keywords in groups, such as all keywords that start with the letter *A*, type the competitor's URL followed by a question mark (?) and the first letter of the keyword — for example, www.visualseobook.com?a. This command generates all keywords for www.visualseobook.com beginning with the letter *A*.

To generate keywords on an even more granular level, you can type a series of letters or a specific keyword to return your competitor's keywords of a similar type. To perform this function, type the competitor's URL followed by a question mark (?) and your specific command, such as www.target.com?toys or www.target.com?apparel.

Keyword Research with KeyCompete

① Navigate to www.keycompete.com.

② Enter a domain in the search field.

③ Click Search.

● Note the five results that appear. These are a small selection of the keywords that the domain is currently bidding on in Google AdWords. KeyCompete rates the keywords from Great to Bad based on search frequency and advertiser competition.

④ Repeat the same process for multiple competitors to see what your competition is bidding on.

⑤ To access more than five results per domain, purchase a KeyCompete.com account.

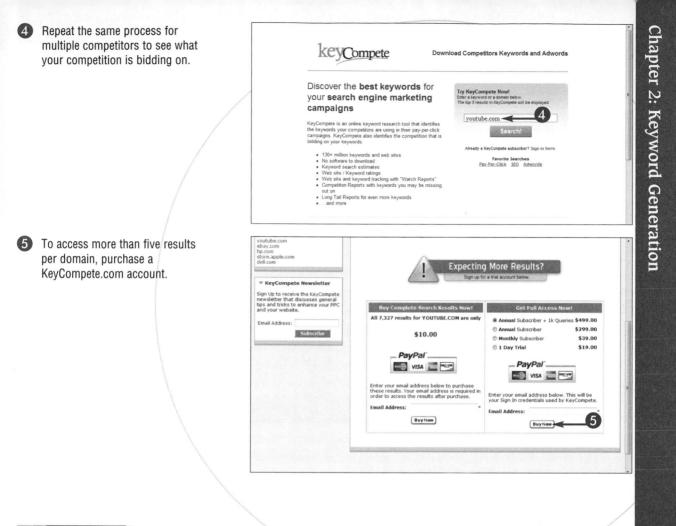

KeyCompete can be used to evaluate the keywords that your competitors are bidding on, as well as to significantly expand your own paid search efforts. KeyCompete should be used as a primary keyword-generation method. An annual membership to KeyCompete is under $500, but it can save you significant time and money in your overall keyword-generation efforts compared to other tools that are currently on the market.

KeyCompete offers many of the same benefits of a traditional keyword-generation tool, such as the ability to search for variations of keywords across all Web sites. For this function, no URL is required; instead, just type a general or specific keyword, and KeyCompete provides you with an extensive list of similar keywords.

A supplement to the KeyCompete keyword-generation tool is KeyCompete's Long-Tail Keyword technology, which allows you to generate large keyword lists that include variations of more general keywords. For example, you can type a general keyword, such as "jelly," and the KeyCompete Long-Tail Keyword tool provides you with an extensive list of specific descriptive keywords such as "gourmet jelly preserve" or "peanut butter and jelly sandwich." This approach allows you to quickly find keywords that may have been overlooked by other keyword-generation approaches.

In addition to KeywordSpy and KeyCompete, other popular, competitive, keyword-generation research tools include Hitwise.com and SpyFu.com.

Keyword Research with KeywordSpy

KeywordSpy (www.keywordspy.com) is a powerful tool that allows you to perform keyword research based on what keywords your competition is bidding for on a pay-per-click basis, as well as what keywords your competition ranks for organically on major search engines like Google, Bing, and Yahoo. Moreover, KeywordSpy offers a real-time keyword tracking tool that allows you to monitor keyword performance of your personal Web site(s) and your competitors' Web sites.

KeywordSpy's real-time keyword tracking technology allows you to easily assess the effectiveness of your keyword ranking, which in turn can influence your keyword research strategy. By simply typing your domain into the tracking tool, KeywordSpy produces a report of the keywords you rank for organically and on a pay-per-click basis. The keyword list of your organic rankings should serve as an excellent reference source for your ongoing keyword research and generation efforts.

Having real-time access to your organic rankings allows you to discover keywords that you rank for, but that were not a primary part of your keyword-generation process. In fact, sometimes you will find that you rank for keywords that you were not even trying to rank for. This insight allows you to modify the ongoing keyword research process by helping to focus your attention on keywords that search engines have already ranked your Web site for. For example, if you discover that your Web site ranks organically especially well for a specific subcategory of the business you are in, it makes sense to focus on building additional keywords around that category.

Analyzing your organic ranking also allows you to find new keywords to add to your pay-per-click campaigns. Keyword research and generation is not an exact science. Therefore, you need to take advantage of data such as the organic search ranking data provided by KeywordSpy's real-time tracking tool to help you fine-tune your keyword research efforts.

Keyword Research with KeywordSpy

① Navigate to www.keywordspy.com and log in using your account.

② Type in a competitor keyword. For example, type www.patagonia.com.

③ Click Search.

● Note the competitor's activity with PPC advertising, including estimated daily ad budget and average cost per click.

④ Click the PPC Keywords tab.

- Note your competitor's various PPC keywords.

5 Click the Organic Keywords tab.

- Note your competitor's various organic keywords.

Extra

If you are an affiliate marketer or want to make some additional income by being an affiliate marketer, you can use KeywordSpy's Affiliate Intelligence tool to uncover important keyword data about the pay-per-click activities of your competition. (See Chapter 14 for more information about monetizing Web traffic through affiliate marketing.) KeywordSpy's Affiliate Intelligence database includes more than 127 million keywords and allows you to target your competition based on the specific affiliate network they use to generate income.

The KeywordSpy Affiliate Intelligence tool allows you to search its database by competitor domain, keywords, destination URLs, or ad copy.

KeywordSpy provides a limited lifetime free trial account to test the technology. This gives you an opportunity to immediately track down your competition and produce a preliminary list of keywords for you to analyze your competition. The full KeywordSpy Affiliate Intelligence membership is $89.95 per month.

Analyze Your Competition with SEMRush

An effective approach to generating keywords for your Web site is to analyze where your competitors rank on the search engines for keywords that you want to rank for. You can use tools such as SEMRush, located at www.semrush.com, to determine how well you rank for specific keywords versus your competition, as well as to determine other important factors, including popularity and a rough estimate of how much search volume each individual keyword receives.

SEMRush offers a free tool that allows you to easily determine the top keywords that your competitors rank for organically on Google.com. SEMRush offers two options for accessing competitor keywords. Nonregistered users are allowed up to five free domain searches per hour, and registered users are provided up to ten domain searches per hour. Another benefit of registration is a function called *site-wide search*. The site-wide search function allows you to search for the top 20 rankings for every single page of a Web site, as opposed to just searching the home page rankings. Registration is free and only requires verifying your e-mail address.

In addition to organic ranking, SEMRush provides you with important information on keyword popularity. Observing the keyword popularity of your competitors' organic rankings is important because it can be used to determine the relative amount of traffic your competitor is receiving for a particular keyword placement. The SEMRush keyword popularity function also provides a rough idea for how much traffic you can possibly gain by increasing your rankings for your keywords. For example, if your site is ranked between spots 7 and 10 for two separate keywords, but one receives double the monthly searches, you stand to gain the most from optimizing further for the higher volume keyword.

Analyze Your Competition with SEMRush

① Navigate to www.semrush.com.

② Enter a domain into the domain field. For example, www.bradsdeals.com.

● Note that you can search by domain, keyword, or URL.

③ Click Search.

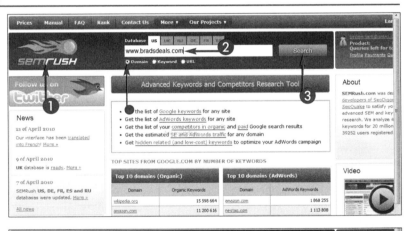

● Note the results that appear. Search results represent the top five organic search listings on Google for the domain www.bradsdeals.com.

● Search results represent the top five search listings on Google AdWords for the domain www.bradsdeals.com.

④ Click Full Report.

- Note the results that appear. Search results represent the top organic search listings on Google for the domain www.bradsdeals.com.

⑤ Click Competitors in Google.

- Note the results that appear. Search results represent a list of competitors within the organic search results on Google for the domain www.bradsdeals.com.

Extra

Another popular tool to evaluate your competition's keywords is the Shoemoney Search-Engine Results Pages (Serps) tool, which is part of Shoemoney Tools and located at www.shoemoneytools.com. As a reader of this book you can sign up for a trial membership to Shoemoney Tools for $4.95 by entering code SEOBLUEPRINT. Shoemoney Tools includes a range of tools for improving search-engine optimization and pay-per-click marketing.

Unlike Seodigger, the Shoemoney Serps tool allows you to evaluate ranking for only one keyword and URL at a time. Organic ranking results are provided across Google.com, Yahoo.com, MSN.com, and AltaVista.com with unlimited usage requirements.

The Shoemoney Serps tool is also a quick and effective way to check in on your own Web site's rankings for your main keywords. It is extremely fast, and provides a great snapshot of your Web site's overall organic strength by showing the rankings across numerous engines.

When the Shoemoney Serps tool displays the ranking results, the name of each search engine serves as a link to the actual keyword search that was done to obtain the results. By clicking any search-engine name, you can see what other Web sites are ranking for your target keywords, and what Web sites you may need to keep an eye on to ensure you defend your top rankings.

Using the Wordtracker Keyword Suggestion Tool

Wordtracker, located at www.wordtracker.com, offers a useful keyword suggestion tool that comes in free or subscription-fee versions. Similar in functionality to Keyword Discovery, Wordtracker provides you with a list of related keywords and the estimated search volume for each keyword. Wordtracker collects search volume data from two search engines, dogpile.com and metacrawler.com. Together, these engines account for roughly 3.5 million searches per day. Given the large size of the Wordtracker database, search volume estimates have proven to be fairly reliable and should provide you with a good idea of the kind of volume a given keyword generates across various search engines.

Wordtracker breaks search-volume estimates down into daily figures, as opposed to the monthly numbers the Keyword Discovery Global Premium Database provides. Having quick access to the daily number of searches for your potential keywords can prove critical when deciding what keywords to target in your SEO efforts. You can rank in the number-one position for a keyword, but if no one is searching for that keyword, you will not receive any traffic from that top ranking. Before you begin building your site, you should always do extensive keyword research to ensure you are targeting realistic rankings that bring you valuable traffic.

Doing extensive keyword research also provides valuable insight into the online behavior of your potential customers. The keywords with high search volume are the most common ways your audience is currently talking about your product or service. Listen to them, and build your site around the terms they already use. Taking this reverse-engineering approach to building content ensures that you can successfully reach your target audience in the most efficient way possible.

Using the Wordtracker Keyword Suggestion Tool

1 Navigate to http://freekeywords.wordtracker.com.

2 Enter your base keyword into the keyword field.

③ Select your filtering option to remove offensive or dubious keywords or show only adult keywords.

④ Click Hit Me.

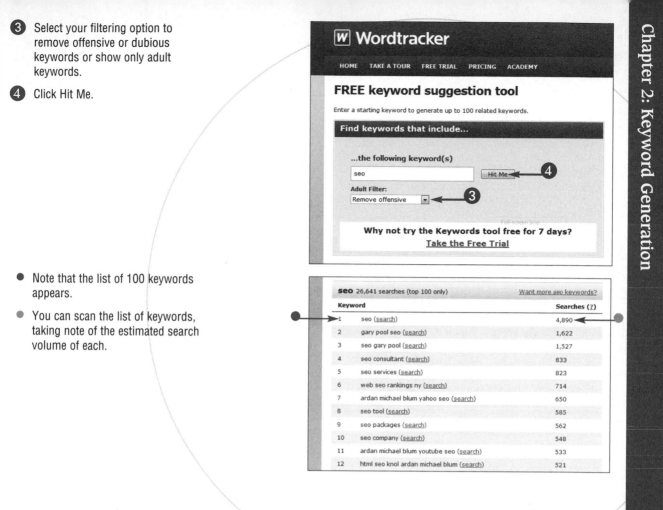

● Note that the list of 100 keywords appears.

● You can scan the list of keywords, taking note of the estimated search volume of each.

The free version of the Wordtracker Keyword Suggestion Tool is limited to 100 results per search. However, the paid version gives you instant access to thousands of keywords, which can prove invaluable when building out large keyword lists for running a PPC account, and when searching for supplemental keywords to use when constructing your content pages for SEO purposes.

Another benefit of signing up for the paid version of Wordtracker is the ability to import a list of keywords and check their search volume. Instead of manually entering each keyword into the free tool one at a time, all you need to do is copy and paste your list into the paid version of the tool; with one click you get the search-volume estimates for every word. This alone can save you hours of time each month.

As with Keyword Discovery, the paid version of Wordtracker also allows you to save your keyword projects for easy access later on. This feature allows you not only to work ahead, but also to build your own expandable database of valuable keyword research.

Using the Google Keyword Suggestion Tool

The Google AdWords Keyword Suggestion Tool, located at https://adwords.google.com/select/KeywordToolExternal, is a free tool Google offers that generates keywords based on a user entering descriptive words or phrases or a Web site URL. Because Google provides this tool, it has the unique advantage of being able to display a measure of *advertiser competition*. Advertiser competition is in reference to the amount of advertisers bidding on each term within the Google AdWords program. This is helpful in finding new keywords for use in your own PPC account because the search volume appears right next to the advertiser competition. Keywords that have a fairly high search volume with a low competition rating can make perfect additions to your own keyword lists.

The Google Keyword Suggestion Tool also shows seasonal trends in keyword searches. This is useful for planning your SEO campaigns. You should always target keywords with a mix of seasonal and constant search volume. You should also begin your link-building efforts for your targeted seasonal terms at least six months before the

period of peak search volume. This ensures that you are ranked as highly as possible for those high-volume periods.

Google's Keyword Suggestion Tool provides you not only with a list of potential keywords to target in your PPC or SEO efforts, but also with a list of potential negative keywords. Negative keywords are essential when putting together a PPC campaign. Your negative keywords are the words that prevent your ad from being triggered for display. The most commonly added negative keyword is "free" because most advertisers do not want their products shown to someone who is searching for something free. However, other keywords that you may initially overlook also may prove to be useful as negatives. For example, the word "picture" is often associated with popular e-commerce terms. If you have a sporting goods business and bid on keywords such as "football" and "baseball," you should use "picture" as a negative keyword because there is a low probability that the keywords "picture of football" or "baseball picture" would convert into a sale.

Using the Google Keyword Suggestion Tool

① Navigate to https://adwords.google.com/select/KeywordToolExternal.

② Enter one or more keywords into the keyword variations field, placing one on each line.

③ Select Use Synonyms if you want Google to return common synonyms of your keywords as results.

④ Enter the phrase shown in the image. This is to prevent requests from automated tools.

⑤ Click Get Keyword Ideas.

- The list of keywords appears.

- Notice all the additional specific keywords that you can use for purposes of search-engine optimization.

- You can sort keywords by Advertiser Competition, Local Search Volume, and Global Monthly Search Volume.

Keywords	Advertiser Competition	Local Search Volume: January	Global Monthly Search Volume	Match Type: Broad
Keywords related to term(s) entered - sorted by relevance				
seo search engine optimization		60,500	49,500	Add
search engine optimization		673,000	823,000	Add
search engine optimizing		4,400	4,400	Add
seo		2,240,000	5,000,000	Add
seo optimization		90,500	90,500	Add
seo search engine		74,000	74,000	Add
seo copywriting		8,100	12,100	Add
seo submission		6,600	12,100	Add
search engine optimization google		8,100	9,900	Add
seo ranking		18,100	18,100	Add
search engine optimization marketing		60,500	90,500	Add
seo keywords		9,900	9,900	Add
seo keyword		27,100	22,200	Add
seo elite		22,200	33,100	Add
seo google		40,500	60,500	Add
seo placement		2,400	2,900	Add
search engine optimization software		12,100	14,800	Add
seo promotion		8,100	14,800	Add
seo optimisation		4,400	5,400	Add
search engine optimization tips		8,100	9,900	Add
seo software		49,500	49,500	Add

6 Select a format and download keywords.

You can examine the list and select the most appropriate keywords for your Web site.

website promotion software		2,400	5,400	Add
pay per click optimization		2,400	3,600	Add
seoinc		2,400	3,600	Add
search engine optmization		590	2,400	Add
pay per click placement		1,300	1,900	Add
search engine placement service		1,000	1,600	Add
high search engine positioning		1,300	1,300	Add
search engine optimazation		880	1,300	Add
search engine positioning service		720	1,300	Add
guaranteed search engine positioning		320	1,000	Add
search engine placement company		480	1,000	Add
affordable search engine placement		590	880	Add
search engine placement companies		720	590	Add
search engine placement specialist		480	590	Add
search engine positioning specialist		320	590	Add
search engine optimzation		720	480	Add
search engine optomization		260	390	Add

Add all 50 »

Download all keywords: text, .csv (for excel), .csv

6

Extra

The Google AdWords Keyword Suggestion Tool provides the option of finding keywords related to the content of any Web page. This is very useful for analyzing keywords that your competition targets. However, a less obvious use for this tool lies in optimizing your own page content. By publishing your Web site to the Web and then looking for site-related keywords with the Google Keyword Suggestion Tool, you get a clear look at the way Google is interpreting your page content.

After generating a list of keywords, you have the option of saving your list in multiple formats. You can save your list as a text file, a CSV file, or a CSV file preformatted for Microsoft Excel. Alternatively, if you are already running a Google AdWords PPC campaign, you can add the keywords directly into your Google AdWords account.

The data from the Google AdWords Keyword Suggestion Tool is primarily used to add keywords to PPC campaigns; however, the tool can be extremely valuable during your keyword-generation efforts for SEO purposes. The Google AdWords Keyword Suggestion Tool allows you to gauge search volume and competition, and see exactly how Google interprets your content, which can be incredibly useful for creating, and tweaking, your Web site content.

Research Keywords with Keyword Discovery

Another extremely effective method for doing keyword research involves using the subscription fee-based Keyword Discovery research tool, located at www.keyworddiscovery.com. Keyword Discovery is available for a monthly or yearly subscription fee and offers a wealth of information to aid in your keyword research.

With Keyword Discovery, you can generate a large list of head and tail terms for any topic you choose, including many industry terms you may not yet be aware of. The Keyword Discovery tool returns a large list of keywords related to the base keyword you use when performing a search. For example, by typing the base keyword "cheese" into Keyword Discovery, you get a list of keywords related to your base keyword "cheese." Your Keyword Discovery search report is sorted by search volume, starting with high-volume head terms at the top of the list down to low-volume tail terms at the bottom of your list. For example, head terms such as "cheese" and "gourmet cheese" appear at the top of your keyword

report, and tail terms such as "gourmet cheese basket" and "Italian hard cheese" appear toward the bottom.

Keyword Discovery keyword documents can help you connect with your target audience because the reports come from aggregate data collected from 200 search engines. Each report provides you with the exact terms your potential customers are using when they search for your product or service online. If you use a representative sample of the keywords downloaded from Keyword Discovery when you generate your content and optimize your Web site, you greatly increase your chances of generating large volumes of traffic through organic rankings.

An added benefit of analyzing the lists Keyword Discovery provides is that you can analyze word popularity. The keywords "dancewear" and "dance wear" are common variants of each other, yet one is searched for nearly 20 percent more often than the other. The more knowledge you have about your keywords and how your audience searches for them, the greater your chances of gaining large amounts of search-engine traffic.

Research Keywords with Keyword Discovery

1. Navigate to www.keyworddiscovery. com and log in to your account.

2. Enter your keyword into the Search Term field.

3. Select the number of results you want to view per page.

4. Select your database.

5. Select the appropriate check boxes for options such as Phrase Match or Include Plurals.

6. Click Search.

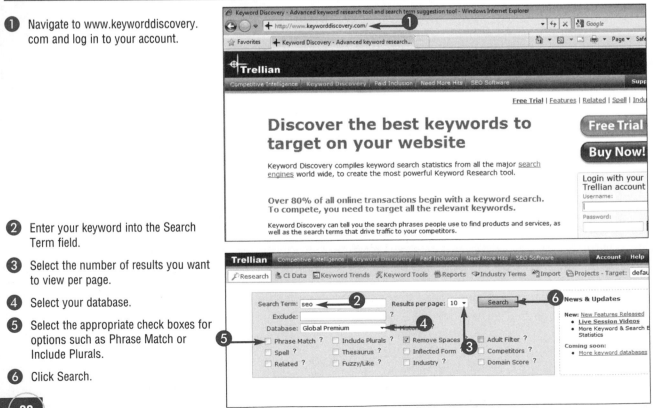

- The defined number of results appears, with their estimated search volume.

7 To chart the results, click the bar graph symbol to break down the number of searches by month for the previous 12 months. Or, you can click the pie graph symbol to break down the market share of the searches by search engine.

- Note the bar graph chart that appears, showing seasonal trends in search volume for the keyword you chose in Step 2.

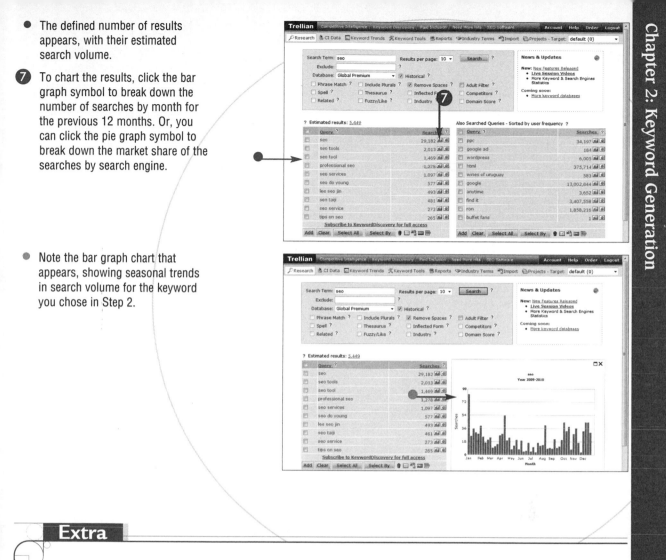

Analyze Keywords with Keyword Discovery

Keyword Discovery includes several useful advanced features that enable you to analyze your lists of keywords, including information on the number of occurrences of a keyword throughout a Web site, overall keyword effectiveness, and predicted daily search volume. Keyword Discovery advanced features allow you to achieve a better understanding of what keyword rankings are realistically available, and the directions in which your SEO work is most likely to achieve positive results.

Keyword Discovery's number-of-occurrences feature provides an estimated number of pages that use a given keyword. The higher this number, the more pages likely competing for the top organic positions for the keyword. Generally speaking, a lower number is better for your Web site.

Keyword Discovery's keyword effectiveness indicator, or *KEI*, is a simplified value scale from 0 to 10 that provides

a snapshot of the potential for each keyword. The KEI compares the number of searches for a keyword with the number of search results to pinpoint what keywords are most effective for your campaign. The general idea is that the higher KEI value a keyword has, the more likely it is to rank well for that particular term. However, this value ignores the strength of the top-ranking sites and focuses instead on the relation of searches to the number of competing sites.

Keyword Discovery's predicted-daily-searches feature provides you with a prediction for how many searches occur daily across the entire Internet for a given keyword. Although Keyword Discovery pulls data from more than 180 search engines, it does not capture data from every search performed. Therefore, keep in mind that the Keyword Discovery predicted-daily-searches feature is an educated estimate of the actual search volume.

Analyze Keywords with Keyword Discovery

① Perform your keyword research, as outlined in the previous task.

② Click the Analyze link.

- Note that the Searches and the Predicted Daily columns are already populated for all terms.

- The Occurrences and KEI columns are populated for commonly searched terms, or terms you have already analyzed.

- The graph icons are present for any terms that have not already been analyzed.

③ Select the check boxes next to the keywords you want to analyze.

④ Click Analyze.

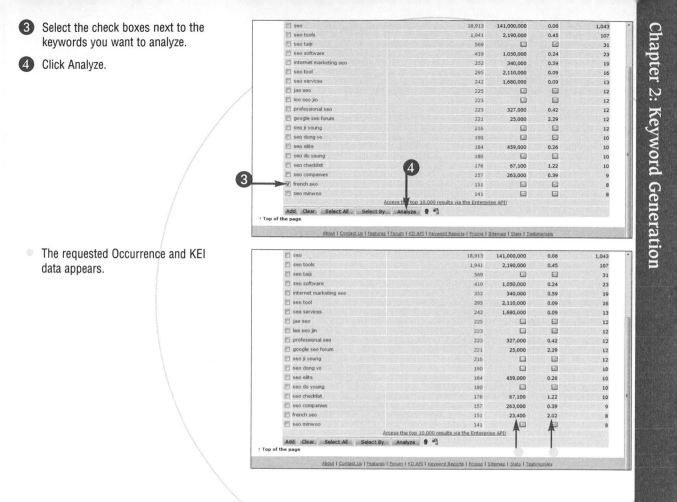

The requested Occurrence and KEI data appears.

When you use the Analyze section of Keyword Discovery, keep in mind that the data is not derived from actual data, but from best guess estimates. This data should be combined with other keyword-generation tools such as KeyCompete.com and Compete.com to form the starting point of your keyword research.

The biggest advantage of the Keyword Discovery tool is the ability to narrow your potential keyword pool down to the most effective words for your Web site. From there, you can look at who is currently ranking for these terms, and use the other tools mentioned in this chapter, such as Seodigger.com and the Google Keyword Suggestion Tool, to find even more information.

The estimated data is derived from a comparison between the engines that Keyword Discovery uses to gather data and the total number of searches done online every day. For example, if the engines that provide data to Keyword Discovery process 5 percent of the monthly searches, multiplying that data by 20 gives a rough estimate of the total search volume actually performed.

Filter Keywords with Keyword Discovery

Keyword Discovery offers a keyword filter tool that is incredibly useful when expanding on existing keywords for both PPC and SEO campaigns. The filter enables you to automatically add a prefix, suffix, or both to each keyword on a list, which is far more reliable than performing similar functions manually. In addition, the Keyword Discovery filter tool can accomplish time-consuming keyword edits and additions in seconds, saving you valuable time. Aside from the prefix and suffix additions, the filter tool also offers a mass find-and-replace tool, which is a valuable option for adding common synonyms into your keyword list.

Using the Keyword Discovery filter tool to expand your preliminary keyword list is very helpful when building out a PPC account for an e-commerce site. For example, the filter tool allows you to easily insert descriptive prefixes and suffixes onto the base keywords commonly used when someone is searching with the intent to make

a purchase. Adding prefixes like "buy" or "discount" and suffixes like "on sale" to your general keywords ensures that your ads are shown to people actively looking to purchase your products.

The filter tool can also help enhance your SEO efforts. When looking for new keywords to target, you can greatly benefit from experimenting with prefixes, suffixes, and synonyms. As with building out a PPC keyword list, you can add common prefixes and suffixes to your base keywords and also introduce common synonyms to further expand your list. This aids in content building because you can also analyze the search volume for all your newly generated keywords. This may lead to the discovery of low-competition phrases with fairly significant volume. Moreover, keywords that contain prefixes or suffixes tend to be easier to rank for than keywords without such extensions.

Filter Keywords with Keyword Discovery

① Navigate to www.keyworddiscovery.com and log in to your account.

② Click the Filter link at the top of the page.

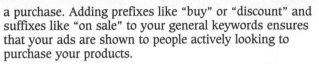

③ Insert your keywords into the field labeled Insert Keywords Here.

④ Fill in the Find What field with the keyword you want to replace.

⑤ Fill in the Replace With field with the word that you want to replace the word from the Find What field.

⑥ Click Filter Keywords.

- Notice the word has been replaced in the Filtered Keyword Results window.

7 Enter a word you want to combine with your keyword list.

8 Click Prefix or Suffix.

- Notice the addition of the prefix.

Extra

Keyword Discovery's keyword filter tool gives you the option to import the *meta keywords* from any Web page URL. Meta keywords are the keywords Webmasters use within the keyword meta tag of a Web site to highlight important keywords for reference by search-engine spiders.

Keyword Discovery's keyword filter tool is very useful when researching your competition. By importing the meta keywords of your competition, you can get a very good feel for the keywords they have decided to target. You can utilize your competitors' selected keywords as a base list and expand on them by using prefixes, suffixes, and synonyms. You can also input each competitor's keywords into the research tool and see if they have missed a higher-volume keyword with manageable competition.

If you have a keyword project already built within Keyword Discovery, you can easily import the list into the keyword filter tool. All you need to do is click the project name in the box labeled Projects, and then click the Load button. You can then make any additions to your list using the keyword filter tools, and save the newly generated keywords to your project by clicking Save Filtered Results to Selected Project. You always want to save your projects, especially because you can combine, compare, and contrast keyword lists generated from various keyword research tools.

An Introduction to Creating Pages

Creating search-engine-optimized Web pages is the core effort of a successful Internet marketing campaign. Taking care of technical on-site factors such as filenames, title tags, meta description tags, meta keyword tags, and meta robots tags is crucial to making sure the search-engine spiders can determine the relevance of your Web site. Think of search-engine spiders as robots that read the content of your Web pages. Optimizing your content with header tags and other text modifiers allows you to stress the main ideas and topics that your content covers. Optimization of images is important for those Web browsers that do not support images, and because search-engine spiders cannot read the content of an image, optimizing images presents an extra avenue to squeeze in more content. Links provide the pathways that search-engine spiders need to find your Web pages. Creating these links with search-engine optimization in mind is necessary for optimal results. Throughout the Web page creation process, try to adhere to the standards set forth by the World Wide Web Consortium (W3C). The consortium works to create standards in Web design and development that ensure Internet-wide compatibility.

Choose Filenames

Every Web page that you create is stored in a file. Every file has a name. Using filenames that are relevant to the content of your Web page is important for numerous reasons. Besides your domain name, the search-engine spiders see your filenames before anything else. If your filenames are not relevant to the content contained on that page, the search engines can algorithmically detect a disconnect. Taking the extra time to ensure that filenames are properly designed can provide an added boost to your rankings.

Optimize Meta Description Tags

Meta description tags allow you to summarize what a particular Web page's content is about. Some search engines use the meta description tags in their results pages directly underneath the Web page titles. Your rankings on these search engines are likely influenced by your meta description tags. Writing a brief yet informative description about your Web page's content and adding it to your meta description tag is a search-engine-optimization tactic that should not be skipped.

Optimize Title Tags

Title tags are an extremely influential search-engine ranking factor. What you place in your Web page title tags has a substantial effect on where and for what terms your page ranks. Just as importantly, the first thing a human visitor sees when finding your page on the search-engine results is your title tag. Title tags should be descriptive of what your Web page is about and compel potential visitors to your site.

Optimize Meta Keyword Tags

Meta keyword tags allow you to indicate the relevance of a particular Web page to certain keywords and phrases. Although many search engines ignore this tag, some likely still use it in their ranking algorithms. For that reason alone, you want to implement this tag on all your Web pages. The keywords and phrases contained in your meta keyword tags work in tandem with the meta description tag to describe the content of a particular Web page.

Create a Meta Robots Tag

Sometimes you may not actually want the search-engine spiders to visit certain pages within your Web site. Although this is often not the case, especially because the goals of search-engine optimization are to increase search-engine-generated traffic, there are situations where the privacy of a particular Web page or Web site is of utmost concern. The meta robots tag allows you to identify what pages the search engines are allowed to index in their results pages, and whether or not they are allowed to follow links on those pages to other Web pages or Web sites. This is especially useful if certain sections of your Web site require payment to access. The last thing you want is search engines sending visitors directly to those locations.

Optimize Images

Search-engine spiders are becoming more sophisticated every day, but the spiders still cannot read any images present on your pages. If images make up a large portion of your content, the search engines will have a difficult time understanding the topic of your content. Using alt image tags to describe your images gives the search engines a readable text description of those images and also aids in compatibility with nongraphical Web browsers.

Benefit with Header Tags

Optimizing your content includes emphasizing your main topics and ideas. A well-structured Web page has a logical hierarchal flow with headings and subheadings fortified with content. These main topics and ideas can be placed within header tags that not only alter the format of the text the Web browser displays, but also tell the search engines and human visitors that these keywords and phrases are important.

Create Links

Your internal linking structure leads the search-engine spiders and human visitors from one Web page to another on your Web site. The structure of your links tells the search engines what the linked Web page is about. Your internal linking structure is taken into consideration by the ranking algorithms that determine where your Web pages rank for target keywords and phrases. Making it simple for both the search engines and human visitors to find every page on your Web site is critical for optimal Web site structure.

Using Text Modifiers

Beyond just optimizing your main topics and ideas, you want to emphasize appropriate keywords and phrases within your content. Your Web page content should speak to visitors, emphasizing words and phrases to express urgency or significance. Using text modifiers, you can emphasize certain blocks of text by bolding, italicizing, or underlining. The search engines also take modified text into consideration when determining your content's relevance to that text.

Validate HTML

Writing valid HTML is just as important as speaking proper English. Improper HTML can cause Web browser incompatibilities that result in your Web site appearing differently across different browsers. The World Wide Web Consortium has gone to great lengths to develop standards for Web development to ensure compliance across all browsers.

Choose Filenames

Choosing correct filenames is an important first task when you create Web pages. Besides your domain name, the first thing search engines discover when spidering through the pages of your Web site are your filenames. Every single page of your Web site resides in a different file. These files can be written in HTML, PHP, ASP, or any other Web programming language. When you title your pages with search-engine optimization in mind, you have a powerful opportunity to establish relevance to a certain topic or keyword. Before you even write your first page of content or acquire that first link back to your site, make sure your filenames are relevant.

Before you generate a Web page, have a specific topic in mind. Just as it makes sense to fill that Web page with keywords relevant to the topic, you should also give the file a relevant name. If you are writing an HTML Web page about San Francisco hotels, and you are trying to rank highly for the search term "San Francisco Hotels," consider naming the HTML file sanfranciscohotels.html or san-francisco-hotels.html.

Making your filenames relevant to the content contained within the page is also important for organizational purposes. If you follow this practice, you name each Web page after the main key phrase that the page is about. Both search engines and your visitors associate the name of the page with the content that it contains. This titling is much more effective than a more conventional naming style like page1.html, page2.html, and so on, especially when you want to make changes to the content of individual pages on a Web site that has grown to hundreds or even thousands of pages.

Choose Filenames

① Open a Web page in any text editor such as Notepad or a Web development program.

② Analyze the content of the page and choose a proper filename when you save it.

③ Upload the file with the optimized filename to your server.

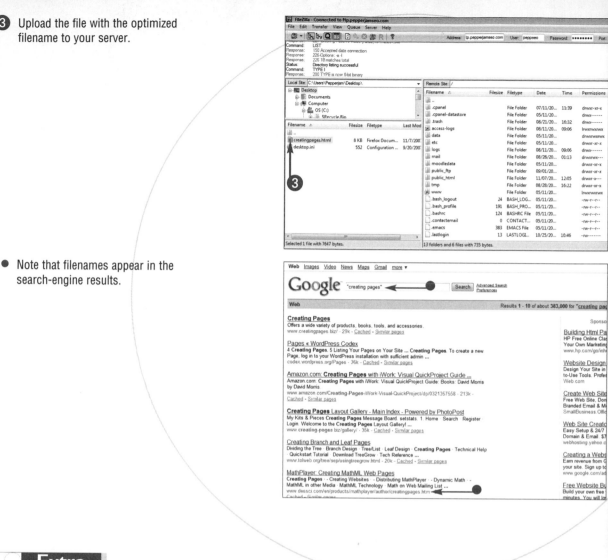

● Note that filenames appear in the search-engine results.

Extra

Authorities at the major search engines have stated that hyphens in URLs and Web page filenames are viewed as spaces by the search-engine ranking algorithms. This is important because hyphen usage in domain names and Web page filenames aids in readability and organization when used in moderation. Overuse of hyphens is considered to be a spamming technique and can result in a penalty by the search engines if used to an unreasonable extent. The search engines do not specify to what extent hyphen usage is acceptable, but try to limit hyphen usage to no more than three hyphens per filename. If possible, use no more than two. Recently, the search engines have begun to treat underscores similar to hyphens, so you should limit your underscore usage as well.

Also, make a consistent effort to keep URL lengths as short as possible. It appears awkward to human visitors if URLs exceed a certain length. Often, Web site visitors take note of the Web pages they visit and commit the URLs to memory. A 30-character URL is far easier to remember than a 300-character URL. Always remember to keep your human visitors in mind when you apply search-engine-optimization techniques.

Optimize Title Tags

The title tag is possibly your most important consideration when you try to raise your search-engine rankings for a particular keyword or phrase. Search engines use the text contained within the title tag as a primary factor to determine what the content of a certain Web page is about. The text that makes up your title tag is also the clickable link text that typically appears on the search-engine results pages when your site appears in the rankings. Title tag text also appears at the top of a Web browser when someone is visiting a particular page on your Web site.

The title tag is located in the header of an HTML document and its syntax is as follows:

```
<HEAD>
  <TITLE>The title of your Web page</TITLE>
  </HEAD>
```

Limit your title tag to 65 characters or less because most search engines do not display any more than that. Your title tag should be a concise statement summarizing the main point of your content, and should be compelling enough to entice search-engine users to click the link text and visit your site. Additionally, your title tag must be unique for each and every page of your Web site and should include the one or two keywords you want the page to rank for.

If you are building a Web site for a business, include the company name in the title tag. If your company name is already well known, search-engine users may try to find it; having the company name in the title tag facilitates that process. If the brand is not well known, including it in the title tag with the key phrase or phrases that describe the field in which it operates provides an opportunity to present that company as an authority in the field.

Optimize Title Tags

① Open a Web page in any text editor such as Notepad or a Web development program and locate the <HEAD> tag.

② Within your <HEAD></HEAD> tags, type <TITLE>, followed by your optimized title text, and close the title tag with </TITLE>.

③ Save the file, and upload it to your Web server.

● The title appears at the top of your Web browser when you visit that page.

To increase relevancy for the keywords or phrases that you have included in your title tags, consider naming your files based on those terms. Your Web page's filenames should relate very closely to those pages' title tags.

Also, when you link from one page to another on your Web site, your link text should be closely related to the title tag of the page linked to. The same applies when acquiring links from other Web sites, which is discussed in more detail in Chapter 8. If those links contain link text that is closely related to the title tag of the page on your Web site, the major search engines are likely to conclude that your Web page is relevant to those terms.

Be mindful to create unique title tags for each page of your Web site. Due to the ranking influence that the title tag possesses, a search-engine penalty is likely to result if the same title tag is repeated across all pages.

Optimize Meta Description Tags

You should optimize each and every meta description tag on your Web site because meta description tags are part of the display information that visitors see when your site is listed in the search engines. The meta description tag contains a brief description of what your Web page is about, and although not as influential as it once was in the search-engine ranking process, the meta description tag is important because you can use it as a method to deliver your marketing message and entice search-engine visitors to click your listing versus clicking your competition.

The meta description tag is located in the header of an HTML document, and its syntax is as follows:

```
<HEAD>
 <META NAME="description" CONTENT="This is a
 brief description of your Web page.">
 </HEAD>
```

At one time, the meta description tag could be stuffed with keywords and phrases in an attempt to trick the search engines into believing a Web page was more relevant for those terms than it actually was. Advances in search-engine ranking algorithms have reduced the impact the meta description tag has on rankings but from a human visitor standpoint, it is still very important. When search-engine users find your page in the search-engine results, the text contained within your meta description tag often appears directly underneath the title tag.

Create a few compelling sentences describing your product, services, or Web site content, and place them in your meta description tag. The description should interest the potential visitor and tempt that person to click your search-engine result link. Make sure all your pages have unique meta description tags. You may be tempted to replicate the same tag throughout your entire Web site, but this practice is likely to hurt your rankings; the major search engines could determine that all your pages are duplicates.

Optimize Meta Description Tags

Create a Meta Description Tag

① Open a Web page in any text editor such as Notepad or a Web development program and locate the `<HEAD>` tag.

② Within your `<HEAD></HEAD>` tags, type `<META NAME= "description" CONTENT="`, your optimized meta description tag, and `">`.

③ Save the file, and upload it to your Web server.

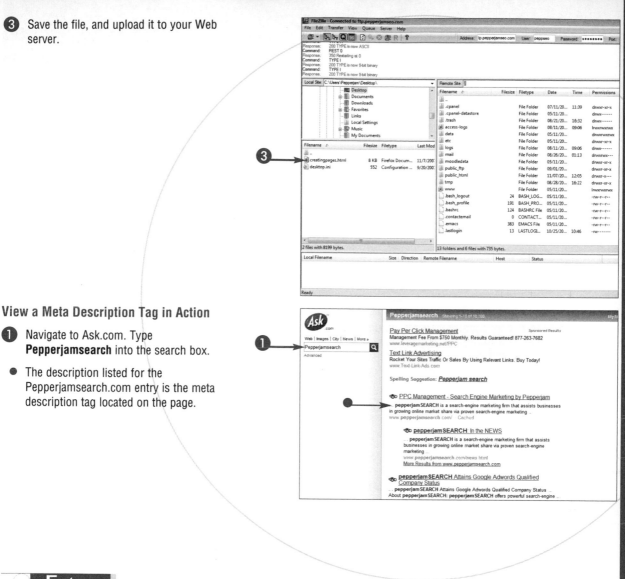

View a Meta Description Tag in Action

① Navigate to Ask.com. Type **Pepperjamsearch** into the search box.

● The description listed for the Pepperjamsearch.com entry is the meta description tag located on the page.

Extra

Not all search engines use the meta description tag in the results pages. Google, for example, generates its own description based on the content contained within the particular Web page. Whether Google uses meta description tags in its ranking algorithms is not known. Still, you should take advantage of the search-engine spiders that do use the meta description tag in their ranking algorithms. Less-popular but still-significant search engines such as Ask.com, AltaVista, AllTheWeb, and Teoma do still use the meta description tag in their results.

Try the free meta tag generator from SeoBook.com at http://tools.seobook.com/meta-medic. Simply enter your preferred page title, a description of the page, and a list of relevant keywords, and this tool generates a complete set of meta tags for you to copy and paste onto your Web page.

Optimize Meta Keyword Tags

Perhaps the least-important factor in optimizing a Web site for search-engine rankings is the use of the meta keyword tag. Similar to the meta description tag, the meta keyword tag contains a list of keywords or phrases, separated by commas, that describe the subject matter of a particular Web page. Today, the search engines give little consideration to meta keyword tags. Still, you should not skip implementing this tag on all your Web pages. What sort of significance the search engines may place on this tag in the future is impossible to know, and although you are not likely to see an increase in your rankings with today's ranking algorithms, anything is possible down the road.

In the mid-1990s, back when search engines were much less sophisticated and had much less computing power, the meta keyword tag was used by the search engines to determine what keywords and phrases a Web page should rank for. As you can imagine, it did not take long before

the meta keyword tag was exploited to obtain search-engine rankings for keywords and phrases that had nothing to do with the actual content of certain pages.

The meta keyword tag is located in the header of an HTML document, and its syntax is as follows:

```
<HEAD>
 <META NAME="keywords" CONTENT="a, list, of,
 keywords, describing, your, web, page,
 separated, by, commas">
 </HEAD>
```

For each page on your Web site, generate a short list of no more than ten keywords or phrases and include them in the meta keyword tag. Do not repeat keywords or phrases, and be sure that each Web page on your site has a unique meta keyword tag. Again, although you may be tempted to duplicate this tag throughout your site, your rankings could decrease as a result due to duplicate content.

Optimize Meta Keyword Tags

① Open a Web page in any text editor such as Notepad or a Web development program and locate the `<HEAD>` tag.

①

```
creatingpages - Notepad
File  Edit  Format  View  Help
<!DOCTYPE HTML PUBLIC "-//W3C//DTD HTML 4.01 Transitional//EN" "http://www.w3.org/TR/html4/loose.dtd">
<HTML>
<HEAD>
<STYLE TYPE="text/css">
<!--
H1 {
Font-size: 25px;
Font-family: Arial, Verdana, sans-serif;
Color: black; }
H2 {
Font-size: 15px;
Font-family: Arial, Verdana, sans-serif;
Color: black;
Padding: 0;
Margin: 0; }
STRONG {
Font-size: 15px;
Font-family: Arial, Verdana, sans-serif;
Color: black; }
-->
</STYLE>
<TITLE>Creating Pages</TITLE>
```

② Within your `<HEAD></HEAD>` tags, type `<META NAME="keywords" CONTENT="`, followed by your optimized meta description tag, and `">`.

②

```
creatingpages - Notepad
File  Edit  Format  View  Help
<!DOCTYPE HTML PUBLIC "-//W3C//DTD HTML 4.01 Transitional//EN" "http://www.w3.org/TR/html4/loose.dtd">
<HTML>
<HEAD>
<STYLE TYPE="text/css">
<!--
H1 {
Font-size: 25px;
Font-family: Arial, Verdana, sans-serif;
Color: black; }
H2 {
Font-size: 15px;
Font-family: Arial, Verdana, sans-serif;
Color: black;
Padding: 0;
Margin: 0; }
STRONG {
Font-size: 15px;
Font-family: Arial, Verdana, sans-serif;
Color: black; }
-->
</STYLE>
<TITLE>Creating Pages</TITLE>
<META HTTP-EQUIV="Content-Type" CONTENT="text/html; charset=utf-8">
<META NAME="description" CONTENT="Creating search-engine optimized Web pages is the core effort of a suc
<META NAME="keywords" CONTENT="file names,title tags,meta description tag,meta keywords tag,meta robots
<META NAME="robots" CONTENT="index,follow">
</HEAD>
```

Save the file, and upload it to your Web server.

● View the source to verify the keywords are placed correctly.

SeoCentro offers an invaluable tool to help analyze meta tags at www.seocentro.com/tools/search-engines/metatag-analyzer.html. The tool analyzes every meta tag of a Web page and offers suggestions to improve those tags. It analyzes the length and relevancy of your title, description, and keywords meta tags. It also verifies that all the tags, including the robots tag discussed in the next task, are formatted correctly. Incorrectly formatted tags can render your HTML unreadable by the search engines, causing a ranking penalty, and they could prevent a Web browser from loading your page correctly, thus rendering it unreadable to human visitors as well.

Try to make sure your meta tags follow the guidelines and suggestions the tool mentions. Keep your title, description, and keywords meta tags within the length requirements. The tool can also be used to analyze your competitors' meta tags if you are curious to see what they have done differently.

The tool also analyzes the size and load time of the page. Pages that are too large or take too long to load can aggravate your visitors and push them out the door.

Create a Meta Robots Tag

You can use the meta robots tag to tell a search-engine spider whether or not the Web page it visits should be indexed or if links on that page should be followed. These search-engine "robots" often need to be controlled. The meta robots tag is not used as extensively now as in the past because much more functionality can be obtained through the use of a robots.txt file, which is discussed in Chapter 5. Depending on your Web hosting, you may not have the ability to create and add a robots.txt file. If that is the case, using the meta robots tag is the only method available to at least partially control the behavior of the search-engine spiders.

The meta robots tag is located in the header of an HTML document, and its syntax is as follows:

```
<HEAD>
  <META NAME="robots" CONTENT="index,follow"> or
  <META NAME="robots" CONTENT="noindex,follow"> or
  <META NAME="robots" CONTENT="index,nofollow"> or
  <META NAME="robots" CONTENT="noindex,nofollow">
</HEAD>
```

The meta robots tag includes directives for the search-engine spiders. The four directives available are `index`, `noindex`, `follow`, and `nofollow`. Including `index` in the meta robots tag tells the spiders to index that page. `Noindex` tells the spiders not to index that page. Including `follow` tells the spiders to follow links on that page. `Nofollow` tells the spiders not to follow links on that page. Use only one of the four variations at a time. You can also use `CONTENT= "all"` in exchange of `"index,follow"` or `CONTENT= "none"` in exchange for `"noindex,nofollow"`.

Normally, you use these directives to block the search-engine spiders from indexing a certain piece of content such as a product or piece of information that a visitor would have to purchase before accessing. You may want to consider investing in a Web hosting service that allows you to use a robots.txt file if that is the case because it provides a more robust layer of protection.

Create a Meta Robots Tag

① Locate a Web page on your site that you do not want the search engines to index.

② Open that Web page in any text editor such as Notepad or a Web development program and locate the `<HEAD>` tag.

③ Within your `<HEAD></HEAD>` tags, type `<META NAME="robots" CONTENT="noindex,nofollow">`.

Note: This meta robots tag prevents the search engines from indexing a page and following any links from that page.

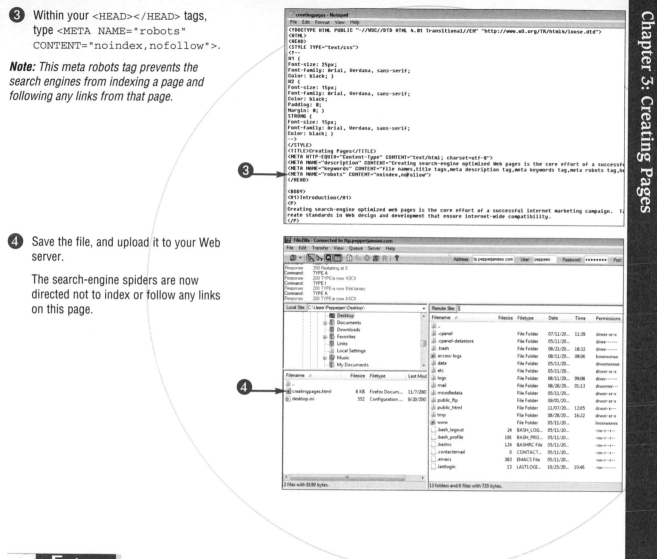

④ Save the file, and upload it to your Web server.

The search-engine spiders are now directed not to index or follow any links on this page.

There are special meta robots tags for both the Google and Bing search-engine spiders. Generally, the normal meta robots tag should be enough to control the activity of these robots, but sometimes you may want a more granular level of control over what spiders are allowed to do.

Google's spider is called Googlebot. To control Googlebot, instead of the NAME attribute being set to robots in your meta robots tag, set it to Googlebot. You have a few extra options besides the index, noindex, follow, and nofollow directives. You can also tell Googlebot not to archive a copy of your Web page in its cache by using the directive noarchive. If you do not want a description of your Web page to show up in the Google results page, you can use the directive nosnippet.

Bing's spider is called MSNBot. To control MSNBot, instead of setting the NAME attribute to robots in your meta robots tag, set it to MSNBot. MSNBot obeys only the noindex, nofollow, and noarchive directives.

Add Emphasis with Header Tags

Y ou can use HTML header tags to apply significance to keywords or phrases within a Web page. Placing a selection of text within a header tag tells the search-engine spiders that the text is of a certain level of importance. Search-engine ranking algorithms place emphasis on text enclosed within header tags when determining where pages should be ranked for these terms. Much like the other tasks of this chapter, the use of header tags is standard practice and should be viewed as a best-practices starting point.

Header tags are arranged in preset levels of importance ranging from `<H1>`, the most important, to `<H6>`, the least important. Unless it is modified through other means, text enclosed within an `<H1>` tag appears larger than its neighboring text on the Web page, and text enclosed within an `<H6>` tag appears smaller.

Header tags can be used anywhere within the `<BODY>` tag of an HTML document, and the appearance of the resulting formatting can be altered with Cascading Style Sheets. Their syntax is as follows:

```
<H1>Text enclosed within a Header 1 Tag</H1>
<H2>Text enclosed within a Header 2 Tag</H2>
```

Beyond using header tags to highlight text on your pages, you can use them to logically format your content into hierarchal topics and subtopics. For example, if you are writing an information page about PPC management, place that key phrase in a header tag like `<H1>PPC Management</H1>`. If within that same topic there is the subtopic "PPC management services," place that key phrase in a subheader like `<H2>PPC Management Services</H2>`.

Do not expect drastic increases in rankings for keywords and phrases highlighted by header tags, but always try to use them wherever appropriate in your Web page creation. You are providing a service to both the search engines and your visitors by visually emphasizing the important topics.

Add Emphasis with Header Tags

① Open a Web page in any text editor such as Notepad or a Web development program and locate a main topic.

② Find text you want to emphasize.

③ Add an `<H1>` tag in front of this text and an `</H1>` tag following the text.

④ Save the file, and upload it to your Web server.

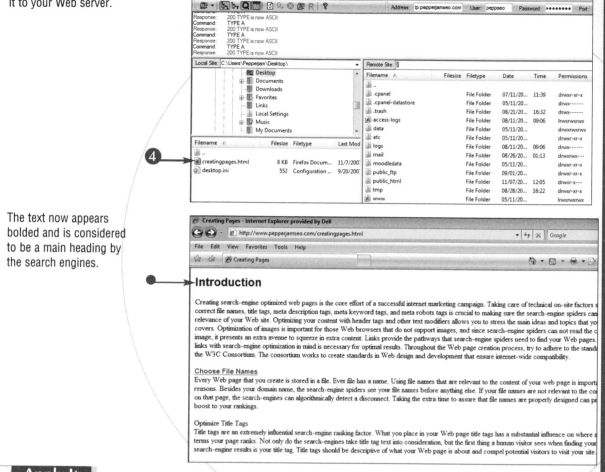

● The text now appears bolded and is considered to be a main heading by the search engines.

Although excellent for search-engine-optimization purposes, header tags are not always visitor and appearance friendly. Header tags have been around since the first incarnations of the HTML language. This was a time when information exchange was the sole function of the Web, long before it became the interactive media outlet that it is today. Luckily, the appearance of header tag text can be modified while preserving its influence on the search-engine ranking algorithms. It requires using Cascading Style Sheets, also called CSS. Add the following code inside your header tag:

```
<style type="text/css">
<! --
H1 {
Font-size: 20px;
Font-family: Arial, Verdana, sans-serif;
Color: blue; }
-- >
</style>
```

Now, any time that you use an <H1> tag within your content, its font is Arial, the color blue, and the size 20. These modifications are useful when you want the header tag text to match the rest of your Web site. To discuss the many uses of CSS requires a book in itself, but many resources on the Web provide free tutorials. A good starting point is the CSS tutorial by W3Schools.com located at www.w3schools.com/css/default.asp.

Using Text Modifiers

As discussed in the previous task, you can modify text on a Web page to emphasize important keywords and phrases to help search engines and human visitors identify the main topic of that page. This can lead to higher rankings for those terms. Besides header tags, you can use other text-modifying tags to place emphasis on certain keywords, phrases, or blocks of text.

These tags include <STRONG>, <EM>, <B>, <I>, and <U>. Usage of these tags works as follows:

```
<STRONG>Strongly emphasized text</STRONG>
<EM>Emphasized text</EM>
<B>Bolded text</B>
<I>Italic text</I>
<U>Underlined text</U>
```

Whereas header tags should be used to emphasize the main topics that logically break content into different sections, use these other text-modifying tags within those bodies of content.

Use the <STRONG> tag to strongly emphasize an important selection of text. If you want to stress a point that you are trying to get across, place it within a <STRONG> tag. Web browsers normally bold the text within a <STRONG> tag.

Use the <EM> tag to emphasize an important selection of text. This tag is similar to the <STRONG> tag, but Web browsers tend to display it in the form of italicized text.

Use the <B> and <I> tags if your intent is purely to bold or italicize text. These tags differ from the <STRONG> and <EM> tags in that they are not intended to portray any semantic meaning. They are strictly presentational elements. The <U> tag should be used to underline text. Much like the <B> and <I> tags, it is not intended to portray any semantic meaning.

Although it is unlikely that use of these tags is going to provide any serious boost to your rankings, it is important to understand that search-engine optimization is a cumulative effort, and the use of these practices together is what provides results.

Using Text Modifiers

1. Open a Web page in any text editor such as Notepad or a Web development program.

2. Find text you want to modify.

3. Add a <STRONG> tag in front of this text and a </STRONG> tag following the text.

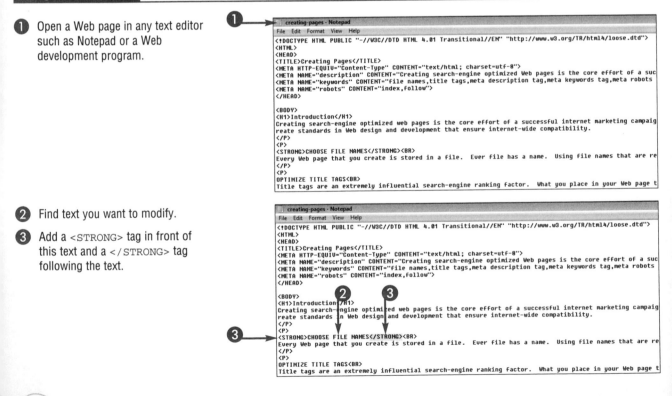

④ Save the file, and upload it to your Web server.

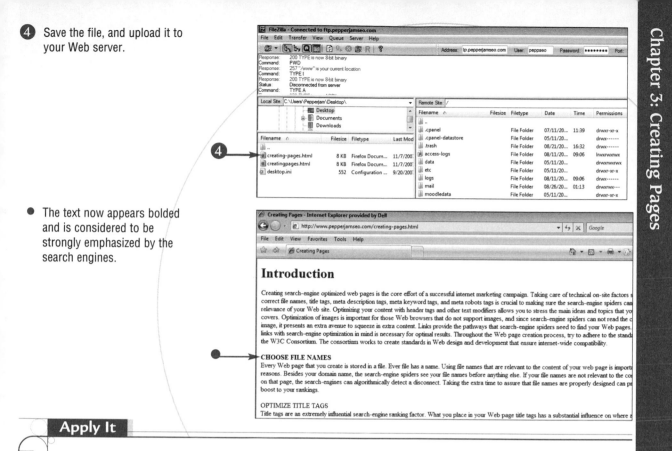

● The text now appears bolded and is considered to be strongly emphasized by the search engines.

Much like header tags, all text modifier tags can be altered using CSS while preserving their search-engine ranking influence. Add the following code inside your header tag:

```
<style type="text/css">
<! --
STRONG {
Font-size: 25px;
Font-weight: bold;
Font-family: Arial, Verdana, sans-serif;
Color: red; }
-- >
</style>
```

Now, any time that you use a <STRONG> tag within your content, its font is size 25, Arial, red, and bolded. These modifications are useful when you want the header tag text to match the rest of your Web site. You may want to use your text modifier tags to emphasize text within your content but not visibly highlight the text in any way. If that is the case, add the following code inside your header tag:

```
<style type="text/css">
<! --
STRONG,EM {
Text-decoration: none; }
-- >
</style>
```

Now, any time you use the <STRONG> or <EM> text modifier tag, the text is not modified in any way. You have still emphasized that text within your HTML document though, and the search engines still understand your intent.

Optimize Images

Sometimes you want to use an image in your content instead of a selection of text, and you can use alt image tags to ensure that search engines understand what the image is about. Search engines cannot accurately read images, so unless you explicitly tell the search engines what your images are about, those images provide no overall search-engine-optimization value to the content of your page. Although images are not necessarily search-engine friendly, they are a vital part of visitor-friendly design. A vibrant, colorful, image-based Web site compels its visitors to stay longer and browse more pages. It can also increase visitor trust and lead to higher sale-conversion rates.

As a general rule you should limit the use of images on your Web page; if you can say what you want to with text, you should. However, if you use images, you should also use alt image tags. An alt image tag is located within an `<IMG>` tag, and its syntax is as follows:

```
<IMG SRC="yourimage.jpg" ALT="A brief
 description of the image.">
```

The alt image tag is a textual replacement for an image. If for any reason an image cannot be displayed, the alt image text appears in its place. It also appears when you position a mouse pointer over the image for a period of time.

Rather than just fill your alt image tags with lists of keywords or phrases, take the time to write a unique, relevant description of the image being described. alt image tags have been historically abused by spammers trying to stuff as many keywords or phrases into their Web pages as they possibly can. Abuse of these tags can lead to a rankings penalty, so be careful when writing your descriptions. Do not repeat the same words over and over again, and never repeat the same alt image tag more than once unless the image itself is repeated.

Optimize Images

① Open a Web page in any text editor such as notepad.exe or a Web development program and locate an image insertion.

② Find the `<IMG>` tag, add `ALT="`, type an optimized image description, and then add a closing quote.

③ Save the file, and upload it to your Web server.

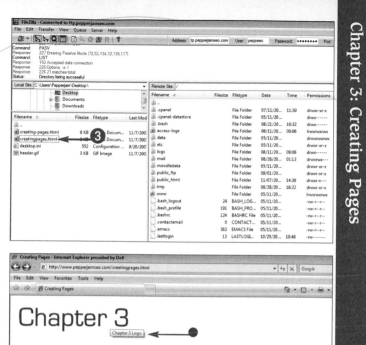

● When you position your mouse over the image, the alt image description appears.

Believe it or not, some Internet users still use nongraphical, text-based Web browsers. This may include visually impaired users who employ screen readers or users who simply prefer very simple displays. These browsers cannot read images, but are sophisticated enough to display alt image tags in their place. Although the number of users of these browsers is very small, they, like all other Internet users, should be able to access your Web page and use the content that you provide.

Images can increase the usability and improve the appearance of your Web site, but whenever possible, use actual text within your content instead of images. The search engines read alt image tags and take that text into consideration when ranking pages, but alt image text is not an equal substitute for actual text included within the body of the page.

Create Links

You can create an internal link structure that allows search-engine spiders, as well as human beings, to quickly and easily navigate your Web site. Just like human visitors, search engines use links to navigate the Internet. As search-engine spiders crawl from page to page within a single Web site and then from page to page across multiple Web sites, each and every link is taken into consideration by individual search-engine ranking algorithms. Although it can be difficult to control how many links point to your Web site from other sources, you can easily control how your own internal links are structured. Link creation may be a basic task, but if done correctly, it can be tremendously influential to your overall search-engine rankings.

A link is created within an HTML anchor tag, and its syntax is as follows:

```
<A HREF="http://www.somesite.com/page.
html">Link Anchor Text</A>
```

`<A></A>` tags are anchor tags and indicate that the element located within will become a hyperlink. HREF stands for *hypertext reference* and its attribute is set to a URL.

Creating effective links involves only two elements. First, be sure to always use absolute URLs even when linking within your own Web site. Instead of `<A HREF="page.html">Next Page</A>`, use `<A HREF="http://www.yoursite.com/page.html">Next Page</A>`. If you use relative URLs, links no longer work if you move pages from one directory to another unless the entire file structure moves with it.

Second, always make sure the anchor text is descriptive. You learn more about the proper use of anchor text in Chapter 8, but for now, know that the search engines use the anchor text of a link to determine what the page being linked to is about. So, if you are linking to a page about LCD televisions, use "LCD Televisions" as your anchor text rather than something more general and nondescript like "Click Here."

Create Links

① Open a Web page in any text editor such as Notepad or a Web development program and find a location to place a link.

② Type `<A HREF="`, the URL of the Web page you are linking to, and `">`.

③ Add descriptive link anchor text and follow it with `</A>`.

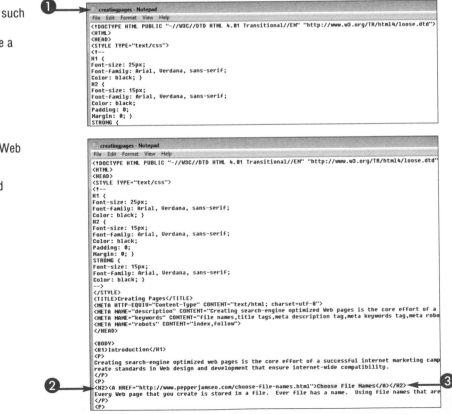

④ Save the file, and upload it to your Web server.

● A hyperlink has been created.

Introduction

Creating search-engine optimized web pages is the core effort of a successful internet marketing campaign. Taking care of technical on-site factors correct file names, title tags, meta description tags, meta keyword tags, and meta robots tags is crucial to making sure the search-engine spiders ca relevance of your Web site. Optimizing your content with header tags and other text modifiers allows you to stress the main ideas and topics that yo covers. Optimization of images is important for those Web browsers that do not support images, and since search-engine spiders can not read the image, it presents an extra avenue to squeeze in extra content. Links provide the pathways that search-engine spiders need to find your Web pages links with search-engine optimization in mind is necessary for optimal results. Throughout the Web page creation process, try to adhere to the stand the W3C Consortium. The consortium works to create standards in Web design and development that ensure internet-wide compatibility.

Choose File Names

Every Web page that you create is stored in a file. Ever file has a name. Using file names that are relevant to the content of your web page is import reasons. Besides your domain name, the search-engine spiders see your file names before anything else. If your file names are not relevant to the c on that page, the search-engines can algorithmically detect a disconnect. Taking the extra time to assure that file names are properly designed can p boost to your rankings.

Optimize Title Tags

Title tags are an extremely influential search-engine ranking factor. What you place in your Web page title tags has a substantial influence on where terms your page ranks. Not only do the search-engines take title tag text into consideration, but the first thing a human visitor sees when finding you search-engine results is your title tag. Title tags should be descriptive of what your Web page is about and compel potential visitors to visit your site

Optimize Meta Description Tags

Meta description tags allow you to summarize what a particular Web page's content is about. Some search-engines use the meta description tags in pages directly underneath the Web page titles. Your rankings on these search-engines are likely influenced by your meta description tags. Writing a descriptive description about your Web page's content and adding it to your meta description tag is a search-engine optimization tactic that should a

Extra

The search engines place more credibility on links assigned to certain locations on a Web page. Generally speaking, the higher a link appears on the page, the more it assists the rankings of the Web page it links to. Also, links embedded within blocks of content hold more value than isolated links. You can use this to your advantage by making sure the most important pages of your Web site are linked to in prominent, content-laden locations. Your overall Web site navigation menu should appear on the top of your page in a prominent location. These links to the main categories of your Web site are of utmost importance for both the search engines and human visitors.

If possible, avoid using images to link to other pages of your Web site. As discussed in the previous task, search engines cannot read images, and thus you lose the opportunity to attach descriptive link anchor text to that page. alt image tag text is not passed as anchor text when linking from an image.

Validate HTML

Valid, properly written HTML allows search engines to easily read your Web page content and underlying HTML code. Much like the English language, there is a right way and a wrong way to write the code that structures your Web pages. The World Wide Web Consortium (W3C), an international group that works to develop protocols and guidelines that ensure the long-term growth of the Web, has developed standards for HTML development. Web browser developers like Mozilla and Microsoft adhere to these standards to guarantee cross-browser uniformity when displaying Web pages.

Search engines read Web sites line by line, and errors in your HTML syntax can trigger a penalty if the invalid code prevents the search-engine spider from reading the content. Invalid code can cause Web sites to look different from browser to browser. Some Web developers apply various patches and band-aids to minimize browser display problems instead of adhering to W3C standards, and although the end result may be browser compatibility, these patches often involve adding a substantial amount of unnecessary code. Avoid applying patches and band-aids by testing your code for standard compliance during the development process.

Use the W3C Markup Validation tool at http://validator. w3.org to test your Web page code for standard compliance. Just enter your Web site URL into the location bar, and the validation tool shows you any errors that your code contains and also gives suggestions to help you fix any problems.

You should make your best attempt to pass the validation test, but do not spend a great deal of time if it appears to be impossible. Many sites do not pass, including Google, Yahoo, and most other heavily visited Internet hot spots.

Validate HTML

① Navigate to http://validator. w3.org.

② In the address bar, enter a URL that you want to test for HTML standard validation.

③ Click Check.

- The results of the validation check appear.

④ Click Validation Output.

W3C° Markup Validation Service
Check the markup (HTML, XHTML, ...) of Web documents

Jump To: Validation Output ◀—— ④

This page is **not** Valid HTML 4.01 Transitional!

Result:	Failed validation, 1 Error
Address:	http://www.pepperjamseo.com/creating-pages.html
Encoding:	utf-8 (detect automatically) ▾
Doctype:	HTML 4.01 Transitional (detect automatically) ▾
Root Element:	HTML

Options

☐ Show Source   ☐ Show Outline   ⦿ List Messages Sequentially   ○ Group Error Messages by type

☐ Validate error pages   ☐ Verbose Output   ☐ Clean up Markup with HTML Tidy

Help on the options is available.

[Revalidate]

↑ TOP

- All the errors appear with suggestions to fix the problems.

↑ TOP

Validation Output: 1 Error

⊗ *Line 14, Column 3:* **end tag for element "P" which is not open.**

`</P>`

The Validator found an end tag for the above element, but that element is not currently open. This is often caused by a leftover end tag from an element that was removed during editing, or by an implicitly closed element (if you have an error related to an element being used where it is not allowed, this is almost certainly the case). In the latter case this error will disappear as soon as you fix the original problem.

If this error occurred in a script section of your document, you should probably read this FAQ entry.

↑ TOP

Home   About...   News   Docs   Help & FAQ   Feedback

Extra

Search engines are unlikely to penalize your site for including invalid code unless it significantly hinders the capability of the search-engine spiders to read your Web pages. W3C Markup Validation is primarily in place to ensure compatibility with all current and future technologies. As use of the Internet becomes more prevalent on portable devices like PDAs and cell phones, and new Web browsers are programmed for these specialty items, adhering to the W3C standards is likely to become more and more necessary if you want your Web site to display properly on these devices.

Valid HTML also tends to reduce the overall amount of code on your Web pages. Optimize your Web pages by not having excess markup code surrounding your main page content. Less markup code means a higher percentage of your page size is actual content.

Although it has not been proven to increase search-engine rankings, writing valid HTML is another weapon in an arsenal of best-practice techniques that are likely to have a cumulative effect on overall search-engine approval.

An Introduction to Basic Web Site Structure

Optimizing the basic structure of your Web site greatly increases the likelihood that search engines will successfully locate and index your content. Search-engine ranking algorithms analyze numerous on-site factors when determining where a Web page ranks for particular search terms. Some of these factors include your Web site content, your domain name, whether or not your Web site works on all browsers, your Web site structure, your navigational linking structure, the accessibility of all your pages, and your credibility. There are many things that you can do to optimize for these factors, including choosing reliable Web hosting, choosing an appropriate domain name, optimizing your site for all Web browsers, creating a logical site structure and navigational menus, generating a sitemap, and creating an About Us page and a Privacy Policy page.

On-site factors are absolutely critical to the process of search-engine optimization, or SEO. A well-optimized design and structure help to improve the overall performance of your Web site, help users to navigate it, and allow search engines to find and index all your content.

During the process of Web site design or redesign, ask yourself the following two basic questions: Does my Web site appeal to visitors? Is it search-engine friendly? Once you answer those two essential questions, build each page as a balance between the needs of the search engines and the experience of the user.

Find Web Hosting

The first step in the process of on-site optimization is choosing a reliable Web hosting company. Web hosting is required to make your Web site accessible on the Internet. If you choose an unreliable or poorly maintained Web host, your Web site faces numerous potential issues such as Web site downtime and potential security concerns. Choosing an appropriate Web host requires you to carefully evaluate and address all technical requirements of your Web site. Careful consideration must be given to your hosting package if you require e-commerce functionality or if you expect your Web site to get a significant amount of traffic. Depending on your needs, you can compare hosting packages based upon price, database needs, and bandwidth limitations, among other things.

Establish a Domain Name

Choosing a good domain name has two potential benefits. First, domain names work toward forming impressions about your online credibility. A well-thought-out domain name gives users the impression of value and trust. The second reason why you need to choose a relevant domain name is that a domain name is often the first thing the search-engine spiders see when indexing your Web site. Written by the software engineers at the search engines, spiders are programs that jump from Web site to Web site, reading content and following links. Search engines and potential Web site visitors view a poor domain name as noncredible and unreliable.

Optimize for Multiple Browsers

It is imperative that your Web site is viewable to users of all the major Web browsers. A Web browser enables a user to display and interact with text, images, and other information typically located on a Web site or local area network. It allows users to easily access information provided through HTML. Popular Web browsers such as Internet Explorer and Mozilla Firefox enable Internet users to view and interact with Web sites. At the same time, millions of people use mobile smart phones and other devices such as the Apple iPad to surf the Web, which requires that you optimize your Web site for multiple types of browsers. Unfortunately, each individual browser does not read HTML code in the same fashion. In fact, you may design a Web site a certain way and view it in Internet Explorer, only to find out later that it looks much different in Firefox. Because of these potential problems, you should test that your Web site is viewable in all browsers. Fortunately, tools are available that help make sure your Web site is compatible with multiple browsers.

Plan and Design a Web Site Structure

An effective Web site structure enhances user experience and allows search engines to determine the subject matter and relevancy of your site. You should create a blueprint of your site before you begin your design and content creation. It is important to keep all related Web site content grouped together into categories. For example, if your Web site is about gourmet food, you would have a cheese section, a sauce section, and a section on dry goods. Each of your categories should have unique directory and filename structures, so that when your Web site is indexed by search engines, your site demonstrates a wide breadth of content related to the subject. By doing this, the search engines can view your Web site as an *authority* across various areas of gourmet food.

You need to spend time working on your Web site structure. Failure to have a properly structured site can make it difficult if not impossible for search engines to properly index your Web site. Such a failure may lead search engines to omit your Web site from the search results and conclude that you are not an authority on the subject matter of your site.

Link within Subject Matter Themes

In order for search-engine spiders to locate and index all your Web site content, you need to develop a linking structure that allows search engines to find each and every page. At the same time, in order to maintain relevancy to particular topics, not every page on your site should be linked to each other because it would cause different categories, or *themes*, of your Web site to "bleed" into each other. Search engines favor pages with similarly themed content and tend to dislike pages that are not part of a larger subject or theme. Think of your linking structure as a means to logically progress from one page of your site to the next. By avoiding a haphazard linking structure, you ensure maximum effectiveness for both the search engines and your users.

Design a Sitemap

An effectively designed sitemap increases the likelihood that your site is indexed by search engines. A well-built sitemap displays the inner framework and organization of your Web site's content to the search engines. A sitemap should reflect the entire navigational framework of your Web site so that search-engine spiders can find and index all your content.

Create a Company Information Page

Adding a company information section to your Web site enhances credibility and provides visitors with important information about your business's history, your management team, and any notable accomplishments or awards received. The company information portion of your Web site allows users to get to know the people behind the Web site and the business. The presence of this page also builds credibility in the eyes of search engines, and they now try to automatically detect the presence of a company information page. Search engines are constantly striving to better the experience of their users, and providing this type of information can bolster your ranking while adding credibility about your Web site to your visitors.

Create a Privacy Policy

Regardless of the type of Web site you have, creating a Privacy Policy page adds credibility and authority to your Web site in the eyes of both search engines and users. Like a Company Information page, search engines now try to detect the presence a privacy policy. A basic privacy policy details all your company's marketing information practices and policies. It shows users how seriously you take their personal and private consumer information and that you are committed to protecting it. A privacy policy page informs your Web site visitors that you will not, under any conditions, sell any personal information, including credit card and contact information, to other companies.

Find Web Hosting

You can evaluate your current and future Web site goals to select an appropriate Web hosting plan for your needs. If you are designing a simple Web site, like a small informational Web site, an inexpensive entry-level Web hosting plan can meet your needs. However, if you are designing a midlevel or large-scale Web site and plan to sell products or services from your Web site, you want to carefully evaluate potential Web hosting companies. This way, you can make sure that you use a Web hosting package that meets your needs.

Your safest bet is to host your Web site with a hosting provider that has both a positive reputation and an established online presence. Choose one that is up 24 hours a day, 7 days a week, 99.9% of the time, so users and search engines are never faced with any errors. Many hosts provide support around the clock, and this can come in handy if an unexpected problem arises. You benefit from working with some of the more popular

hosting service providers, even if they are more expensive; doing so can help you avoid costly downtime that may result in disappointed visitors and lost sales.

One effective way of selecting a reliable and trustworthy Web hosting company is to visit popular review Web sites and forums to see the opinions of other Web site owners and designers. Two of the premier Web hosting review forums are WebHostingTalk at www.webhostingtalk.com and FindMyHosting at www.findmyhosting.com. Both of these forums give detailed information that can help you evaluate various Web hosting companies to determine which fits best considering your needs and technical specifications. For example, FindMyHosting gives information about how much bandwidth and hard drive space is required to meet your Web site specifications and price range, along with a list of Web hosting plans that fall within those specified ranges.

Find Web Hosting

① Navigate to www.findmyhosting.com.

② Review the list of Best 10 Web Hosting Companies.

● Note that you can search for a specific host if you are looking to view ratings and reviews.

③ Click Compare Hosts.

④ Compare Web hosting plans.

● Note the monthly pricing for each plan.

● Note the features for each plan.

⑤ Browse the results, and click a package you find appealing.

⑥ Take note of the company name offering the package you are interested in.

7. Navigate to www.webhostingtalk.com.

8. Enter the name of the company you are interested in into the search field.

9. Click Search Forums.

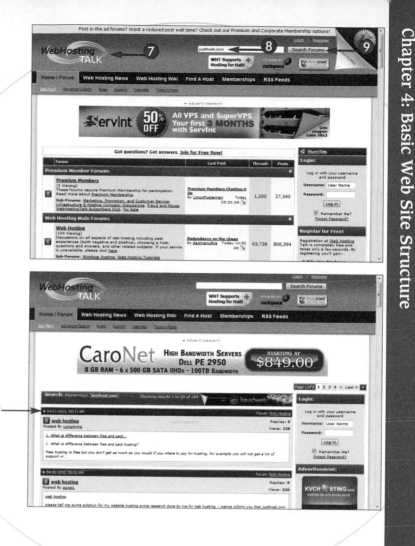

A list of threads appears. Each of these threads contains a reference to the company name you have searched.

You can browse the provided threads to find more information and reviews of the company before making a purchase.

Extra

Some Web hosting providers offer free hosting. Free Web hosting should be avoided if you are looking to build a large-scale Web site with e-commerce functionality, or if you expect to use a significant amount of bandwidth. Free hosting has bandwidth limits that greatly restrict your ability to send large amounts of traffic through your Web site. Free hosting also tends to be advertisement supported, which can be a real problem especially if you cannot control the advertisements.

However, if you are interested only in publishing a blog, you can use free versions of leading blog software such as WordPress, Blogger, or TypePad and even have them host the blog for free. For example, WordPress allows you to either create a blog and host it for free on WordPress.com, or for ultimate flexibility, set up the WordPress software on your own unique paid Web host.

For search-engine-optimization purposes, you should host your own Web site. Many of the free services limit your ability to control the domain that your Web site points to, resulting in a poor-quality domain name. Moreover, major search engines are unlikely to attribute authority to Web sites hosted on free hosting services.

Establish a Domain Name

Your domain name is one of the primary factors that search engines use to rank your Web site. Selecting a domain that relates directly to the theme of your Web site increases the likelihood that search engines such as Google and Yahoo will rank your Web site for related keywords. Generally speaking, you have two options: Choose a domain name that contains the keywords and phrases that your Web site is about, or choose a brandable domain name. Many Web sites, such as Amazon and eBay, began with generic or obscure domain names to build successful Web sites and brand awareness. Such an approach can be more difficult in the beginning when trying to rank for certain search terms because the search engines do use your domain name as a ranking factor.

When choosing a domain name, try to include, if possible, one or two of the major keywords your Web site is trying to rank for. For example, if your Web site is about designer shoes, an ideal domain name would be www.designershoes.com.

If your Web site is trying to create a new brand or develop a new niche in the market, consider registering a domain name that contains as few characters as possible. Make it short and easily recognizable for even the least experienced Web users. Avoid using multiple hyphens in your domain name because hyphens may be seen negatively by search engines. Spammers are known to register multiple hyphen domain names in order to stuff as many keywords as possible into the domain name of the Web site they are creating, in an effort to fool the search engines into top rankings.

Visit reputable registrars such as GoDaddy at www.godaddy.com or 1&1 Web Hosting at www.1and1.com to register your domain. Web sites like these offer easy-to-use tools to help you select relevant domain names based on the keywords you want your Web site to rank for, and also make recommendations for similar domains if the domain you are searching for is unavailable.

Establish a Domain Name

① Navigate to www.godaddy.com.

② Enter a domain name you want to register.

③ Select the top-level domain (TLD) extension.

④ Click Go.

● The selected domain has already been registered.

● If the domain has already been registered, you may be able to register the name by selecting a different top-level domain.

● Alternatively, you can view suggestions from GoDaddy.

⑤ Enter a domain name you want to register.

- The selected domain name is available.

6 Select the top-level domain extensions you want to register.

7 Click Continue to Registration.

8 Proceed through the checkout process.

Extra

It is often necessary to secure variations of your primary domain name in order to prevent cybersquatting. *Cybersquatting* occurs when someone registers a variation of your current domain name. The cybersquatter often profits from the traffic that comes from the domain or may attempt to sell you the domain at an inflated price.

At the same time you register your primary domain name you should also register that same domain with common domain and country extensions. At the least you should register the .com, .net, and .org extensions, as well as .co.uk and any other country with which you may want to eventually conduct direct business.

You should also register common misspellings of your domain name. For example, if your domain name is www.pepperjam.com, you should also purchase www.peperjam.com and www.peppperjam.com, if they are available.

Securing a good domain name is not easy, especially because of a business practice known as domaining. *Domaining* is a business where domain names are purchased, usually in bulk, and monetized. In many cases, domainers own thousands and thousands of domain names, making premium domain names unavailable. If the domain you are looking for is unavailable, you may consider purchasing that domain in the domain secondary market from a Web site such as www.sedo.com, which brokers single domain names for as little as $10 to as much as $10 million.

Optimize for Multiple Browsers

When you design your Web site, you must make sure that it is viewable to users of all the major Web browsers, including the most recent versions of Microsoft's Internet Explorer, Mozilla Firefox, Opera, and Safari. In addition, millions of people use mobile smart phones and other devices such as the Apple iPad to surf the Web, which requires that you optimize your Web site for alternative types of browsers as well. Unfortunately, each individual browser does not read HTML code in the same fashion. It is possible to design a Web site a certain way and view it in Internet Explorer only to find out later that it looks much different in Firefox. One way to assure that each browser is compatible with your Web site coding is to simply download a version of each browser and test your Web site in each. It is important to know that most of the discrepancies you find are because of the different ways

the browsers handle erroneous code. Try to adhere to the HTML standards found at w3c.org as closely as possible. You can save a lot of time and hassle by dealing with this issue as you design your Web site as opposed to waiting until it is finished.

Also, you want to be sure that your Web site is designed with different screen resolutions in mind. If your Web site was designed on a desktop set at 800×600 resolution, but the majority of your visitors use 1024×768, the Web site will appear different on their monitors. Test your Web site with your computer's resolution set to 800×600 and 1024×768. These resolutions are fairly common and should take care of almost all your visitors, including those using widescreen monitors and laptops. Overall, computer users are trending toward higher resolutions, so if you are designing your own Web site, do so with your screen set to 1024×768.

Optimize for Multiple Browsers

1 Navigate to www.anybrowser.com.

2 Click SiteViewer.

● SiteViewer appears.

③ Scroll down and enter the URL you want to view.

④ Select the HTML level you want to check your Web site against.

⑤ Click View Page.

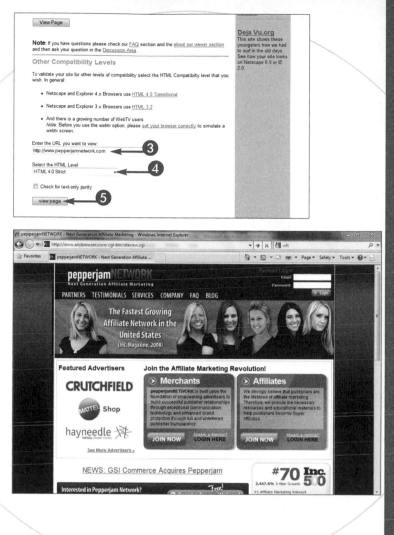

Your Web site appears as it would within the selected HTML level.

⑥ Return to SiteViewer and check your Web site in multiple HTML levels.

Extra

Anybrowser.com offers a variety of tools that help you make sure your site is compatible with multiple browsers. The SiteViewer tool eliminates certain HTML programming tags that do not work in all browsers and shows you what your Web site looks like without those tags. Using nonuniversal HTML tags can cause havoc in browsers that do not support those tags. If you can view your site correctly with this tool, you can also be assured that it will display correctly to the majority of your visitors. If not, you should try to eliminate the HTML tags that are causing the display problems. Use this tool in conjunction with the AnyBrowser HTML validation tool located at www. anybrowser.com/validateit.html to assist in finding problems.

AnyBrowser also offers a useful Screen Size Test tool at www.anybrowser.com/ScreenSizeTest.html. This is a rather simple tool that saves you some time by showing how much of your Web site will show to visitors using various screen resolutions. You can use this tool instead of constantly changing your screen resolution back and forth.

Plan and Design a Web Site Structure

When designing your Web site, you want to approach it with a developed plan in place for your Web site structure. A well-structured and organized Web design ensures the search-engine spiders' ability to read every page of your Web site, provides a positive experience for visitors, and makes changing the design or adding pages much easier.

The most significant idea behind choosing a theme for your Web site is to find one and stick with it throughout the entire Web site. Nothing draws the ire of the search engines more than a Web site with no clear focus or real benefit to a user. If you create a Web site about computers but write content about cars and then link to other Web sites which deal with gardening, you are preventing the search engines from recognizing that you are an authority on computers.

Start with a Plan

Before you start any design work on your Web site, decide how best to structure your Web site. If you sell a variety of products spanning a large number of categories, your Web site will be structured differently from a single-themed informational Web site.

Once you have made a decision on the overall theme of your Web site, your next step is to begin designing the structure of the site. Start by planning out all the necessary categories and subcategories that your Web site will consist of. Think of the planning stage as a blueprint that enables both your visitors and the search-engine spiders to easily navigate your content.

Build Your Web Site around a Thematic Structure

Once you have completed planning the layout of your Web site and decided on its overall structure, your next step is to divide the Web site into different categories, or themes. A well-thought-out thematic structure helps maintain a clear delineation between the different content areas of a Web site. In order to achieve high search-engine rankings, you need to appear as an authority on these main topics. Therefore, it is beneficial to design your Web site in well-organized and structured themes that do not confuse users or search engines. An additional benefit for organizing your Web site in this way is that it allows you to target specific keywords and phrases within each particular section.

A Web site theme represents a group of subject-specific content on your Web site much like chapters of a book outline specific content and ideas. The home page describes the overall subject in the introduction of the Web site and then breaks down into different subsections that support that major subject.

Take a Web site dealing with Internet marketing as an example of a Web site employing the use of thematic structures. Each subsection of the Web site then focuses on just one aspect on the subject of Internet marketing. Write content and link only to similar content on the subject for each subsection. A subsection on paid search should have pages of content dealing only with paid search. Design your file structure to represent these themes. For example, if your major categories are pay-per-click marketing, search-engine optimization, and online media buying, your file structure should represent this. Use folders for your main categories like www.example.com/pay-per-click, www.example.com/seo, and www.example.com/media-buying.

Although search engines reward Web sites that have large amounts of unique content, it is important that your content does not dilute the individual thematic categories of your site. By adhering to the structure outlined above, you are assuring that the search engines see that you are an authority site for each topic. The purpose of these thematically structured sections is to reinforce the overall subject relevance of your Web site.

Link within
Subject Matter Themes

Proper linking between pages on your Web site enables search-engine spiders to find, index, and rank each page. If the search engines cannot crawl every page of your site, some pages will be left out, not found, and therefore not included in

search-engine results. A proper linking structure not only allows search engines to find all your pages, but also helps search engines determine the theme or themes of your Web site.

Link in a Hierarchy

Be sure to link from your home page to all the major themes or categories of your site. Do not link directly from your home page to individual pages within your site's main categories. Instead, link to those documents from your main category pages. Through your linking structure, you should logically guide both users and the search engines from page to page. Your linking should create a hierarchy of your pages from the top-level main categories down through your individual content documents or product pages.

Avoid Broken Links

You can use free software like Xenu Link Sleuth, found at http://home.snafu.de/tilman/xenulink.html, to check your Web site for broken links or pages that do not exist. If you link to a page that does not exist, the search-engine spiders may try to crawl and index that page. You can be negatively penalized by the search engines if too many of these broken links exist, either as internal or external links on your Web site. If you are linking to external pages on other Web sites, do frequent checks to make sure they have not been taken down or moved. Although you cannot control the actions of other Webmasters, you can at least make sure that you do not link to pages that no longer exist or whose content has changed.

Link Directly

You should avoid linking from one page to another on your site if the pages are not directly related to one another. For example, if you have a site that sells cell phone accessories, try not to link from a page about Verizon headsets to a page about AT&T chargers. When doing this, you tend to dilute your themes. Remember, search engines consider links very strongly in their ranking algorithms, and not just links to your site, but also links from your site. If you link from one page to another page that is not directly related to the first, even if both are located on your own site, you can give the search engines the impression that these pages are directly related. If linking those pages makes sense, you can learn about how to link them properly using the `nofollow` attribute in Chapter 5.

Avoid Error Messages

Most Web hosting packages come with entry-level Web site statistics. Check these statistics often to see if your visitors are receiving any error messages. The problem may be that other Webmasters are linking incorrectly to pages on your Web site. If so, your visitors may be receiving 404 Page Not Found errors, which should show up in a Web site statistics package. Incorrect links of this type can be addressed by setting up 301 redirects to the correct pages, which is discussed Chapter 5.

Design a Sitemap

Y ou can create a sitemap to function as an outline or index of your entire Web site. You should structure it using the same hierarchy that you used when you created your Web site structure. Start off with your home page and build out from there with all the pages linking to it. Link all the major subsections plus your company information page and privacy policy page from the home page. All subsequent pages are placed and categorized under that subsection in your sitemap as well. Although not strictly necessary, consider naming the sitemap either *sitemap.html* or *sitemap.php*. Such names help the search engines recognize that the file is indeed a sitemap. Automatic sitemap generators like the one at XML-Sitemaps.com help automate this process.

A benefit of having a sitemap is that it gives visitors a place to potentially find what they are looking for without getting lost in the navigation of the Web site. Sometimes, no matter how well you design your internal linking structure, your visitors may have a hard time finding exactly what they are looking for. A sitemap can help your visitors understand the Web site layout, and give them a quick access tool for all the pages within the Web site.

As you add new pages to your Web site, be sure to add them to your sitemap. Search engines tend to reward Web sites with fresh and up-to-date content. A sitemap enables search engines to quickly find those Web pages recently added or changed on your Web site.

Design a Sitemap

① Navigate to www.xml-sitemaps.com.

② Read through the sitemap generator's instructions.

③ Enter your Web site address.

④ Select your Web site's change frequency.

⑤ Select a modification option.

⑥ Select Automatic Priority.

⑦ Click Start to begin the crawling of your Web site.

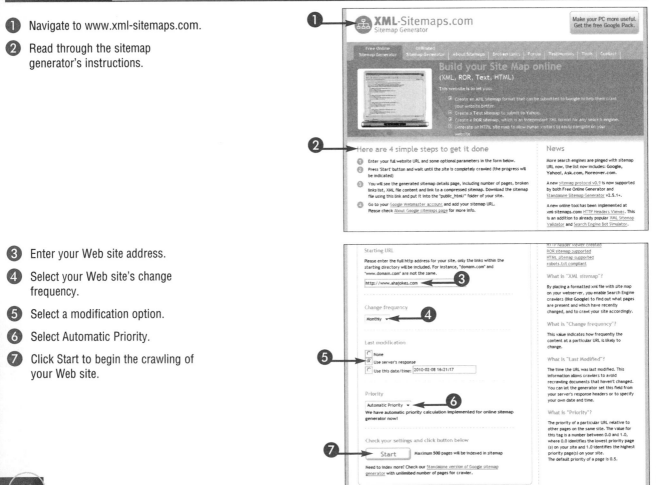

- XML-Sitemaps generates a sitemap. Note that the sitemap code is available in other formats, including HTML, ROR, and text.

⑧ Save the XML version of your sitemap to your hard drive.

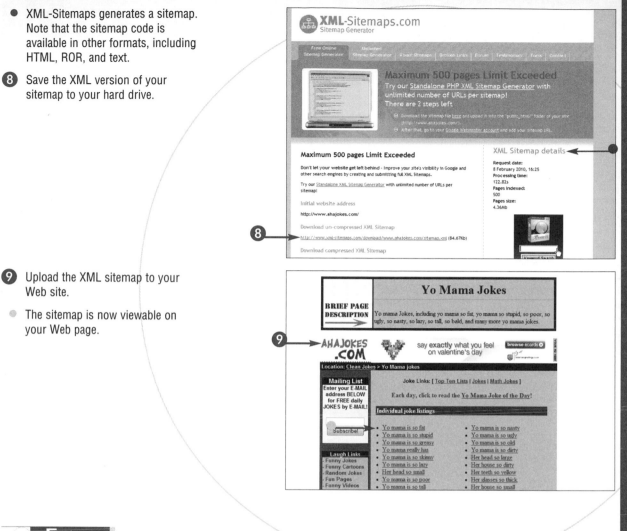

⑨ Upload the XML sitemap to your Web site.

- The sitemap is now viewable on your Web page.

Create a Company Information Page

Trust and credibility are becoming increasingly major issues for Internet users. You can create a company information page to help strengthen your reputation in the eyes of both your audience and the search engines. A company information page helps build trust with your viewers by providing company biographies, history, and even photos to explain who you are and where you come from.

Creating a company information page is good practice in general, but for search-engine-optimization purposes, it is important for Google to see this page during its indexing process. A lot of less reputable Web sites do not contain any type of company information section. Spammers, who generate mass numbers of Web sites automatically, do not usually include this specific company information. Therefore, many in the search-engine-optimization

community theorize that having a company information page may help improve your appearance of legitimacy and trustworthiness in the search-engine ranking algorithms.

Place a link for your company information section on the home page of your Web site. Label the link as About Us, Company Information, or something similar so that users can easily find it. This link needs to be clearly visible and prominent on your home page. There is no reason to hide this link on the bottom of your home page or bury it in a navigational menu. If you are selling a product, your consumers want to know who you are, where you come from, and why they should trust your business. Even if you are not selling a product, having a company or personal information page can help build your reputation as an expert in your particular niche.

Create a Company Information Page

Note: This task uses the Web site www. seomoz.org as an example.

Decide Upon Home Page Link Placement

1 Go to the home page of your Web site.

● Notice on SEOmoz.org there is a link to the About Us section at the top of the home page.

2 Decide where on your Web site's home page to place a link or links to the About Us section.

● Notice that SEOmoz.org uses an additional link to the About Us section at the bottom of the home page.

Write an About Us Section

1. Write an About Us section including information about you and your company.

2. Include information such as what your business does and any contact information such as a phone number or e-mail address.

Include a Biography Section

1. Write a brief biography about yourself.

2. Include a few photos of yourself or your company.

● Notice SEOmoz.org's Rand Fishkin includes information about his personal, educational, and professional background.

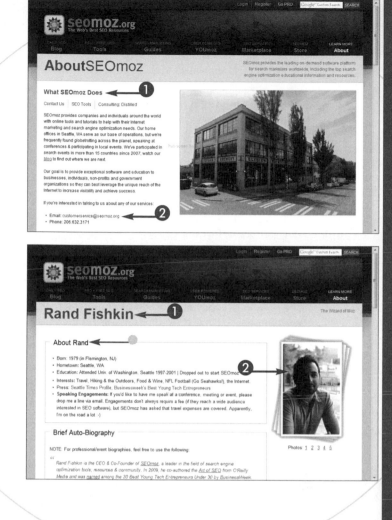

Extra

Statistics show that your Web site's Company Information or About Us page is likely to be one of the most clicked pages of your entire site by new visitors. Because this is the case, you should spend ample time creating a compelling and complete profile of both you and your business. Some extra information to include on this page would be a mission statement or a biography of your management team. Additional information can include the history behind your business, what sets you apart from your competitors, and contact information. Including an actual address and a phone number can help to provide a sense of confidence in your visitors, which is especially important if you run an e-commerce Web site. When visitors do make purchases, they want reassurance that your company can offer some level of customer service if something breaks or otherwise goes wrong. You can address issues like this on your Company Information or About Us page and instill a sense of trust in your visitors.

Create a Privacy Policy

Y ou should create a privacy policy to ensure your users are aware of your information-collecting policies. Similar to your Company Information page, a privacy policy page is regarded as good practice in general, as well as for search-engine-optimization purposes. You want to have open communication with your audience and let them know what is being done with any information collected during their time visiting your Web site. Many in the SEO community theorize that having a privacy policy page can help to show the search-engine algorithms that you are in fact a legitimate business. Companies and organizations such as FreePrivacyPolicy.com at www.freeprivacypolicy.com and the Direct Marketing Association at www.the-dma.org have tools to assist in creating privacy policies.

The purpose of having a privacy policy is to prove to your visitors that you are committed to protecting the privacy of their personal information. Privacy policies are particularly important if you collect e-mail addresses or any other type of demographic information about your visitors. Do not just copy a privacy policy from another Web site solely for the purpose of having a policy. Besides being unethical, different Web sites often have different policies in place. You are better off seeking professional guidance to ensure that appropriate policies are included.

Try to keep your privacy policy simple and make it easy to read, easy to understand, and easy to find on your Web site. Place the policy link next to your company information page link. Be sure to stay current with any changes in your business and the business environment. Update your privacy policy as much as needed to comply with any implemented changes, and always alert your customers when a change takes place. Remember, a well-written privacy policy puts consumers in charge of their personal information.

Create a Privacy Policy

① Navigate to www.freeprivacypolicy. com.

② Click the Create Your Free Privacy Policy Now button.

● Note the Why You Must Have a Privacy Policy section.

③ Review the entire Privacy Policy sample.

④ Click Create a Free Policy Now.

5 Click the Free Click Here button.

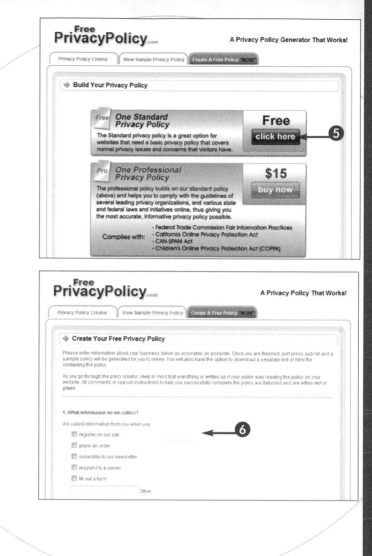

6 Enter the requested information to generate your free Privacy Policy.

An Introduction to Advanced Web Site Structuring

Proper Web site design and structure is an integral part of any search-engine-optimization campaign. Although the techniques discussed in this chapter are not required for success, having this knowledge in your arsenal allows you to take an advanced, streamlined approach to problems that would otherwise be difficult to solve. Many Webmasters are not even aware that these issues exist let alone know how to deal with them when they arise. Mastering these tactics requires the willingness to dig deeper than the surface and delve into some fairly technical tasks. Ultimately, the world's premier search-engine-optimization experts must develop advanced skills and techniques to keep their Web sites on top of the search-engine results pages.

The search-engine ranking algorithms are constantly evolving. More and more Web site owners are losing their spots in the rankings as their competition becomes more technically competent and adept at the technical side of

search-engine optimization. Consider the tasks in this chapter as stepping stones to a more advanced understanding of how search-engine-optimization efforts can be enhanced. You can use these techniques to streamline much of the tedious work involved with search-engine optimization. For example, using the `mod_rewrite` module discussed in the "Using Mod_Rewrite to Rewrite URLs" task can, depending on the size of your Web site, shave hours or even days off the amount of time normally required to rewrite every URL on your Web site. Adding a simple line of text to a robots.txt file as discussed in the "Create a Robots.txt File" task can save your Web server from an overflow of search-engine spider traffic. This traffic can waste a tremendous amount of server resources and even force your Web host to charge you extra money for bandwidth overcharges. These are just a few examples of potentially daunting tasks that can be simplified using these techniques.

Create a Robots.txt File

Creating a robots.txt file is a way of speaking directly to the search-engine spiders when they arrive at your site. These spiders are simply robots programmed to obey certain commands. There are numerous scenarios where such an exchange is useful. Perhaps you would rather the spiders not visit certain sections of your site. Or maybe you want to instruct them to visit every single page. Other times you may want to control the frequency at which the spiders visit your site. A robots.txt file allows you to tell the spiders what they may and may not do once they arrive at your domain.

Using the Nofollow Attribute

Attaching a `nofollow` attribute to a link is your way of telling the search-engine spiders that they should not follow that link or view that link as anything of significance when determining ranking. Although the `nofollow` attribute was developed to prevent the influencing of search-engine rankings through spamming blogs and guest books, it can also be used to funnel relevance and authority throughout the individual themes of your Web site. The `nofollow` attribute can also be used to link to other Web sites that are not directly related to the content of your own Web site. More recently, Google has asked that all paid links be tagged with the `nofollow` attribute to indicate that the links should not affect ranking influence.

Structure URLs Correctly

Structuring your URLs correctly is a critical step when developing a search-engine-optimization plan of attack. Both the search engines and search-engine users appreciate static-looking, descriptive URLs. From a mechanical standpoint, they are easily spidered, and from a user's standpoint, they are easily understood. The search engines also take into consideration the keywords and phrases contained within your URLs and use these to influence your rankings. Properly designed URLs provide a solid foundation upon which to build more pages while maintaining an efficient organizational structure. Make a strong effort to create your URLs correctly the first time through because changing URLs later can be a daunting task.

Redirect Non-WWW Traffic to WWW

You may be amazed to learn that some search engines see the example.com and www.example.com variations of your domain name as two totally separate Web sites. This is called a *www/non-www canonical issue* because there is confusion as to which version is standard. This technical weakness can lead to less-than-optimal rankings — one version of your domain name may rank alongside another version of your domain name even though they share the same content. The search engines may believe you are proliferating duplicate content and penalize your Web site's rankings. It is important to set up your server to redirect all traffic to one variation to prevent any confusion by the search engines.

Protect Yourself with an .htaccess File

Modifying your Web server's functionality is possible through the use of an .htaccess file. An .htaccess file is the Apache Web server's configuration file. It is a straightforward yet powerful text file that can accomplish a wide variety of functions. It enables you to protect your Web site from content-stealing robots and allows you to dynamically rewrite poorly formed URLs generated by shopping cart or blog software. Most Web site owners have never seen an .htaccess file or know of its existence. Although normally left to expert server administrators, an .htaccess file can help you avoid several potential problems.

Redirect with 301 Redirects

If you move pages around or even decide to move your entire Web site from one domain to another, you need a method of alerting the search engines to this move. If not, you lose all your previous rankings, and the time and effort put into achieving them becomes a waste. 301 redirects provide you with the means to tell the search engines that not only have you moved your site, but you want all your rankings to move with it. This is a very important and often overlooked issue.

Using Mod_Rewrite to Rewrite URLs

Throughout this book are many references to the importance of proper URL structure for search-engine optimization. The `mod_rewrite` module of the Apache Web server gives you the power to rewrite poorly formed URLs on the fly as well as manipulate the appearance of any filename you choose. Using the `mod_rewrite` module may appear difficult at first, but tools are available to simplify the complex parts, and the benefits of using this module to its fullest extent far outweigh the steep learning curve.

Create a Robots.txt File

You can create a robots.txt file to prevent search-engine spiders from consuming excessive amounts of bandwidth on your server and also to prevent potential copyright infringements. A robots.txt file provides the search-engine spiders with information about which pages should be crawled and indexed and which should not. It is a text file that resides in the root directory of your Web server. If you do not provide a robots.txt file, search-engine spiders assume that the entire site should be crawled and indexed.

Depending on the content of your Web site, you may have a large number of images stored on your server. These images may be spidered by the search engines and indexed in various image search engines such as Google Images. This could lead to a potentially unexpected and unwanted increase in server bandwidth if your images are found and viewed through a search engine. Prevent this by

creating a robots.txt file that disallows search-engine spiders from crawling and indexing your /images directory.

If you sell a copyrighted informational product or piece of software on your Web site, the search engines may be able to find and index your intellectual property. Instead of paying for and then downloading your product, a savvy Internet user can potentially download for free. Prevent this by creating a robots.txt file that disallows search-engine spiders from crawling and indexing the directory where your product is located; or, you can disallow the search engines from indexing a particular file.

To create a robots.txt file, you need nothing more than a simple text editor such as Windows Notepad and a thorough understanding of just what parts of your Web site should and should not be crawled by the search-engine spiders and indexed in the search engines.

Create a Robots.txt File

Create a Robots.txt File

1 Open any text editor, such as Notepad.

2 Type User-Agent: *. This line describes which search-engine spiders should obey this rule. The * refers to all robots.

3 To disallow all robots from crawling your /images directory, add this text: Disallow: /images/. You can also add any other directories that you would prefer not be crawled.

4 To disallow a certain file from being crawled and indexed, add this text: Disallow: /directory/file.html.

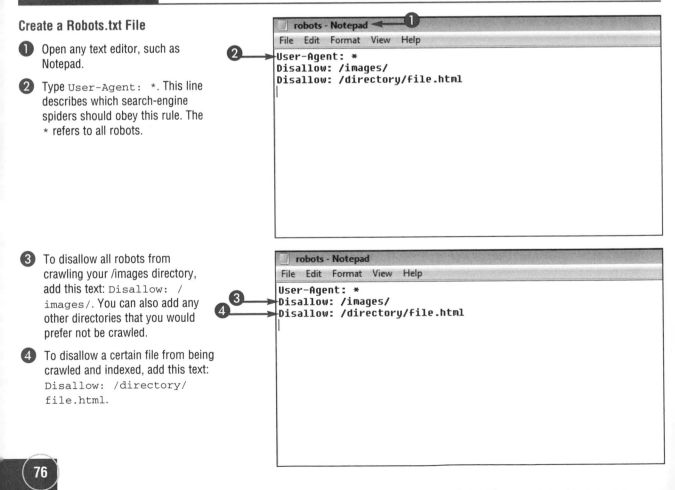

⑤ Save the file, and name it robots.txt.

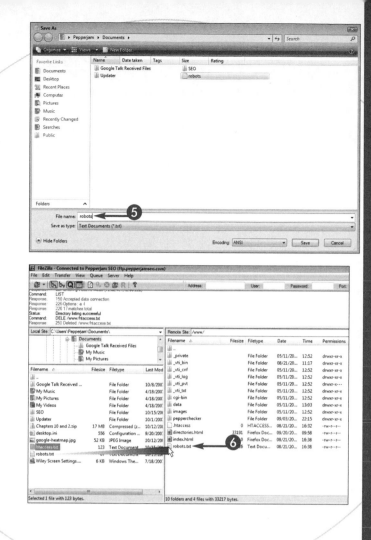

Upload to Server

⑥ Upload the file to your Web root directory.

The robots.txt file now prevents search-engine spiders from entering the /images directory and indexing /directory/file.html.

Extra

A robots.txt file can also be used to tell the search-engine spiders where a sitemap is located with this text: Sitemap: http://www.example.com/yoursitemap.html. A new robots.txt standard has been introduced that adds more commands, such as the ability to force certain crawl delay rates. You can dictate that the search-engine spiders crawl only one page per a certain time period and also specify that they may crawl only during certain hours of the day. This can aid in bandwidth preservation because some search-engine spiders crawl pages at a very fast rate.

You can use the robots.txt generator at www.mcanerin.com/EN/search-engine/robots-txt.asp to simplify the robots.txt-creation task. You specify a crawl delay rate and the location of your sitemap and either disallow all spiders or choose from a list of the most common. The tool then automatically generates the robots.txt file information that should be pasted into your robots.txt file and uploaded to your server via FTP.

Using the Nofollow Attribute

Nofollow is an HTML attribute value applicable to hyperlinks that informs the search engines not to follow that link. Linking to another Web page can influence that page's rankings in the search engines. If you want to link to a page but not influence that page's rankings, use the nofollow attribute. You can apply the nofollow attribute to any hyperlink by attaching rel=nofollow to the HTML anchor tag. It was developed to deter forms of Web spamming such as comment spamming and guestbook spamming. Many blog and guestbook software applications now automatically attach this attribute to all user-posted hyperlinks.

If your site is broken down into sections — for example, baseball, football, and basketball — and each section contains pages about your favorite players in each sport, for example, it would not make sense to the search engines to see a link between pages about your favorite

baseball players and pages about your favorite basketball players unless there is some direct relation between the two. If you believe it is beneficial to your visitors to link between two unrelated pages, use the nofollow attribute to prevent the search engines from following that link.

If your Web site has numerous categories or themes, interlinking between those categories could hurt your search-engine rankings. The search-engine spiders follow links from page to page within your Web site. If those pages are not related, the search engines may have a difficult time determining the theme or topic of your content. Consider adding a nofollow attribute when linking between pages within your site that reside in differing thematic categories. This prevents dilution of your themes when cross-linking between unrelated pages and helps to build relevancy and authority for the different content areas of your Web site.

Using the Nofollow Attribute

Build Relevancy

① Navigate to www.pepperjam.com.

② Click the View Source icon to view the page's HTML source code.

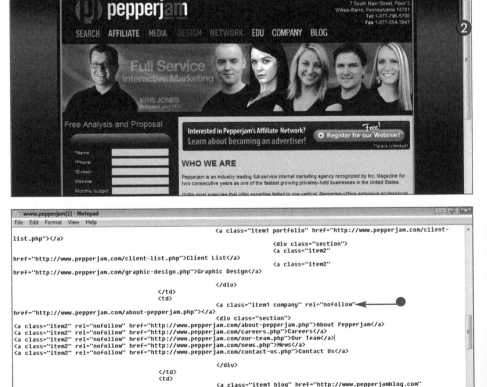

● Notice that the link to the Company section of the Web site includes a nofollow attribute. The link from Pepperjam.com's main page does not influence the ranking of the Company page.

Prevent Blog Spam

① Navigate to www.pepperjamnetwork.com/blog.

② View any blog post that contains comments, such as www.pepperjamnetwork.com/blog/2008/08/15/kris-jones-jr/#comments.

③ Click the View Source icon to view the page's HTML source code.

● Notice that links to URLs within the comments contain the `nofollow` attribute. This link can no longer influence the search-engine rankings of the linked page.

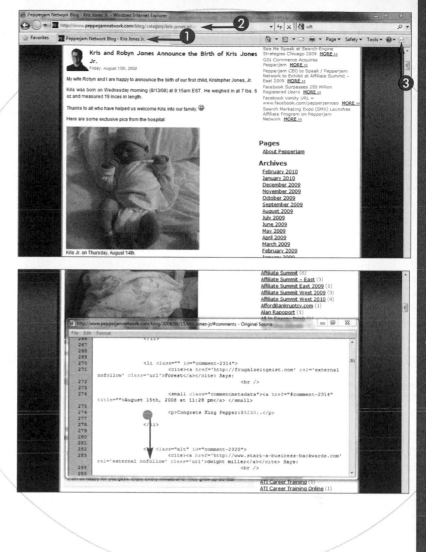

Extra

`Nofollow` is also used to prevent the passing of PageRank, or *PR*, from one page to another. Chapter 8 discusses the importance of PageRank as part of Google's ranking algorithm. PageRank passes from page to page within your Web site, and dilutes as it passes throughout your site. Essentially, adding the `nofollow` attribute to a link tells the search engines not to use that link as a positive factor in their ranking algorithm.

You may not be interested in certain pages ranking, such as a company information page or a page that contains contact information. Normally, you link to these pages directly from the main page of your Web site. Add a `nofollow` attribute to these links throughout your Web site, and you prevent wasting the passing of PageRank to these pages.

Google introduced the `nofollow` attribute in early 2005, and both Yahoo and Microsoft's Bing search engine claim to adhere to its rules as well. Some theorize that Yahoo and Bing do not take this tag into consideration when crawling through links.

Structure
URLs Correctly

Structure URLs correctly and you may see an increase in both your rankings as well as the percentage of people who click your link, called your *click-through rate*. Search-engine marketers have long recommended inserting relevant keywords into page URLs, and although the positive effects of this may not be as prevalent today as they were in the past, you will want to structure your URLs in an organized, hierarchal manner. Both search engines and search-engine users alike take URL structure into consideration when they make decisions about your Web site's relevancy and authority.

As mentioned in the previous chapter, you should organize your Web site into themes or categories that contain individual Web pages full of content relevant to the parent theme. Regardless of whether your site is an information portal or an electronic commerce platform selling thousands of products, the same best practices apply. Think of your Web site as being broken down into containers full of related information. Each container

should be labeled appropriately with a URL. Your Web site's baseball section should be located at www.example.com/baseball, and your Web site's football section should be located at www.example.com/football. Individual pages about baseball topics should be placed within their respective containers. Suppose you created a page about your favorite baseball player, Manny Ramirez. Place his page at www.example.com/baseball/manny-ramirez.html.

Structure your page URLs in this manner, and you create an easily spidered, organized, user-friendly Web site navigation system. The search engines can easily find each content-rich page and relate it back to its parent category. Search-engine users prefer clean, well-structured URLs when searching for a page. If searching for a page about Manny Ramirez, a large majority of search-engine users would be more inclined to click a URL like www.example.com/baseball/manny-ramirez.html versus www.example.com/player1.html.

Structure URLs Correctly

Correctly Structured URL

① Navigate to www.google.com.

② Search for search engine optimization.

● Notice Wikipedia.org ranks #1 with the URL http://en.wikipedia.org/wiki/Search_engine_optimization. This is an example of a well-structured, relevant URL.

Correctly Structured Subtopic URL

① Navigate to www.pepperjam.com.

② Position your mouse pointer over the link to Search in the upper navigation frame.

● Notice the URL structure www.pepperjam.com/search.

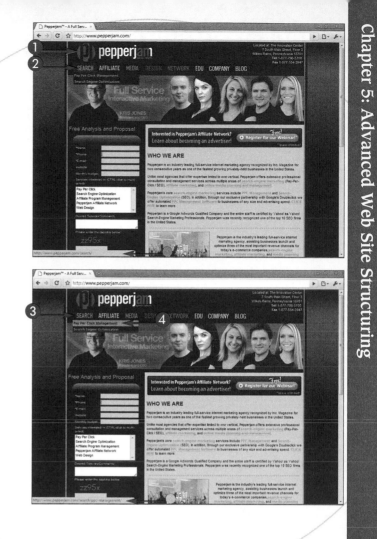

③ Click Search.

④ Position your mouse pointer over the link to "Pay Per Click Management."

● Notice the URL structure www.pepperjam.com/search/ppc-management. This is another example of a well-structured, relevant URL.

Extra

Structuring your URLs correctly provides you with benefits beyond just improving your search-engine-optimization efforts. Well-structured URLs provide you with a blueprint for creating other advertising campaigns. One such example is a paid search, or pay-per-click, advertising campaign, which is discussed in Chapter 11. A paid search, or pay-per-click, advertising campaign involves purchasing advertising space directly on search engines when users search for particular keywords relevant to your products or content. A properly categorized Web site gives you a head start in developing the keyword lists necessary to properly construct a paid search advertising campaign.

Search engines like Google incentivize Web sites that partake in proper search-engine-optimization techniques in both their organic rankings as well as in their paid search rankings. For that reason, you should properly construct your URLs for reasons beyond just an increase in the organic rankings. You may actually see a price decrease in your paid search efforts as well.

Protect Yourself with an .htaccess File

An .htaccess file is the configuration file for the Apache Web server. It allows you to control the functionality of your server and has many other uses, including rewriting URLs and redirecting Web traffic. It enables you to use numerous forms of protection ranging from password-protecting directories, banning visitors from certain sources, and preventing bandwidth theft from image linkers. An .htaccess file is a simple text file, and it can be created in any simple text editor, such as Notepad. It can be uploaded to the root directory of your Web server or any directories underneath it. Rules located in an .htaccess file uploaded to your images directory take precedence over the root file. Take full advantage of the server modification effects of .htaccess, and you can prevent your hard work from being abused or even stolen.

At some point, you may find that you are receiving an excessive amount of Web traffic from bots that are unrelated to search engines. Or you may want to stop the malicious use of the Linux `Wget` command that can retrieve your Web site content. Hundreds of bots are crawling the Web for a variety of reasons ranging from archiving Web content to collecting Web content to be used in spamming engines. Although normally harmless, these bots can eat up an impressive amount of bandwidth as your site becomes further established. Prevent this by using .htaccess to ban these bots.

If your Web site contains a large number of images or videos, other Webmasters may link directly to your images. Although the intent may be harmless, you may find that this also is eating a large amount of bandwidth. You can use .htaccess to block direct linking to your images, and instead even send a replacement image that relays a message to the offending Webmaster that you are not happy with his practices.

Protect Yourself with an .htaccess File

① Open any text editor, such as Notepad.

Block Bad Bots

② Type `RewriteEngine On` to activate the `mod_rewrite` module.

③ To disallow content retrieval from your Web site through use of the `Wget` command, add `RewriteCond %{HTTP_USER_AGENT} ^Wget [OR]`.

④ On the next line, add `RewriteRule ^.* - [F,L]`. This prevents the use of the `Wget` command to access your Web site.

Prevent Image Theft

⑤ To allow visitors from your own Web site, add `RewriteCond %{HTTP_REFERER} !^http(s)?:// (www\.)?yourdomain.com [NC]`.

⑥ To match all image file extensions, add `RewriteRule \.(jpg|jpeg|png|gif|flv|swf)$ - [NC,F,L]`.

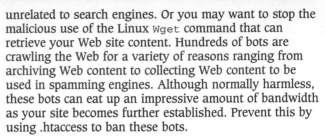

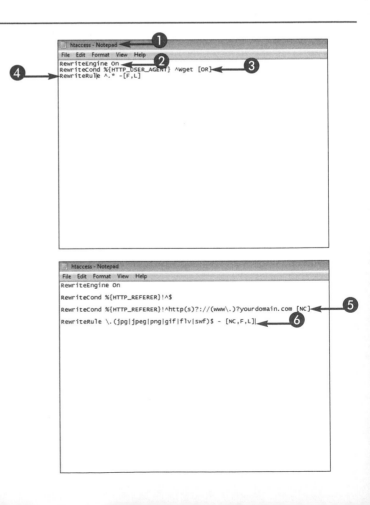

7 Save the file as htaccess.txt. This file will be renamed later using your FTP program to .htaccess.

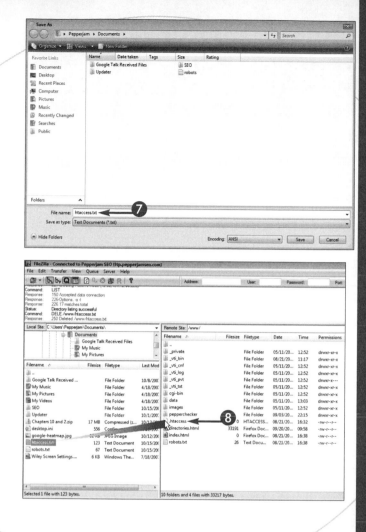

Upload to Server

8 Upload the htaccess.txt file to your Web server root directory and rename it .htaccess.

The .htaccess file prevents other Web sites from directly linking to your images and videos.

Using Mod_Rewrite to Rewrite URLs

Mod_rewrite is an Apache Web server module that enables you to redirect users from one URL to another URL without the user experiencing any indication that the redirect took place. Mod_rewrite can be used in conjunction with what you have learned about proper URL structuring to generate both search-engine-friendly and user-friendly URLs with ease. This is especially relevant for Web sites that employ any type of content management system that generates URLs dynamically. These dynamically generated URLs are rarely constructed with search-engine optimization in mind, and due to limitations in the content management software, it can be impossible to fix without the use of mod_rewrite.

Throughout the Internet, you find examples of Web sites that have been generated dynamically by content management systems. These sites can be information portals or large e-commerce Web shops, and the URLs often resemble something similar to www.example.com/viewproduct.php?cat=pets&subcat=dogs&type=food. Numerous reasons have already been discussed regarding why this URL structure is inefficient for both the search engines and your visitors. Use mod_rewrite to easily and noninvasively restructure the URL to look like www.example.com/pets/dogs/food. The new URL is more logical, well structured, and in the eyes of search engines and users alike, more relevant and authoritative.

Activate mod_rewrite by adding the text RewriteEngine On to your Web root directory's .htaccess file. If the file does not already exist, create a blank file and upload it to your Web root directory. The mod_rewrite module is not present on all servers, so be sure to contact your Web hosting administrator to make sure that it is installed. If it is not installed or if your host does not use the Apache Web server, ask if an alternative solution is available.

Using Mod_Rewrite to Rewrite URLs

Rewrite a Static URL

① Open any text editor such as Notepad, or open your current .htaccess file.

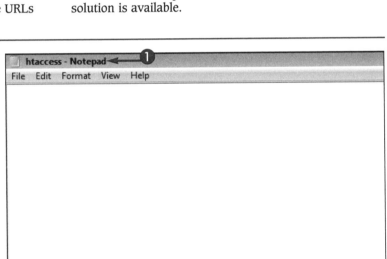

② Type RewriteEngine On to activate the mod_rewrite module.

③ To rewrite a single static URL, add RewriteRule ^old\.html$new.html [R].

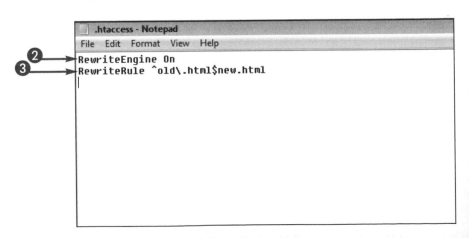

Rewrite a Dynamic URL

④ To rewrite a dynamic URL, add `RewriteRule ^([^/]*)\.html$ /viewproducts.php?category=$1 [L]`. This redirects all traffic going to www.example.com/viewproducts.php?category=sports to www.example.com/sports.html.

```
.htaccess - Notepad
File  Edit  Format  View  Help
RewriteEngine On
RewriteRule ^old\.html$new.html

RewriteRule ^([^/]*)\.html$ /viewproducts.php?category=$1 [L]
```

④

Upload to Server

⑤ Upload the htaccess.txt file to your Web server root directory and rename it .htaccess.

The `mod_rewrite` module rewrites the URLs to make them appear static.

⑤

Extra

`Mod_rewrite` can be very complex and difficult to use if you are not a skilled Web programmer. Luckily, it is so commonly used that many tools have been developed to help. An excellent, free tool can be found at www.generateit.net/mod-rewrite to assist in rewriting dynamic URLs into well-structured URLs that appear static.

The tool itself can seem complex at first, but with a little practice, it is an invaluable resource. First, enter an example of the type of dynamic URL, and then choose which variables you want to remain static. You also have the option to add any relevant keywords as a prefix or suffix. Generate individual rewrites for specific pages, or take it a step further and generate general rules that rewrite an entire set of pages.

For example, if your Web site contains a dynamically generated shopping mall with product pages of the form www.example.com/products.php?category=health&subcat=eyes&prodid=1, the URL can be rewritten to www.example.com/health/eyes/1.html; you can also automatically rewrite www.example.com/products.php?category=sports&subcat=baseball&prodid=3 to www.example.com/sports/baseball/3.html. As long as your link structure is consistent throughout your entire Web site, only one `mod_rewrite` rule is necessary.

Redirect Non-WWW Traffic to WWW

You have probably noticed that you can visit most Web sites by visiting either example.com or www. example.com. Although the true location of a site is example.com, the most common naming convention normally includes the www. Unfortunately, despite progress over time, many of the search engines, even large engines like Google, continue to index and rank both URL variations. This can lead to various problems, including duplicate content penalties and dilution of incoming link benefits. Chapter 8 discusses the search-engine-optimization benefits of building links back to your Web site. If some Webmasters link to www.example. com and others link to example.com, the ranking influence of those links becomes spread out over two separate entities as the search-engine spiders follow the links to what they assume to be separate destinations. This problem is often referred to as a *non-www/www canonical issue*. You can redirect all this traffic to one variation or the other to maintain optimal search-engine rankings and quality user experience.

Fortunately, you can easily address this problem by adding a small amount of code to your Web root directory's .htaccess file to set up a 301 redirect from example.com to www.example.com or vice versa. A 301 redirect is also known as a *permanent redirect*. It tells Web browsers and search-engine spiders that a page has permanently moved from one location to another. This location may be a page on the same server or an entirely different domain name. The browser or search-engine spiders are then immediately redirected to the proper location instantly. 301 redirects are the preferred method of redirection because Google attempts to pass all the ranking influences to the new destination. By focusing all your links and traffic on one variation of your domain, you may experience an overall ranking increase.

Redirect Non-WWW Traffic to WWW

Redirect Non-WWW to WWW

① Open any text editor such as Notepad, or open your current .htaccess file.

② Add `RewriteEngine On` to activate the `mod_rewrite` module.

③ Add `RewriteCond %{HTTP_HOST} !^www\.example\.com$`.

④ Add `RewriteRule (.*) http://www.example.com/$1 [R=301,L]`.

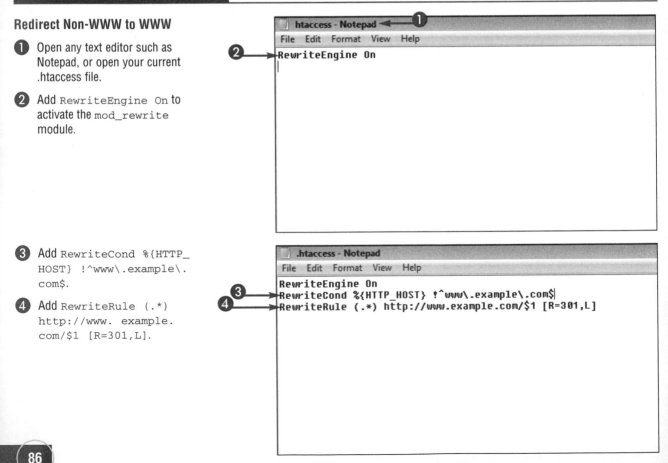

Rewrite WWW Traffic to Non-WWW

5 Add `RewriteCond %{HTTP_HOST} !^ example\.com$`.

6 Add `RewriteRule (.*) http:// example.com/$1 [R=301,L]`.

Upload to Server

7 Upload the htaccess.txt file to your server and make sure to rename it .htaccess.

The `mod_rewrite` module creates a search-engine-safe 301 redirect.

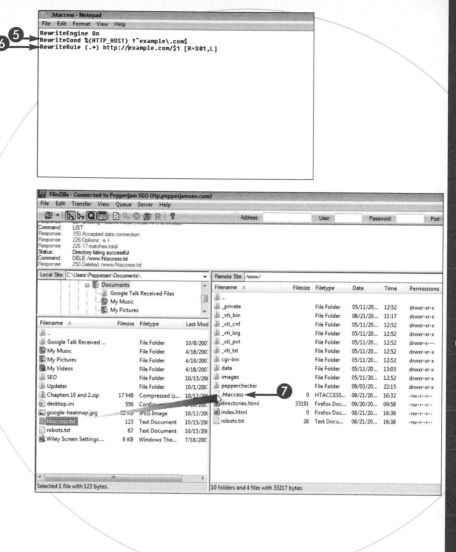

Extra

Despite making progress in the effort to combine the results for both www.example.com and example.com, the major search engines, including Google, still struggle to completely blend the two entities. You should always set up the 301 redirect discussed in this task, and you may be curious to see if you have a large canonical issue with your www/non-www domain entries.

To check, visit www.google.com and type **site:*newdomain.com*** into the search bar. Replace *newdomain.com* with your domain name. This should show every single page Google has indexed of your Web site. If you find both www. yourdomain.com and yourdomain.com in the list, you have an issue. Also, take note of the total number of pages indexed in the upper right corner of the search results. Next, type **site:www.*newdomain.com*** into the search bar. If the results differ dramatically from the results of the previous query, you probably have a canonical issue. Note that if you purposely employ the use of other subdomains besides www., the results cannot be compared accurately.

Redirect with 301 Redirects

There will surely come a time when you feel a total redesign of your Web site is necessary. Unfortunately, search engines are not necessarily friendly when you make Web site changes. Suppose you move a page from www.example.com/mistydogpic1.html to a more organized, well-structured URL such as www.example.com/pictures/dogs/misty.html. If the search engines have already spidered and indexed your original URL and your Web site visitors have added the page to their browser bookmarks, you want to be sure that both your visitors and the search engines know the page has moved. You can set up a 301 redirect to accomplish this task, and both search-engine spiders and Web browsers automatically redirect to the new location. For search-engine-optimization purposes, this also preserves most if not all of your search-engine ranking factors.

If you want to move your entire Web site from one domain to another, a 301 redirect is your best bet to keep your current search-engine rankings. Once the search engine updates its Web page index, it should recognize the status change and update your listings accordingly. Keep in mind that this update does not happen instantly. Search engines make major ranking adjustments as often as once a month or as infrequently as every few months. Do not be alarmed if your redirect is not reflected immediately. Also, keep in mind that any changes you make to your Web site can negatively or positively influence your search-engine rankings. Although a 301 redirect is the proper way to make the changes mentioned in this task, your rankings may immediately return to their previous levels.

Redirect with 301 Redirects

Redirect a Single Page on the Same Server

① Open any text editor such as Notepad, or open your current .htaccess file.

② Add Redirect 301 / oldpage. html http:// www.example.com/newpage. html.

Redirect to a New Domain

3 Add `Rewriterule (.*) http://www.newdomain.com/$1 [R=301,L]`. This redirects everything on your original domain name to your new domain name.

htaccess - Notepad
File Edit Format View Help
`RewriteRule (.*) http://www.newdomain.com/$1 [R=301,L]`

Upload to Server

4 Upload the htaccess.txt file to your server and make sure to rename it .htaccess.

The `mod_rewrite` module creates a search-engine-safe redirect from one page to another on your Web site.

FileZilla - Connected to Pepperjam SEO (ftp.pepperjamseo.com)

Filename	Filesize	Filetype	Date	Time	Permissions
..					
_private		File Folder	05/11/20...	12:52	drwxr-xr-x
_vti_bin		File Folder	08/21/20...	11:17	drwxr-xr-x
_vti_cnf		File Folder	05/11/20...	12:52	drwxr-xr-x
_vti_log		File Folder	05/11/20...	12:52	drwxr-xr-x
_vti_pvt		File Folder	05/11/20...	12:52	drwxr-x---
_vti_txt		File Folder	05/11/20...	12:52	drwxr-xr-x
cgi-bin		File Folder	05/11/20...	12:52	drwxr-xr-x
data		File Folder	05/11/20...	13:03	drwxr-xr-x
images		File Folder	05/11/20...	12:52	drwxr-xr-x
pepperchecker		File Folder	09/03/20...	22:15	drwxr-xr-x
.htaccess	0	HTACCESS...	08/21/20...	16:32	-rw-r--r--
directories.html	33191	Firefox Doc...	09/20/20...	09:58	-rw-r--r--
index.html	0	Firefox Doc...	08/21/20...	16:38	-rw-r--r--
robots.txt	26	Text Docu...	08/21/20...	16:38	-rw-r--r--

10 folders and 4 files with 33217 bytes.

Extra

It is important to use 301 redirects any time you move a page from one location to another on your Web site. Do not expect the search engines to understand your intentions. You may consider moving a page to be a logical and intelligent decision, but the search engines initially see nothing but a missing page. When you remove pages that are no longer necessary for your site, consider adding a 301 redirect for those pages back to your site's home page. Otherwise, if you remove the pages and the search-engine spiders continue to crawl the missing pages, they may penalize your entire site despite the deletions being intentional.

If you own the .com, .net, .org, or other extension of your domain name, you can use 301 redirects to automatically force all .net and .org visitors to redirect to the .com extension or whatever extension you choose. If your brand recognition is strong, you may own various misspellings of your domain name. 301 redirects can be used to automatically redirect any misspelled traffic to your actual domain name. See Chapter 4 for more about domain names.

An Introduction to Creating Content

ontent is the lifeblood of your Web site — it is what visitors use to determine value and what search engines evaluate to rank your Web site. Well-written, original content is essential to the success of your Web site efforts. The quality of your content is directly proportional to how well you are likely to rank in search engines and whether a customer will purchase something from your Web site. Content written for the purposes of search-engine optimization, or *SEO*, is

designed to achieve organic rankings by appealing to the reader and to the search engine. Web sites with keyword-rich, naturally flowing, original content are judged better than Web sites that simply stuff keywords into otherwise poorly written text. This chapter instructs on the mechanics and proven methods for writing authentic and effectual content that not only gets visitors to take action, but also significantly increases your odds of attaining desirable search-engine rankings.

Write for People, Not Search Engines

Original, naturally flowing, well-written content provides your readers with a positive, enjoyable user experience while greatly improving your chances of top search-engine ranking. Search engines strive to keep their ranking systems as close to a meritocracy as possible: the best rankings for the best Web sites. The algorithms of today's popular search engines are sophisticated enough to determine whether a page is acceptable for human consumption; search engines tend to favor and reward high rankings to Web sites with well-written original content.

All the traffic on the Net is worthless without user click-through and conversions. The most utilized feature on the Web is the Back button; the crux of this problem lies with insipid and ineffectual content creation. Keeping your content flavorful and persuasive is the best way to accomplish superlative rankings and consistent conversions.

Using Proper Keyword Density

The goal of search-engine optimization is to make sure that your Web site ranks at the top of the search results when high-converting, target keywords related to your product or service are typed into popular search engines as search queries. Using proper *keyword density* is a process that includes the strategic repetition of select, target keywords and the minimization of nontarget keywords throughout your content, so that search engines deem your Web site relevant to search queries that you want to rank for. Proper keyword density is a fundamental component of on-site search-engine optimization. By using available tools to maximize optimal keyword density, you can incorporate a substantial number of target keywords through your content without compromising the natural flow of the writing.

Avoid Duplicate Content

Avoiding duplicate content is critical to achieving and maintaining favorable, long-standing, organic search-engine rankings. A trustworthy content writer understands the importance of writing and maintaining original content on a Web site. Search engines award original content and penalize identical content, making it absolutely necessary that you write unique content for your Web site. You also want to ensure that no plagiarists utilize your content for use on their pages. The discovery of duplicate content on your Web site prompts search engines to penalize you with lower rankings or omit your pages from the search results altogether. Tools exist that allow you to scan the Web for instances of duplicate copy and prevent plagiarism of your work from ever happening.

Using Latent Semantic Content

Search engines use latent semantic indexing to determine a site's thematic relevance to a particular search query. Latent semantic indexing allows the content writer to establish a site's relevance through thematically linked terms. You can use latent semantic content to create relevancy while maintaining the organic flow of your content. For example, if your page is about the Washington Redskins, you can use words like "football" and "Washington, D.C." in your content to establish relevancy. You can use these connected terms to legitimize your site as relevant without inundating your copy with the keywords "Washington Redskins."

Keep Content Current

Keeping your content current is essential to maintaining favorable organic search-engine rankings. It is vitally important to your Web site's success that you update content on a fairly regular basis. Search engines consider fresh content to be of greater value than outdated content, penalizing Web sites that remain unchanged and stagnant and rewarding Web sites that maintain fresh content. There are many ways to keep content fresh and original. Manually changing your content on a routine basis is time consuming, tedious, and often results in less-authentic prose. Self-perpetuating systems of content creation are preferred over the manual insertion of fresh content. User-generated content from testimonials, forums, and blogs, as well as content through content-aggregation networks, are highly recommended methods of supplying your site with fresh, stimulating content.

Optimize Non-HTML Documents

Search-engine algorithms were originally capable of indexing only HTML documents. However, with advances in technology, search engines are now indexing other documents such as Microsoft Word, Microsoft Excel, Microsoft PowerPoint, Rich Text Format (RTF), and Adobe Portable Document Format (PDF). Therefore, it is acceptable to include non-HTML types of document files within the body of your Web site content; however, these files must be optimized to improve the results when search engines index them.

For SEO purposes, you should fill your page primarily with textual content rather than image files. A simple rule is that even if your image contains information that is viewable to humans, search engines cannot read the image unless it also appears in a basic text format. Image files might be visually stimulating and eye-catching to a reader, but they are of little value as far as search engines are concerned. The fact is that although some search engines are capable of reading some aspects of PDF files and other kinds of images, search engines cannot read text or messages within image files, and tend to disregard them as empty space on your site.

It is prudent and beneficial to infuse your site with text that search-engine spiders can recognize. Include a call-to-action phrase in a text box, or use a creative textual format, which stands out to the reader. Textual content is not as visually pleasing as images, but it garners the necessary attention from search engines. Bottom line: Text lends itself to SEO; images do not.

Write for People, Not Search Engines

Search engines grant high rankings to Web sites deemed most relevant and valuable to the user; therefore, writing for search engines and writing for people are not mutually exclusive concepts. By strategically weaving a few target keywords into original, well-written content, you can accomplish superior organic rankings and persuade readers to become customers.

The ultimate goal of any search-engine-optimization (SEO) campaign is to achieve long-standing, organic rankings with popular search engines such as Google and Yahoo. Although content is not the only thing that search-engine algorithms take into consideration when ranking a Web site, content is arguably the most important. Therefore, if your goal is to obtain high organic rankings for your Web site, you must produce high-quality, original content that contains the keywords that you want to rank for.

Write Original, Persuasive, and Natural Content

If your content is original, persuasive, and has a natural tone, search engines tend to recognize it as worthwhile and therefore rank it positively. Conversely, if your content is overtly — or even worse, covertly — stuffed with keywords and the only purpose of the content is to manipulate search-engine results, search engines will eventually remove your content from the search results. Packing too many keywords into your content creates an awkward tone and unnatural flow. Even worse, when a search-engine spider detects superfluous keyword use, it deems a site "spammy" and devalues it accordingly.

Structure Your Content with Your Reader in Mind

For a beginner copywriter, it is beneficial to view content as your Web site's salesperson. It is enormously important to outline and structure your content to be as helpful and informative as possible. Your content must address the gamut of possible questions and concerns your reader may have regarding your product, service, or message. List the benefits of your product, service, or message and provide information that addresses any questions or concerns you might have as a reader. Supply genuine, thought-provoking product information rather than hollow, stale slogans. Writing distinctly helpful and user-friendly content makes your page appealing to humans and search engines alike. Before writing any content, ask yourself some questions: What are the benefits of the product, message, or service? What concerns would I have as a consumer or reader? What is truly exceptional about this product? By answering these types of questions, you alleviate any confusion or apprehensions your reader may have regarding your product, increasing your chances of conversion. People and search engines alike value comprehensive, useful information, not slogans and vague appraisals.

Avoid Poor Grammar

Search engines value the elegance and accessibility of your writing. The search-engine spiders are aware that clumsy sentences and poor grammar are displeasing to human readers; therefore, your grammar should be of the highest caliber. Search engines tend to devalue any content containing awkward sentences, clichés, erroneous grammar, or writing considered aesthetically abrasive to a reader. By keeping your prose elegant and distinctive, you increase your Web site's chance of attaining high search-engine rankings. It is also important to keep your content accessible to the average reader. Content that is too academic or esoteric in nature is going to confuse the average reader, costing the Web site potential conversions. Do not alienate the average reader by writing in a style more befitting to a doctoral dissertation than a Web page. However, content that comes across as elementary is going to generate minimal excitement and make your site look unprofessional. The key to writing accessible yet impressive content is determining the level at which your target audience reads. Besides overly academic diction, the use of colloquial language, slang, and industry jargon also detracts from the universal accessibility of content, which may lead to poor organic rankings.

Write Useful and Informative Content

It is important that your content be informative, concise, and easy to navigate. Readers on the Web are said to have an exceptionally short attention span, so avoid verbosity in your ad copy. Write in a concise manner and use headings, subheadings, bold type, and similar formatting that illustrate the information contained in each subsequent section of your page. Start all subheads, paragraphs, and bullet points with information-carrying words or action phrases that users can notice while scanning down your content. Keep in mind that users visit your Web site with a specific objective in mind. Readily accessible information increases the reader's chances of achieving an objective in a timely fashion. Readers are more likely to purchase or subscribe to your product or service if you make it easy for them.

Write with an Original Voice

With practice, copywriting becomes a learned skill. The process of becoming a skilled writer includes paying special attention to the originality of the writing. Originality requires you to make certain that your voice is the most powerful component of the content. Even if you are writing content that is technical in nature, you need to spend time to understand the material well enough to explain to the reader with your own voice. Writing with an original voice makes your content valuable to search engines and naturally compelling to readers. Writing in a manner natural to you translates as natural to your audience.

Using Bold-Type Headings

Provide bold-type headings that inform on the nature of each subsection, affording the reader an overview of the site's benefits at a glance. Furnishing readers with easily accessible, detailed information is the best way to keep them reading. Many inexperienced copywriters make the mistake of writing their material in one large block of content without headings that grab the reader's attention. Some readers are looking for specific information, and consider the task of reading the giant blocks of content to be too time consuming.

Using Call-to-Action Statements

Present your readers with readily accessible call-to-action options such as *Sign Up Today* or *Register Here*, prompting them to act on the information you provide. Make your call-to-action prompts eye-catching, reminding readers that they can take action whenever they feel ready. Calls-to-action make your site's user experience more engaging, allowing users to read and act at their own pace. Do not assume that average readers are inclined to read on to the bottom of your site before they make a decision.

Write Interesting Content in a Friendly Tone

Use the tone of your writing to capture your readers' attention and keep them interested in your work. Employing a friendly tone in your writing results in a positive response from virtually all readers. You can use a friendly tone and humor in your copy to make your Web site more personal and engaging. One of your main goals is to keep readers engaged long enough for them to read all the facts; the best way to accomplish this goal is to entertain while informing. Keep your content interesting and persuasive, and you will be pleased to find that not only people but also search engines will enjoy it. It is a fact that the vast majority of content that is ranked on the front page of major search engines also tends to be the content that is deemed most valuable and interesting to readers. Therefore, write quality content that people like, and search engines will rank it accordingly.

Avoid Duplicate Content

O ne of the essential characteristics of building and maintaining a Web site that ranks well in search engines is avoiding instances of duplicate content. Avoiding duplicate content issues allows you to eliminate penalties that are applied by search engines when duplicate content issues are discovered. Instances of duplicate content arise in one of two primary ways: You copy someone else's content for use on your page, or someone else copies your content for use on their page.

Duplicate content infractions occur when multiple Web sites contain identical or similar content. Although this problem may seem trivial, especially if you feel that you have not copied anyone else's content, you still must remain vigilant because someone may very well attempt to poach your content. It is also important to appreciate that search-engine algorithms do not have a good basis for determining who stole whose content. As a result, you may very well be the original author, but you may be penalized because Google's real concern is minimizing duplicate content, not arbitrating the rightful owner.

The discovery of duplicate content on your Web site prompts search engines to either omit your Web site completely from all search results, or place your content within the dreaded *supplemental results*. Supplemental results are not part of the main search results index and rarely if ever appear to a search-engine user. Getting your Web site kicked out of the index or placed within the supplemental results must be avoided.

Fortunately, tools exist that allow you to search for instances of duplicate content. One of the most commonly used tools is Copyscape, located at www.copyscape.com. Copyscape is a free service that searches the Web and identifies pages with content similar or identical to your own. In addition, Copyscape offers a free plagiarism warning banner that you can display on your Web site to deter others from stealing your work. You can sign up for Copyscape Premium if you want advanced protection from plagiarists. The premium membership carries a fee but provides unlimited searches for copies of your Web pages and helps to track and eliminate acts of plagiarism.

Avoid Duplicate Content

① Navigate to www.copyscape.com.

② Type the URL of your Web site into Copyscape's search box.

③ Click Go.

● The Web sites in which Copyscape found occurrences of duplicate content appear.

④ Click the Cached link to view the duplicate content.

- The page's content appears. Copyscape highlights certain items and/or blocks of content. The highlighted material is identical or nearly identical to content found on your page.

from **Become an SEO Professional & Dominate Google's Search Results** : SEO Book.com, 5 hours ago

The SEO Book is a 328 page downloadable ebook currently available for only $79. Since 2004, over 10,000 SEO professionals reading The SEO Book. Published as an ebook, you benefit from no shipping charges and access to an immediate download.

read more... »

"This Is YouTube Material!" - Cry of a New Generation?

from InsideGoogle, 4 hours ago

Boing Boing has the story of British potsmoking idiot who did something truly awful to a 50-year old dying disabled woman involving a buck shaving cream and a phone video camera.

read more... »

Free Prize Inside, or Mr.-Shouty-Trousers?

from Traffick: Search Engine Enlightenment | Grab the feed: traffick.com/atom.xml, Yesterday 7:54 PM

Recent news in <a href="http://en.wikipedia.org/wiki/CKVR-TV">VR-land</a> suggests that the Muskoka Tourism Association is proposi innkeepers levy a <a href="http://www.huntsvilleforester.com/huntsvilleforester/article/46868">3% "tourism tax."</a> that would then be fun

- You can find a link for Copyscape Premium anywhere on the Copyscape Web site. Click Premium to go to the Copyscape Premium sign-up and information page.

Copyscape

Search for copies of your page on the Web.

http://www.seobook.com   [Go]

PAGE PROTECTED BY COPYSCAPE DO NOT COPY
Defend your site with a plagiarism warning banner!

Premium - Unlimited searches, copy and paste. **Copysentry** - Automatic web monitoring.

About Example Plagiarism Press Testimonials Forum Log In

Extra

One of the most common forms of content theft occurs when content spammers create automated systems that steal content and simultaneously post it to so-called *Made-for-AdSense* Web sites. Made-for-AdSense, or MFA, Web sites attempt to monetize Web traffic from contextual advertisements, usually from Google AdSense or the Yahoo Publisher Network, by using unethical search-engine-optimization tricks, including the use of plagiarized content, which can result in top search-engine rankings.

If your content has been copied by someone attempting to profit from an MFA or similar Web site, your best bet is to immediately report the spam to the search engines. You can submit reports of spam to Google at www.google.com/webmasters/tools/spamreport?hl=en&pli=1, but you are required to log in to your Google account first. You can submit reports of spam to Yahoo at http://help.yahoo.com/l/us/yahoo/search/spam_abuse.html. You can submit reports of spam to Bing at http://help.live.com/Help.aspx?market=en-US&project=WL_Webmasters&querytype=topic&query=WL_WEBMASTERS_PROC_ReportSpam.htm.

Another common occurrence of duplicate content arises when e-commerce merchants distribute product data to content distribution partners such as comparison shopping engines and affiliate marketers. Duplication of content occurs when the product titles and descriptions sent to the comparison engines or affiliates are identical to the content on the merchant's Web site. The most successful way to minimize this common problem is to write unique titles and descriptions for all your products when submitting them to comparison engines and affiliates.

Using Proper Keyword Density

The goal of search-engine optimization is to make sure that your Web site ranks at the top of the search results when high-converting, target keywords related to your product or service are typed into popular search engines as search queries. Using *proper keyword density* is a process that includes the strategic repetition of select, target keywords and the minimization of nontarget keywords throughout your content, so that search engines deem your Web site relevant to search queries that you want to rank for. Proper keyword density is a fundamental component of on-site search-engine optimization. By using available tools to maximize optimal keyword density, you can incorporate a substantial number of target keywords through your content without compromising the natural flow of the writing.

Keyword density tools allow you to minimize the over-repetition of nontarget keywords, while ensuring that you have the proper density of your target keywords. WeBuildPages.com offers one of the most user-friendly and powerful keyword density tools, located at www. webuildpages.com/seo-tools/keyword-density. This tool provides a keyword density analysis of any Web site you request. The process is as easy as typing a URL, selecting basic preferences, and clicking Go.

The We Build Pages keyword density tool breaks down occurrences of two- and three-word terms, displaying them as density percentages. The tool can ignore terms of less than two words, eliminating words like *the, and,* and *of* from the analysis. If you want to exclude or include other parameters after your initial breakdown, go to the bottom of the page and reset the preferences.

Keyword density tools can help you to gain useful competitive research information on your competition. Once you identify the competitors that rank #1 for the keywords you want to rank for, use the keyword density tool to look for similarities among them that you can use to also rank well.

Using Proper Keyword Density

① Navigate to www.webuildpages.com/seo-tools/keyword-density.

② Under Keyword Density select your search preferences.

③ Type the URL of the Web site you want to analyze.

④ Click the Submit button.

● The keyword analysis of the Web site appears. This page displays the occurrences and percentages of the page's target keywords.

Note: *You can analyze any site. Performing a keyword analysis of top-ranking sites can help you understand optimal keyword density for certain search queries.*

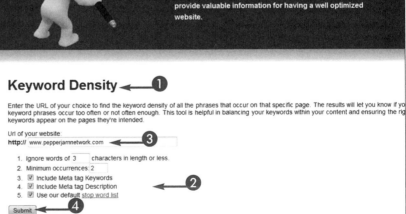

When it comes to good SEO there is no substitute for time, testing and research. Fortunately, there are a wide variety of tools to help make the process a little easier. SEO tools can provide valuable information for having a well optimized website.

Keyword Density ← ①

Enter the URL of your choice to find the keyword density of all the phrases that occur on that specific page. The results will let you know if yo[u] keyword phrases occur too often or not often enough. This tool is helpful in balancing your keywords within your content and ensuring the rig[ht] keywords appear on the pages they're intended.

Url of your website:
http:// www.pepperjamnetwork.com ← ③

1. Ignore words of 3 characters in length or less.
2. Minimum occurrences: 2
3. ☑ Include Meta tag Keywords
4. ☑ Include Meta tag Description ← ②
5. ☑ Use our default stop word list

[Submit] ← ④

Keyword Density for http://www.pepperjamnetwork.com
Total Words: 25   2 Word Phrases: 5   3 Word Phrases: 2

Word	Count	Density	2 Word Phrases	Count	Density	3 Word Phrases	Count	Density
affiliate	17	7.62%	affiliate marketing	9	4.04%	affiliate program pepperjam	2	0.90%
pepperjam	14	6.28%	launches affiliate	3	1.35%	launches affiliate program	2	0.90%
marketing	10	4.48%	program pepperjam	2	0.90%			
network	9	4.04%	affiliates merchants	2	0.90%			
publisher	5	2.24%	build successful	2	0.90%			
2010	4	1.79%						
pepperjamnetwork	3	1.35%						
launches	3	1.35%						
affiliates	3	1.35%						
publishers	3	1.35%						
program	3	1.35%						
advertisers	3	1.35%						
build	3	1.35%						
full	3	1.35%						

5 To change your search parameters, create another search.

6 You can change your search preferences for a more focused keyword analysis.

In this example, the boxes for meta tags are unchecked. This excludes the meta tag keywords and descriptions from the next search.

7 Click Submit to conduct a new search.

● Adjusted search results appear.

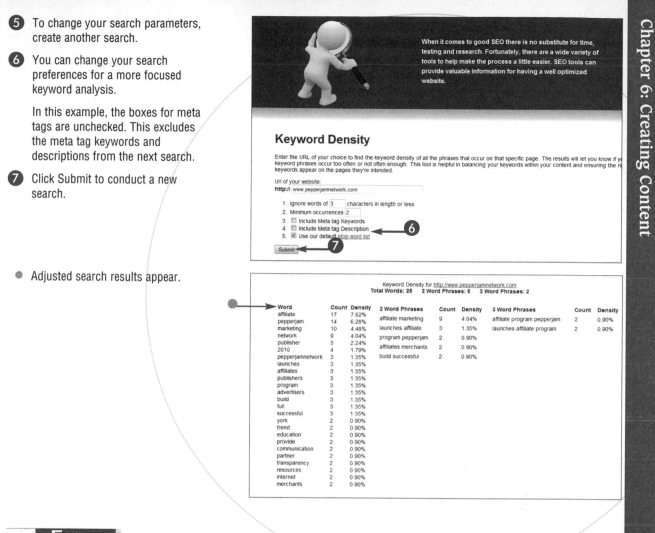

When it comes to good SEO there is no substitute for time, testing and research. Fortunately, there are a wide variety of tools to help make the process a little easier. SEO tools can provide valuable information for having a well optimized website.

Keyword Density

Enter the URL of your choice to find the keyword density of all the phrases that occur on that specific page. The results will let you know if your keyword phrases occur too often or not often enough. This tool is helpful in balancing your keywords within your content and ensuring the right keywords appear on the pages they're intended.

Url of your website:
http:// www.pepperjamnetwork.com

1. Ignore words of 3 characters in length or less.
2. Minimum occurrences 2
3. ☐ Include Meta tag Keywords
4. ☐ Include Meta tag Description
5. ☑ Use our default stop word list

Submit

Keyword Density for http://www.pepperjamnetwork.com
Total Words: 25   2 Word Phrases: 5   3 Word Phrases: 2

Word	Count	Density	2 Word Phrases	Count	Density	3 Word Phrases	Count	Density
affiliate	17	7.62%	affiliate marketing	9	4.04%	affiliate program pepperjam	2	0.90%
pepperjam	14	6.28%	launches affiliate	3	1.35%	launches affiliate program	2	0.90%
marketing	10	4.48%	program pepperjam	2	0.90%			
network	9	4.04%	affiliates merchants	2	0.90%			
publisher	5	2.24%	build successful	2	0.90%			
2010	4	1.79%						
pepperjamnetwork	3	1.35%						
launches	3	1.35%						
affiliates	3	1.35%						
publishers	3	1.35%						
program	3	1.35%						
advertisers	3	1.35%						
build	3	1.35%						
full	3	1.35%						
successful	3	1.35%						
york	2	0.90%						
trend	2	0.90%						
education	2	0.90%						
provide	2	0.90%						
communication	2	0.90%						
partner	2	0.90%						
transparency	2	0.90%						
resources	2	0.90%						
internet	2	0.90%						
merchants	2	0.90%						

Extra

In the past, keyword density was a much more important aspect of the search-engine-optimization process than it is today. All you had to do was repeat a particular keyword on a Web page eight to ten times and you stood a great chance of ranking for that term. Search-engine algorithms have improved tremendously and have become far more complex and much less transparent. Regardless, keyword density analysis should still be performed.

As a rule of thumb, search algorithms apply more weight to the title of your Web page than the density of the keywords on it. Therefore, your most important target keywords should be contained in your title and should also be dispersed throughout the content of your Web page. Keywords should not be repeated more than four to six times per 350 words of content. It is best to optimize each page of text, including title, for no more than two keywords or phrases.

The idea of using latent semantic content, which is covered in the next task, is replacing the idea of applying basic keyword density principles. As search engines continue to change their algorithms to combat spam and reduce fraud, keyword density is likely to become less and less important because it is one of the easiest things to manipulate. Instead, search engines will continue to build complex algorithms that favor original, well-written content over content riddled with keywords.

Using Latent Semantic Content

L atent semantic indexing allows the search engines to determine a page's relevance based upon its subject matter, rather than keyword density. Search engines consider a Web site's overall theme and then rank it based on topical relevance and authority, not on the density of its target keywords. You can construct your sentences and paragraphs using semantically linked words to help make your pages extremely relevant to your particular search terms. Covering as many thematically linked terms as possible helps establish high relevancy and a natural tone within your content.

In the world of organic search, latent semantic content refers to words that are connected thematically to a specific search query. For example: *Kevin Kolb*, *Philadelphia*, and *football* are all connected to *Philadelphia Eagles*. If the theme of your Web page is *Philadelphia Eagles*, the Web site does not need the keyword *Philadelphia Eagles* repeated numerous times in your content in order to rank

for that term. Instead, you can build content around related topics such as *Kevin Kolb* or *football*. These topics are fundamentally linked to *Philadelphia Eagles*.

Latent semantic content is an invaluable tool to use during the construction of your Web site. If a page in your Web site deals with Apple products, your Web site would benefit from covering subjects like *Macs*, *Macintoshes, Steve Jobs, iPads, iPhones, and iPods*, terms synonymous with *Apple*.

A Google tool is available to assist you in finding terms related to your search. If you perform a synonym search for *~apple* on Google, the result pages then show several terms highlighted in bold type. Google considers these terms to be semantically linked to the subject of *Apple Computers*. Quintura.com is also an excellent source for latent semantic keyword research.

Using Latent Semantic Content

Google's Latent Semantic Tool

① Navigate to www.google.com.

② Type **~apple** as your search term.

● Note bolded terms that appear such as *computer*, *QuickTime*, and *Mac*.

③ Type **~windows** as your search term.

● Note the bolded *Windows* and *Microsoft* that appear.

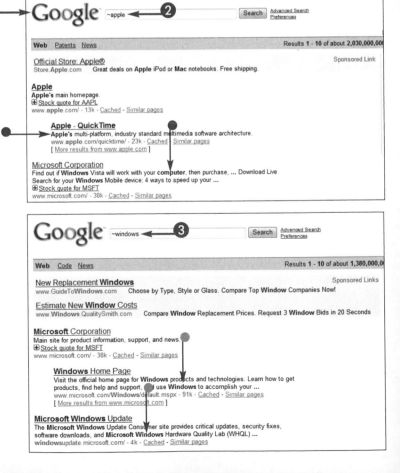

Quintura.com

① Navigate to www.quintura.com.

② Type **apple** as your search term.

Search results appear.

③ Position your mouse pointer over *apple* in the keyword cloud.

● Notice the bolded terms that appear, such as *ipod*, *macintosh*, *mac*, and *computers*. These terms are related to the term *apple*.

④ Position your mouse pointer over *ipod*.

● Notice the terms that appear such as *nano*, *parts*, and *itunes*. These terms are related to the term *ipod*.

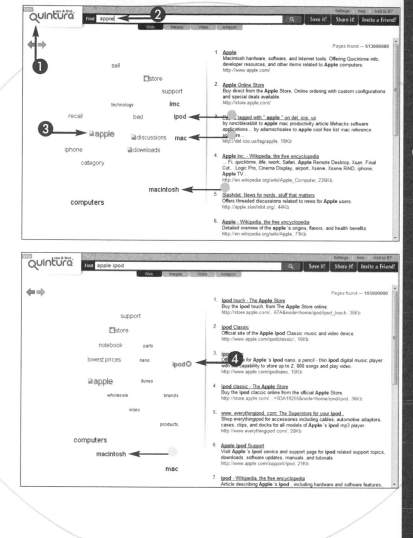

Keep Content Current

Search engines favor Web sites that have fresh content. Keeping your content current is fundamental and necessary to achieving and maintaining high search-engine rankings. Search engines consider fresh content to be of greater value than outdated content, penalizing Web sites that remain unchanged and rewarding Web sites that maintain fresh content.

Short of having to draft your own content on a daily or weekly basis, several proven strategies exist that allow you to keep your content fresh and original. For example, the most streamlined and least expensive approach to keeping your content current is to allow your users to create content for you. User-generated content from testimonials, forums, and reviews provides your users and the search engines with fresh content, while also providing valuable feedback to you and your users about the highlights of your Web site.

Another approach to keeping content current is through the use of free content aggregation systems such as

Really Simple Syndication, or RSS. RSS technology allows you to subscribe to various content sources, such as relevant news and blog feeds, and then automatically post that content to your Web site. For example, you can use RSS to update your Web site on a daily basis with select content on subjects that deal directly with the theme of your Web site.

Keep in mind that although use of content aggregation systems helps to keep some of your Web site content fresh, content aggregation systems alone cannot lead your Web site to a high search-engine ranking. Because RSS syndicates duplicate content, which can cause search engines to penalize your search-engine ranking, you also need to make weekly or monthly updates to the original content on each of your Web pages.

Integrating RSS feeds into your Web site requires moderate to advanced technical skills. The most common approach to integrating RSS feeds is using the programming language PHP.

Keep Content Current

1 Navigate to www.freshcontent.net.

2 Click Directory of Newsfeeds.

- A variety of newsfeed categories is available for you to choose from.

3 Click a newsfeed that is relevant to the content of your Web site.

④ Scroll down the page, and copy the JavaScript code to the Clipboard.

⑤ Paste the JavaScript code into your HTML wherever you want the Freshcontent.net content to appear.

Extra

A plethora of free content aggregation systems is available. For example, just about every popular blog allows you to join its RSS feed, and other sources exist such as Google News and Yahoo News. Free content aggregation provides a quick and easy approach to updating your Web site with fresh content, especially if the theme of your Web site is broad and not overly technical. If your Web site deals with very specific issues, such as medical services, programming, or aeronautics, you should consider a paid content aggregation service such as YellowBrix.

YellowBrix, located at www.yellowbrix.com, is a leading paid online content aggregator that offers real-time, online syndicated content from reliable and respected premium sources and numerous industry-specific trades. The YellowBrix aggregation system offers up to 130,000 breaking news stories a day gathered from thousands of trusted sources such as *USA Today*, the *Washington Post*, the BBC, and the Associated Press. YellowBrix offers a free 30-day trial demonstration, along with several different levels of paid service once your trial expires.

Another approach to keeping content fresh is to launch a company blog. A blog can serve several useful purposes, including keeping your visitors informed and educated, and allowing your Web site to build authority in the eyes of search engines.

Optimize Non-HTML Documents

Beyond basic HTML files, search engines now index other file formats such as Microsoft Word, Microsoft Excel, Microsoft PowerPoint, Rich Text Format (RTF), and Adobe Portable Document Format (PDF) documents. If you choose to post non-HTML files to your Web site, you can optimize each document to improve the results when search engines index them.

The basic rule for whenever you attempt to optimize a non-HTML document for search-engine purposes is to make sure that it contains readable text. Images that contain text cannot be read and therefore are not properly indexed by search-engine spiders.

Optimizing a PDF document is very much like optimizing a Web page. Treat each PDF file like it is a separate Web page and link to it from your sitemap the same way you would an HTML page. Whenever possible, the anchor text to the PDF file should contain keywords. Make sure your PDF file contains text and that it contains a nice blend of

your target keywords and phrases. Include your target keywords in the title of your PDF document. Consider breaking your PDF document into several smaller documents if it is very large or if it contains multiple topics. Avoid search-engine indexing pitfalls associated with large PDF files by creating an HTML-formatted abstract of the PDF file that links to the PDF.

Although most leading search engines can now read and index the content of a PDF file, some have certain restrictions and may index only the first thousand or so characters of the document. Therefore, PDF files should be used sparingly, and large PDF files should be minimized.

Sometimes you may want to convert HTML into PDF and other times PDF into HTML. HTMLDOC 1.8.27 from Easy Software Products, located at www.easysw.com/htmldoc, is a tool that provides a free 21-day demo license for first-time users.

Optimize Non-HTML Documents

Convert HTML to PDF

1. Click Start → HTMLDOC.

2. In the Input tab, select Web Page.

3. To convert an HTML file located on a Web site, click Add URL.

   If you are converting an HTML file located on your computer, click Add Files.

4. Type the address of the Web site you want to convert to a PDF file.

   If converting an HTML file on your computer, browse to the file and click OK.

5. Click the Output tab.

6. Select an output path.

7. Select PDF as the output format.

8. Select output options and the compression level.

9. Click Generate, and HTMLDOC creates a PDF file in your selected output path.

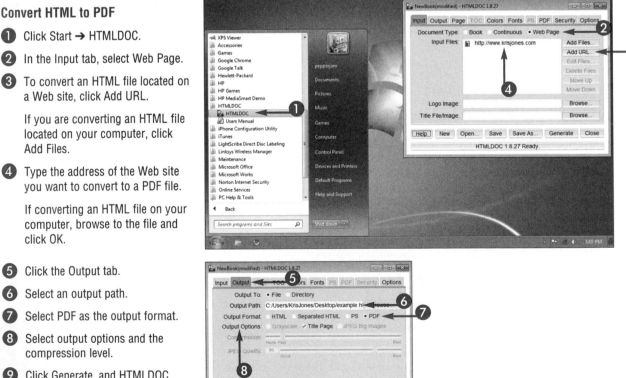

Convert PDF to HTML

1 Click Start → HTMLDOC.

2 In the Input tab, select Book.

3 To convert a PDF file located on your computer, click Add Files.

If you are converting a PDF file located on a Web site, click Add URL.

4 To convert a PDF file on your computer, browse to the file and click OK.

If you are converting a PDF file located on a Web site, type the address.

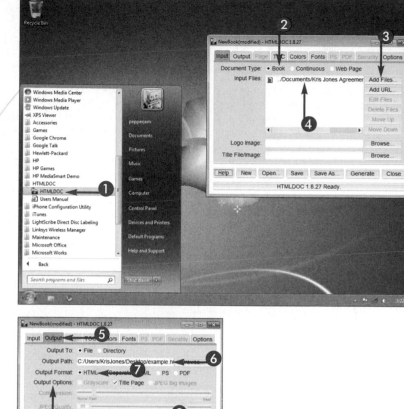

5 Click the Output tab.

6 Select an output path.

7 Select HTML as the output format.

8 Select output options.

9 Click Generate, and HTMLDOC creates an HTML file in your selected output path.

Extra

PDF files can be used to help your Web site generate leads. For example, you can set up your PDF files so that an unregistered user can read only the first page or two of the file. If that user wants to read the remainder of the document, you can require him to submit contact information to you, such as an e-mail address, name, address, and anything else that you want to track. Also, because many search engines refuse or are unable to index very large PDF files, you can break the PDF into several separate files so that search engines will read and index them.

If you have a very popular PDF file, you may want to consider structuring it as an e-book and charging your visitors to view it. An *e-book* is the equivalent of a conventional printed book, but it is made available only online or through special e-book readers. The downside of an e-book is that because you restrict access to it, search engines do not index it and therefore your Web site is not ranked based on the content of the book.

An Introduction to Creating Communities

Creating a community on your Web site is one of the most effective ways to keep your content fresh, and also helps establish your site as an authority for your area of business. Moreover, communities help build trust and provide a venue for your visitors to get interested and educated about your products or services. Two of the primary approaches to building online communities are blogs and forums. Blogs provide an opportunity for you to position yourself as an authority, and also attract participation from your visitors by allowing them to comment and provide feedback on your blog posts. Forums provide an opportunity for

multiple discussions to occur simultaneously around your area of business and stand as a meeting place for people who are interested in your products or services. Another very successful approach to building community on your Web site is to allow visitors to add reviews about your products. User reviews, blogs, and forums are exceptional ways to build user-generated contact on your Web site. Building large amounts of fresh content around your area of business is a prime strategy to build links and rank well in the search-engine results.

This chapter explores different approaches and strategies for creating successful communities on your Web site.

Create a Blog with WordPress

WordPress is a popular blog software service that allows you to quickly and easily create weblogs. Aside from the fact that the product is easy to install and manage, it is also free to use. WordPress allows you to build a community by educating, entertaining, and providing useful information to the consumer through a blog. You can use your WordPress blog to educate your customers about the benefits of your products. Moreover, you can use your blog to share special offers and deals with your customers and to elicit feedback on how you can improve your business.

Create a Blog with Tumblr

Tumblr is a next generation blogging platform that enables users to post text, images, video, links, quotes, and audio to a short-form blog. Tumblr is similar in many respects to Twitter and Facebook, including the ability for users to "follow," as well as "like" or "reblog" other blogs on the site. Tumblr is often favored by social media bloggers over other blog platforms such as WordPress and Blogger because of its customizability, ease of use, and social media attributes.

Create a Blog with Blogger

Similar to WordPress, Blogger is a free blog software service that allows you to quickly and easily create weblogs. There are pros and cons to using Blogger over WordPress. For example, with Blogger you can easily edit template layouts, styles, and colors, or install a third-party theme. With WordPress there is no template editing, and style sheet editing is available only as a paid upgrade. WordPress provides you with 3GB of image storage, and Blogger provides up to 1GB for free. If you intend to use a lot of high-resolution images and want to minimize your cost, WordPress may be a better option for you.

Write Search-Engine-Optimized Posts

If you are going to use your community as a way of generating traffic to your Web site, you should make sure that your blog and forum posts are search-engine optimized. The first thing you should do is use keyword research tools such as the Yahoo Search Suggestion Tool to explore what your audience is searching for. You can utilize the keyword research tool to identify keywords that you want to target within your blog title, headlines, and posts. See Chapter 2 for more about keyword generation.

After you have identified your target keywords, you are ready to generate a blog post. You should highlight your target keywords in various ways, including adding them to headlines and using bold or italic font to make your keywords stand out. The benefit of search-engine-optimizing your blog posts is that when search engines index your Web site, you are more likely to rank for target keywords.

Make Your Blog Successful

One of the most successful approaches to getting your Web site to rank well in the organic search results is to create a blog. A blog allows you to continually provide fresh content on your Web site while building a community of readers who look to your site as an authority. Your blog does not necessarily need to be educational in nature. You may also want to entertain and reward your readers for being part of your community.

Making your blog successful requires a serious time commitment and is likely to require the resources of an expert on your particular area of business.

Create a Community with vBulletin

vBulletin is a community forum software program that lets your visitors interact, take part in discussions, ask questions, give answers, and express opinions, giving you an instant community. Unlike a blog, a community forum is more of a discussion board where members and forum moderators interact by posting questions and answers and discussing common problems. A forum encourages your visitors to return again and again by allowing interaction and information sharing.

Create a Community with phpBB

phpBB is a popular open source bulletin board software package written in the PHP programming language. Unlike vBulletin, phpBB is free. However, depending on your needs, phpBB can serve as acceptable entry-level community forum software and provide you with the ability to add user-generated content to your Web site.

Make Your Forum Successful

Creating a forum on your Web site provides an excellent opportunity for your visitors to become part of your Web site community. Because forums are ultimately message boards where people ask and answer questions, a forum can provide a great place to refer a customer who has a question that may be shared by other members of the community. If a visitor has a question about the durability of a particular product or is unsure about one product over another, a forum provides a venue to get feedback and to generate interest in your products. At the same time, a forum is a great way to produce user-generated content on your area of business, which search engines tend to reward with high ranking in the search results.

Add Reviews to Your Web Site

Similar to the effect of adding a blog or forum to your Web site, adding reviews to your Web site can have a positive impact on your search-engine rankings while enhancing the overall credibility and sales of your Web site. Reviews provide an opportunity for your Web site visitors to learn from previous customers while providing you with fresh user-generated content, which search engines love.

User reviews have the same selling power as a testimonial. If you offer a product or service, other users' reviews can help increase sales. People find comfort knowing that others have used the product or service with good results. Although you may be concerned that users may provide negative reviews of your products, the positive effect of having user reviews on your Web site far outweighs the risk of an occasional negative review.

Create a Blog with WordPress

WordPress, located at www.WordPress.com, offers free blog software that allows you to quickly and easily create weblogs. A *weblog*, also known as a *blog*, is an online journal or diary that is frequently updated by an author and typically allows readers to interact by providing comments after each blog is published. Although individuals have traditionally used blogs as a way of entertaining and sharing opinions and expertise, businesses also effectively use blogs as a way of building community through educating, entertaining, and providing useful information to the consumer.

Hosting a blog through WordPress allows you to interact with your Web site visitors and customers. A blog creates a community on your Web site that you can use for various purposes to increase Web site traffic and improve customer relations. For example, you can use your blog to

educate your customers about the benefits of your products. Moreover, you can use your blog to share special offers and deals with your customers and to elicit feedback on how you can improve your business. By encouraging interaction and rewarding your readers, you can steadily build loyal readership and repeat customers.

Hosting a blog through WordPress on your Web site is a highly effective approach to maintaining fresh content. Because search engines favor Web sites with fresh content, hosting a blog not only allows you to build a community with interesting content, but also increases your chances of ranking well on the search engines. In addition, posting fresh content on your blog helps demonstrate to the search engines that you are an authority on a topic. Authoritative Web sites with fresh content rank higher in the search engines.

Create a Blog with WordPress

① Navigate to www. wordpress.com.

② Click Sign Up Now.

③ Choose a username and password, and fill in your e-mail address.

④ Select the check box associated with the WordPress legal terms of service.

⑤ Click Next.

6 Choose your subdomain and blog title.

7 Select your language and privacy options.

8 Click Signup.

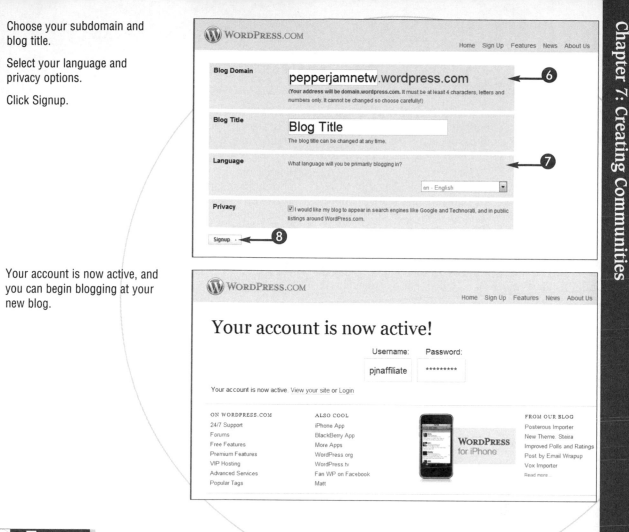

Your account is now active, and you can begin blogging at your new blog.

Extra

WordPress is used by more than 1 million bloggers from around the world. One of the primary reasons bloggers choose WordPress is because it is free and easy to use. In fact, WordPress can even host your blog for you, but that is not recommended because you can receive greater search-engine benefit by hosting your blog on your own Web site. However, if you want to host your blog, you need to meet a few technical requirements before you can start posting content to it.

To host your blog, your Web host must support the execution of PHP scripts. PHP is the programming language in which WordPress is written, and thus for WordPress to run at all, your Web host must support it. Another technical requirement is that your Web host must also include a MySQL database engine because WordPress stores its data and all your blog entries in a special file called a *database*, which allows easy and fast retrieval of content for your users.

WordPress also allows you to install numerous plugins that you can use to enhance your blog usability and search-engine optimization. For example, a popular usability plugin that reduces comment spam is Spam Karma, which you can read about at http://unknowngenius.com/blog/wordpress/spam-karma. A useful search-engine-optimization plugin is Optimal Title v3.0, located at http://downloads.wordpress.org/plugin/optimal-title.3.0.zip.

Create a Blog with Blogger

Blogger, located at www.blogger.com, is completely free blog software offered by Google that allows you to quickly and easily create weblogs. Blogger is a competitor to WordPress, and there are pros and cons to using one over the other.

With Blogger you can easily edit template layouts, styles, and colors, or install a third-party theme. With WordPress there is no template editing, and style sheet editing is available only as a paid upgrade. Keep in mind that you should host your own blog and customize it to fit the look and feel of your Web site. Therefore, using Blogger is free, but if you use WordPress you may have to pay an additional fee depending on exactly what customizations you want to make.

With Blogger you are unable to import blog entries from other blogs you may manage. WordPress allows you to import entries from Blogger, TypePad, LiveJournal, Movable Type, or another WordPress blog. Therefore, if

you have an existing blog, your best choice for blog software may be WordPress because you can easily import your content.

WordPress provides you with 3GB of image storage, and Blogger provides only 1GB for free. If you intend to use a lot of high-resolution images and want to minimize your cost, WordPress is a better option for you. If storage is still a problem, you can choose a free image storage service such as Flickr, located at www.flickr.com, which will allows you to upload 100MB of images a month.

One additional consideration between Blogger and WordPress deals with comment moderation and editing. With Blogger you can moderate comments, but you cannot edit them. In contrast, WordPress provides you with more flexibility by allowing you to both moderate and edit comments. If you expect your blog entries to generate a lot of comments, WordPress provides the better solution for moderating comments.

Create a Blog with Blogger

① Navigate to www.blogger.com.

② Click Create Your Blog Now.

Note: If you do not already have a Google account, you need to create one by navigating to www.google.com/accounts.

③ Fill in your personal information, including name and e-mail address.

④ Click Continue.

5 Choose a name and address for your blog.

6 Click Continue.

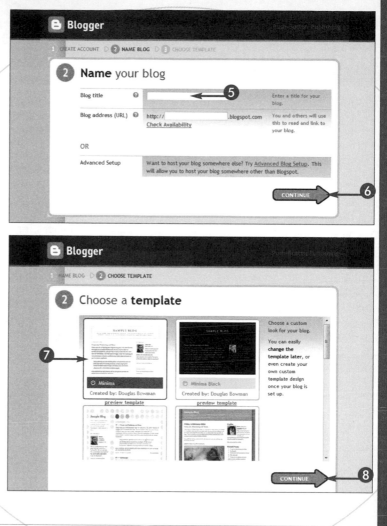

7 Choose a template for your blog.

8 Click Continue.

Your new blog has now been created.

Extra

One of the biggest challenges with managing your own blog is limiting the amount of comment spam you receive. Although you can moderate and review comments prior to their being published, you may prefer a solution that automatically publishes comments but reduces or eliminates comment spam. If you want an automated solution, you can use a CAPTCHA, install anti-spam software, and require users who comment to log in. The term CAPTCHA is an acronym for "Completely Automated Public Turing test to tell Computers and Humans Apart." A CAPTCHA is commonly displayed as an image showing warped or obscured letters and numbers and is used to reduce robotic comment spam by requiring the user to type a series of letters and numbers prior to submitting a comment. Although the goal of using a CAPTCHA is to make sure that the entity leaving the comment is a human, several sophisticated comment spamming robots can crack the CAPTCHA and therefore bypass the fix.

Another approach to minimizing comment spam is to download software. One of the most popular pieces of software is Akismet, located at www.akismet.com.

You can choose to accept comments only from people who have already logged in to a registration system that you run on your blog. Although requiring a login reduces comment spam, it cannot completely eliminate it because robots exist that can complete the required login steps and spoof you into believing the commenter is human.

Create a Blog with Tumblr

Tumblr, located at www.tumblr.com, is a Web 2.0 blogging platform that allows users to post text, images, video, links, quotes, and audio to a short-form blog, also called a *tumblelog*. Tumblr includes many similar attributes to popular social networking sites such as Twitter and Facebook, including the ability for users to "follow" other users and see their posts together on their dashboard, as well as "like" or "reblog" other blogs on the site.

The Tumblr text post allows you to easily upload content and share it with your readers in the form of a published weblog. You have the choice to edit your content through the Tumblr Text Editor or by using HTML. Photos can be added as part your Tumblr text post or can be added separately through what is known as a Tumblr photo post.

The Tumblr photo post makes it easy to upload photos that have been saved to your computer by supplying the URL of the image you want uploaded, or simply taking a picture through your computer's Webcam. You can write a caption using text or HTML for each photo and can also set a click-through link. Keep in mind that for search-engine optimization purposes the caption section of a Tumblr post should be used to specifically describe the image being posted, whereas the click-through link should go to the specific page you want ranked by search engines (see Chapter 13 for more info on optimizing images for Google image search).

Another common way to use Tumblr is to post video through a Tumblr video post. The Tumblr video post makes it easy to share a video that you like or have created through popular video Web sites such as YouTube or Vimeo. Similar to photo posts, you are able to provide a caption that allows you to customize the video to your specific post.

Create a Blog with Tumblr

1 Navigate to Tumblr.com and log in using your e-mail address and password.

2 Click the Text button to create a new text post.

● Note the different types of posts you can create, including Photo, Quote, Link, Chat, Audio, and Video posts.

③ Write the title of your post.

④ Write the body of your blog post.

⑤ Add tags to your post. Tags are descriptors that describe your post and are used by others to better understand what your post is about.

⑥ Set a custom post URL using descriptive keywords for SEO purposes. For example, post/123456 is about Google's consideration of pulling its search engine from China, so the custom post URL is google-china.

● Note that you can preview your post before publishing it.

⑦ Click Create Post.

⑧ Navigate to your Tumblr blog by typing **yourblog.tumblr.com** to view your blog post. For example, www.pepperjam.tumblr.com.

⑨ View your blog.

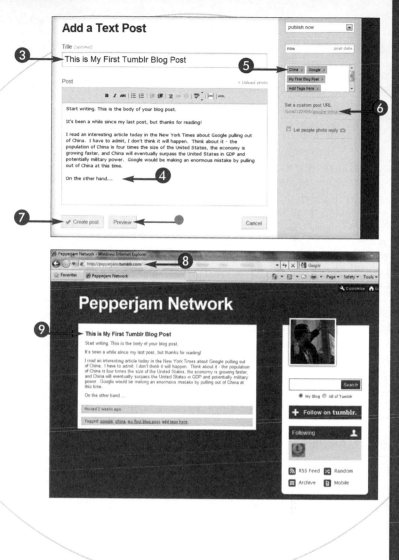

Tumblr tends to be favored by social media bloggers because of its customizability, ease of use, and social media attributes. For example, Tumblr offers a "like" button that allows you to tell another Tumblr user that you like her content. The Tumblr like functionality is similar to the popular "like" feature provided by Facebook that allows you to easily tell a Facebook friend that you like the comment that he posted on Facebook. The more "likes" that you have on a given Tumblr post, the more popular your post is perceived by the Tumblr community of bloggers.

Another popular social media feature of Tumblr is the "reblog" button, which reposts content from one Tumblr blog onto another. The Tumblr reblog feature can serve as a good source of traffic to your blog, especially if you produce interesting and useful content that others want to share. In fact, with nearly 1 million Tumblr users there is a chance that your content can be shared virally within the Tumblr community, resulting in a substantial increase in your Web site traffic.

Write Search-Engine-Optimized Posts

Writing search-engine-optimized blog posts is important if you want your content to rank well in search engines. You should familiarize yourself with how your blog software formats your content and make adjustments where necessary for search-engine-optimization purposes.

Use keyword research tools such as the Google AdWords Search Suggestion tool, located at https://adwords.google.com/select/KeywordToolExternal, to explore what your audience is searching for. The idea of using a keyword research tool is to identify keywords that you want to target within your blog title, headlines, and posts. See Chapter 2 for more about keyword generation.

For example, if you are writing a post about a specific kind of acne treatment, you should perform keyword research around that broad topic and select five to ten keywords to include throughout the body of the post. All the keywords you select should be related to the topic of your post.

The primary topic of your post should be included in your title tag and within any post headlines. For example, if your post is about your Web Design firm, your title and any headlines should reflect just that. Your title tag would read something like "My First Post on KrisJones.com – Thanks Unique Blog Designs!" Any headlines should mention the words Unique Blog Designs, such as "Why I Decided to Hire Unique Blog Designs to build my Blog."

When linking to your blog post from other posts within your Web site, you should use keyword-rich anchor text. For example, if you just created a new post about how impressed you are with a certain Web design firm for building you a Web site that exceeded your expectations, you may want to link back to your original post praising the Web design firm with the anchor text "Unique Blog Designs." See Chapter 8 for more about anchor text.

In general, you should selectively use bold or italic type to note your target keywords from the rest of the text. However, keep in mind that your post should ultimately be seen as natural to your readers and to the search engines. Do not just simply stuff keywords where they do not belong. Instead, write keyword-rich posts and make sure to highlight your most important keywords.

Write Search-Engine-Optimized Posts

1 Navigate to www.WordPress.com and log in using your username and password.

2 Select Add New under the Posts menu on the left navigation bar.

3 Enter your title in the field below the Add New Post heading.

4 To make a piece of text bold or italic, select the text.

5 Click the corresponding button in the toolbar.

6 To make a text a hyperlink, select the text.

7 Click the chain button.

8. Enter the URL you want to link to in the field labeled Link URL.

9. Click Insert.

   Your link is now included in your blog post.

10. When you are done writing your blog post, click Publish.

- Your new blog post is now visible on your blog.

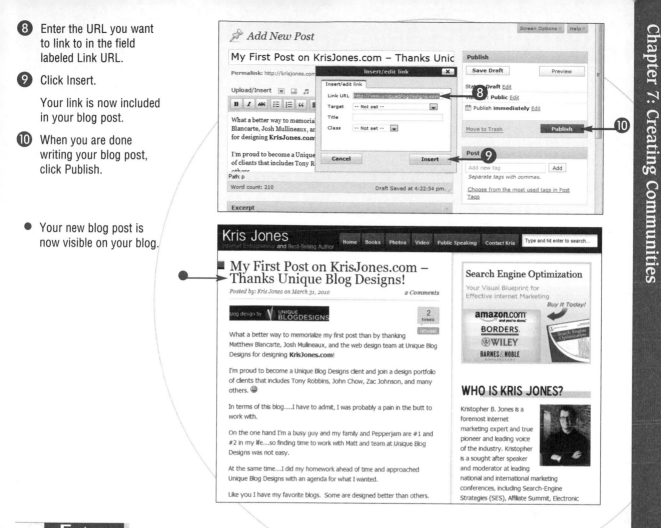

Make Your Blog Successful

One of the most successful approaches to getting your Web site to rank well in the organic search results is to create a blog. A blog gives you the opportunity to continually provide fresh content on your Web site, while building a community of readers who look to your site as an authority. Your blog does not necessarily need to be educational in nature. You may also want to entertain and reward your readers for being part of your community. Regardless, if you choose to create and maintain a blog, you can do a number of specific things to make your blog successful.

Keep in mind that creating a successful blog requires a serious commitment of time and resources. Although you can launch a blog for free through blog software vendors such as WordPress.com or Blogger.com, your blog is likely to require that you have a Web host that can handle your traffic, server, and database demands. Expect your blog to be a significant distraction from your normal course of business. Writing interesting and useful blog posts requires a significant amount of time. In many cases, you must perform some research to back up or support your writing, and you may also need to request permission if you want to use particular images or screenshots in your work. In short, remember that launching a blog requires your absolute commitment for it to be successful.

Using Experienced Writers with Industry Knowledge

Your blog should be maintained by a high-level individual at your business who understands your products and services very well. This person does not need to be an executive-level person, but should be someone with enough experience with your products to come across as educated and knowledgeable. If your goal is to use your blog as a resource for others in your industry, make sure that all the claims that you make are factual and that you are not questioned about the authenticity of your writing.

Using an Administrator

Your blog should have an administrator. An administrator acts as a moderator by approving or declining comments and manages the overall goals of your community. For example, you may want your administrator to provide perks to those members who comment frequently. Recognizing your most active members is a great way to keep those members coming back and to build community. A great example of building community through recognizing members is done by expert blogger Jeremy Schoemaker of Shoemoney.com. Shoemoney.com recognizes the ten most frequent commenters by placing the members' Web site names with a link on the www.shoemoney.com home page. Because most of Shoemoney's readers are from the SEO community, a link on Shoemoney's home page is highly valued.

Hold Contests and Giveaways

One way of getting interest in your blog is to periodically hold contests or giveaways. For example, you can create a blog post in the form of a poll that asks your readers to guess what your top selling product will be for any given week. Each guess counts as one entry in the contest. You can select the winner at random from the correct answers and give the top selling product or some other incentive as a prize. Holding contests keeps your readers interested in your blog and provides incentive for them to talk about your business and frequently visit your Web site.

Offer RSS Technology

Another approach to getting people to frequently follow your blog is to offer your content through Really Simple Syndication, or *RSS*. RSS allows your readers to keep up with your blog in an automated manner and is easier for them than checking your blog randomly for new content. The most popular blog feed management provider is FeedBurner, which is a free service located at www.feedburner.com. Once you join FeedBurner and add a FeedBurner icon to your Web site, your readers can easily join your RSS feed. For example, via the FeedBurner blog feed management system, your readers can elect to receive an e-mail notification every time you write a new blog post. The e-mail contains either a summary of your content or the full text with a link to your Web site.

Interview Experts

There are several strategies that you can use to recruit new readers to your blog. One of the most effective ways to get new readers interested in your work is by interviewing experts and other well-known people associated with your particular industry. You should ask questions that are provocative as well as interesting, including questions about your interviewee's personal life. For example, your business may be in the manufacturing industry. An example of a provocative question might include something about why most manufacturers have not taken proactive steps to control water and air pollution. A softer approach might be to ask the expert about the pros and cons of offshore manufacturing. Asking the expert about family and favorite pastimes is another way of making your interview personable and attractive to your readers.

Break News or Piggyback News

Another approach to attracting new readers to your blog is by breaking news or piggybacking a news story that affects your area of expertise. For example, you can use your blog to talk about exciting news that is happening at your company. Also, you can provide an interpretation or a summary of a popular news story that occurs within your industry. If possible, you should spin the story by making some predictions about what the news means for your industry or why the news is good or bad. Remember that your goal is to come across as a credible authority in your field, so you should make sure that your opinions are substantive and not entirely speculative.

Participate on Social Media Web Sites

A proven effective approach to marketing your blog is through participation on social media Web sites such as Facebook, Twitter, Google Buzz, Digg, Technorati, Flickr, and others. For example, if you use images on your Web site, you should also upload those images to Flickr, which is a popular photo-sharing Web site. If your blog post is especially provocative, you should definitely make sure one of your readers submits it to Digg, a popular social news Web site that can have a profound impact on your Web site traffic if the Digg community embraces your content. Submitting your blog to Technorati is another great way to market your blog. Technorati is a popular blog search engine that millions of potential readers visit every day to find interesting and informative content. See Chapters 10 and 13 for more about social media Web sites and Technorati, respectively.

Making your blog successful is an achievable process if you are willing to dedicate the requisite time, energy, and creativity to making it work. In addition, a successful blog helps you to promote your products or services and increases the likelihood that other people link to your Web site, which helps to improve your organic search-engine rankings.

Create a Community with vBulletin

VBulletin is community-forum software that gives you the ability to create a community that lets your visitors interact, take part in discussions, ask questions, give answers, and express opinions. Unlike a blog, a community forum is more of a discussion board where members and forum moderators interact by posting questions and answers and discussing common problems. A forum encourages your visitors to return again and again by allowing interaction and information sharing.

vBulletin is powerful, scalable, and fully customizable forum software. vBulletin is easy to install, user friendly, and easy for new members to learn to use. vBulletin has been written using the Web's quickest-growing scripting language, PHP, and is complemented with a highly efficient and ultrafast back-end database engine built using MySQL.

One of the clear benefits of vBulletin is that the software is search-engine friendly. Moreover, controlling the meta tags for each page of your forum is done through the easy-to-use vBulletin admin panel. Within the vBulletin admin panel you can set up your meta keywords and

meta descriptions, among other things. See Chapter 3 for more about meta tags.

vBulletin allows you to customize the look and feel of your forum. You can get free *skins* and different forum style sheets at www.vbulletin-faq.com/skins-styles.htm. Skins refer to preselected template designs that allow you to change the look and feel of your forum or Web site. You should make sure that your forum's look and feel are consistent with the look and feel of your Web site. You should also set up the forum on the domain of your Web site, such as www.example.com/forum or forum.example.com.

By building a community on your Web site with vBulletin, you are making the case to Google and other search engines that your Web site is an information hub for the particular area of your business. Aside from creating content on a regular basis yourself, hosting a community forum or a blog is the best way for you to rank well in the search engines.

Create a Community with vBulletin

① Navigate to https://www.vbulletin.com/order and order your copy of vBulletin.

② Create a /forum/ directory on your Web site and upload the vBulletin files.

③ Your forum software is now publicly available for new user registration and posting.

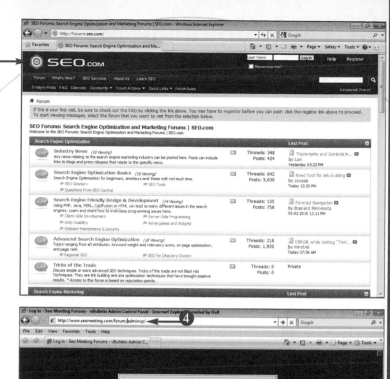

④ To make changes to your forum, log into the administrative area located in the /admincp/ directory of your Web site.

Extra

One of the steps that you should take to prevent search-engine spiders from visiting private areas of your forums is to create a robots.txt file. See Chapter 5 for more about robots.txt files. A private area of your Web site may be an area that is accessible only to paid members, or an area where you have concerns about search engines indexing duplicate content.

Here is an example of the code you can upload to your public_html directory to prevent private pages from being indexed:

```
User-agent: *
Disallow: /forums/memberlist.php
```

A complete list of code that you can upload to your public_html directory is located at www.vbulletin-faq.com/optimize-vbulletin-server.htm. If you use something other than /forums/ for your forums directory, adjust the paths accordingly.

Create a Community with phpBB

phpBB is a popular open source, bulletin board software package written in the PHP programming language. Unlike vBulletin, phpBB is free. However, depending on your needs, phpBB can serve as acceptable entry-level community forum software and provide you with the ability to add user-generated content to your Web site.

phpBB offers a large and highly customizable set of key features, including the ability to implement forum modifications and style changes. Because phpBB is open source, there is a large range of existing modifications that have been written by other phpBB users and programmers, which you may find useful. Existing phpBB modifications such as Attachment modification provide you with the option to attach different types of files to your posts. The Show Replies and Views in Topic modification displays the number of replies and views of the topic that your visitor

reads. An extensive database of validated modifications is located at www.phpbb.com/mods.

phpBB version 3 uses a powerful templating system that keeps the PHP code separate from the HTML code and gives you complete freedom to customize your forum the way you want. However, if you want to download additional styles and new graphics for your forum, you can do so at www.phpbb.com/styles.

phpBB has an easy-to-use administration panel and a user-friendly installation process, which allows you to have your basic forum set up in minutes. However, if you want to customize your forum, you can expect the process to take much longer, and it may require moderate-to-advanced expertise with PHP, CSS, HTML, and MySQL.

You can download phpBB at www.phpbb.com/downloads. However, be sure to read and fully understand the license agreement before you download and use the software.

Create a Community with phpBB

 ❶ Navigate to www.phpbb.com.

❷ Click Downloads in the main menu.

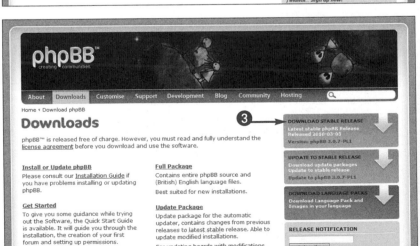

The Downloads page appears.

❸ Click Download Stable Release.

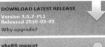

The File Download dialog box appears.

④ Click Save, and then click OK.

You have successfully downloaded phpBB.

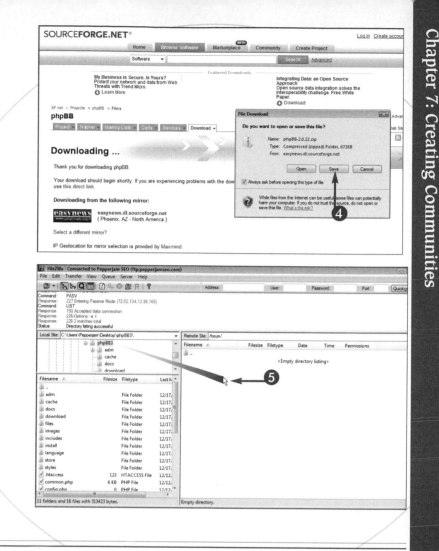

⑤ Create a /forum/ directory on your Web site, and upload phpBB.

Extra

Selecting appropriate forum software is challenging, especially if you have an e-commerce Web site. If you have a minimal budget, your best bet is to go with phpBB because it is free. However, the other leading forum software, vBulletin, is inexpensive and is likely to be a better choice if you have an e-commerce Web site. There are a number of different factors to consider, and there is likely no better way of evaluating your options than finding out what other people in your situation have done.

HotScripts, located at www.hotscripts.com, is a popular Internet directory that compiles and disseminates Web programming-related resources and opinions. You can use HotScripts when you are exploring the pros and cons of different available forum and community software. Through HotScripts, you can access user reviews from a variety of current and former phpBB and vBulletin users. Moreover, HotScripts allows users to provide a rating on a one-to-five scale of user satisfaction with each forum. Ratings and reviews are broken down by date because often forum software vendors provide regular updates to improve the software based on user comments, so older reviews may not be relevant.

Make Your Forum Successful

A community forum provides you with the ability to better communicate and interact with your Web site visitors, while enabling your users to generate substantial amounts of relevant content. Because the content generated by your users is likely to be fresh and substantial, a community forum is a good way to rank higher in the search engines. Creating a community forum has numerous potential benefits.

Having a community forum encourages user interaction and participation on your Web site. You can use your forum as a tool to communicate with your visitors frequently and closely. For example, your forum is a great place to refer visitors who have specific questions about your products or services, including the benefits of selecting one product over another. In addition, if you find that your customers tend to ask the same question over and over, you can use the forum as a place to offer a comprehensive response. Your forum could also be a place where you proactively pose answers to questions you know your customers are going to have based on a policy decision. For example, if you must increase shipping charges, you can use your forum to provide details on why you made that decision.

Allow Users to Post Questions

Most community forums allow users to post customer service-related questions to be answered by a forum moderator or by other members. This is a great way to reduce the demand typically placed on your customer service team because one customer's questions or concerns are likely to be shared by others. Moreover, if you have a moderator control the forum, you will be made aware of a problem and can deal with it quickly before it becomes more widespread and difficult to manage.

Optimize for Search Engines

One of the clearest benefits to having a community forum is that the content created on the forum helps you rank higher in the search engines. The primary reason that forums rank well within search engines is that they tend to contain fresh, concentrated content. Content on forums is typically focused around a very specific niche area. By allowing your members to express opinions and share expertise on your particular area of business, you are communicating to Google and other search engines that you are an information hub. In this way, existing members keep coming back to participate on your forum and hopefully buy your products, and you also create content that ranks well in the search engines, thereby generating new users for your Web site.

Evaluate Consumer Feedback

Having a forum allows you to understand more about your visitors by reading the conversations and discussions between them. Your visitors are likely to talk about your products, services, and Web site, which is hopefully a good thing. Regardless of whether it is good or bad, consumer feedback can be invaluable and can help you market your products or services more effectively. Keep in mind that the idea of having a forum on your Web site does not solely have to be about promoting your products and services. Equally valuable is the information that you can get from your customers to improve your overall Web site initiatives.

Dedicate Requisite Time and Resources

Making your forum successful requires a substantial dedication of time. However, you can have your existing customer service team or a key employee or two help moderate the forum. In addition, once your forum is established and a few key members emerge based upon frequency of participation, you can ask them to help moderate the forum. In general, you need not spend more than 10 to 15 hours per week managing the forum, especially if you have active members looking after the board and providing responses to other members. However, if you want to be proactive and post questions before a member asks them, you may need to dedicate more time to managing the board.

Conduct Contests or Giveaways

One way of generating participation on your forum is to periodically hold contests or giveaways. For example, you can give away a $100 iTunes gift card to the person who submits the most compelling testimonial about your products or services. Another idea might be to provide a giveaway like a logo T-shirt or mug whenever someone on your forum exceeds a certain number of posts. Many successful forums offer active members milestone awards. As mentioned earlier, one way of rewarding your most active members is by giving them a moderator or similar status. Moderator status is usually designated by an icon or some other symbol that notes the status of the member.

Ask Friends and Colleagues to Post Questions and Comments

When you first launch your forum, ask your friends and employees to post on it. Your employees can start out by posting common questions and concerns shared frequently by your customers. For example, you can start a forum post around what products have sold best during the holiday season. Your friends and employees can simply respond with their opinions and you can step in with the answer based on your experiences. You can also use your first few forum posts to ask members what they want to know more about and how you can best use the forum to help them. Finally, your first few forum posts could be on topics about which you are interested in requesting feedback from customers. For example, you can pose questions about desired shipping methods or experiences with packaging.

Set Rules

In order to create a successful forum, you need to have very specific rules about what is and is not allowed. You may decide that the forum is a place where you allow members to promote their own services. For example, you should have a policy that disallows or minimizes members from posting self-serving links to their Web sites for SEO purposes. Moreover, you may want to have a policy that forbids competitors from coming to your board and posting advertising messages or maliciously stirring rumors or posting false information. Finally, a forum is supposed to be a place where the community helps to set rules and standards. Therefore, you should consider asking your most active members what rules and policies they think should be implemented on your forum in order for it to attract new members and provide existing members with valuable information.

Share Information about New Products

Probably the most effective use of a forum if you have an e-commerce Web site is to share information about new products as well as to inform members about promotions and special incentives. For example, you may provide an exclusive percentage-off offer to all your members or a special free-shipping coupon to active members of your forum.

Regardless of your approach, a forum is a great place to keep your customers interested in your products and informed about special deals and offers.

Add Reviews to Your Web Site

Adding reviews on your e-commerce Web site can have a positive impact on your search-engine rankings, while enhancing the overall credibility and sales of your Web site. Reviews provide an opportunity for your Web site visitors to learn from previous customers, while providing you with fresh user-generated content, which search engines love.

User reviews have the same selling power as a testimonial. If you offer a product or service, other user reviews can help increase sales. People find comfort in knowing that others have used the product or service with good results. Although you may be concerned that users may provide negative reviews of your products, the positive effect of having user reviews on your Web site far outweighs the risk of an occasional negative review.

Adding the ability for users to review products on your Web site is an effective approach to keeping your content fresh. Each user review adds original content to your Web

site that is often keyword rich for your product or service. User-generated content is free and tends to be favored by search engines because it is seen as authentic.

User reviews get your users involved and active on your site. A user who may be considering purchasing a product on your site may check back frequently to read new reviews to help in the decision-making process. The more active your users are on your Web site, the more likely they are to find your site credible and useful, and the more likely the user is to become a customer.

Adding a review script to your Web site is easy and inexpensive. For example, Review-Script, located at www.review-script.com, provides an Amazon-style review script that allows users to rank a product or item on a scale of one to five stars and make comments related to the product for other users to read. The Review-Script Web site includes a demo so that you can preview the script and get some ideas for how you can use it on your Web site.

Add Reviews to Your Web Site

1 Navigate to www.review-script.com.

2 Click Demo.

- The demo area shows an example of a bare-bones design that is ready to be customized.

3 Scroll down the page to see example uses of Review Script.

- Note that Review Script allows you to list the top rated reviews on your site.

- Note that Review Script also allows you to list the most useful reviews on your site.

④ Create a /review/ directory on your Web site and upload the review script files.

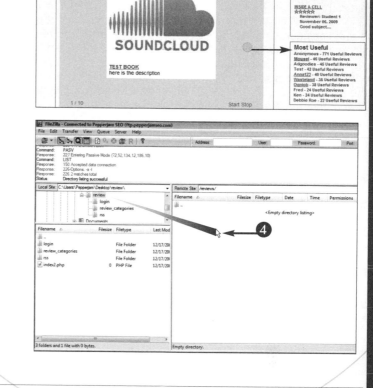

Review-Script.com uses a PHP script with a MySQL database back end. If you prefer working with ASP instead of PHP, you can use EasyReviewScript v1.0, located at www.easyreviewscript.com. Both Review-Script and EasyReviewScript require only a basic understanding of ASP or PHP and MySQL. In addition, a basic level of HTML is required during the installation process and is necessary if you want to make significant alterations to the appearance of the script.

EasyReviewScript is easy to install and requires very little configuration and support. You can customize EasyReviewScript to the look and feel of your site using HTML or CSS, which is essential if you intend to add your forum community to an existing Web site.

EasyReviewScript allows your visitors to rate and review products, pictures, articles, and more using a star rating system based on a one-to-five scale. EasyReviewScript also allows you to log the IP address of each reviewer so you know where the reviews are coming from. The EasyReviewScript review software also has a fraud prevention system that validates e-mails before submission to keep users from submitting fraudulent e-mails.

An Introduction to Building Links

In a fraction of a second, Google's search algorithm computes how many Web sites link to your Web site and the value of each individual link. Google automatically performs this process millions of times every day: Google believes that calculating links and taking into consideration such things as what those links say, along with the quality of the Web sites they come from, is an effective method of determining a Web site's authority. Google ranks sites based on how authoritative they are in their respective markets. Delivering relevant results and determining authority is the foundation of the Google search engine.

In short, if you have a lot of quality Web sites that link to your Web site, you are probably doing well in Google's organic, or nonpaid, results. However, if you have just a few links, you are probably scouring resources to figure out what you can do to improve your search-engine ranking. This chapter represents a step-by-step guide on how to effectively build links to your Web site so that Google and other search engines will determine that your Web site is an authority and thereby rank it well in the organic search results.

Evaluate Competition

The first step to effectively building links is to evaluate your competition. What works for your strongest competitors can also work for you. At this early stage of the link-building process, your goal should be to build the foundation for an effective search-engine-optimization business plan. You should take the process of evaluating competition seriously and spend the requisite time necessary to rank your competition and take advantage of their success.

Gather Link Intelligence with Linkscape

Linkscape is a link analysis tool that provides basic or advanced intelligence of the links pointing to a particular Web site. The basic Linkscape intelligence report provides general information about the number of links pointing to a particular Web site, as well as the relative popularity of that Web site. The advanced Linkscape intelligence report provides extensive information about a particular Web site, including detailed lists of the top links pointing to the site, the most common anchor text, and much more.

Acquire Quality Links

You can save yourself a measurable amount of time by approaching the link-building process from the standpoint of building quality links versus building a high quantity of links. Too often, Web site owners believe that they need thousands of links to rank well in the search engines. That is simply not true, regardless of what vertical, or industry, your Web site is in. For optimal success, your approach should be dictated by quality over quantity.

Developing the skill set required to quickly evaluate potential link partners includes learning how to identify the age of a domain, the uniqueness of content, and the potential for incoming traffic. Evaluating potential link partners for quality and focusing on those quality links is a key part of the link-building process, and provides an opportunity for you to focus on some of the important factors that search engines take into consideration when determining the quality of the Web sites that link to your Web site.

Evaluate Potential Linking Partners

Not all links are created equally, so you should evaluate each potential linking partner for quality. This can be accomplished by analyzing numerous link-quality factors. By focusing on quality links, the major search engines are more likely to recognize you as a quality contributor to your Web site's subject matter.

Using Effective Anchor Text

Once you have identified potential link partners, you want to determine the anchor text to use for each link. This part of the Google algorithm focuses not on how many links you have pointing back to your Web site, but on what those links say. Approaching the rest of the link-building process with a list of keywords that you want to use as anchor text is essential to your link-building success. You should use a variety of anchor text throughout your link building to ensure that the search engines can determine the overall theme of your site.

Link and Article Directory Submissions

Submitting links to free and paid online directories represents an easy and proven method of building links, but submitting articles to Web sites and content distribution services works especially well. Among other things, article submission strategies allow you to tailor content so that it maintains the specific theme you are looking to be associated with. Getting an article published on a popular, authoritative Web site with links back to your Web site is a surefire way to rank well in the search engines.

Community Participation

Participating in communities such as blogs and forums that allow you to post a link back to your Web site is a fun and effective strategy for generating Web site traffic and building links. However, keep in mind that your participation on blogs and forums should be substantive and relevant. Although commenting on relevant blogs and forums seems tedious, it is one of the quickest approaches to building links and also presents the opportunity to learn more about what people in your industry are talking about. Participating in these conversations not only allows you the opportunity to increase your own Web site traffic and search-engine rankings, but it can also help you learn how to grow your business in other ways.

Request One-Way Links

Another method for building links is to request one-way links directly from Web sites. This involves screening potential Web site linking partners for quality and then sending a link request through e-mail. These Webmasters may not have ever considered selling a link, and contacting them could potentially give you the opportunity to acquire high-quality links for a very low price.

Buy Links

Buying links can be done through link broker networks. Link broker networks allow you to search through a large database of Web site owners who have agreed to sell Web site links. You should try to buy links primarily from Web site owners that have Web content that is related to your product or service. Often these Web sites have already been prescreened for quality factors, thus saving you a good amount of time and energy. You can also choose your specific link anchor text.

Pay-per-post networks allow you to hire bloggers to write a post about your product or service and place your link within the body text. Often you can choose more than one variety of link anchor text. These links are generally purchased for a one-time fee as opposed to a recurring monthly subscription, and for that reason they can be an inexpensive way to build high-quality, relevant links. Pay-per-post networks can be used to effectively generate buzz about your product or service. Keep in mind that you should primarily select blogs that are substantively related to your Web site. At the same time, be careful about whom you select to blog about your product or service. Some readers devalue paid posts and conclude the content must be biased because payment is involved.

Finally, this chapter explores the practice of building links through writing and distributing search-engine-optimized press releases. Search-engine-optimized press releases provide the added benefit of generating buzz and lots of Web site traffic, and include the ability to strategically optimize the press release for specific keywords you want to rank for on the search engines.

Evaluate Competition

O ne of the most effective ways to find potential quality link partners is to mimic the efforts of your most successful competition. What works for your high-ranking competition can also work for you. Any Web page that links to a competitor of yours is a prime candidate to link to your Web page as well.

Because the number of quality incoming links plays such a large role in Google's organic ranking algorithm, you should put together a list of Web pages that link to your top performing competitors. First, determine who your top competitors are. Focus on pages that target the same audience that you intend to target. Then, find out where all their links are coming from and attempt to acquire links from those sites to your own.

The simplest tools available to find your competition's backlinks are the search engines themselves. Google and Yahoo provide a way to find all the links pointing to a particular Web page. You can use Google's link query and

Yahoo's linkdomain query. These tools allow you to find what sites link to any other site.

Yahoo seems to keep the most updated and comprehensive list of these links. Also, Yahoo allows you to exclude a domain when searching for links. For example, you may want to find how many sites are linking to your own site, but you do not want to see your own internal links. Yahoo also allows you to find links from other domains to any pages on your site.

Keep in mind that not all links are created equally, so after generating this list of prospective linking partners, you should evaluate each one on an individual basis before spending a great deal of time trying to make the acquisition. The next task explains more about evaluating links. After narrowing down your list, you should contact the Web page owners directly to discover what the owner might require to obtain a link, as discussed in the task "Request One-Way Links."

Evaluate Competition

Note: This task uses the Web site www.pepperjamnetwork.com as an example.

Google's Link Query

❶ Navigate to Google.com.

❷ Enter **link:** followed by the Web site in the search box.

● Notice that 56 pages link to the Web site.

Yahoo's Linkdomain Command

❶ Navigate to Yahoo.com.

❷ Enter **linkdomain:** followed by the Web site in the search box.

● Notice 101,000 pages link to the Web site.

Additional Yahoo.com Queries

① Click the Show Inlinks arrow and choose Except from This Domain.

② Click the To arrow and choose Only This URL.

● This command shows links from sites other than pepperjamnetwork.com that point directly to www.pepperjamnetwork.com.

③ Click the To arrow and choose Entire Site.

● This query shows links from sites other than pepperjamsearch.com that point to any page on www.pepperjamnetwork.com.

Extra

Using the link search query on a domain in Google shows you only a small sampling of the total number of incoming links recognized by Google; however, people familiar with the search-engine marketing industry speculate that these are the links that Google considers the most influential to your site's rankings.

There are some advanced competition evaluation tools available. One such tool is called Link Harvester, which can be found at http://tools.seobook.com/link-harvester. Link Harvester provides a detailed look into an individual site's incoming links, breaking down the list into links that come from unique domains, from unique C-class IP addresses, and from .edu, .mil, or .gov sources.

Another extremely valuable tool is called Hub Finder, which can be found at http://training.seobook.com/hubfinder. Hub Finder searches Yahoo, Google, or both for a specific search term, returns a list of the top ranking sites, and then examines the sites' incoming links to determine which links they share. Enter a search term you are interested in increasing your rankings for into the tool. If all or even just a few of the top ranking sites for that term share an incoming link from a particular page, make an effort to obtain a link from that page for your own site.

Evaluate Potential Linking Partners

You can determine what is considered a quality link by analyzing a number of factors. One of the most important factors to consider is the age of the domain you are trying to acquire a link from. Google tends to treat older domains that have been around for several years with more respect than domains registered recently. If you can acquire a link to your page from a domain that was registered in 1995, it is likely to have a greater effect on your organic rankings than a link from a domain that was registered last month.

You should also try to acquire as many links as possible from domains with .edu and .gov top-level domain extensions. The search engines know that these educational and governmental establishments are much less likely to link to low-quality pages than a typical .com

or .net domain. If you cannot find any .edu or .gov links to directly link to you, try to find pages that do have a large number of .edu or .gov links and prospect those site owners for a link.

Make sure that pages you are prospecting for links have unique and relevant content to your page's subject matter. The search engines can determine easily whether or not content is duplicated from another source, and they diminish the impact of links obtained from sites that publish duplicate content.

Also, try to focus on acquiring links from pages that already rank well for the keywords and terms that you are targeting. Those pages are obviously already considered authorities on those topics, and a link can pass some of that authority onto your own site.

Evaluate Potential Linking Partners

Find the Age of a Domain

① Navigate to www.DomainTools.com.

② Enter a domain name in the Whois Lookup search box.

③ Click Search.

④ Scroll down to Whois Record.

● You can determine the age of the domain from the Created date.

Find .edu Links in Yahoo

1 Navigate to www. Yahoo.com.

2 To find .edu links pointed to a Web site, type **linkdomain:**, the Web site, and then **inurl:.edu** in the search box.

3 Click Search.

● .edu links appear.

Find Other .edu Links

1 Navigate to AlltheWeb.com.

2 To find .edu links pointed to a Web site, type **linkdomain:**, the Web site, and then **inurl:.edu** in the search box.

3 Click Search.

● .edu links appear.

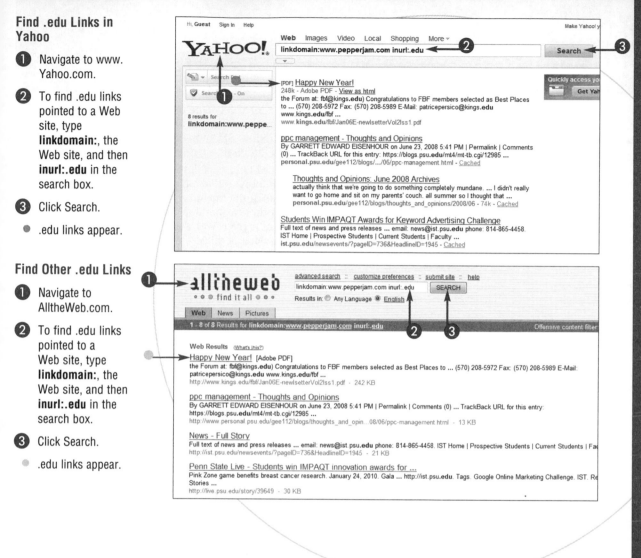

Extra

You may want to consider examining other factors when analyzing potential linking partners. Make sure that sites you are trying to acquire links from have incoming links that are relevant to their own content. If so, that site is likely an authoritative and trusted resource for that subject matter. You should also take into consideration the number of and quality of outbound links from a particular site. An outbound link is a link from a page of one site to another site. If you acquire a link from a site that is linking to hundreds of other unrelated sites, search engines are likely to discount the link.

Also, you should acquire links from high-traffic pages. Those sites will then have the potential to pass some of their traffic along to your own page. Visit www.alexa.com and enter the domain name of the potential linking partner into the search box. The more traffic the site receives, the lower the Alexa number is. Aim for sites with Alexa rankings of less than 100,000.

Gather Link Intelligence with Linkscape

Linkscape, located at www.seomoz.org/linkscape, is a link analysis tool that provides basic or advanced intelligence of the links pointing to a particular Web site. The basic version of Linkscape is free, whereas a paid, advanced version is available for as little as $79 per month.

The basic Linkscape intelligence report provides general information about the number of links pointing to a particular Web site, as well as the relative popularity of that Web site. Although the basic version of Linkscape is free, it provides only a limited amount of intelligence about links pointing to a given Web site. The basic version of Linkscape may provide some value if you are just looking to get a quick, high-level view of the links that point to your Web site or as an initial tool to evaluate the links of your competition. However, if you are looking to gather in-depth intelligence about links pointing to a particular domain, you want to purchase the advanced

version of Linkscape. One of the benefits of upgrading to the advanced version of Linkscape is that you also gain membership into SEOmoz PRO, which provides you with access to additional search-engine-optimization tools.

The advanced Linkscape intelligence report provides extensive information about a particular Web site, including detailed lists of the top links pointing to the site, the most common anchor text, and details about the relative popularity of a given Web site based on analyses of links in the form of what is called mozRank and mozTrust.

mozRank is a numerical score provided on a scale from 0 to 10 that depicts how popular a page is on the Web based on an analysis of how many links point to a given site, as well as the popularity of those links. mozTrust is a numerical score provided on a scale from 0 to 10 that depicts the cumulative trustworthiness of a page based on the links pointing to it from other trustworthy pages.

Gather Link Intelligence with Linkscape

Run a Basic Report

1 Navigate to www.seomoz.org/linkscape.

2 Enter a URL to analyze.

3 Click Run Basic Report.

- The Basic Intelligence Report appears. Note the link intelligence information.

4 Click Choose SEOmoz PRO to purchase premium membership.

- Note that an SEOmoz PRO Membership entitles you to gain access to Linkscape advanced reports, as well as many other premium search-engine-optimization tools.

Run an Advanced Report

1 Log into your SEOmoz PRO account at www.seomoz.org/linkscape and run a basic report using a URL you want to analyze.

2 Click Run Advanced Report.

● An active window appears requiring you to confirm that you want to run an advanced report.

3 Click OK.

4 Review your advanced Linkscape report.

5 Scroll down the page to view entire advanced report.

Acquire Quality Links

You can save yourself a tremendous amount of time and effort by focusing your energy on acquiring a few high-quality, authoritative links versus a large quantity of low-quality links that are not related to your Web site. You can easily build a huge quantity of links back to your page by either manually submitting or purchasing software that mass-submits your Web page to thousands of online guest books, forums, blogs, directories, and other link sources. However, this type of activity is often detected as spam by search engines and therefore should be avoided. Search engines are becoming increasingly sophisticated and capable of detecting the difference between natural, relevant links, and unnatural, irrelevant links such as those typically submitted by software.

Just one or two high-quality links can provide the same if not greater search-engine-optimization benefit than hundreds of low-quality links. All the major search engines, particularly Google, embrace this approach to link building.

Google uses a numerical system called *PageRank*, or *PR*, to express an opinion on the relative authority of a Web page. Google assigns every Web page on the Internet a PageRank value of 0 through 10 based on a calculation of the quantity and quality of backlinks. Typically, the higher the number and quality of backlinks, the higher the PageRank. When prospecting link partners, you can easily check the PageRank of their page and get a general feel for how important that link may appear in Google's eyes. You can easily check a site's PageRank by installing the Google Toolbar (available for download at toolbar.google.com) or by visiting www.pagerank.net (a Web site not owned by Google).

Many industry insiders believe that Google and other leading search engines such as Yahoo rank Web sites based on how "trusted" they are in their individual niches. In fact, Yahoo published a paper, located at www.vldb.org/conf/2004/RS15P3.PDF, that uses a technique called *TrustRank* for semiautomatically separating useful Web pages from spam. This score, known as a site's TrustRank, is not made available to the public; however, you can assume that sites ranked highly by Google and Yahoo's algorithm for competitive keywords likely possess a high trust score.

Acquire Quality Links

① Navigate to www.pagerank.net/seo-tools.

② Click PageRank Checker.

3 To check the PageRank of the domain www.pepperjamnetwork.com, type **http://www.pepperjamnetwork.com** into the text box. Be sure to include the http://.

4 Enter the word verification.

5 Click Generate.

● The PageRank for the domain in question appears.

6 To check the PageRank of multiple sites, enter more than one site in the text box in Step 3. Be sure to include the http://.

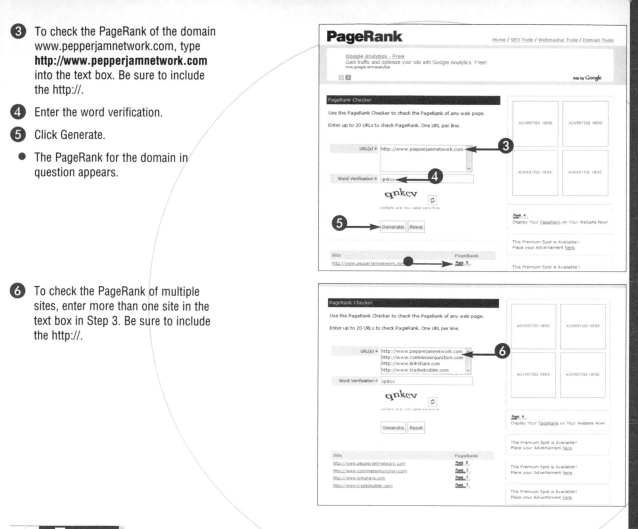

Obtaining links from highly trusted sites can have a greater effect on your search-engine rankings than obtaining links from sites with high PageRank alone. You can take advantage of this knowledge by focusing your link-building efforts on sites that appear to meet Google's TrustRank criteria. Sites that meet such criteria have been in existence for a long period of time, contain a substantial amount of unique content, possess a large number of quality incoming links, and rank highly for many keywords related to their niche.

Aaron Wall from SEObook.com offers a fantastic free Firefox extension called SEO for Firefox at http://tools. seobook.com/firefox/seo-for-firefox.html. After you install this plugin, your Google and Yahoo search results will contain information about each result's PageRank, age, incoming links, and more. This tool gathers information for you about each page that would otherwise take a great deal of time to find.

According to SEO experts, including Aaron Wall, TrustRank algorithms appear to focus on tendencies and linking patterns of trusted versus nontrusted Web pages. For example, Aaron suggests that trusted Web pages rarely link to poor, nontrusted Web pages, whereas nontrusted Web pages often link to trusted Web pages in an attempt to convince search-engine algorithms that the nontrusted page is more important than it actually is. Aaron also suggests that TrustRank is attenuated or weakened as it passes from Web site to Web site.

Using Effective Anchor Text

Choosing appropriate anchor text for both your incoming and outgoing links can play a large role in increasing your search-engine rankings for the terms and keywords your site is targeting. *Anchor text* is the clickable text attached to a World Wide Web hyperlink.

You often see links with the clickable text "Click here." In this case, the anchor text of the link is "Click here." You must use the context around that link to determine the topic of the page you are about to visit. A more effective use of anchor text is to describe the content of the page being linked to directly in the anchor text. For example, a link to a page about search-engine optimization could have the anchor text "search-engine optimization," "SEO," or something else related to search-engine optimization.

When building links to your Web page, you should always attempt to acquire links with highly descriptive anchor text. Search engines use anchor text to determine the theme of the page being linked to, and anchor text is an important factor in search engines' ranking algorithms. Throughout your link-building efforts, you usually have the opportunity to specify what anchor text you want attached to your link. You want the anchor text of your incoming links to directly relate to the keywords and terms for which you want to increase your search-engine rankings. Do not overuse a specific variation of anchor text. The search engines rank you more highly for more terms if you include some variety in your anchor text selection.

Do your fellow Webmasters a favor and always link to other Web sites with relevant anchor text. This helps their search-engine optimization efforts as well as your own.

Using Effective Anchor Text

Anchor Text in Search Results

1. Navigate to www.google.com.

2. Search for PPC Management.

- Note that www.pepperjam.com/search is ranked #6.

Anchor Text on Jpsimbulan.com

 1 Navigate to http://bit.ly/cNK7Vx.

● Notice the link with anchor text PPC Management pointing to www.pepperjam.com/search. This helps www.pepperjam.com/search rank well for a search for the term PPC Management.

Anchor Text on Duless.com

 1 Navigate to http://bit.ly/9wQlVu.

● Notice the link with anchor text PPC Management pointing to www.pepperjam.com/search. This helps www.pepperjam.com/search rank well for a search for the term PPC Management.

Extra

If you already have incoming links to your Web site, you may want to analyze and potentially alter the anchor text of these links. Webconfs.com offers a backlink and anchor text analysis tool located at www.webconfs.com/anchor-text-analysis.php. Entering your Web site URL into this tool gives you a list of pages that link to your site as well as anchor text associated with each link. Although the tool is not 100 percent accurate, you can get a substantial list of incoming links and associated anchor text.

If you find many incoming links to your site that do not have descriptive anchor text, contact the owners of those sites and politely ask them if they would consider changing the anchor text to something more relevant to the content of your site. Make a suggestion about what the anchor text of the link should be. Many Webmasters agree to this request because a link with descriptive anchor text provides a better experience for their own visitors, as well as allowing them the opportunity to fit a few more keywords into their own page.

Link Directory Submissions

There are hundreds if not thousands of Web page directories on the Internet. A link directory is simply a large Web page link database broken down into categories. Most of these directories allow you to choose a specific category and offer either free or paid link placement within that category. Although directory links are not quite as useful now as they were in the past for search-engine-optimization purposes, a few directories can still provide your Web page with a high-quality, authoritative link that makes a difference.

Your first directory submission should be to Yahoo. Yahoo is one of the largest and most visited Web sites on the Internet. Yahoo offers free submissions to noncommercial categories and also a paid submission option for $299 that can be used to submit your site to any category. Inclusion is not guaranteed whether you pay or not, but by paying you are guaranteed a response

within seven business days. If you are accepted into a commercial category, your site is reviewed on a recurring yearly basis. In order to stay listed, you must continue to pay $299 per year.

The Best of the Web directory, found at BOTW.org, has existed since 1994, making it one of the first directories on the Web. It offers a free category sponsorship for 60 days and provides options to get listed in the directory for a fee. To get your Web site reviewed and listed on BOTW, expect to pay $149.95 annually or a one-time fee of $299.95. Bulk discounts are available if you want to submit 20 or more Web sites.

The Open Directory Project, also known as DMOZ, is also a directory submission candidate. Located at www.dmoz.org, DMOZ is one of the oldest and most respected directories on the Web. You can submit your site for free into any of its hundreds of categories.

Link Directory Submissions

Yahoo Directory Sign-up

1. Navigate to https://ecom.yahoo.com/dir/submit/intro.

2. Log in to your Yahoo account.

3. Click Get Started and confirm your password.

4. Fill in the required site information.

5. Explain the content of your Web site to ensure proper placement.

6. Enter billing information and submit to the directory.

   Within two weeks, you will receive an e-mail from Yahoo regarding the acceptance or rejection of your directory submission.

Note: Yahoo's submission service does not guarantee a placement in the directory.

BOTW Directory Sign-up

1 Navigate to http://botw.org/helpcenter/sponsor.aspx.

2 Click Get Started Today.

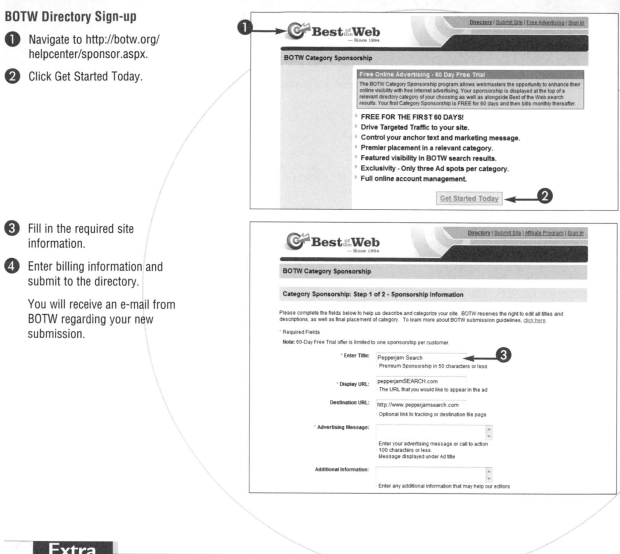

3 Fill in the required site information.

4 Enter billing information and submit to the directory.

You will receive an e-mail from BOTW regarding your new submission.

Extra

Besides those listed above, there are other directories that are worth the time it takes to submit your link. For example, Joeant.com is a human-edited directory with a history of listing high-quality sites. Another popular directory is AboutUs.org, which is a wiki for and about businesses, organizations, blogs, forums, and interesting Web sites. Keep in mind that you should always submit your URL to the category that is most relevant to your site's content. If you attempt to submit your site to a nonrelevant category, it is much more likely to get declined. Also, for search-engine-optimization purposes, a link from a relevant directory category is more beneficial than a link from a nonrelevant category.

Do not rely too strongly on directory submissions to raise your search-engine rankings. Due to the ease with which these links can be obtained and the sheer number of directories that exist, they are not given as much credibility by the search engines today as in the past. Focus only on directories that have been in existence for at least a few years, possess a large number of incoming backlinks, and maintain a PageRank of 6 or greater.

Article Directory Submissions

Y ou can generate a large number of relevant links back to your site by writing unique articles and submitting them to article directories, where they can be picked up by other Webmasters and placed on other Web sites. One of the most sought-after commodities by Webmasters is unique content relevant to the theme of their Web site. Article directories are public content depositories where Webmasters can search for and select content to place on their own sites. Usually, this content is in the form of an article written by the Webmaster of another Web site. That Webmaster has the option to include a link to his or her own site that must be left intact when the article is copied by others.

Try to write articles between 300 and 1,000 words in length. Make them unique, and also make sure they have proper spelling, grammar, punctuation, capitalization, and sentence structure in order to have the best chance at being accepted.

There are hundreds if not thousands of article directories scattered throughout the Internet, but you should focus your submission efforts on only those that have a large visitor base to give yourself the best chance at exposure. For example, Ezinearticles.com is one of the largest article directories on the Internet. Founded in 1999, it has grown to contain hundreds of thousands of unique articles written by tens of thousands of authors. Your article will be human reviewed before it is selected and placed into the Ezinearticles directory. The directory is visited by hundreds of thousands of visitors every day, so you should make submitting your articles to this directory a priority. Other examples of high-quality article directories include Goarticles.com, ArticleDashboard.com, and Isnare.com.

Article Directory Submissions

1 Navigate to www.ezinearticles.com.

2 Click Submit Articles.

3 Fill out the account creation form.

You will receive an e-mail with a link you must visit to verify your application.

4 Once you have completed the registration form and verified your e-mail address, return to Ezinearticles.com and enter a login name and password.

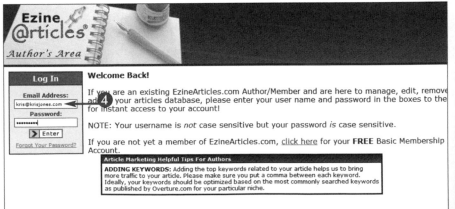

5 Enter your article topic, title, keywords, and summary.

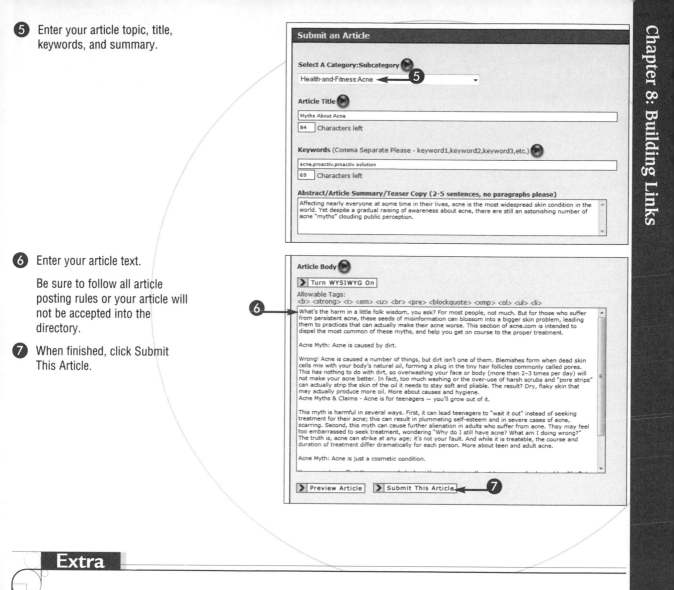

6 Enter your article text.

Be sure to follow all article posting rules or your article will not be accepted into the directory.

7 When finished, click Submit This Article.

Extra

Consider writing a few variations of your articles and submitting a different variation to each directory. It is common for high-quality articles to get ranked by themselves in the search engines. If you submit duplicate content to each directory, the chance of more than one of the articles getting ranked is small. If the content is slightly different, the search engines may not penalize the articles due to duplicate content, and more than one variation could be ranked.

You can also search the Web for sites that compete in your niche and offer them a variation of your article to be used on their site in exchange for including a link back to your site.

If you need help writing your articles or simply do not have enough time to do it yourself, consider outsourcing the writing. Depending on the quality you expect, typical prices for a 300-to-1,000-word article range from $5 to $50. Create an account on www.elance.com and submit a proposal for free. You will get many responses to your request, and you can choose the price that best suits your budget.

Community Participation

Participating in online communities such as blogs is an effective strategy for building links and generating traffic. Blogs allow you to provide comments and feedback on each blog entry that the author of the blog posts. Commenting on a blog requires you to submit your name and e-mail for verification purposes, as well as for a link back to your Web site.

Because blog comments tend to be moderated, you should provide useful and constructive responses to avoid being labeled as spam. Adding value to the community increases the likelihood that your link and comment are posted.

Comment on blogs that are as closely related to the theme of your Web site as possible. Also, try to find blogs that have a PageRank higher than 4 and possess a large number of relevant incoming links. You can find these blogs by searching for a keyword related to your site in a

blog directory such as http://blogsearch.google.com or www.blogcatalog.com. Then, perform an evaluation as you would for any other potential linking partner. Do not waste time submitting comments to blogs that are unrelated to the content of your site. Such comments are viewed as spam and are deleted by the moderators.

Acquiring links through blog participation works especially well to achieve rankings in Yahoo and Microsoft's Bing search engine, but is not as effective a strategy to use in Google. This is due to most blog owners attaching a `nofollow` attribute to links in blog comments. This tag is supposed to prevent the search engines from following and taking into account that link in their ranking algorithm. Google appears to follow this rule more strictly than the Yahoo and Bing search engines.

Community Participation

Participate in a Blog

1 Navigate to http://blogsearch.google.com.

2 Enter the topic of your Web site into the search box.

● Google lists blog posts based on relevance.

3 Select a blog post that is relevant to your Web site's content.

4. Enter your name.

5. Enter your e-mail address.

6. Enter your Web site.

7. When leaving a comment, be sure to stay on topic and make a useful contribution to the blog.

8. Click Submit.

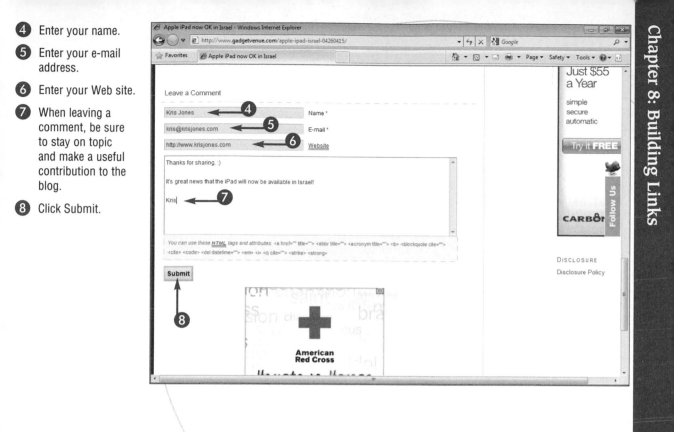

Extra

The nofollow attribute was developed to prevent excessive spamming on blogs. It deters spammers from wasting their time with automated blog-commenting programs. Despite Google's claims that it does not take blog comments or any other links with a nofollow attribute into consideration in its ranking algorithm, the search engine likely still sees that those links exist. The search engines want to see natural growth in your site's linking patterns as well as that your link is found on related sites. It is natural for your site to have a mixture of incoming links that do and do not have a nofollow attribute attached.

It is usually impossible to place a link directly into your blog comment; however, if your site is relevant enough to the topic being discussed, and you are truly providing a valuable resource to the blog readers, the link may be accepted. If your site is impressive enough, the blog owner may end up using your link in a future blog post. Such links are very valuable, and the traffic you can receive from a highly trafficked blog is substantial.

continued ➡

Participating in online communities like forums is also an effective strategy for building links and generating traffic. Forums are Internet message boards that allow you to start new discussions or participate in ongoing discussions about a variety of topics. Most forums allow you to participate by simply signing up for a free account with your e-mail address and very little personal information.

Forums tend to be moderated, but unlike blogs, your forum posts are often posted for public viewing without having to go through a review process. You should still provide useful and constructive responses to avoid having your posts being labeled as spam. Adding value to the community increases the likelihood that your link and

comment stay posted and that the other forum participants will visit your site.

Join and participate in forums that are as closely related to the theme of your Web site as possible. Also, try to find forums that have a PageRank higher than 4, have high traffic, and possess a large number of relevant incoming links. You can find these forums by searching for a keyword related to your site in one of the major search engines. As an example, if your site is related to pets, a simple query like "pet forums" provides a good list to start with. Do not waste time submitting posts to forums that are unrelated to the content of your site. Such posts are viewed as spam and are deleted by the moderators.

Acquiring links through forum participation works well to increase your rankings in all the major search engines as well as your overall site traffic from the forums themselves.

Community Participation (continued)

Register to Participate in a Web Forum

1. Visit a Web forum related to your site's content.

2. Register as a user.

Note: *Although forums are powered by different software, most have a link for you to register as a user.*

3. Enter the necessary information such as your name and username to create an account.

   You will receive an e-mail with a link to verify your account.

Make a Post

1 Search for a thread relevant to your Web site's content.

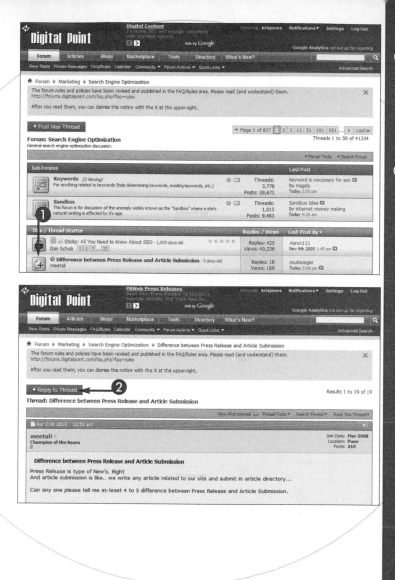

2 Participate in the conversation and include your link in the post if it is relevant and useful to the topic at hand.

Extra

Unlike blog comment links, forum post links do not contain a `nofollow` attribute, making them useful for increasing your rankings in all the major search engines. Some forums allow you to place a link directly into your forum *signature*, which is simply a personalized line of text that follows each of your posts. This method of acquiring links on a forum is less obvious than placing a link directly into your forum posts, and it is often encouraged by the forum moderators.

You can use the search engines to find forums relevant to the content of your site by creatively constructing search queries. As opposed to searching for something as simple as "pet forums," consider trying a query like "inurl:forum pets." This query returns only results that contain the word "forum" in the URL and the word "pets" in the content of the page. Because many forums are located on a URL such as www.mydomain.com/forum, this type of query should provide almost 100 percent forum results.

Request One-Way Links

Y ou should spend the majority of your link-building efforts on directly requesting one-way links from pages that are relevant to the theme of your own site. A one-way link request involves sending an e-mail or making a phone call to a Web site owner expressing interest in obtaining a link to your Web site from a page on his or her Web site. It can be the most difficult method of obtaining quality links, but it is likely to produce the best results because the links are coming from handpicked sites that meet the quality criteria that you want.

Most of the sites you should be targeting when doing one-way link requests should come from your competition-evaluation efforts. Target only those links that meet quality link criteria. Also, make sure you request descriptive anchor text with your link.

You can also search for relevant keywords in the major search engines and contact the owners of the top results. One of the best resources for potential one-way link requests is DMOZ.org. DMOZ lists many old and established Web sites whose owners normally do not sell links. Often, these owners are unaware of the value of such a link, and they may not require compensation of any kind.

To ensure the best shot possible at obtaining a link from a Web site owner who you contact, try to establish a conversation related to the content of the site with the owner before requesting a link. This conversation can result in more than just obtaining a link; you are creating a relationship with another Web site owner interested in your niche.

Request One-Way Links

1 Navigate to DMOZ.org.

2 Search for sites related to your content. As an example, search for "spinach lasagna."

The search results appear.

Browse through the Web sites and look for sites that appear relevant to your content. Look for sites that meet the link quality criteria discussed earlier in this chapter.

3 Click a site. In this example, click the www.igourmet.com link to Spinach Lasagna Val d'Aosta.

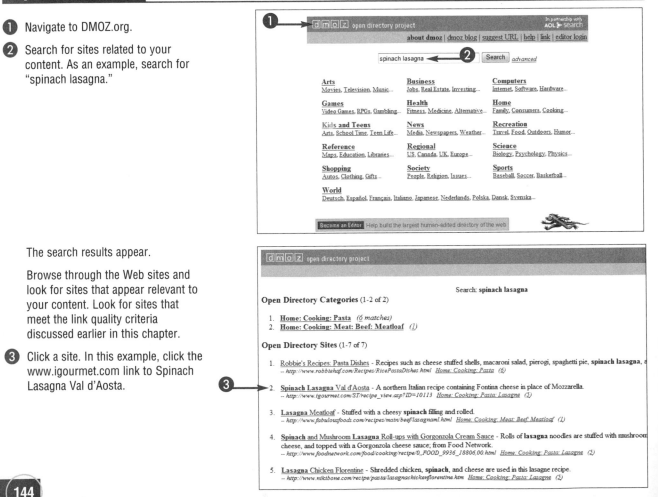

4 Look for a method to contact the Web site owner to request a link. In this example, click Customer Service and look for an e-mail address or contact form.

5 Write a thoughtful e-mail to the owner of the Web site requesting a link back to your own Web site.

● Be sure to include the link as you want it to be added including the proper anchor text. Consider offering some financial compensation or a piece of useful content.

Chapter 8: Building Links

Extra

When you contact fellow Webmasters for a link request, remember that you are asking them to take time out of their day to review your own site and add the link to their site. In other words, you are creating work for them. Be sure to go out of your way to show a sincere interest in the site you are requesting a link from. Perhaps you can comment on an article on the site, or alert the Webmaster to a mistake you noticed. A good link request appears genuine and authentic. A bad link request comes across as spam.

Some site owners may be inclined to add the link without any sort of compensation because they genuinely feel that the content of your page can provide their visitors serious value. Most owners look for something in return. In some cases, you can offer to write a relevant article for their site. In other cases, you may want to offer financial compensation. If you can broker a link from a high-quality, authoritative site in your niche, it will be well worth the trouble.

Buy Links

Y ou can effectively supplement your link-building efforts through strategically buying links on publisher Web sites. *Link buying* is the process of paying for specific link placements on Web sites in an effort to improve your Web site traffic and ranking within the search engines.

Link broker networks provide you with a very efficient way of buying links. Link broker networks act as intermediaries between Web site publishers and advertisers. Membership to link broker networks is free, but requires you to sign up by providing your name, e-mail, and telephone number, and by selecting a log-in password. You must have a major credit card or a PayPal account to pay for any purchases you make.

Link broker networks enable you to search for links from a large database of publisher Web sites, such as blogs, forums, and other content-rich Web sites. You can refine your search for links by such qualities as popularity,

geography, Web site category, and domain type. Individual link-placement fees are prepaid on a monthly basis, and prices range from $10 to as high as $1,000 per Web site.

Link broker networks, such as Text-Link-Ads.com, allow you to select the exact advertiser Web sites you want to purchase a link from and give you important information about the host Web site, including description, traffic ranking, link popularity, placement location, and availability of inventory.

One of the benefits of buying links through a link broker network is that the network allows you to choose your desired anchor text. Anchor text gives Web site visitors relevant descriptive or contextual information about the content of the link's destination, but more importantly, anchor text is a factor Google uses to determine the theme and authority of the page. The anchor text you choose includes the specific keywords you want to rank for on the search engines. For more on anchor text, see the task "Using Effective Anchor Text."

Buy Links

Link Broker Networks

1. Navigate to text-link-ads.com.

2. Click Create My Account Now.

3. Fill in the required information.

    You will receive an e-mail with a link to verify your account. Follow this link to your active advertiser account at Text Link Ads.

4. Search for a keyword relevant to your site.

- You can sort the results by criteria such as Domain Authority Score, Link Popularity, Alexa Rank, and Ad Price, among other factors.

⑤ Analyze the information on the available sites.

⑥ Click the Add to Cart link for each link you would like to purchase.

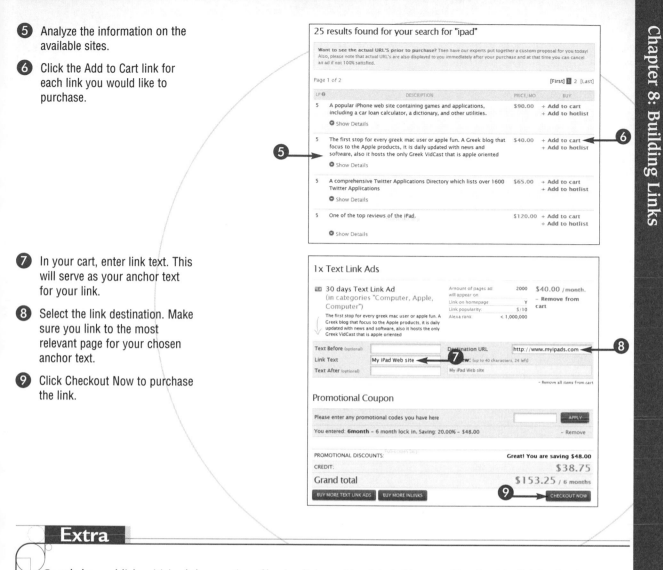

25 results found for your search for "ipad"

Want to see the actual URL'S prior to purchase? Then have our experts put together a custom proposal for you today! Also, please note that actual URL's are also displayed to you immediately after your purchase and at that time you can cancel an ad if not 100% satisfied.

Page 1 of 2   [First] **1** 2 [Last]

LP	DESCRIPTION	PRICE/MO	BUY
5	A popular iPhone web site containing games and applications, including a car loan calculator, a dictionary, and other utilities. ⊙ Show Details	$90.00	+ Add to cart + Add to hotlist
5	The first stop for every greek mac user or apple fun. A Greek blog that focus to the Apple products, it is daily updated with news and software, also it hosts the only Greek VidCast that is apple oriented ⊙ Show Details	$40.00	+ Add to cart + Add to hotlist
5	A comprehensive Twitter Applications Directory which lists over 1600 Twitter Applications ⊙ Show Details	$65.00	+ Add to cart + Add to hotlist
5	One of the top reviews of the iPad. ⊙ Show Details	$120.00	+ Add to cart + Add to hotlist

⑦ In your cart, enter link text. This will serve as your anchor text for your link.

⑧ Select the link destination. Make sure you link to the most relevant page for your chosen anchor text.

⑨ Click Checkout Now to purchase the link.

1x Text Link Ads

📷 30 days Text Link Ad
(in categories "Computer, Apple, Computer")

The first stop for every greek mac user or apple fun. A Greek blog that focus to the Apple products, it is daily updated with news and software, also it hosts the only Greek VidCast that is apple oriented

Amount of pages ad will appear on	2000	$40.00 /month.
Link on homepage:	Y	– Remove from cart
Link popularity:	5/10	
Alexa rank:	< 1,000,000	

Text Before (optional) [ ]   Destination URL [http://www.myipads.com]

Link Text [My iPad Web site]   ...ew: (up to 40 characters, 24 left)

Text After (optional) [ ]   My iPad Web site

– Remove all items from cart

Promotional Coupon

Please enter any promotional codes you have here [ ] APPLY

You entered: **6month** – 6 month lock in. Saving: 20.00% – $48.00   – Remove

PROMOTIONAL DISCOUNTS: **Great! You are saving $48.00**

CREDIT: $38.75

Grand total   **$153.25** / 6 months

BUY MORE TEXT LINK ADS   BUY MORE INLINKS   CHECKOUT NOW

Extra

Google has publicly criticized the practice of buying links and has labeled it spam. Despite this, link buying is a practice used by leading search-engine-optimization firms and remains an effective way to build quality links. However, you should be selective with where you buy links, and you should avoid associating with any known link broker network or individual Web site that has been banned or penalized by Google.

Danny Sullivan of SearchEngineLand.com reports that not all paid links are bad, only those that positively influence PageRank by attempting to manipulate Google's ranking algorithm. Therefore, you should avoid buying links from advertiser Web sites that include excessive unrelated links, as well as those Web sites that fail to disclose that links are paid.

Aside from link broker networks, you can buy links directly from Web site owners. Approach the Web site owner or Webmaster and ask for a link in return for a flat one-time fee or for a monthly recurring fee for the life of the link. You can also purchase links from pay-per-post blog networks, which is covered on the next page.

continued ➡

You can effectively supplement your link-building efforts through paying bloggers and other content providers to review your Web site. Paying content providers to review your Web site has numerous potential benefits, such as providing constructive feedback, building buzz, and generating one or more anchor text links back to your Web site.

Pay-per-post networks provide you with an efficient way of getting content providers to link to your Web site. Pay-per-post networks act as intermediaries between content providers and advertisers. Membership to pay-per-post networks is free but requires you to sign up by providing your name and e-mail, as well as selecting a username and password. You must have a major credit card to fund your account prior to making a purchase.

Pay-per-post networks, such as PayPerPost.com, enable you to offer content providers such as bloggers money to review your Web site. You are required to provide the prospective content provider a brief overview of what you want them to write about and where you want them to link. In this way, you maintain flexibility if you want the content provider to link to your home page or to a specific page within the Web site.

PayPerPost.com allows you to apply restrictions and set minimum standards when choosing prospective content provider partners. Restrictions include minimum length, post type, tone, and category. Minimum standards include traffic ranking, Web site popularity, and blog type.

PayPerPost.com requires you to select whether you want the content provider to link to your Web site, and allows you to designate your desired anchor text for the link.

Buy Links (continued)

Pay-Per-Post Networks

① Navigate to payperpost.com.

② Click the Signup Now button under the advertisers section of the Pay-Per-Post homepage.

③ Enter your e-mail and select a password.

④ Check the box to verify that you are over the age of 18.

⑤ Click Signup.

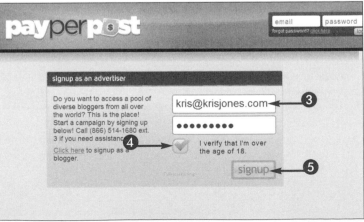

6 Type a name to identify your new Pay-Per-Post opportunity.

7 Click the Create Opp button to open a new Pay-Per-Post opportunity.

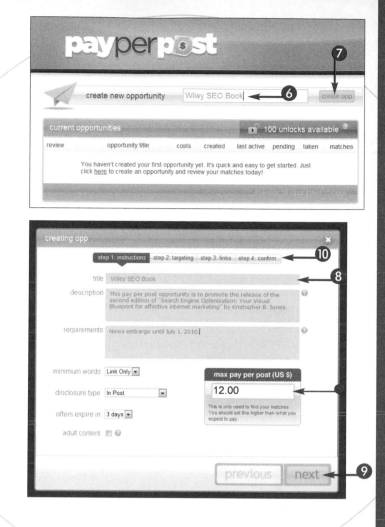

8 Fill in the fields to describe your opportunity, including the title, description, requirements, minimum words, disclosure type, and the expiration date of your opportunity.

● PayPerPost also gives a suggested offer per post, but this number is not mandatory.

9 Click Next to continue with your submission.

10 The next steps include targeting the bloggers you want to blog about your Web site and defining your anchor text and other link factors.

Extra

If you are simply making an announcement, a press release opportunity through PayPerPost.com is an easy way to spread the word and gain links. To use this type of opportunity, you can copy and paste your press release into the PayPerPost system and provide a few additional parameters. Content providers identify what they believe is newsworthy and help you spread the word about your announcement via their blog or Web site.

Unlike buying links through traditional link-buying networks, pay-per-post networks appear to be acceptable to Google and the other major search engines. According to search-engine-optimization expert Rand Fiskin, as long as the paid posts are not too far off-topic to the theme of the host Web site, the search engines are unlikely to discount links from paid posts. Therefore, if you are opposed to traditional link-buying networks, pay-per-post networks are an effective alternative method for building links, as long as you purchase posts from Web sites with a similar theme to the topic of your post.

ReviewMe.com is another pay-per-post network that allows content providers to review your Web site and includes benefits such as site traffic, feedback, word-of-mouth buzz, and links with target anchor text.

An Introduction to Google Analytics

Google Analytics is a free analytics solution designed to give you a complete view of every aspect of activity on your Web site. Understanding how to properly analyze and implement the numerous types of data that Google Analytics provides gives you a considerable edge over your competition in the quest for top search-engine rankings. A robust analytics program is an often overlooked but entirely vital part of a successful search-engine-optimization, or *SEO,* campaign. After all, without

knowing what is currently working for your Web site, you have no idea what areas need to be improved, or what successes can be expanded upon. The use of Google Analytics presents you with multiple advantages as a site owner, from the ability to track goals and sales to the knowledge of where your visitors exit your Web site. The first step is to ensure you properly install the tracking code on your Web site. Next, you begin the process of learning how to use Google Analytics as a tool to improve your Web site performance.

Install Google Analytics

To use Google Analytics with your Web site you must create an account and install tracking code on your Web site. Installing tracking code is what allows Google Analytics to capture, collect, and analyze the information about the way users reach and interact with your Web site. The most important detail in the installation process is making sure that your tracking code is correctly placed on every single page of your Web site. This ensures that all of your Google Analytics reports are as accurate as possible. Without proper installation, you cannot make accurate judgments about the performance of your Web site, which can severely damage the success of your SEO campaigns.

Set and Track Goals

If your Web site includes some sort of lead generation such as a newsletter subscription, catalog request, or even something as simple as a contact page, goal tracking can make gauging the success of your online marketing campaigns simple. Any goal action can be traced back to the original source of the visitor, which allows you to determine what traffic sources are working for your site, what search keywords are performing the best, and what methods are ineffective. The Google Analytics goal-setting feature is especially useful when targeting keywords in your SEO efforts. Knowing ahead of time what keywords are already converting for your site and targeting those keywords until you reach the top organic positions is a very effective SEO strategy.

Apply Filters

The tracking code for Google Analytics tracks the user behavior for each visit to your site. At times, you may want to track certain parts of your site separately, or exclude certain traffic from reports. For these reasons, Google Analytics has made it simple to apply filters to your Web site profile to ensure your data is as accurate and useful as possible. Adding filters to exclude your own IP address prevents your own internal traffic from skewing the data about your true Web site performance. This ensures certain statistics such as time on

site, pages per visit, and visitor loyalty are derived from actual site performance.

You can also use Google Analytics filters to track specific directories located on your Web site. This filter is best utilized in a separate Web site profile, and is very useful for quickly analyzing a section of your Web site. It is most useful for larger sites that have multiple areas, such as a forum, a blog, a resource directory, or an e-commerce section.

Track External Clicks

If you are setting up any traffic trades, or promoting any affiliate offers on your Web site, keep track of how many clicks you are sending to external sites. For traffic trades, this information can help you negotiate better link placement if you are sending a substantial amount of traffic. For affiliates, this information is invaluable if you monitor the accuracy of the affiliate program statistic reporting. Another added benefit of tracking your external clicks is explaining *bounce* rates. A bounce occurs when a Web site visitor leaves your Web site without visiting any other pages. If your home page has numerous external links and a high bounce rate, you can research exactly how many of the recorded bounces came from a user clicking an external link.

Automate Reporting

If you want to keep a separate archive of your Web site's progression, setting up automatic e-mail reporting can be extremely useful. This feature of Google Analytics allows you to specify what information you want to have reported, and the time interval between reports. The reports can be e-mailed to you, or anyone else you choose, in a variety of formats including PDF and CSV. This makes sharing information and tracking your Web site growth extremely easy, and the PDF option allows you to keep separate hard copies of your Web site data. Having past data available for quick and easy reference can prove extremely useful when making decisions about future campaigns.

Find Keywords

An extremely efficient strategy for deciding what keywords to target in your SEO efforts involves looking at what is already working for your Web site. Terms for which your Web site is already ranking in the top 50 results are typically easier to dominate than terms where your Web site is not ranked at all. Looking through your traffic sources in Google Analytics is a very simple way of finding out what keywords are sending you traffic. When analyzing your list, if you come across a keyword that is sending a considerable amount of traffic despite a ranking on the bottom of the first, or on the second page of results, you have found a fantastic target for SEO purposes. Finding these keywords ensures that you target only keywords that send sufficient traffic. Also, when using this method in combination with goal tracking, you can focus your SEO efforts toward keywords that you know convert well.

Track E-Commerce

If your Web site lists products for sale, using Google Analytics to track your orders can be an invaluable tool to your SEO, pay-per-click (PPC), and media campaigns. If properly installed, Google Analytics can track a purchase at your Web site to the original source of the visitor who made the purchase. This allows you to track exactly how much revenue was generated from each keyword that is currently driving traffic to your Web site. When you have accurate data about which traffic sources are sending sales, you can push to extract more traffic from those sources to ensure high profits from your search-engine marketing efforts.

Create an Account

I n November 2005, Google announced that the analytics tracking software then known as Urchin would be renamed Google Analytics and available at no cost to all Web site owners. Google Analytics provides detailed statistics about your Web site and allows you to efficiently monitor important aspects of your Web site from one centralized location. Google Analytics provides detailed reporting features including graphs and charts to give you a visual look at your Web site statistics.

Google Analytics is available in a variety of languages, including English, Spanish, French, Italian, and German.

You can access Google Analytics with your Google account. If you do not have a Google account, you can open one for free at www.google.com/accounts. If you already have a Google account, you can log in to Google Analytics at www.google.com/analytics. The only requirement for signing up for Google Analytics is a valid e-mail address.

Once you have created your account and logged in to Google Analytics, you may add your first Web site profile. Adding a new Web site profile to your Google Analytics account is as simple as entering your Web site address and selecting your time zone. You are then provided with a piece of code you paste into your Web pages, and within 24 to 48 hours, you can view your reporting data. If you own multiple Web sites, you can add a profile for each site, and access each site's reports from your Google Analytics account home page.

The data provided by Google Analytics allows you to make accurate, informed decisions about everything from search-engine optimization and pay-per-click advertising success, to your Web site design, linking partners, and marketing campaigns. Google Analytics is an extremely cost-effective and robust tracking- and Web-site-analytics software that allows you to effectively analyze and monitor your Web site statistics in near real-time.

Create an Account

Create a Google Account

① Navigate to www.google. com/accounts.

② Click Create an Account Now.

The Google Accounts Create page appears.

③ Fill in the required information and click I Accept. Create My Account.

You have successfully created a Google account.

Sign Up for Google Analytics

1 Navigate to www.google.com/analytics and log in using your new Google account.

2 Click Sign Up to activate Google Analytics.

Google Analytics
Getting Started

Improve your site and increase marketing ROI.

Google wants you to attract more of the traffic you are looking for, and help you turn more visitors into customers.

Use Google Analytics to learn which online marketing initiatives are cost effective and see how visitors actually interact with your site. Make informed site design improvements, drive targeted traffic, and increase your conversions and profits.

Sign up now, it's easy – and free!

(5M pageview cap per month for non AdWords advertisers.)

Sign Up for Google Analytics

You are just a few steps from Google Analytics. Click on the **Sign Up** button to get started.

Sign Up » ← **2**

© 2010 Google | Analytics Home | Terms of Service | Privacy Policy | Contact us | Analytics Blog (in E

The Google Analytics Profile Addition page appears.

3 Enter the URL, Account Name, Time Zone, and Country of the Web site you want to track.

Note: The Account Name is the name you assign to your Web site within Google Analytics.

4 Click Continue.

5 Fill in the required personal information in the next step, select the type of domain(s) you are tracking, and accept the user agreement.

You have successfully added your first Web site profile in Google Analytics.

Google Analytics
Getting Started

Analytics: New Account Signup

General Information > Contact Information > Accept User Agreement > Add Tracking

Please enter the URL of the site you wish to track, and assign a name as it should appear in your Google Analytics reports. If you'd like to track more than one website, you can add more sites once your account has been set up. Learn more.

Website's URL: http:// ▼   www.krisjones.com   (e.g. www.mywebsite.com) ← **3**

Account Name: www.krisjones.com

Time zone country or territory: United States ▼

Time zone: (GMT-04:00) Eastern Time ▼

Cancel   Continue »   **4**

© 2010 Google | Analytics Home | Terms of Service | Privacy Policy | Contact us | Analytics Blog (in E

Extra

If you have multiple sites that you want to track with Google Analytics, you can add additional Web site profiles. Once you add additional Web site profiles and log in to your Google Analytics account, a drop-down menu that includes all of your profiles appears. There is currently no limit to the amount of Web sites you can track with Google Analytics.

Google Analytics gives you the option to grant additional users the ability to view your Web site profiles. This is done by entering the Access Manager from the initial Settings page, and clicking Add User. You must then enter the e-mail address of the person to whom you want to grant access, as well as his or her first and last name. Note that the e-mail address you enter must already be a valid Google account. If the user does not have a Google account, he or she can sign up for free at www.google.com/accounts.

Next, select the account type, which either limits the additional user to a view-reports-only setting, or grants him full administrative abilities. Google Analytics allows you to restrict or grant user access to reporting features of your choosing.

Install Tracking Code

In order for Google Analytics to track your Web site data, the tracking code must be correctly installed on each page you want tracked. You can find this code at any time inside your Analytics Profile Settings. After you install this code, you can capture a wide variety of data about your Web site visitors. Among other statistics, Google Analytics tracks and reports the number of visitors, the average time users spend on your Web site, the paths users take to navigate your content, and the points at which visitors completely exit your site.

To avoid receiving inaccurate data, you should install the tracking code on every page of your site. This ensures that your reports are not skewed by visitors navigating to a page on your site that is not tracked. The optimal place for the Google Analytics tracking code is right before the `</head>` tag on each page. If you have a template-based design, you may only have to paste the code in once to your template file. However, in some cases, a Webmaster must manually insert the tracking into each page.

Be cautious when installing your tracking code: If you do not correctly insert the entire code, Google Analytics cannot receive any data from your site. For this reason, the tracking code is presented inside a text box. This allows you to simply highlight the code and copy it to the Clipboard. After you paste the tracking code into your pages, double-check that you have inserted correctly.

Install Tracking Code

① Log into your Google Analytics account at www.google.com/analytics.

② Click Edit under the Actions column for the site you want to track.

The Google Analytics Profile Settings page appears.

③ Click Check Status above the upper right-hand corner of the Main Website Profile Information box.

The Google Analytics Tracking Code page appears.

④ Copy your tracking code from the Tracking Code page.

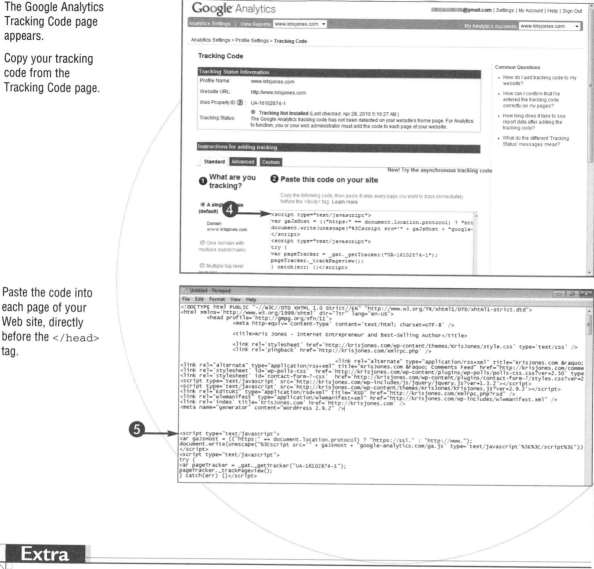

⑤ Paste the code into each page of your Web site, directly before the </head> tag.

Extra

Google Analytics provides a simple tool to check the proper installation of tracking code. At your Google Analytics home page, click Edit under the Actions column of the Web site profile you want to check. You are then taken to that site's Settings page. In the upper right-hand corner, above the Main Website Profile Information, is a link named Check Status. Click the Check Status link, and you are then taken to a page that displays whether your Google Analytics tracking code has been correctly installed. The response "Receiving Data" means your code has been installed successfully.

After you have correctly installed your code, you can begin fully reporting data in approximately 24 hours. The statistics that Google Analytics reports are not real-time, and reports are generally updated every 24 hours. Delayed reporting is why the default date range in your reports does not include the current date, ending instead with the previous day's statistics. This allows for a more accurate report because partial data from the current day is excluded.

Set Conversion Goals

Google Analytics gives you the option of defining specific conversion goals to help gauge the success of your marketing efforts. Conversion goals can consist of things like newsletter signups, catalog requests, product purchases, or filling out a contact form. Creating conversion goals, and the conversion funnels that may accompany them, is as simple as entering the URLs of the pages in your goal settings.

Setting conversion goals is a very important part of the analytics process and is especially useful because specific events can be tracked to the source of the visitor. Tracking the source of your visitor enables you to see where your highest quality traffic is originating from, and then target that source more aggressively. For example, if you discover that half of all the visitors to your Web site who come from example.com end up requesting a catalog

of your products, you should try to receive more traffic from example.com.

An important part of setting conversion goals is defining the details of each goal. For example, you must decide the match type for each goal. The three available matching types are *head*, *exact*, and *regular expression*. A head match matches identical characters starting from the beginning of the string up to and including the last character in the string you specify. Use this option when your page URLs are generally unvarying but when they include additional parameters at the end that you want to exclude. An exact match is a match on every exact character in your URL without exception from beginning to end. Use this when your URLs for your site are easy to read and do not vary. Finally, a regular expression uses special characters to enable wildcard and flexible matching. This is useful when the stem and trailing parameters, or both, can vary in the URLs for the same Web site page.

Set Conversion Goals

① Log into your Google Analytics account at www.google.com/analytics.

② Click Edit under the Actions column for the site you want to track.

The Google Analytics Profile Settings page appears.

③ Click Add Goal.

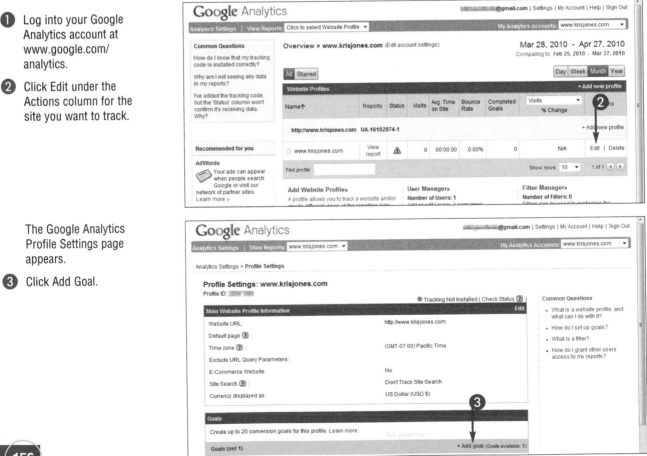

The Google Analytics Goal Settings page appears.

④ Give the goal a relevant name, Contact Page, for example.

⑤ Select On to activate the goal.

⑥ Select your goal position. Goal position allows you to control the order in which your goal appears from the Goals tab in your reports, or lets you move a goal from one set to another.

⑦ Select your goal type, URL Destination, for example. The URL Destination goal lets you specify a page with its own URL as a goal.

⑧ Select your match type based on your individual goals.

⑨ Enter your Goal URL. This URL can be your home page, or another page that acts as the beginning of your conversion goal cycle.

● You can choose a goal value and set up a goal funnel during this stage of the setup process.

⑩ Click Save Goal.

Google Analytics ⋯⋯⋯@gma

Analytics Settings | View Reports: www.krisjones.com ▾ My A

Analytics Settings > Profile Settings > Goal Settings

Goals (set 1): Goal 1

Enter Goal Information

Goal Name: [Contact Page] ◄ ④
Goal name will appear in conversion reports.

⑤ Active Goal: ➤ ◉ On ◎ Off

Goal Position: [Set 1, Goal 1 ▾] ◄ ⑥
Changing goal position will not move historical data for this goal

Please select a goal type
⑦ Goal Type: ➤ ◉ URL Destination
◎ Time on Site
◎ Pages/Visit

Goal Details

Match Type ⑦: [Head Match ▾] ◄ ⑧

⑨ ➤ [http://krisjones.com/cor] (e.g. For the goal page "http://www.mysite.com/thankyou.html" enter
Goal URL ⑦: "/thankyou.html")
To help you verify that your goal URL is set up correctly, please see the tips here .

Case Sensitive: ☐ URLs entered above must exactly match the capitalization of visited URLs.

Goal Value [0.0] optional

Goal Funnel ◄ ●

A funnel is a series of pages leading up to the goal URL. For example, the funnel may include steps in your checkout process that lead you to the thank you page (goal).

+ Yes, create a funnel for this goal

[Save Goal] Cancel ⑩

Extra

Currently, you can have up to five conversion goals for each Web site profile in your Google Analytics account. Each goal can also have a designated *funnel*, or path to the ending goal page. Setting up a funnel allows you to see where your visitors abandon your conversion goal cycle. This feature helps you find potential problem areas of your Web site. For example, if 70 percent of your visitors get to Step 3 of a goal funnel such as a contact form and then leave your site, you should look at the design and content of that particular page and attempt to find out why so many visitors are exiting at that point. This metric can prove to be invaluable in locating and addressing issues within your Web site and goal cycle.

You can get around the limit on goals by creating an additional profile for the same Web site. This is done by clicking Add a Web Site Profile from the Analytics Settings page, and then selecting Add a Profile for an Existing Domain. You then select the domain from the drop-down menu, and enter a new name for the additional profile. You can then set up an additional four conversion goals in this new Web site profile. This process can be repeated as many times as needed.

When creating new goals, you can set a monetary value for each goal conversion. For example, if each newsletter subscriber at your Web site is worth an average of $1.00, you can set this amount as the value of the goal. Your Analytics reports then show this value for each conversion, and provide you with an accurate snapshot of the general worth of your traffic from any given source.

Note that because Google Analytics does not provide real-time data, you must make your decisions based on daily, weekly, or monthly historical trends and not hourly changes or fluctuations.

Exclude Your IP Address with Filters

You can use the filter settings in Google Analytics to prevent your own internal or network traffic from appearing in your reports. This feature is useful because you likely will browse your own Web site on a regular basis to check for broken links, broken images, typos, and so on. Also, you likely will set your Web site as your default homepage. All of these browsing habits can lead to inaccurate data in your analytics reports.

When looking at your reports in Google Analytics, be sure to have your information as accurate as possible because you will use this information to make informed decisions about many aspects of your Web site including design, content, and conversion goal funnels. Including your personal browsing data skews your reporting, which could possibly lead you to incorrect assumptions about

your site, so you want to exclude it from your analytics reporting.

To ensure your reports are accurate, you should always filter out your own internal traffic on your Web site. You can accomplish this by filtering out your IP address from the data that Google Analytics collects. Applying this filter is a very straightforward process, and is effective immediately.

You may also want to exclude an IP range if more than one person from one network works on a site. In this case, adding an exclude filter to the range is much more efficient than blocking each IP address individually. Once a network filter is correctly put in place, Google Analytics filters out all of your internal network traffic before displaying your reports.

Exclude Your IP Address with Filters

① Log into your Google Analytics account at www.google.com/analytics.

② Click Edit under the Actions column for the site you want to track.

The Google Analytics Profile Settings page appears.

③ Click Add Filter in the Filters Applied to Profile box.

The Google Analytics Add Filter to Profile page appears.

④ Leave Add New Filter for Profile selected.

⑤ Give the filter an appropriate name.

⑥ Leave Predefined Filter selected.

⑦ Select Exclude traffic from the IP addresses that are equal to from the Filter Type menus.

⑧ Enter your IP address in the corresponding field.

⑨ Click Save Changes.

The Profile Settings page appears.

● Note that your new filter has been added to your profile.

Google Analytics

                                                        ....@gmail.com

Analytics Settings | View Reports: www.krisjones.com ▼   My Analytics

Analytics Settings > Profile Settings > Create New Filter

Create New Filter

Choose method to apply filter to Website Profile

Please decide if you would like to create a new filter or apply an existing filter to the Profile.

④ ● Add new Filter for Profile   OR   ○ Apply existing Filter to Profile

Enter Filter Information

Filter Name: Exclude My IP   ⑤

⑥ ● Predefined filter ○ Custom filter
Filter Type:

Exclude ▼ traffic from the IP addresses ▼ that are equal to ▼ ⑦

IP address 63 - 212 - 171 - 12   (e.g. 63.212.171.12) ⑧

⑨ Save Changes   Cancel

Goals

Create up to 20 conversion goals for this profile. Learn more.

Goals (set 1)	+ Add goal (Goals available: 4)
Contact Page	Edit
Goals (set 2)	+ Add goal (Goals available: 5)
Goals (set 3)	+ Add goal (Goals available: 5)
Goals (set 4)	+ Add goal (Goals available: 5)

Filters Applied to Profile ?   + Add Filter

	Filter Name	Filter Type	Settings	Remove
1.	Exclude My IP	Exclude	Edit	Remove

Users with Access to Profile ?   + Add User

Extra

When adding an IP address, or an IP range to your filters, use *regular expressions*. Regular expressions are commonly used when performing textual data manipulation tasks. When using an exclude filter, which is used when excluding an IP address or range, Google Analytics excludes the visitor data only if the information from the regular expression matches the data in the corresponding field. Fields may include IP address, visitor location, screen resolution, and language settings, among others. For basic filters, use of regular expressions is fairly limited. Note that Google Analytics also offers good examples to work off of when you are going through the basic filter addition process.

If one filter is going to be common to several Web site profiles, you do not need to remake each filter. You can simply create the filter once, and then add the additional Web sites through the Filter Manager. This can be accessed through the initial Analytics Settings page, through the Filter Manager link in the bottom right section of the page. Simply click Edit next to the appropriate filter, add the desired domains, and save your changes.

Exclude Traffic from a Particular Domain

Y ou can filter out traffic from your Google Analytics reports by excluding all traffic from a particular domain. Excluding traffic from a particular domain does not exclude the referring site that sent you the traffic, but instead the Internet service provider (ISP) of the actual visitors.

You can use the Google Analytics domain filter to remove a company network from your reporting. For example, if you are the administrator of Google Analytics on your company's blog, you may not want the traffic from your co-workers to show up in your reports because the number of people in your office visiting the company blog is not an accurate reflection of the actual growth of the

blog. Including this type of data may skew important reporting data such as average time on site and visitor loyalty. Therefore, you may choose to filter out traffic coming from any network to which you may be connected.

You must use caution when using the Google Analytics domain exclusion filter because you may end up excluding significant traffic sources from your analytics reports. For example, if you were to exclude all traffic from comcast. com, you would in effect be excluding the data from any of your visitors who have Comcast Internet service. This type of exclusion could have a very large effect on your reporting data, which may skew your numbers.

Exclude Traffic from a Particular Domain

① Log into your Google Analytics account at www.google.com/ analytics.

② Click Edit under the Actions column for the site you want to track.

The Google Analytics Profile Settings page appears.

③ Click Add Filter in the Filters Applied to Profile box.

The Google Analytics Create New Filter page appears.

④ Leave Add New Filter for Profile selected.

⑤ Give the filter an appropriate name.

⑥ Leave Predefined Filter selected.

⑦ Select Exclude traffic from the domains that are equal to from the Filter Type menus.

⑧ Enter the name of the domain you want to exclude.

Note: *This example excludes google.com.*

⑨ Leave Case Sensitive deselected.

⑩ Click Save Changes.

The Profile Settings page appears.

● Note that your new filter has been added to your profile.

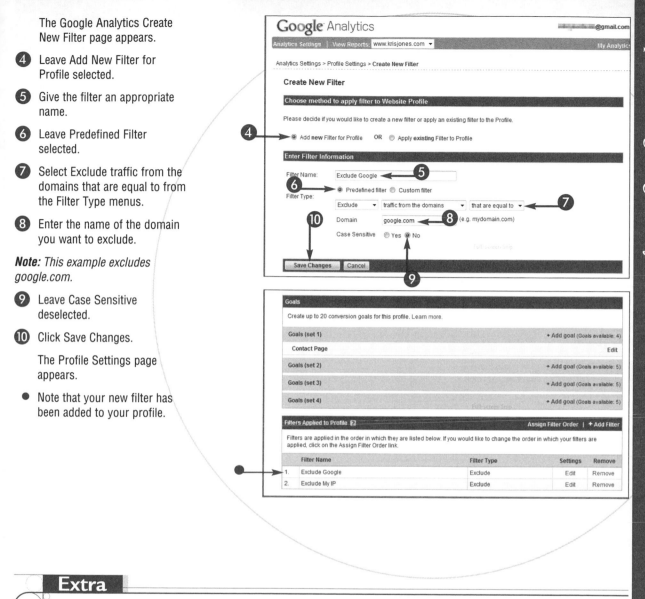

Extra

If you are going to exclude an ISP from your reports, you should create an additional profile before adding this filter. This ensures your ability to view statistics of your Web site with and without the domain exclusion filter in place. Keep in mind that filtering out an entire ISP can remove a valuable amount of data from your reports, and may lead to inaccurate analytics. Having separate accounts allows you to still retain that critical data.

Excluding an ISP is especially useful if your city is serviced by a small, local Internet service provider. Excluding your local ISP effectively removes all traffic from your family and friends who live in your area. This ensures that your data is as reliable as possible. In this situation, having multiple profiles displays the amount of local traffic you are receiving. Simply compare the data from the account with the local ISP filtered out to the account without the filter. The difference between these two equals the total amount of traffic you are receiving from your local ISP.

Include Only Certain Directories

Google Analytics gives you the ability to specify and include or exclude tracking to any location of your Web site. This procedure is useful if you want to analyze only specific landing pages, or any other specific area of your Web site. Also, if your Web site is broken up into multiple categories or themes, you may want to track each of these separately. For example, if you sold cell phone ringtones and wallpapers, applying this filter would allow you to analyze the conversions and goal funnels for each section separately. To do this, you would simply make a new profile for the existing domain, and then apply the filter to track only a certain directory. Repeat this process for each separate directory you want to track.

Despite the fact that aggregate data would be viewable if you were to set only one profile and track the entire domain, you would have to do some digging through the Web site statistics on the Content Drilldown page, which is discussed in the task "Track External Links." Applying the filter and tracking a directory separately allow you a quick look at the performance of that part of your Web site. Having certain directories sectioned off also allows you to share reports about just that portion of your site, without sharing the information about your entire domain. Similarly, you can add an additional user to this profile, giving her access only to the directory you want her to see.

The Google Analytics directory exclusion filter also gives you a quick way to view reports on incoming traffic sources, as well as external clicks for a particular directory. This information is very useful when negotiating rates with potential advertisers. For example, being able to accurately report the traffic volume of specific areas of your site allows you to provide prospective advertisers with detailed statistical information, which is vital to maximizing the amount of money you can charge for advertising space.

Include Only Certain Directories

① Log into your Google Analytics account at www.google.com/analytics.

② Click Edit under the Action column for the site you want to track.

The Google Analytics Profile Settings page appears.

③ Click Add Filter in the Filters Applied to Profile box.

The Google Analytics Create New Filter page appears.

④ Leave Add New Filter for Profile selected.

⑤ Give the filter an appropriate name.

⑥ Leave Predefined Filter selected.

⑦ Select Exclude traffic to the subdirectories that are equal to from the Filter Type menus.

⑧ Enter the name of the subdirectory you want to include.

⑨ Leave Case Sensitive deselected.

⑩ Click Save Changes.

The Profile Settings page appears.

● Note that your new filter has been added to your profile.

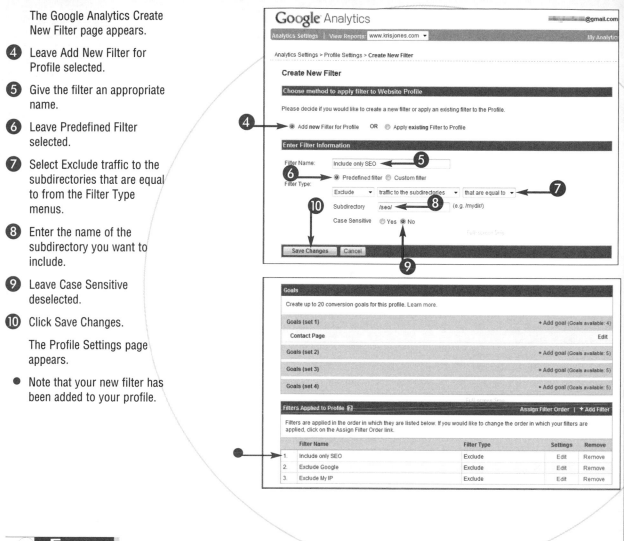

Extra

Although you will likely find tracking a certain directory of your Web site separately useful, you may also find having reports available for your entire domain a good idea, too. For this reason, you should make a new Web site profile whenever you want to track an individual directory. To set up an additional profile, click Add Web Site Profile from your main settings page. Select Add a Profile for an Existing Domain and then choose the domain you want to use. After selecting a relevant name, you can then go ahead and apply the appropriate filter to this new copy of your Web site profile.

Try to avoid picking a name for your new profile that leaves room for confusion as to which profile is tracking the full domain and which profile is tracking an individual directory of the site. This becomes important if and when you want to share reports with someone else. Following these rules has the added benefit of minimizing the possibility that someone with restricted analytics access accidentally receives data from restricted sources. Carefully selecting descriptive names in the beginning keeps your directories more organized and may save you time and energy in the long run.

Track External Links

When constructing your Web site, you are likely to have both internal and external links. Internal links refer to the links that send the visitor to other pages within your site, and external links refer a visitor to a Web site other than your own. Google Analytics can show you how your visitors navigate your internal links, but what if they leave your site by clicking an external link? By tweaking the way you construct your external links, Google Analytics can keep track of how many visitors you are sending out, despite the absence of your tracking code on these outside pages.

If you choose to monetize your Web site with offers from affiliate marketing or cost-per-action (CPA) networks, you should keep your own data on how much traffic you send to each of these external sites. This allows you to compare your own figures with those the affiliate program or ad network provides. In the event that you find large differences between what you seem to be sending out and what the affiliate network is reporting as received for the same period, ask your affiliate manager to look into this for you.

If you do any reciprocal link trading, you will want to keep track of how much traffic you are sending out to your link partners. If you send a site double the clicks that that site sends you each month, you may want to negotiate a better placement of your link, or reconsider the trade pending on the quality of traffic the site sends. As with everything else, the more information you have about your site, the better.

Track External Links

① Open the source file for the page that contains the external link you want to track.

② Locate the link in the source file.

③ Insert the following at the end of the link:
```
onClick=
"javascript:
urchinTracker'/
outgoing/
example_com';".
```

④ Repeat this process for each link you want to track.

⑤ After 24 to 48 hours, view your Web site statistics in the Content Drilldown page.

● Clicks on the tracked outbound links are then logged as page views for the name you gave each individual link.

Extra

Designing and using a relevant and easy to remember structure for tracking your outbound links is very important. The first step is to decide on a folder name that is not being used in your actual Web site. Some examples may include "outgoing," "external," or "clicks." This keeps all of the pages for external clicks organized.

Second, the best practice for separating sites is to use the URL of the site you are linking to. Using the name of the Web site may get confusing and does not allow you to distinguish where you sent the visitor if you have multiple external links to various pages on another domain. Some examples of good names include "example_com" or "example_com_pagename." Keeping accurate track of where you are sending your visitors allows you to gauge the general value of your Web site to your linking partners in terms of traffic.

Logging clicks on your outbound links can also provide you with a supplement to your bounce rate. If a page has a high bounce rate, you may be wondering where all that traffic is going. However, if you log your outbound clicks, you can determine how many of your visitors clicked external links, and went elsewhere instead of to other pages on your site.

Automate Reporting

Google Analytics can be set to automatically e-mail you selected reports on a daily, weekly, monthly, or quarterly basis. Daily reports show the data for the previous day, and are sent out each morning. Weekly reports show the data for the previous Monday through Sunday, and are sent out each Monday morning. Monthly reports are sent out on the first of the month, and provide the data for the previous month. Quarterly reports are sent on the first day of each quarter, and report all the collected data for the previous quarter. Any portion of your reports can be added to the automated e-mail feature, giving you, or other people of your choice, full access to the most important data from your Web site.

Google Analytics automated reporting is also extremely useful because it allows you to automatically e-mail

reports to other people who are involved with your company or Web site in some way, without giving them access to view all of the collected data in your Analytics reports. For example, you may want to show a consultant ongoing reports on your page views, but not on your revenue or traffic sources.

Be cautious when deciding the frequency of your automated Google Analytics reports. If you have a limited amount of storage space in your e-mail inbox, you may quickly reach your limit if you have several PDF files being mailed to you on a daily basis. It is also important to remember that Google Analytics does not include any data from the current day when your report is sent. Your reports show the collected data up to the last fully completed day.

Automate Reporting

① Log into your Google Analytics account at www.google.com/analytics.

② Click View Report under the Reports column for the site you want to track.

The Google Analytics Dashboard page appears.

③ Navigate to the report that you want to have e-mailed to you on a regular basis.

④ Click Email under the report title.

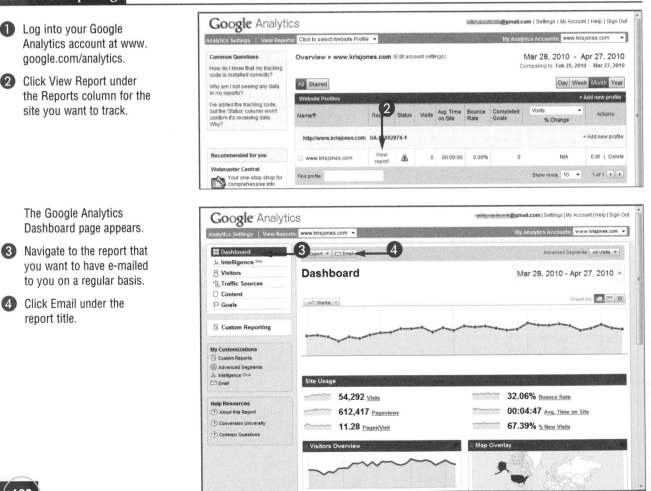

The Set Up Email page appears.

5 Click Schedule.

6 Make sure the Send to Me check box is checked.

7 Add a relevant subject and description.

8 Select the file format you want to receive.

9 Select the date range you want.

10 Click Schedule.

Your reports are now scheduled.

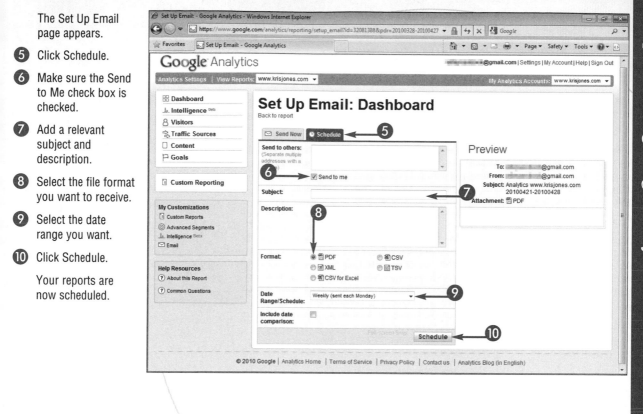

Extra

Adding additional e-mail recipients to existing Google Analytics e-mail reports is easy. At any time, you can include additional e-mail addresses to your pre-existing schedules by simply clicking Email on the left side menu on any page of your Analytics reports, selecting the schedule you want to edit, and adding the new e-mail address. Similarly, this method can be used to remove an e-mail address from receiving any additional reports.

You may also delete any scheduled e-mail report by clicking Email on the left side menu on any page of your Google Analytics reports, and then clicking the trash can icon across from the schedule you want to remove. Be aware that the removal of these schedules is effective immediately.

The reports can be sent in a variety of formats, including PDF, XML, CSV, and TSV. The PDF option is ideal if you want to print your reports in order to have hard copies for your own records, or for sharing with others. The XML, CSV, and TSV files are ideal for building long-term databases of your Web site statistics.

Using Analytics to Find New Keywords

You can use the Traffic Sources report in Google Analytics to locate new keywords to add to your pay-per-click campaigns and search-engine-optimization efforts. Selecting a traffic source like Google or Yahoo presents you with a list of keywords. These are the words your viewers are searching for and using to eventually land at your Web site. You can also view the number of hits, goal conversions, and the e-commerce value of each individual keyword.

Many of the top searched keywords in your report will also be the keywords you have already been targeting in your marketing efforts. However, if you take the time to mine the data contained in the report, you are likely to find keywords that will significantly improve your overall business efforts. For example, a specific keyword related to your product or service may have sent you only 30

visitors over the course of the month, but if those few visits resulted in three conversions, that keyword is a valuable target.

Another advantage of mining the data contained in your keyword reports is locating the potential for large traffic sources. For example, imagine you find a keyword that has sent you a few hundred visitors from Google in the past 30 days, but is not one of the keywords you have been actively targeting. Go to Google and do a search for that keyword. Are you on the first page of results? The second? If a keyword is already sending you a fair amount of volume, and you are listed as result number eight for that keyword, imagine the traffic you would receive if you were in the top three results. This method can help you locate some high-volume keywords that you may have missed or underestimated in your initial keyword generation.

Using Analytics to Find New Keywords

1 Log into your Google Analytics account at www.google.com/analytics.

2 Click View Report under the Reports column for the site you want to explore.

The Google Analytics Dashboard page appears.

3 Click Traffic Sources in the left side menu.

The Google Analytics Traffic Sources page appears.

④ Click the search engine you want to use to find new keywords.

- The keywords from the search engine appear.

- You can view 100 keywords by adjusting the Show Rows option.

  Scan the list for words or phrases that you have not actively targeted, but that are sending in traffic.

Extra

Searching through your keyword reports may also help you identify common words or phrases that your target audience is using when looking for your products or services. By tapping into commonly used phrases about your topic, you can develop a successful campaign that targets low-volume but high-converting keywords.

When looking through your keyword reports, limit yourself to analyzing at least 30 days of historical data or more. Looking at these large time ranges gives you a more accurate view of the potential in your referring keywords. For example, just because a particular keyword may have sent you one visitor and one conversion in the same day does not mean that that pattern will continue over a period of time. On occasion, an isolated conversion slips in without being an indication of any sort of pattern. Similarly, a keyword may send you 20 visitors one day, but only 3 visitors the next day. Looking at larger time frames gives you a much more accurate estimate of actual traffic volume and value.

Set Up E-Commerce Tracking

I n order to properly gauge what traffic sources are the most successful for an e-commerce Web site, you must track all of your Web site transactions. Tracking e-commerce transaction allows you to attach a solid dollar value to each keyword that brings visitors to your site, as well as an average value per visit from each of your traffic sources. Once you have e-commerce tracking properly installed, you can order your traffic sources and referring keywords by their dollar value. This process allows you to prioritize the most valuable keywords and other traffic sources for your Web site.

Before you can track any of your Web site transactions or view reports that attach dollar values to your traffic sources, you must first correctly set Google Analytics to catch the order data from your shopping cart. The first step in this process is letting Google Analytics know that you are running an e-commerce Web site.

Having access to Google Analytics e-commerce data such as keyword profitability enables you to aggressively target the keywords that have the highest conversion ratio for your site. If there are a lot of sales coming in from a certain linking partner, you can consider a media buy to get more exposure to that audience. This form of selective targeting ensures that you reap the largest return possible from your SEO and marketing efforts, by making sure your promotions go toward keywords that your reporting data predicts will consistently convert into sales. This is a perfect example of a way you can work smarter instead of harder. A lot of the time there is no need to reinvent the wheel. Instead, just improve on what you know already works for your particular Web site.

Set Up E-Commerce Tracking

1 Log into your Google Analytics account at www.google.com/analytics.

The Google Analytics Settings page appears.

2 Click Edit under the Actions column of the site you want to track.

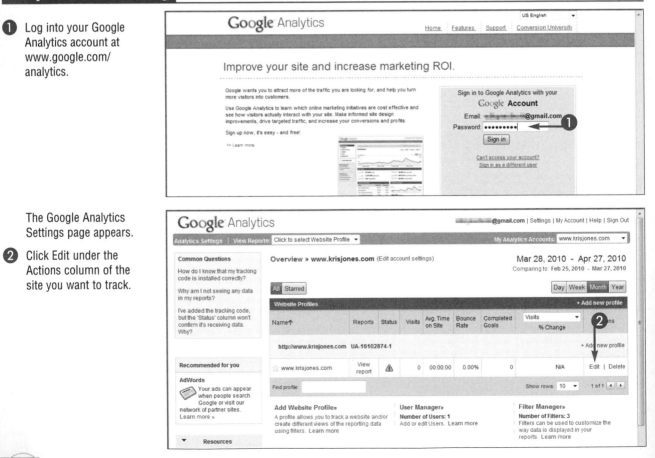

The Google Analytics
Profile Settings page
appears.

③ On the Profile Settings
page, click Edit in the
Main Website Profile
Information box.

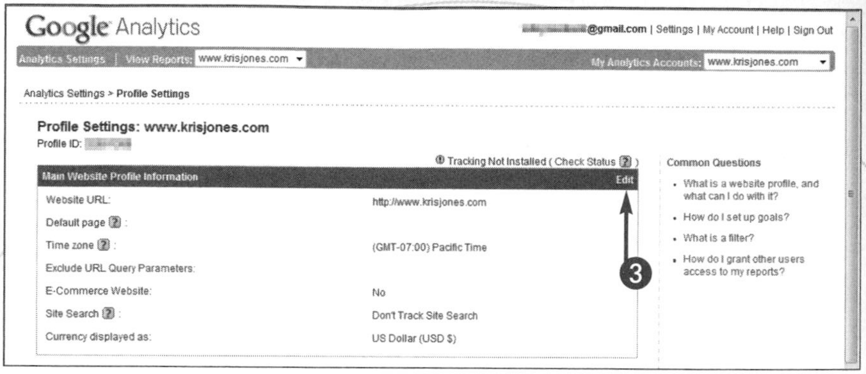

The Google Analytics
Edit Profile Information
page appears.

④ Select the E-Commerce
Website option.

⑤ Save your changes.

Google Analytics now
recognizes your Web
site as an e-commerce
store.

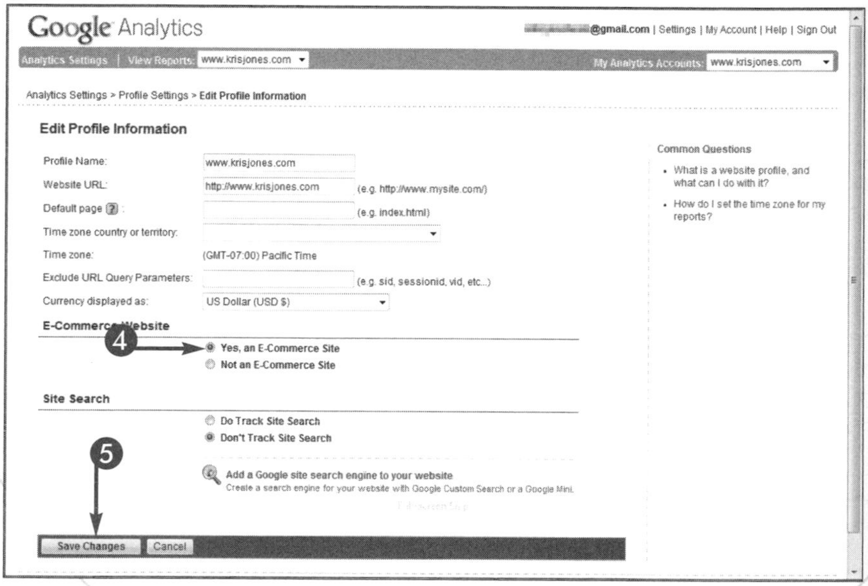

Extra

After e-commerce tracking is successfully installed, allow time to pass so that enough meaningful data is collected
to allow you to make accurate decisions. Depending on your sales volume, a month or less should be a sufficient
time frame to collect meaningful data. View the E-commerce report for your Web site profile. In the bottom right
corner, your sales sources are listed. Click any of these links that are search engines. For example, use Google
Organic. Clicking Google Organic opens the list of your top keywords for the month. Click the Revenue column to
sort your keywords by the amount of revenue each accounted for. You now have a list of your most valuable
keywords.

Next, visit www.google.com and start searching for your top keywords from that list you just viewed. Where is
your site ranking for those keywords? If the answer is not position one, you have found some potential targets for
search-engine optimization, and possibly even for pay-per-click. Targeting your top keywords and making sure you
are ranked as highly as possible for them ensures that you make the most revenue from your search-engine efforts.

Insert Tracking Code on Your Thank You Page

You can track your e-commerce transactions by inserting the tracking code on your Thank You or receipt page. This is the page customers see after their orders have been processed, and typically has a recap of what products were purchased, their price, and the total amount. By placing the tracking code on this page, Google Analytics can catch all of these variables, and bring them into your Web site analytics reports.

From there, you can incorporate this sales data into your reports on traffic sources and content, as well as visitor information. As was mentioned in the first task of e-commerce tracking ("Set Up E-Commerce Tracking"), having the sales information attached to your visitors and the way they reached your site can prove invaluable. Be cautious about who you show your e-commerce data to.

Your top keywords should be kept extremely confidential. The last thing you want to do is tip your competition off on some profitable keywords they may have overlooked.

The variables that are included in the code you place on your receipt page will vary depending on the shopping cart software that you use. If your Webmaster is unsure of the actual variables, check the documentation of your shopping cart software. Alternatively, if you have a shopping cart that is hosted by a third party, contact the company that hosts your cart and ask the company to identify each of the variables for you. Identifying these variables and implementing them into your tracking code is the most complicated step of the process because there is no simple, standard solution.

Insert Tracking Code on Your Thank You Page

1 Ensure that the regular Google Analytics tracking code is correctly installed on your Thank You or receipt page.

```
  <a href="http://www.pepperjam.com/search/" alt="Pepperjam Search" title="Pepperjam
Search">SEARCH</a> <b>&middot;</b> <a href="http://www.pepperjam.com/affiliate/" alt=
title="Pepperjam Afiliate">AFFILIATE</a>  <b>&middot;</b>  <a href="http://www.pepperja
Media" title="Pepperjam Media">MEDIA</a> <b>&middot;</b> <a href="http://www.pepper
alt="Pepperjam Technology" title="Pepperjam Technology">TECHNOLOGY</a>  <b>&middot;</b
href="http://www.pepperjam.com/client-list.php" alt="Portfolio" title="Portfolio">PORTFOLIO</a> <
href="http://www.pepperjam.com/about-pepperjam.php" title="Company" alt="Company">COMPANY</a
href="http://www.pepperjamblog.com" alt="Blog" title="Blog">BLOG</a>
<hr color="#999999">
&copy; 1999 - 2007 - Pepperjam. All Rights Reserved.<br>
</div>


  </div>

  <script type="text/javascript">
  var ddm1 = new DropDownMenu1('menu1');
  ddm1.position.top = -1;
  ddm1.init();
  </script>

<script src="http://www.google-analytics.com/urchin.js" type="text/javascript">
</script>
<script type="text/javascript">
_uacct = "UA-1111111-11";
urchinTracker();
</script>
```

2 Below the regular tracking code, paste the portion of code that catches the variables from your shopping cart.

You must replace the placeholders inside the brackets with the actual variables for whichever shopping cart your site is using. Do not include the brackets in your final code.

```
</div>

  <script type="text/javascript">
  var ddm1 = new DropDownMenu1('menu1');
  ddm1.position.top = -1;
  ddm1.init();
  </script>

<script src="http://www.google-analytics.com/urchin.js" type="text/javascript">
</script>
<script type="text/javascript">
_uacct = "UA-1111111-11";
urchinTracker();
</script>

<form style="display:none;" name="utmform">
<textarea id="utmtrans">UTM:T|[order-id]|[affiliation]|
[total]|[tax]| [shipping]|[city]|[state]|[country] UTM:I|[order-id]|[sku/code]|[productname]|[category]|[price]|
[quantity] </textarea>
</form>
```

3 Edit the body tag of the receipt page to include the `utmSetTrans` function:
```
<body onLoad=
"javascript:__
utmSetTrans()">.
```

4 If you cannot edit the body tag, the `utmSetTrans` function can be called separately by inserting a piece of JavaScript:
```
<script type=
"text/javascript">
__utmSetTrans();
</script>
```

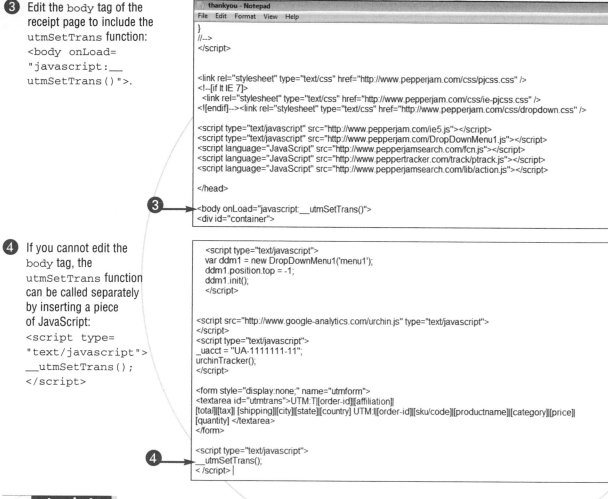

```
thankyou - Notepad
File  Edit  Format  View  Help
}
//-->
</script>


<link rel="stylesheet" type="text/css" href="http://www.pepperjam.com/css/pjcss.css" />
<!--[if lt IE 7]>
  <link rel="stylesheet" type="text/css" href="http://www.pepperjam.com/css/ie-pjcss.css" />
<![endif]--><link rel="stylesheet" type="text/css" href="http://www.pepperjam.com/css/dropdown.css" />

<script type="text/javascript" src="http://www.pepperjam.com/ie5.js"></script>
<script type="text/javascript" src="http://www.pepperjam.com/DropDownMenu1.js"></script>
<script language="JavaScript" src="http://www.pepperjamsearch.com/fcn.js"></script>
<script language="JavaScript" src="http://www.peppertracker.com/track/ptrack.js"></script>
<script language="JavaScript" src="http://www.pepperjamsearch.com/lib/action.js"></script>

</head>

<body onLoad="javascript:__utmSetTrans()">
<div id="container">
```

```
    <script type="text/javascript">
    var ddm1 = new DropDownMenu1('menu1');
    ddm1.position.top = -1;
    ddm1.init();
    </script>


<script src="http://www.google-analytics.com/urchin.js" type="text/javascript">
</script>
<script type="text/javascript">
_uacct = "UA-1111111-11";
urchinTracker();
</script>

<form style="display:none;" name="utmform">
<textarea id="utmtrans">UTM:T|[order-id]|[affiliation]|
[total]|[tax]| [shipping]|[city]|[state]|[country] UTM:I|[order-id]|[sku/code]|[productname]|[category]|[price]|
[quantity] </textarea>
</form>

<script type="text/javascript">
__utmSetTrans();
</script> |
```

Apply It

Here are the variables that you must edit, along with a brief explanation.

Transaction line variables

[order-id]	Order ID number
[affiliation]	Store affiliation optional
[total]	Total amount
[tax]	Tax amount
[shipping]	The shipping cost
[city]	City
[state/region]	State/Province
[country]	Country

Item line variables

[order-id]	Order ID number same as transaction line
[sku/code]	The Products SKU code
[product name]	Name of the product
[category]	Product category
[price]	Price of the product per unit
[quantity]	Quantity of the product ordered

Using Third-Party Shopping Carts

Smaller e-commerce sites often use third-party solutions for shopping carts. Third-party shopping carts allow e-commerce merchants to accept credit cards as a payment option and have the added benefit of being hosted by a third-party. It can be a lot easier during the initial setup, but when you want to track third-party shopping cart transactions with Google Analytics, you must take some extra steps. If you host your own shopping cart, you can skip this task because it does not apply to you. However, if you use any sort of remotely hosted or third-party shopping cart service, this task will prove useful.

The basic idea behind tracking while using third-party shopping carts is to get the information about the sale transferred from the remote cart back to your Web site, which may not seem like a problem at first because you can include your tracking code on the remote page. However, you want to know the original source of those customers. Because of this, you must pass along some information about your customer to the secure site that hosts your cart.

This transfer of information is done by making additions to the links from your Web site to the third-party shopping cart. These pieces of code pass along all the information that Google Analytics has collected, including initial referral, time on site, and the path the customer took through your site while making a purchase. These are all infinitely valuable pieces of information that you definitely do not want lost in the transition to the remote shopping cart. Correctly installing these tags is of the utmost importance to tracking every one of your sales, and putting that knowledge to good use.

Using Third-Party Shopping Carts

① If you use a third-party shopping cart on a different domain than your Web site, adjust your Google Analytics tracking code to fit the format shown here. Note that you need to insert your actual Google Analytics user ID:

```
<script src="http://
www.google-analytics.
com/urchin.js"
type="text/javascript">
</script>
<script type="text/
javascript">
   _uacct="UA-xxxx-x"
   _udn="mystore.com";
   _ulink=1;
   urchinTracker();
</script>
```

② Edit the links from your domain to the shopping cart domain to fit the following format:

```
<a href=" https://
www.securecart.
com/?store=parameters"
onclick="__
utmLinker(this.href);
return false;">Purchase
Now</a>
```

```
thankyou - Notepad
File  Edit  Format  View  Help
<!--
function openWin(theURL,winName,features) {
  window.open(theURL,winName,features);
}
//-->
</script>

<link rel="stylesheet" type="text/css" href="http://www.pepperjam.com/css/pjcss.css" />
<!--[if lt IE 7]>
  <link rel="stylesheet" type="text/css" href="http://www.pepperjam.com/css/ie-pjcss.css" />
<![endif]--><link rel="stylesheet" type="text/css" href="http://www.pepperjam.com/css/dropdown.css" />

<script type="text/javascript" src="http://www.pepperjam.com/ie5.js"></script>
<script type="text/javascript" src="http://www.pepperjam.com/DropDownMenu1.js"></script>
<script language="JavaScript" src="http://www.pepperjamsearch.com/fcn.js"></script>
<script language="JavaScript" src="http://www.peppertracker.com/track/ptrack.js"></script>
<script language="JavaScript" src="http://www.pepperjamsearch.com/lib/action.js"></script>


<script src="http://www.google-analytics.com/urchin.js" type="text/javascript">
</script>
<script type="text/javascript">
  _uacct="UA-xxxx-x"
  _udn="none";
  _ulink=1;
  urchinTracker();
</script>
```

```
thankyou - Notepad
File  Edit  Format  View  Help
<p align="right">
Located at: The Innovation Center<br>
7 South Main Street, Floor 3<br>
Wilkes-Barre, Pennsylvania 18701<br>
<b>Tel</b> 1-877-796-5700 <br>
<b>Fax</b> 570-408-9863
</div>
<img src="http://www.pepperjam.com/images/silverhead.jpg" width="778" height="150" style="position: absolute; top: 107px; left: 11px;">
<div id="dropdownmenu">
<table cellspacing="0" cellpadding="0" id="menu1" class="ddm1">
<tr>
<td><img src="http://www.pepperjam.com/images/dropdownleft.jpg" width="13" height="32" /></td>

<td>
<a class="item1 search"
href="http://www.pepperjam.com/search/"></a>
<div class="section">


<a href=" https://www.securecart.com/?store=parameters" onclick="__utmLinker(this.href); return false;">Purchase Now</a>
```

③ If you use forms to submit the data to the third-party shopping cart, use the form shown in the example. This passes the information along correctly to the shopping cart domain:

```
<form action=
"http://newdomain.
com/form.cgi"
onSubmit=
"javascript:__
utmLinkPost(this)">
```

thankyou - Notepad
File Edit Format View Help

```
<p align="right">
Located at: The Innovation Center<br>
7 South Main Street, Floor 3<br>
Wilkes-Barre, Pennsylvania 18701<br>
<b>Tel</b> 1-877-796-5700 <br>
<b>Fax</b> 570-408-9863
</div>
<img src="http://www.pepperjam.com/images/silverhead.jpg" width="778" height="150" style="position: absolute; top: 107px; left: 11px;">
<div id="dropdownmenu">
<table cellspacing="0" cellpadding="0" id="menu1" class="ddm1">
<tr>
<td><img src="http://www.pepperjam.com/images/dropdownleft.jpg" width="13" height="32" /></td>

<td>
<a class="item1 search" href="http://www.pepperjam.com/search/"></a>
<div class="section">


<a href=" https://www.securecart.com/?store=parameters" onclick="__utmLinker(this.href); return false;">Purchase Now</a>


③ ▸    <form action="http://newdomain.com/form.cgi" onSubmit="javascript:__utmLinkPost(this)">
```

④ Ensure that any calls to `utmTracker` or `utmSetTrans` are above any of the links to the third-party shopping cart.

thankyou - Notepad
File Edit Format View Help

```
④ ▸    <script src="http://www.google-analytics.com/urchin.js" type="text/javascript">
</script>
<script type="text/javascript">
 _uacct="UA-xxxx-x"
 _udn="none";
 _ulink=1;
 urchinTracker();
</script>



</head>

<body>
<div id="container">

<div id="header">
<a href="http://www.pepperjam.com/" alt="Pepperjam Home" title="Pepperjam Home" border="0">
<img src="http://www.pepperjam.com/images/pjlogo.jpg" width="200" height="69" style="border:0px; position: absolute; top: 2px; left: 33px;"></a>
<div id="contact">
<p align="right">
Located at: The Innovation Center<br>
7 South Main Street, Floor 3<br>
Wilkes-Barre, Pennsylvania 18701<br>
<b>Tel</b> 1-877-796-5700 <br>
<b>Fax</b> 570-408-9863
</div>
<img src="http://www.pepperjam.com/images/silverhead.jpg" width="778" height="150" style="position: absolute; top: 107px; left: 11px;">
<div id="dropdownmenu">
<table cellspacing="0" cellpadding="0" id="menu1" class="ddm1">
<tr>
```

Extra

If you run into a situation where the company that hosts your third-party shopping cart claims it is unable to allow you to set up Google Analytics to track your sales, you should strongly consider selecting another e-commerce shopping cart provider. Some of the issues you may want to consider include, first, what kind of service are you paying for when you are unable to use the largest and most encompassing free analytics tool? Second, would it be worth it to host your own shopping cart?

Hosting your own shopping cart can be a bit of work, but it makes tracking your transactions much easier. As was previously mentioned in the task "Set Up E-Commerce Tracking," using the e-commerce feature of Google Analytics provides access to the absolute metric for success: the total revenue generated for any given period. Not having this information means you could be missing the opportunity to discover some real gems in the form of overlooked keywords that convert at a high rate.

If the remotely hosted shopping cart solution does not work out, hosting your own shopping cart is highly recommended. Not having this information about your traffic sources simply is not an option if you want to maximize your Web site's revenue potential.

An Introduction to Social Media Optimization

Social media optimization, or *SMO*, is a form of marketing that focuses on generating traffic and buzz by participation in various social media Web sites, including Facebook, Digg, and YouTube. Social networks allow you to build large lists of contacts and supporters that can help to spread the word about your business and Web site. Social news services provide a platform for others to vote on your content and share your story with others. Finally, video sharing Web sites allow you to upload, view, and share video clips with millions of potential visitors.

This chapter outlines how you can use social media Web sites to generate traffic and buzz, and to build links to your Web site. Social media optimization is an extension of your search-engine-optimization (SEO) efforts, emphasizing the use of social media Web sites to build links that can get your Web site ranked well organically in search engines.

Network with Facebook

Facebook is a popular social networking Web site that allows you to build lists of friends and interact with people all over the world through profile pages, pictures, videos, message boards, and various technology applications. Facebook is one of the top ten most trafficked Web sites in the United States, boasting more than 400 million active members and growing quickly. You can use Facebook to interact with current and prospective business associates while generating considerable traffic to your Web site and buzz about your business. Facebook is a service used by businesses of all sizes and people of all ages to network and communicate in real time.

Create a Fan Page on Facebook

Facebook allows you to create dedicated pages, commonly referred to as "fan pages," to promote your business. With more than 400 million active users on Facebook it is essential that you create a dedicated fan page for your business. A dedicated Facebook fan page allows you to provide fans with your company overview, Web site(s), contact info, press releases, videos, blog RSS, Twitter updates, company news, and status. You can also interact with your fans by responding to comments they post to your fan page, as well as through other social networking tools made available through Facebook.

Network with MySpace

MySpace is a leading social networking Web site that allows you to build lists of friends and interact with people all over the world through profile pages, pictures, videos, and blogs. The MySpace community has more than 200 million members and is one of the most popular Web sites in the United States. Despite the common misconception that MySpace is only for young people, millions of adults and businesses use MySpace as a vehicle to manage reputation, build brand recognition, promote products, and generate buzz.

Maximize Exposure with StumbleUpon

StumbleUpon is a peer and social networking technology that includes a toolbar that you install in your Web browser. The StumbleUpon toolbar allows you to discover and rate Web pages, videos, photos, and news articles. Getting your Web pages, videos, photos, and news articles submitted to StumbleUpon is an effective way to generate buzz and traffic, and to build backlinks to your Web site.

StumbleUpon is a great resource to locate interesting Web sites and videos. Using StumbleUpon regularly provides countless examples of the kind of content that most users find interesting — interesting content that people like is what you want to produce to maximize your exposure on StumbleUpon and other social networks.

Micro-Blog with Twitter

Twitter is a free social networking service that allows you to micro-blog by sending short "updates" of 140 characters or less to others via a text message from your mobile phone, by typing a message from the Twitter site or using instant messaging from Jabber or Google Talk. Twitter is the most widely used micro-blogging network in the world. Micro-blogging is a very powerful and increasingly popular way to communicate with friends and clients, build buzz, and generate prospective business leads. Many celebrities, as well as popular bloggers and writers, use Twitter to network with friends in real time.

Build Followers with Twitter Search

Twitter Search is Twitter's powerful and increasingly popular real-time search engine. Unlike major search engines such as Google, Bing, and Yahoo that update their search indexes every few days or weeks, Twitter Search updates its entire database of news and personal updates, also known as *tweets*, as they occur. The most powerful way to use Twitter Search and build the number of people who follow you on Twitter is to type keywords into Twitter Search that relate to your specific product or service. When Twitter delivers search results, you should follow those users who mention the target keyword.

Network with Google Buzz

Google Buzz is a social networking tool that allows you to share updates, photos, videos, and more. Similar to Twitter and Facebook, Google Buzz allows you to easily start conversations with followers and friends about the things you find most interesting. Google Buzz is integrated directly into Google's popular e-mail service Gmail, which makes joining very easy if you are an existing Gmail user.

Connect with LinkedIn

LinkedIn is a popular business-oriented social networking site that allows you to network with business professionals and build a list of contacts. By building a database of contacts with people you know and trust in business, you have access to a large network of friends with whom you can conduct business, offer jobs, and promote your business. The people in your LinkedIn contact list are referred to as *connections*. You can invite anyone, regardless of whether he is a LinkedIn user or not, to become one of your connections.

Share Videos with YouTube

YouTube is a video sharing Web site that allows users to upload, view, and share video clips. Posting videos on YouTube is easy and requires minimal time and investment on your part.

Successful videos on YouTube can generate thousands or even millions of unique views, which can result in significant exposure to your business. Videos that make it to the coveted YouTube home page are often covered by national news media. Posting interesting videos on YouTube can help to generate buzz and get people and news Web sites talking about your Web site or business.

Take Advantage of Digg Traffic

Digg is a social news Web site that allows users to post and vote on user-submitted content. Digg users submit news stories, such as content that bloggers generate, which are then promoted to the front page through a user-based ranking system maintained by the Digg community. Stories and Web sites that make the front page of Digg.com can lead to thousands of unique visitors within a very short period of time and can lead other Web sites, typically blogs and news Web sites, to link to your Web site. The primary advantages of submitting your content to Digg include increased Web site traffic and links back to your Web site from bloggers and news services that use Digg to find cool stories to write about.

Network with Sphinn

Sphinn is a social news Web site that allows you to read, submit, and vote on content; read and take part in online discussions; and network with others. The Sphinn Web site is an extension of the popular search-engine marketing Web site SearchEngineLand.com, and consists primarily of search-engine and interactive marketing professionals interested in a broad range of topics in the technology field.

Sphinn is a great place to generate interest in your business, especially if what you do is related in some way to online marketing or technology.

Network with Facebook

Facebook, located at www.facebook.com, is a popular social networking Web site that enables you to build lists of contacts and interact with people all over the world through profile pages, pictures, videos, message boards, and various technology applications. Facebook is one of the top ten most trafficked Web sites in the United States and boasts more than 400 million active members. You can use Facebook to interact with current and prospective business associates while generating considerable traffic to your Web site and buzz about your business.

Similar to other leading social network Web sites such as MySpace, your Facebook profile page represents your primary vehicle to communicate and share information about yourself and your business with other members of the Facebook community. Use your profile page to tell other members of the Facebook community about yourself and why your product or service is useful, unique, and valuable.

Your Facebook profile should include accurate data about yourself, including contact information and links to any personal or business Web sites that you want to promote. You should include any relevant information about your past, including education and work history. Moreover, you should upload a picture to stand as your profile avatar, and you should also consider uploading additional pictures of yourself, your company, and any relevant pictures of your products or services.

A useful feature on your Facebook profile page is called the *Wall*. The Wall is a space on your profile page that allows you and your contacts, also known as friends, to post messages for you and your friends to see. Your Facebook Wall is a good place to promote what you want to promote and also allows you to get feedback from your Facebook friends.

Network with Facebook

Create a Facebook Profile

1 Navigate to www.facebook.com and go to your profile page.

2 Click Edit My Profile.

3 Add relevant information about yourself and your business or service.

4 Click Done Editing once you have added information to your profile.

Leave a Wall Post

1 Navigate back to your profile page.

2 Locate the box with the statement *What's on your mind?* This box represents your Wall. Any post you make is viewable by any or all of your friends depending on your privacy settings.

3 Click Share.

● Your Wall post is now active.

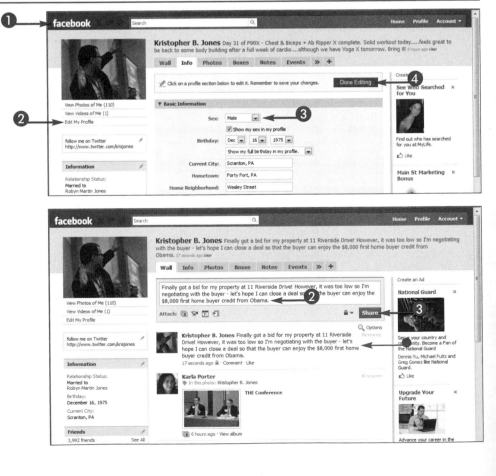

Find and Join Facebook Groups

1. From your Facebook home page, search for the topic you are interested in.

2. Click Groups.

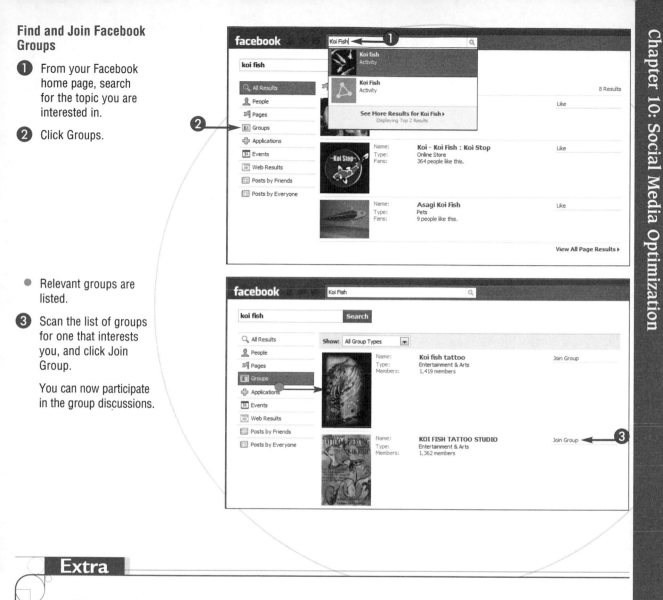

● Relevant groups are listed.

3. Scan the list of groups for one that interests you, and click Join Group.

You can now participate in the group discussions.

Extra

One of the newer features of Facebook is called the Facebook Marketplace. The Facebook Marketplace, located at www.facebook.com/marketplace, is a free self-service classified listing solution that allows you to list items for sale, housing for rent, jobs available, and more. For example, you can use Facebook Marketplace to buy or sell books, furniture, electronics, tickets, cars, and more.

To buy a product or post a product for sale on Facebook Marketplace, you must join a *network*. Facebook defines a network as a city, workplace, school, or region. For example, if you are from the Philadelphia suburbs, you can choose Philadelphia as one of your networks.

Another important Facebook feature is called the Facebook Platform. The Facebook Platform provides a framework for developers to create applications that interact with core Facebook features. Two of the more popular and useful applications derived from the Facebook Platform include Top Friends, which allows you to select and display your favorite friends within your Facebook profile, and Graffiti, which is an application that gives you a visual version of Facebook's Wall.

Create a Fan Page on Facebook

In addition to Facebook profile pages, which tend to be more personal than business focused, Facebook allows you to create dedicated pages, commonly referred to as "fan pages," to promote your business. With more than 400 million active users on Facebook, it is essential that you create a dedicated fan page for your business.

A dedicated Facebook fan page for your business allows you to provide fans with your company overview, Web site(s), contact info, press releases, videos, blog RSS, Twitter updates, company news, and status. Moreover, you can interact with your fans by responding to comments they post to your fan page, as well as through other social networking tools made available through Facebook.

A key element of building a successful Facebook fan page is by adding applications to it. Facebook provides you with access to hundreds of different applications to add to your fan page. Applications add particular functions to your

business fan page, such as the ability to automatically update your page with posts made to your corporate blog through an application called Social RSS. Other popular applications allow you to easily add videos, publish Twitter updates, and add notes to your Facebook fan page.

Your Facebook fan page can serve at least three purposes. First, you can use your fan page as a resource portal by providing information about your products and services. Second, you can use your fan page as an extension of your brand and to build brand loyalty. Third, you can use your fan page to offer contests and coupons exclusively to Facebook users.

Regardless of whether you build a Facebook fan page as a resource portal, brand builder, or as a medium to distribute exclusive promotions, the key to a successful fan page is to engage and interact with fans. Keep in mind that you need to update the page regularly and work proactively to build fans.

Create a Fan Page on Facebook

① Navigate to www.facebook.com/pages/create.php.

② Select the appropriate category type and subcategory from the drop-down menu.

③ Name your new Facebook page.

④ Click to verify that you are authorized to build your new Fan page.

⑤ Click Create Official Page.

⑥ Change your picture to reflect your new Facebook page.

⑦ Click a profile section and edit it to reflect your new Facebook page.

⑧ Click Done Editing.

⑨ Save Changes.

- Notice the changes made to your picture and profile.

- Consider expanding your page by adding photos and commenting on your Wall.

10 Suggest your page to Facebook friends.

- Notice that you have the ability to select and invite existing Facebook friends to join your new page.

Network with MySpace

MySpace is a leading social networking community that enables you to build lists of contacts and interact with people all over the world through profile pages, pictures, videos, and blogs. According to Alexa, MySpace is one of the top 20 most popular Web sites in the United States and the second most popular social network internationally behind Facebook. The MySpace community has more than 200 million members and includes people of all ages and demographics. Despite the common misconception that MySpace is used only by teenagers, millions of adults and businesses use MySpace as a vehicle to manage reputation, build brand recognition, promote products, and generate buzz.

The first step to becoming a member of the MySpace community is to open a free account and create a profile page. The name of your profile page serves as your URL extension on the www.myspace.com domain. For example, if your profile name is "pepperjamsearch,"

then your public MySpace profile address would be www.myspace.com/pepperjamsearch. Therefore, when you use MySpace for business purposes, you should try to name your profile page after your business, or you can name your profile page using keywords that describe the products or services you sell.

Although MySpace was created as a personal social networking Web site and not as a place to conduct business, thousands of companies use the MySpace community as a "test group" to gauge new products or advertising campaigns. When you use MySpace to promote your business or build interest around a new product or service, you can use the About Us portion of your profile to provide potential contacts with a concise overview of your company or product and its key benefits. You should explain why your product is unique and why a potential visitor might want to take action and learn more. You can use your MySpace profile page to further explain the benefits of your company, or add pictures, videos, and more.

Network with MySpace

Create a MySpace Profile

① Navigate to www. myspace.com.

② Log in using your e-mail address and password.

③ Click Edit Profile.

④ Fill the various sections with relevant information about yourself and your business or service.

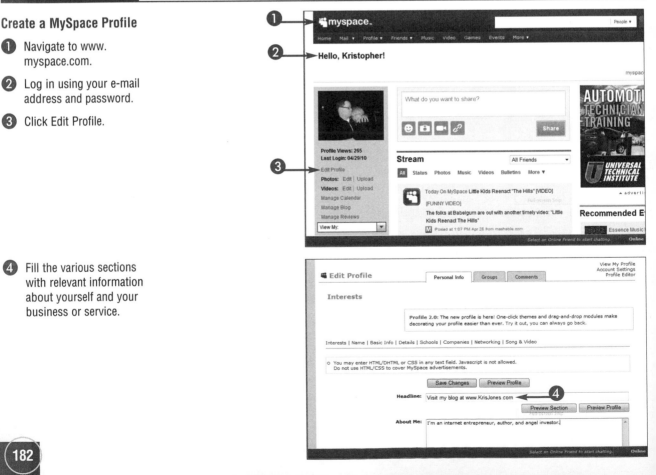

Update Your Status on MySpace.com

1. Navigate to your MySpace home page.

2. Type a message about what you are doing or thinking to update your status.

3. Click Share.

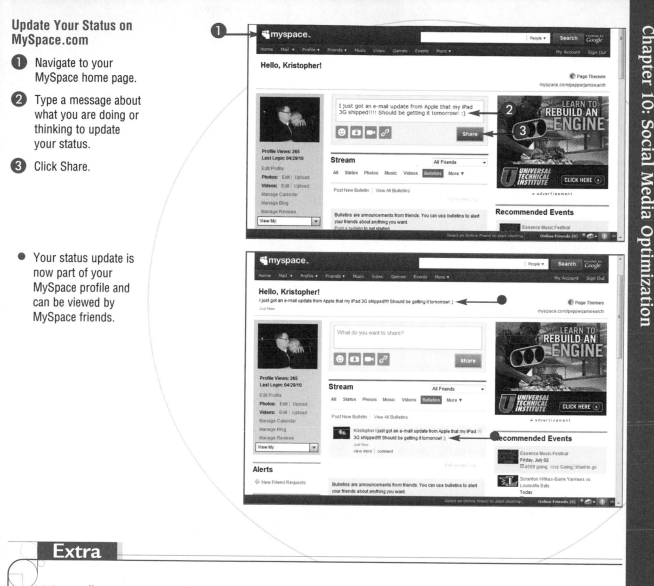

- Your status update is now part of your MySpace profile and can be viewed by MySpace friends.

Extra

MySpace allows you to customize your profile page using HTML in areas such as About Me, I'd Like to Meet, and Interests. You can add videos and Flash-based content using HTML. Users also have the option to add music to their profile pages via MySpace Music, a service that allows bands to post songs for use on MySpace. Using MySpace editors, a user can change the basic appearance of his page by entering a CSS element to override the page's default style sheet. You can use MySpace editors to tweak fonts and colors, but users complain of limitations due to poorly structured HTML used on the default MySpace profile page. User-added CSS is located in the middle of the page instead of being located in the `<head>` element, which means that the page begins to load with the default MySpace layout before changing to the custom layout. A special type of modification is a `div` overlay, where the default layout is dramatically changed by hiding default text with `<div>` tags and large images. Several independent Web sites offer MySpace layout design utilities that let users select options and preview what their pages will look like with the design utility. MySpace has recently added its own Profile Customizer to the site, allowing users to change their profiles through MySpace. Using this feature bypasses the CSS-loading delay issue because the MySpace default code is changed for the customized profile.

Maximize Exposure with StumbleUpon

StumbleUpon is a peer and social networking technology that includes a toolbar that you install in your Web browser; you can use this toolbar to discover and rate Web pages, videos, photos, and news articles. The StumbleUpon service also allows you to submit your own Web pages, videos, photos, and news articles, all of which can help you generate buzz and traffic, and build backlinks to your Web site.

As an Internet user you surf the Web and encounter countless Web sites throughout the day that you like and dislike. By installing and using the StumbleUpon toolbar, you can vote for Web sites you like and dislike simply by clicking the Thumbs Up button on the toolbar when you are on a Web site you like, and clicking the Thumbs Down button when you see a Web site you dislike.

In addition to voting on Web sites you come across on your own, the StumbleUpon toolbar allows you to randomly visit other Web sites by clicking the Stumble button. When you click the Stumble button, the StumbleUpon algorithm displays Web sites that you may find interesting based upon your personal interests and previous voting behavior. The Stumble button allows you to find cool Web sites and vote on whether you like them or not.

The key to generating buzz, traffic, and links from StumbleUpon is to make sure that your content is submitted and available to other StumbleUpon users. You may want to have other people submit your content so that you can vote positively on it and not come across to other StumbleUpon users as partial. The best kind of content to submit to StumbleUpon is entertaining, informative, or unique.

Maximize Exposure with StumbleUpon

Join StumbleUpon

1 Navigate to www. stumbleupon.com.

2 Click Get the Add-on.

3 When prompted, click Run to install the StumbleUpon add-on.

4 Fill in the required information.

5 Click Sign Up to become a member of StumbleUpon.

Add Your Web Site to StumbleUpon

6 After installing the add-on and becoming a StumbleUpon member, visit your Web site — in this example, www.pepperjamnetwork.com.

7 Click I Like It.

8 Click Stumble. When you stumble, you will see only pages that friends and like-minded StumbleUpon users have recommended.

● This is an example of a recommended site for the author's StumbleUpon account.

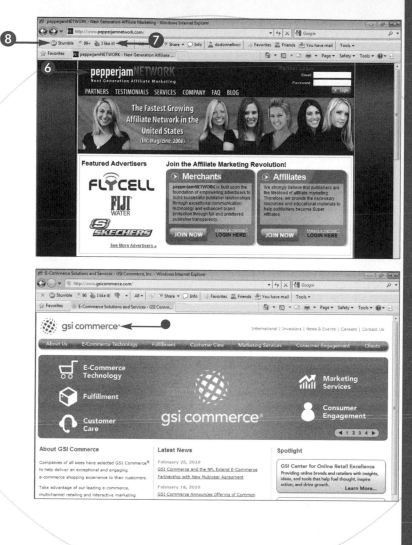

Extra

StumbleUpon has an online video service called StumbleVideo that can provide a large amount of traffic to your videos. StumbleVideo shows users online videos based upon user preferences along with popularity as determined by votes from other members of the StumbleUpon community.

Unlike StumbleUpon, StumbleVideo does not require registration, and you are not required to download the StumbleUpon toolbar to watch videos. Instead, you simply go to the video.stumbleupon.com Web site, select a video, and then click the Stumble button whenever you want to watch another video. StumbleVideo offers users several useful features including the ability to search for other popular videos and to share videos with friends via e-mail.

You do not submit videos to StumbleVideo. Instead, StumbleVideo gets videos from sources such as YouTube, Metacafe, MySpace TV, Google Video, and other popular video sites. Therefore, if you want to get into StumbleVideo, upload your video to one of the sites listed above. StumbleVideo is a great source for you to generate ideas for creating your own videos that you can submit to the popular video Web sites, as well as host on your own Web site.

Micro-Blog
with Twitter

A very powerful and increasingly popular way to communicate with friends and clients, build buzz, and generate prospective business leads is through *micro-blogging*. Micro-blogging is a form of blogging that allows you to write brief text updates, usually less than 200 characters, and publish them, either to be viewed by anyone or by a restricted group you choose. Micro-blogging is a form of social networking that enables you to keep your followers up-to-date with what you are doing at any given time of the day.

The most widely used micro-blogging network is Twitter. Twitter, located at www.twitter.com, is a free social networking service that allows you to micro-blog by sending short "updates" of 140 characters or less to others via a text message from your mobile phone, by typing a message from the Twitter site, or by using instant messaging from Jabber or Google Talk.

Keep in mind that when you sign up for Twitter via the Twitter Web site, your communication settings are automatically set to public. By keeping your communication settings to public, your updates automatically go to both your friends and to the public timeline, which is automatically posted and updated for public viewing every 4 minutes to the Twitter Web site. If you intend to use Twitter to build buzz about your business or generate traffic to your Web site, keep the public settings.

One of the ways you can use Twitter to generate Web site traffic and buzz is by sharing daily deals, special offers, or exciting product news with your readers. If you have an e-commerce Web site, you may want to send out a message each morning announcing your top-selling products. For example, "Yesterday we sold over 1,000 red widgets. We have less than that left in inventory, so order now to guarantee shipment."

Micro-Blog with Twitter

Sign Up for Twitter

➊ Navigate to www.twitter.com.

➋ Click Join Today and then fill in the required information to create your account.

Follow People on Twitter

Twitter allows you to build a list of friends and associates who view your micro-blogs.

➌ Navigate to http://twitter.com/invitations/suggestions.

➍ Select the topics you are interested in. Find people you are interested in and follow them.

• Note that Twitter offers additional tools to add new followers, including Find Friends and Find on Twitter.

➎ Click Home to navigate to your personal Twitter start page.

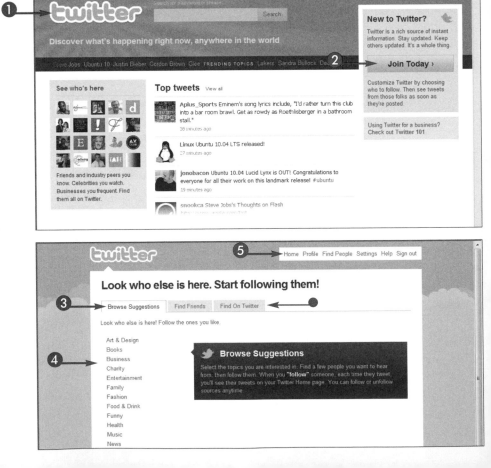

6 Fill in the What's Happening field with your marketing message.

7 Click Tweet to make a Twitter post.

● Note that your post is now live and part of the main Twitter stream.

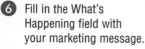

Extra

Twitter is a tool that allows you to quickly communicate and share news with your friends and within the Twitter community. For example, if you manage a music Web site, you can use Twitter to break news about concerts and entertainment gossip. To promote yourself or your Web site, you can simply include a tag at the end of each message such as "Brought to you by X.com."

You can send any of your friends a private message using Twitter. To send a friend a text message, click Message from the Twitter profile page or simply click Direct Messages and choose the recipient from the drop-down box. If you want to send a private message from your phone, use the following command: D + username + message. Note that a person's username and screen name may be different. To ensure that your private message is sent to the proper person, you can verify the accuracy of the person's username by going to her profile page and looking at the URL at the top of the page. The username follows the www.twitter.com domain: for example, www.twitter.com/wileyseobook.

Another useful feature of Twitter is the retweet. A *retweet* is when you share a tweet posted by another Twitter user with your own Twitter followers. The typical format of a retweet is RT followed by the message. For example, RT @wileyseobook: Pepperjam Founder Kris Jones to Speak at Upcoming SES NY Conference. Keep in mind that others may also retweet your posts, which can result in exponential exposure to your tweet.

Build Followers with Twitter Search

Twitter Search, located at www.search.twitter.com, is Twitter's powerful and increasingly popular real-time search engine. Unlike major search engines such as Google, Bing, and Yahoo that update their search indexes every few days or weeks, Twitter Search updates its entire database of news and personal updates, also known as tweets, as they occur.

The immense popularity of Twitter has resulted in a new trend in search-engine marketing called "real-time" search. In late 2009, Google and Bing began incorporating real-time Twitter updates as part of their standard search results. This move, coupled with the fact that Twitter continues to become a primary resource for breaking news and information, such as the death of Michael Jackson to the latest update to Google's search algorithm, demonstrates the importance of incorporating Twitter into your search marketing and Web promotion strategy.

The most powerful way to use Twitter Search and build the number of people who follow you on Twitter is to type keywords into Twitter Search that relate to your specific product or service. When Twitter delivers search results, you should follow those users who mention the target keyword.

Build Followers with Twitter Search

① Navigate to www.search.twitter.com.

② Type a keyword related to your business into the Twitter search bar.

③ Click Search.

● Observe real-time results for affiliate marketing.

④ Click any profile picture.

⑤ Click Follow to begin following the user — in this case, the author of this book, @krisjonescom.

You can return to search results to follow more users interested in your original search.

⑥ For another search, navigate back to www.search.twitter.com.

⑦ Type a keyword related to your business into the Twitter search bar.

⑧ Click Search.

Extra

One of the most effective uses of Twitter Search is to monitor what people are saying about your brand. By simply typing your brand name into Twitter Search, you can access all the instances where your brand was mentioned on Twitter. Accessing Twitter search results allows you to see what people are saying about your brand, which can be especially useful if someone is happy or unhappy with some aspect of your product or service. If someone is unhappy, you can immediately reach out to him and work to address the problem publically or through Twitter's private messaging system.

If you are lucky enough to have someone tweet how great your brand is or if you want to address a negative tweet, Twitter allows you to easily publicly thank her by responding to her original tweet with an @ symbol followed by the username of the person you want to respond to. For example, "@krisjonescom — thanks for saying you enjoy our widgets! We strive to constantly improve so if you have any additional feedback, positive or negative, please share" or "@krisjonescom — I'm sorry you had a bad experience with our product. Please direct message me your address and I'll be sure to send you a replacement immediately."

Network with Google Buzz

Google Buzz, located at www.google.com/buzz, is a social networking tool that allows you to share updates, photos, videos, and more. Similar to Twitter and Facebook, Google Buzz allows you to easily start conversations with followers and friends about the things you find most interesting.

Google integrated Google Buzz directly into its popular e-mail service Gmail, which makes joining very easy if you are an existing Gmail user. Once you are signed into your Gmail account, you can opt-in to the Google Buzz service from the left navigation bar. If you are not a Gmail user, you can sign-up for free at http://mail.google.com.

Similar to Twitter, Google Buzz is a service that allows you to voluntarily follow other Google Buzz users, and in turn they can opt to follow you. In addition, Google Buzz makes recommendations to you for new people to follow based on how often you interact with the person via Gmail.

Once logged into Google Buzz, Google recommends posts it believes you will find interesting and weeds out posts you are likely to skip. When you share something on Google Buzz you have the option to share publicly or only share with other users that you follow. Google claims that public posts are indexed instantly, and may show up in Google's real-time search results. Therefore, you should select the public option only when you want to share your post with the world, whereas you should select the private option when you intend to share your post only with people who follow you.

All your public activity on Buzz is visible through your Google Profile Page. Similar to your public posts, your profile page is eligible to be ranked on Google. Your Google Profile Page should include important biographical information that you want to share with the public, and allows you to share photos and links to your favorite Web sites.

Network with Google Buzz

① Navigate to www.google.com/buzz.

② Watch the video to learn more about Google Buzz.

③ Click Try Google Buzz in Gmail. If you do not have a Gmail account, follow the instructions to open a new account.

● Note the posts. Google recommends posts it believes you will find interesting and weeds out posts you are likely to skip. Posts are updated in real time.

● Note that you are able to comment, like, or e-mail each post.

④ Write a post.

● Note that you can add a link directly to your post. When you add a link Google automatically pulls the title tag of the link and shares it as part of your post.

⑤ Click Post.

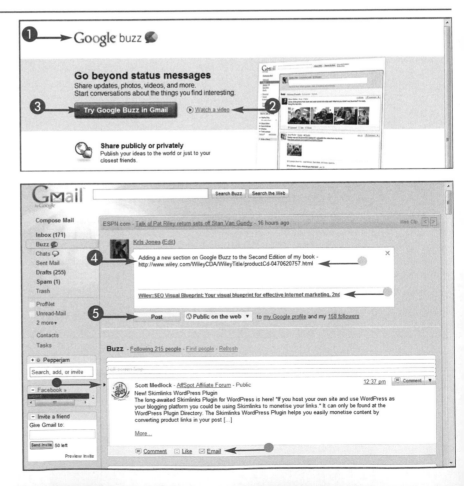

- Note that your post is now public.

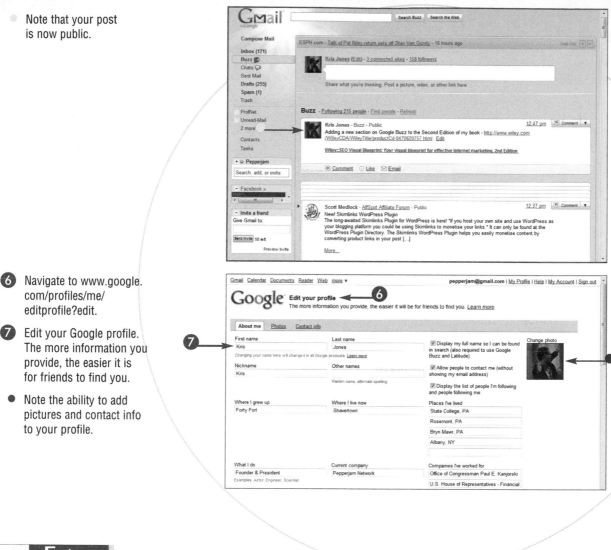

(6) Navigate to www.google.com/profiles/me/editprofile?edit.

(7) Edit your Google profile. The more information you provide, the easier it is for friends to find you.

- Note the ability to add pictures and contact info to your profile.

Extra

Buzz for mobile, located by typing **buzz.google.com** into your mobile browser, is the mobile version of Google Buzz. Buzz for mobile provides comparable functionality to that found on your personal computer, while also providing mobile-only features that allow you to create posts through voice-recognition technology and easily share your location through GPS technology.

One of the distinct features of Buzz for mobile is the ability to post updates without having to type. Buzz for mobile voice-recognition technology is available on Google Maps for the Blackberry phone, in the quick search widget on Android, and in the Google Mobile App on iPhones.

Another key feature of Buzz for mobile is the ability to easily share your location with people on Google Buzz. Sharing your location and being able to see other Google Buzz users in your nearby location allows you to see a wider collection of public messages around you, including messages from people you do not know, as well as updates that are specifically about a nearby location.

Connect with LinkedIn

Linkedln, located at www.linkedin.com, is a popular business-oriented social networking site that enables you to build a professional network of contacts. The primary purpose of this social network site is to allow you to maintain a list of contact details of people you know and trust in business. The people in your LinkedIn contact list are referred to as *connections*. You can invite anyone, regardless of whether or not the person is a LinkedIn user or not, to become one of your connections.

Each time you add a new connection to your LinkedIn network you gain access to that person's connections. For example, by adding a new connection, you gain indirect access to that person's direct connections (your second-degree connections) and also the connections of your second-degree connections (called third-degree connections). Every time you create new connections, you are, in turn, tapping into a potentially large network of business leads that you can use to help grow your business.

For example, you can use your network of business connections to recruit employees by sending an internal message through LinkedIn outlining your needs to your contacts. In addition, you can use your connections to explore various business opportunities and to attract people to your Web site.

The LinkedIn service allows you to quickly build your contact list by searching for LinkedIn members you know from your current and past place of employment or from your past educational institutions. Moreover, as part of the sign-up process, you have the opportunity to build a profile page that others can see. Your profile page includes basic information about you, as well as more specific information about your present and past educational and business activities.

Connect with LinkedIn

① Navigate to www.linkedin.com.

② Log in to your account with your username and password.

③ Search for people in your field of interest by entering your industry into the Search field.

④ Click the search button.

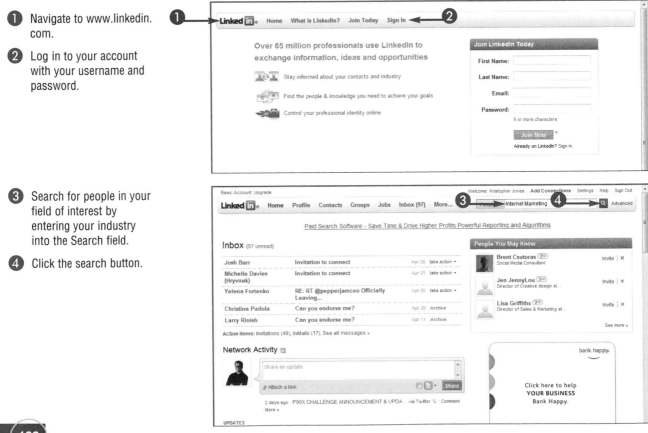

- Scan the list for potential new contacts in your field.

- You can click the results to visit the person's profile page and add her as a contact.

5 You can also search LinkedIn for potential job opportunities by selecting Jobs from the Search drop-down menu.

6 Search for your field of interest.

- Job search results appear.

Extra

The basic LinkedIn service is free, but there are limits on the amount of InMail you can send and on how many *open introductions* you can have at any given time. Open introductions refer to the number of contact requests your contacts can make on your behalf to other LinkedIn members that are neither accepted nor declined. InMail is LinkedIn's internal e-mail system, and introductions let you contact or be contacted by LinkedIn users in your network through the people you know. In this way, your connections can introduce you to anyone in your network (or introduce anyone to you) by forwarding messages through a chain of trusted professionals.

Although the basic LinkedIn service allows you to build a large professional network of connections, you may want to consider opening one of LinkedIn's premium accounts, which is a paid service, if you intend to use LinkedIn for larger-scale job recruiting or other purposes. For example, a LinkedIn Business Plus Account provides 10 InMails per month, premium content access, one-business-day customer service, and 25 introductions open at a time, among other benefits.

Another useful LinkedIn service is called LinkedIn Answers. LinkedIn Answers is a free service that allows you to pose questions to the LinkedIn community to answer.

Share Videos with YouTube

Video Web sites such as YouTube provide one of the most powerful forms of communication for you to attract potential visitors and get them interested in your products, services, and Web site. YouTube, located at www.youtube.com, is a video sharing Web site that allows users to upload, view, and share video clips. Posting videos on YouTube is easy and requires minimal time and investment on your part.

Users of all kinds, including small and large businesses, amateur videographers, and everyday people, have successfully posted videos to YouTube. Your goal in creating a video may be to inform or entertain your audience. You can create videos that both inform and entertain your viewers, but videos that entertain tend to create more buzz and result in more viewers than informational videos. Regardless of whether your goal is to inform, entertain, or both inform and entertain, try to make your videos interesting so that people will want to share your video with friends.

Successful videos on YouTube can generate thousands or even millions of unique views, which can result in increased brand recognition and customer leads. Top videos are typically featured on the YouTube home page and are often covered by national news media. Posting interesting videos on YouTube can help to generate buzz and get people and news Web sites talking about your Web site or business.

Posting videos on YouTube is free, but requires membership. As a YouTube member, you can post unlimited videos to your YouTube Channel. Your YouTube Channel is another name for your YouTube member name. Because your YouTube Channel is where all your videos will be posted once you upload them, choose a name that best represents your business. For example, if your business is the Royal Bank of Canada, your YouTube Channel should be RBC, RoyalBankofCanada, or something very close so that your frequent viewers can easily find you.

Share Videos with YouTube

1 Navigate to www. youtube.com.

2 If you do not already have a YouTube account, click the Create Account link, fill in the required information, and create a YouTube account.

3 Sign in to your YouTube account.

4 Click Upload.

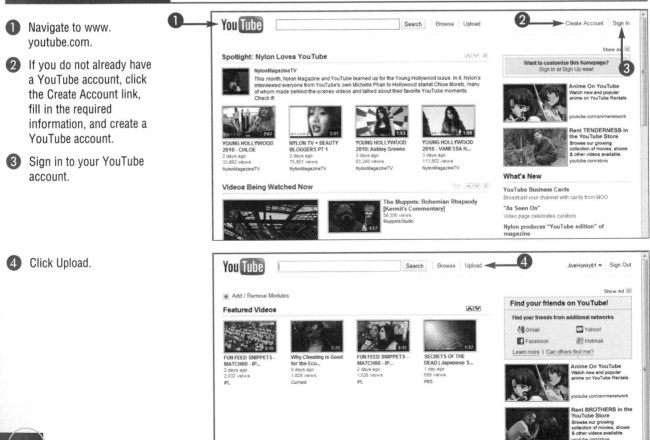

5 Click Upload Video.

6 Select a video to upload.

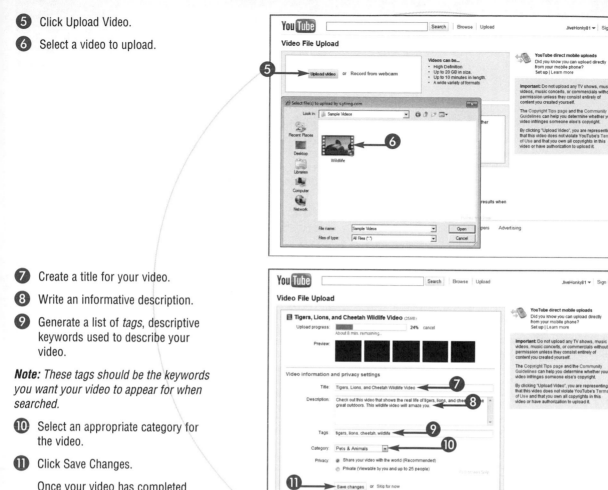

7 Create a title for your video.

8 Write an informative description.

9 Generate a list of *tags*, descriptive keywords used to describe your video.

Note: These tags should be the keywords you want your video to appear for when searched.

10 Select an appropriate category for the video.

11 Click Save Changes.

Once your video has completed uploading it can be found through searches of the YouTube database. You may also share this video with friends or associates.

Extra

Videos that receive widespread acceptance and attention, usually resulting in millions of video views, are said to be *viral*. Viral videos are original works that are so unique, funny, or sensational that viewers share them with friends and strangers through blogs, e-mail, and other forms of communication.

Creating a viral video can catapult your business in the search-engine rankings because others are likely to write about you and link to your Web site. However, you will need to be creative to make sure that you receive credit for your work. For example, you can wear a promotional T-shirt featuring your business during the video, or simply add your Web site URL to the credits at the end of each of your videos. Phrases like "Sponsored by Business A" or "Learn more at Business.com" are typical. Another approach is to include a trailer about your business at the beginning or end of each video.

Take Advantage of Digg Traffic

Digg is a popular social news Web site that allows users to post and vote on user-submitted content. News stories and Web sites are submitted by users and then promoted to the front page through a user-based ranking system. Stories and Web sites that make the front page of Digg.com can lead to thousands of unique visitors within a very short period of time and can lead other Web sites, typically blogs and news Web sites, to link to your Web site.

You can significantly increase your chances of getting users to vote your content or news story to the front page of Digg by following several basic strategies. Do not submit your own Web site or story to Digg. Content submitted by the content creator rarely makes the front page of Digg. Instead, ask a friend, preferably an active

Digg user, to submit your story. Once the story is submitted, you can vote and comment on your own story.

As a member of Digg, you can add friends to your member account. Adding lots of friends is a good idea because your friends will often vote on the same stories that you do. When you vote on your own story, you increase the likelihood of your friends voting on your story by having lots of friends.

Story titles that capture users' attention are more likely to get voted on and make the front page of Digg. Titles with sensational, compelling headlines and interesting summaries tend to work best. Therefore, make sure that your story title and summary are interesting and stand out. If you are not an experienced writer, you can hire a professional writer to draft interesting content about your Web site and then have one of your friends submit it to Digg.

Take Advantage of Digg Traffic

Add a Web Site to Digg

1. Navigate to www.digg.com.

2. Log in using your username and password.

3. Click Submit New.

4. Enter your URL.

5. Choose the type of submission.

6. Click Continue.

7. Fill in an attention-worthy title and description.

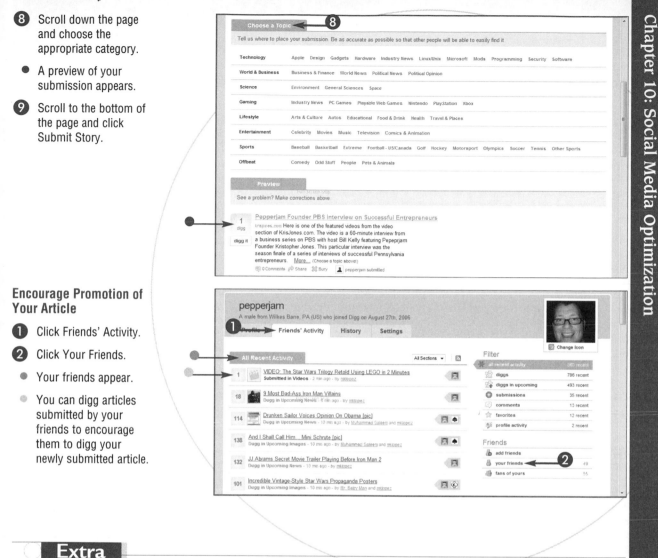

8 Scroll down the page and choose the appropriate category.

● A preview of your submission appears.

9 Scroll to the bottom of the page and click Submit Story.

Encourage Promotion of Your Article

1 Click Friends' Activity.

2 Click Your Friends.

● Your friends appear.

● You can digg articles submitted by your friends to encourage them to digg your newly submitted article.

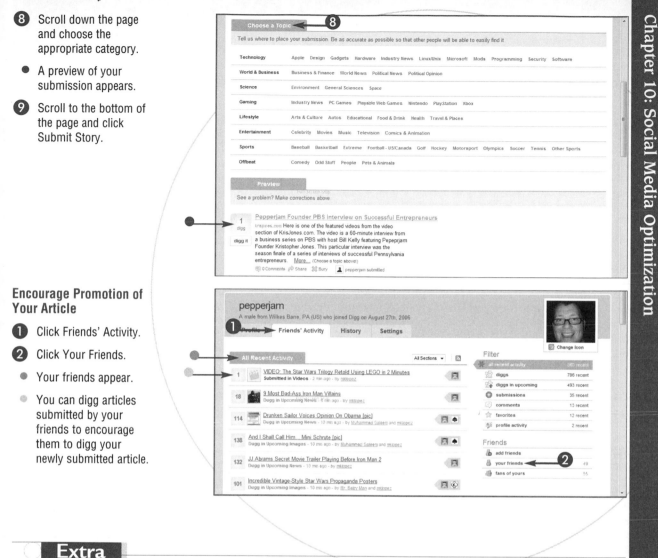

Extra

If you are using Digg to generate buzz and traffic and to build links to your Web site, you must make sure your server can handle the traffic. For example, getting your story voted to the front page of Digg results in massive traffic to your Web site in a very short period of time, and therefore can dismantle your Web site, making it inaccessible if you do not have adequate server requirements. Typically, increasing your bandwidth limits prior to receiving large amounts of traffic increases the likelihood that your server can handle the load.

Social communities find new, unknown members coming in and attempting to sell anything offensive. As a rule, your story will not receive enough votes to make the front page of Digg if users believe the submission was for the sole purpose of selling something. Therefore, if your intention is to sell something, you need to be creative about how you capture the attention of the Digg community. Do not post your press releases on Digg.com. Digg users are looking for interesting, impartial stories that are posted on their merit by other community members. Instead of posting your own press release, have a well-known blogger interpret your release and then have one of your top Digg friends post the release as interpreted by the blogger.

Network with Sphinn

Sphinn, located at www.sphinn.com, is a social news Web site that allows you to read, submit, and vote on content; read and take part in online discussions; and network with others. The Sphinn Web site is an extension of the popular search-engine marketing Web site SearchEngineLand.com. The Sphinn community consists primarily of search-engine and interactive-marketing professionals interested in a broad range of topics in the technology field.

You can generate quality traffic to your Web site or blog by having your content submitted to Sphinn, although keep in mind that others should submit your content. Submitting your own content may appear to readers as an attempt to spam or self-promote, which is typically frowned upon within the social networking space. Sphinn is similar to the popular social news Web site Digg.com in that stories with the most votes from members of the community are deemed most popular and therefore gain premium placement on the coveted Sphinn home page.

On the Sphinn home page you can sort the most popular news stories by current or previous day, week, or month.

Remember that the Sphinn community is a niche community made up of marketing professionals who are looking for interesting and useful content related to search-engine and interactive marketing. Therefore, content unrelated to Internet marketing is unlikely to do well on Sphinn.com.

You can read stories on Sphinn.com without becoming a member, but if you want to submit content, leave comments, or take part in community discussions, you must sign up for a free membership and create a personal profile. Your profile includes information that allows other Sphinn members to get to know you and understand your background, as well as your involvement on other social networks, both of which can lead to additional traffic, buzz, and links. For example, through your Sphinn profile you can provide other members with your profile names and Web addresses for other leading social networking Web sites and discussion boards, such as Digital Point, SEOmoz, Digg, Facebook, and MyBlogLog. You can also add your personal and business blog feed to your profile page.

Network with Sphinn

1. Navigate to www.sphinn.com.

2. If you do not already have a Sphinn account, click Join Us and choose a username, password, and e-mail address.

3. Log into your Sphinn account.

4. Click Submit News to submit a new article or story.

5. Enter the article or story's URL.

Note: *Make sure you follow the submission guidelines. Not following these guidelines could result in your submission being turned down.*

6 Select a category for your submission.

7 Select a descriptive title for your submission.

8 Scroll down the page and add a short summary of the article or story.

9 Click Preview and Submit.

Your article or story is now viewable by Sphinn users.

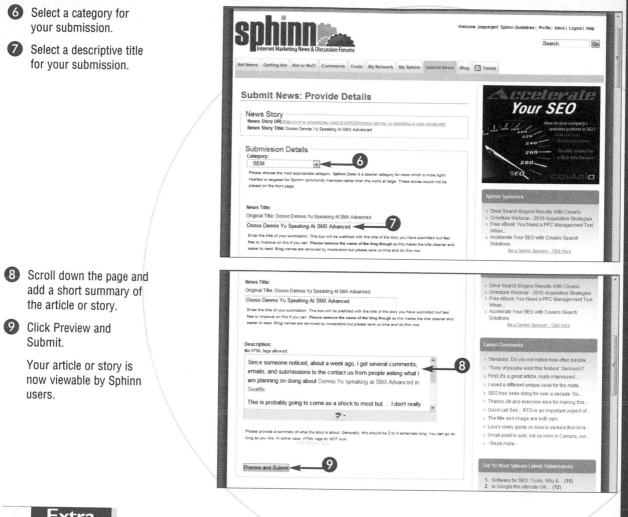

Extra

The Sphinn.com Web site allows you to sort news stories by five main sections, including Hot Topics, What's New, Greatest Hits, Comments, and Submit. In addition, you can break down each content section into numerous categories, including Google, Yahoo, Microsoft, Search Marketing, Social Media, and Online Marketing. Sorting content by category is especially useful if you want to quickly review information related to specific topics. For example, if you want to research content related to changes in Google's quality score algorithm, Sphinn allows you to easily sort content by selecting the Google or Search Marketing category.

- The Hot Topics section is the default Sphinn.com home page setting and provides you with the top stories across all categories as voted on by Sphinn members. You can sort Sphinn Hot Topics stories by current or previous day, week, or month.

- The What's New section provides you with the most recently submitted news stories. You can sort stories by how recently they were submitted, as well as by the amount of votes.

- The Greatest Hits section includes a ranking of the most popular stories ever submitted to Sphinn.com. The Greatest Hits section is a great place to get ideas for the type of content you should be submitting to Sphinn if you are looking to generate a lot of buzz and Web site traffic.

- The Comments section provides a list of the most recent comments from Sphinn members.

- The Submit section allows you to create a new discussion or submit news to the Sphinn community.

An Introduction to Pay-Per-Click Campaigns

In February 1998, Bill Gross of Idea Labs launched the first pay-per-click, or *PPC*, search engine, GoTo.com. The GoTo.com search engine pioneered the process of *pay-per-click* advertising, which allows advertisers the option of bidding on how much they would be willing to pay to appear at the top of results in response to specific searches. GoTo.com later became known as Overture, which was eventually acquired by Yahoo and renamed Yahoo Search Marketing.

In the fall of 2000, Google followed suit and introduced its own PPC service, Google AdWords. Similar to Yahoo Search Marketing, Google AdWords lets prospective advertisers sign up and show advertisements triggered by keywords on the Google search engine and its syndicate partners. Within the matter of a few years, Google AdWords quickly became the largest and most used PPC advertising platform in the United States and remains so to this day.

The basic concept of PPC advertising is very simple. Although the goal of search-engine optimization, or *SEO*, is to rank "naturally" for any given keyword, PPC allows advertisers to bid against each other for a particular keyword or phrase. Advertisers therefore compete for the highest ad placement in the sponsored results, which typically appear above and to the right of the organic results. Organic results are the nonpaid results located below the sponsored listings on the center of the search results page.

Testing has shown that having both a high sponsored and high organic ranking greatly increases the credibility of your Web site and, therefore, increases the traffic to your Web site. If you think of the search results page as a piece of real estate, a powerful strategy is to get your company's name onto that piece of property as many times as you can.

Structure an AdWords Account

There are three major levels within a basic Google AdWords PPC account: Account, Campaign, and Ad Group. This chapter will help you understand the basic structure of a PPC account, why some advertisers choose to open multiple accounts, and why Google sometimes requires advertisers to do so. AdWords allows you to manage multiple accounts with a Client Center, which is specifically designed for larger advertisers.

Target Your Campaign

You can use targeting when you want your text ads shown only to a specific geographic area. You can also target specific languages. Google lets you implement advanced targeting strategies, which is one of the major reasons advertisers have embraced the AdWords online advertising platform. Google enables you to target your PPC ads to virtually any geographical location you want, including local, regional, state, national, and international location targeting.

Open an AdWords Account

When you open a Google AdWords account, you should be prepared to create your first campaign, ad group, text ad, and keywords. If you have not already created a Web site for your product, you must do so before you can create a PPC campaign. Be prepared to fill in the required information including names for your campaigns and the text ad that will be shown on the search results. You should have a pretty good idea about what you want to accomplish before you begin.

Write Effective Ad Copy

Text ads are the link between your Web site and the search results pages. The more targeted and effective your ad copy is, the more quality customers will be directed to your Web site. There are many approaches to writing ad text. You will want to come up with a few variations and test them against one another. PPC advertising platforms such as Google AdWords simplify the process of creating and testing ad copy.

Using Keyword Matching Options

An important aspect of optimizing your PPC account is selecting the correct matching option for each keyword. There are three main options: broad, phrase, and exact. These matching options determine how much and what kind of traffic your text ads receive. Negative keywords help you eliminate unwanted clicks from users who will not benefit from your site. Whether you are trying to get rank organically or with paid search, the keywords you choose are a large factor in your online marketing strategy.

Set Bidding Strategies

When you set a bid within the Google AdWords platform you are telling what you are willing to pay for a click. Setting the right bids helps your PPC campaign succeed. There are various bidding strategies that you can choose from; you can explore different options while you experiment with your account. Do not be afraid to spend a little more if the return is worth it.

Run PPC Reports

One of the major benefits of advertising online is robust, real-time, keyword-level PPC reporting. Google AdWords is no exception to this — it lets you run PPC reports on an account, campaign, ad group, and even keyword level. All of the information you will ever need to make intelligent decisions is at your fingertips. In order to master PPC advertising, you first have to master the art of reporting.

Track Conversions

In order to run the most valuable reports for your PPC account, you must be able to track what customers are doing when they visit your site. The installation of conversion tracking code on your Web site allows you to track visitor behavior and Web site *conversions*, including e-commerce transactions, e-mail submissions, lead form completions, or any other conversion that you choose. You can track whatever information is important to you and your online efforts and make decisions based upon this data.

Using Google Adwords Editor

As your AdWords account grows larger, it also grows more difficult to manage. AdWords Editor is an offline tool that allows you to bulk edit and seamlessly manage your campaign so that you can make the most of the time you spend working on your PPC account. The program is offered by Google for free and can help you bulk edit Google AdWords keywords and ad copy. Google Editor is the tool that professionals use, and it is very easy to use even for a beginner.

Optimize Your Account

Do not forget that once you have your account up and running, you still have a lot of work to do to get things moving in the right direction. You must maintain your PPC account on a daily basis if it is going to grow and succeed. Try a lot of different approaches to see what works best based on your particular needs.

When you combine all of the available options of PPC advertising, you possess a powerful marketing tool that can hardly be matched. Your text ads can reach the widest audience you choose, or the thinnest; the range is up to you. Remember, however, that these accounts spend money in real time. If you make a change, you need to watch that change and how it affects your account. A careless mistake that slips through the cracks can spend a lot of money before anyone notices.

PPC advertising could be a valuable tool in your toolbox if you take your time and build a high-quality account. Combined with your organic traffic, PPC traffic can help you capture all the clicks available for your particular list of keywords. If there is a term you just cannot seem to get your site ranked naturally for, PPC is the answer.

The more important thing to remember is to be creative. Find the keywords that nobody else is bidding on. Write the ad copy that sets you apart from the competition. Drive your traffic to the most relevant destination page on your Web site. What you take away from your PPC campaign depends on what you put into it.

Learn About
AdWords Accounts

You can use a Google AdWords account to purchase pay-per-click advertisements on the Google.com search engine and the Google Search Network. The Google Search Network consists of Google partner Web sites, including highly trafficked Web sites such as AOL.com, Netscape.com, and Ask.com. There are three major levels within a Google AdWords PPC account: Account, Campaign, and Ad Group. An account is a unique e-mail address and password with unique billing information. Your account is targeted to the time zone and currency you select. An advertiser can have multiple accounts linked together into a Client Center.

The second level of a Google AdWords PPC account is the Campaign level. Each of your accounts can contain various campaigns. You should think of a campaign as a particular strategy. One campaign may be just for keywords related to your trademark, and another campaign may target a certain demographic or relate to a seasonal offer that your site runs every year. You can have up to 25 campaigns in your Google AdWords account. Each of your PPC

campaigns has start and end dates, daily budgets, Google Network Preferences, and language and location targeting. *Google Network Preferences* allow you to choose whether your ads are shown on Google syndicate partner Web sites such as AOL.com, and also allow you to designate your participation in the Google Content Network. Usually one campaign is sufficient for a smaller advertiser; two or more are appropriate for a larger site. Each of your campaigns contains your unique ad groups.

The third level of a Google AdWords PPC account is the Ad Group level. An account can have up to 100 ad groups. Ad groups can contain hundreds of keywords and complementary ads that show when those keywords are searched. Ad groups are usually broken down into related groups.

Finally, you have keywords and ad copy. These are the meat and potatoes of the AdWords account. The number of people who see your ads depends on how popular the keywords are that you choose. The amount of clicks those keywords generate depends on the ad copy you write to accompany the keywords.

Learn About AdWords Accounts

① Navigate to www.google.com/intl/en/adwords/professionals.

● You can join the Google AdWords Certification Program as a company or an individual.

② Click Join the Program and fill in the necessary information to open a Google Certification Program account.

③ Click My Exams Page.

④ Click The Learning Center.

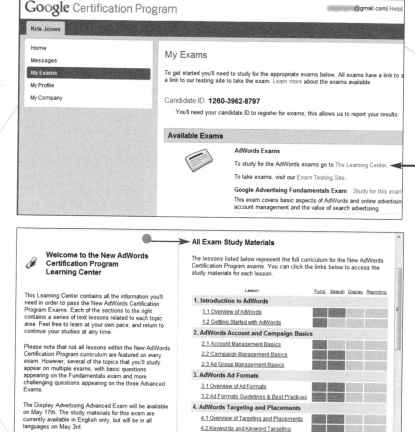

● The Learning Center provides detailed study aids to help you learn more about Google AdWords and prepare to take the certification exam.

Create an AdWords Campaign

Y ou should be prepared to create your first campaign, ad group, text ad, and keywords when you open an AdWords account for the first time. The system requires new advertisers to not only enter basic Web site information, but also complete the steps required to display an actual PPC advertisement before the account creation process can be completed. There is a one-time charge of $5, which you should be prepared to pay with a major credit card prior to account activation.

When you first begin to create your account, you can create a Starter Edition or a Standard Edition AdWords account. The examples in this book use a Standard Edition account; choose a standard account to ensure that your screen matches those depicted in the step-by-step instructions.

The Google AdWords sign-up wizard takes you through the steps necessary to create your account. Once your account is created, you must create a campaign. AdWords campaigns allow you to configure numerous features

such as the daily budget for the campaign, where your advertisements appear, and the language you are targeting. On the campaign level you may also decide whether to show your ads on the Google Content Network. You can also choose to display your advertisements at certain times of the day by using the dayparting feature.

When creating your first campaign, you must also create your first ad group. To do this, you must create an ad variation, select a group of keywords associated with that ad, and configure your maximum, or default, cost-per-click values. Note that if you select default cost-per-click values your default bid will apply to all keywords within a given ad group; however, you may also choose to select maximum cost-per-click values by keyword, which is strongly recommended. Once your first ad group is created, you can always go back and generate more ad groups within that same campaign.

Create an AdWords Campaign

① Navigate to http://adwords.google.com and sign into your AdWords account.

② Click New Campaign.

③ Name your campaign.

④ Choose the geographical locations you want your ads to appear.

⑤ Select the language that your customers speak.

⑥ Complete the remainder of the campaign generation process. When complete, click the Save and Continue button.

Select campaign settings ⟩ Create ad group

Select campaign settings

Load settings ⑦   Campaign type ▾ or Existing campaign ▾

General

Campaign name   Rolex Watches ◄——— ③

Locations and Languages

Locations ⑦   In what geographical locations do you want your ads to appear?
○ Bundle: **All countries and territories**
④ ——► ◉ Bundle: **United States; Canada**
○ Country: **United States**
○ State: **Pennsylvania, US**
Select one or more other locations

⑤ ——► ̇guages ⑦   What languages do your customers speak?
English Edit

Networks and devices

Networks ⑦   ◉ All available sites (Recommended for new advertisers)
○ Let me choose...

---

⑦ Name your ad group.

⑧ Create your first ad.

⑨ Scroll down the page to the Keywords section.

✓ Select campaign settings ⟩ Create ad group

Create ad group

Name this ad group

An ad group should focus on one product or service. Each ad group can contain one or more ads and a set of related keywords, placements, or both.

Ad group name: Oyster Perpetual ◄——— ⑦

Create an ad

◉ Text ad   ○ Image ad   ○ Display ad builder   ○ Mobile ad (WAP only)

Enter your first ad here. You can create more ads later. Help me write an effective text ad.

Headline	Rolex Oyster Perpetual ◄——— ⑧	**Ad preview**
Description line 1	Timeless Elegance & Distinction	Rolex Oyster Perpetual
Description line 2	Official Website of Rolex	Timeless Elegance & Distinction
Display URL	http://www.rolex.com	Official Website of Rolex
Destination URL ⑦	http:// ▾ http://www.rolex.com	http://www.rolex.com

---

Extra

If you already have a Google account such as Gmail or iGoogle, you should use it as your AdWords login. Otherwise, choose a secure e-mail address that you use often and create a password with at least seven characters, both letters and numbers.

You can edit your information, with the exception of currency and time zone, at any time after you verify your account. According to Google, "AdWords is built for change" and it is okay to make mistakes. This is true not only for changing billing information, but also for any of your PPC advertising campaigns. For example, Google provides numerous tools that allow you to make quick edits or mass edits to any of your advertisements. Moreover, with Google you can easily locate ads that are not appearing and quickly determine what needs to be done in order for the ad to show live on the Google search engine.

Note that Google is the largest of all PPC advertising platforms. The other top-tier PPC platforms include Yahoo, MSN, and Ask.com. Second-tier search engines include Miva.com, LookSmart, Kanoodle, and Enhance.com, among others.

continued ——►

T here are many adjustments that you can make to your campaign settings to take advantage of the advanced functionality Google AdWords offers. On the most basic level, you can set a campaign ending date in the case that you are only interested in running your campaign up to a certain date. On a more advanced level, you can choose to set different maximum bids for clicks generated at different times of the day.

Be sure to accurately set a campaign daily budget and select whether you want your budget spent on a "standard" or "accelerated" basis. Choose the Standard setting to allow Google to spread your clicks throughout the day while hitting your daily budget. Choose the Accelerated setting to spend your daily budget as quickly as possible. If you spend your entire daily budget in the

first hour of the day, your ads cannot run for the remaining 23 hours. Try starting with an accelerated ad display to determine how long it takes to spend your daily budget.

Other important options to consider are the opportunity to display your ads only at certain times of the day. Use the AdWords Ad Scheduling feature to adjust the display times of your ads. You can choose to turn your ads on and off throughout the day in 15 minute intervals. You may find that the overnight hours provide traffic but that the traffic does not convert as well as afternoon traffic. In this case, you should either shut down your ads overnight, or you can use a more advanced feature to decrease your maximum keyword bids by a certain percentage during certain hours of the day.

Create an AdWords Campaign *(continued)*

10 Select your keywords.

11 Scroll down the page to the Ad Group Default Bids section.

12 Set your default and content bid.

13 Click Save Ad Group.

● Your ad is now enabled.

14 You can edit your campaign settings at any time; for example, click Add Keywords.

Ad group: Oyster Perpetual

Last 7 days
Apr 23, 2010 - Apr 29, 2010

Rolex Oyster Perpetual
Timeless Elegance & Distinction
Official Website of Rolex
www.rolex.com

1 of 1

● Enabled

Ad group default bids (Max. CPC) Edit ⑦
Default bid $0.05   Content bid $0.05

Settings   Ads   Keywords   Networks   Audiences ▾

All but deleted
Keywords ▾   Segment ▾   Filter ▾   Columns ⦿ ⬇   [   ] Search

These keywords refine search, and determine which placements are good matches for your ads.

View

Apr 23, 2010

14 → + Add keywords   Edit ▾   Change status... ▾   See search terms... ▾   More actions... ▾

		Keyword	Status ⑦	Max. CPC	Clicks	Impr.	CTR ⑦	Avg. CPC ⑦	C
☐	●	rolex oyster perpetual	💬 Eligible	$0.05	0	0	0.00%	$0.00	$0

● Note that you may now add new keywords to your ad group.

Rolex Oyster Perpetual
Timeless Elegance & Distinction
Official Website of Rolex
www.rolex.com

1 of 1

● Enabled

Ad group default bids (Max. CPC) Edit ⑦
Default bid $0.05   Content bid $0.05

Settings   Ads   Keywords   Networks   Audiences ▾

All but deleted
Keywords ▾   Segment ▾   Filter ▾   Columns ⦿ ⬇   [   ] Search

These keywords refine search, and determine which placements are good matches for your ads.

Apr 23, 2010

Add keywords

Enter one keyword per line
You may enter as many as you like Add keywords by spreadsheet

Sample keywords,
For more keywords

```
buy oyster perpetual
official oyster perpetual
```

Category: oyster p
« Add all from t
« Add   oyster
« Add   oyster
« Add   oyster
« Add   oyster

Extra

Another feature offered within the campaign settings is *position preferencing*. If you find that your ads convert best when showing in the second or third position, you can set a position preference for those positions, and the AdWords system attempts to show your ad only when it ranks in the second or third position and not otherwise. If your ad ranks higher than the second or third position, AdWords attempts to lower your maximum cost-per-click so that it falls into your specified range. This feature is similar to what many of the expensive bid management solutions offer. Through constant monitoring of your account, you can determine the optimal position of your ads and use the position preferencing feature to ensure that your ads show in that position. Note that the position preferencing feature takes three to four days to accumulate enough data to make these changes to your ad positions, and that every time you change your position preference the data accumulation process must be repeated. Read more about position preferencing at https://adwords.google.com/support/bin/answer.py?answer=31788&ctx=tltp.

Target Your Campaign

Sometimes you may want to create a new campaign rather than add a new ad group. Language and geographical targeting are established on a campaign level. If you want to isolate different regions with different ad text, you can create a new campaign with specific location and language settings to be sure that your ads are relevant to the users who are searching for them. You can also set separate daily budgets at the campaign level. Many advertisers create a separate campaign for trademarked terms. Trademarked terms tend to lead to a much higher conversion rate than nontrademarked keywords and therefore should be shown at the highest position in the sponsored results. Having trademarked keywords in a separate campaign allows you to set a higher daily budget and separate these unique metrics from the rest of your account, which results in more traffic and more accurate reporting.

Google AdWords allows you to set specific start and end dates for any campaign. You may not want to run certain keywords all year long, but only during a holiday season. If you keep these keywords separate from the rest of your account by placing them in a separate campaign, you can set them to automatically turn on and off when you want them to. You do not ever have to worry about forgetting to run a promotion again.

Finally, Google allows you to run your ads on various partner networks outside of Google.com. You can choose to run your ads on just Google.com, or you can choose to run them on the Google Search Syndication Network, which includes Web sites such as AOL.com, Ask.com, Netscape.com, and many others. Google only allows you to show your ads on all or none of its partners. You do not have the option of choosing among various network partners. The network participation setting is exclusively available at the campaign level. Before you opt out of Google's Syndication Network, you may want to test your ads on the various networks to maximize your return-on-investment.

Target Your Campaign

① Navigate to http://adwords.google.com and sign into your AdWords account.

② Click the Settings tab.

③ Click the Show Ads All Days and Hours link to target your campaign by day and time.

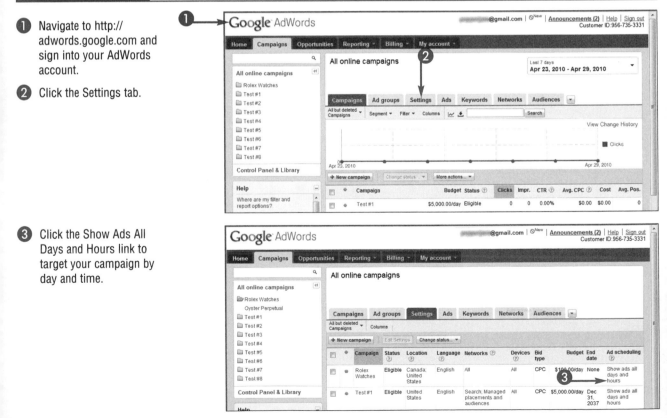

- Note that you can target ads to show only during specific days or specific times of the day.

4 Click any time period to edit the time of day you want your ad to appear. You also have the option of selecting not to show an ad on any particular day.

5 Click Save to save the days and hours you want your ad to appear.

Ad schedule

Edit days and times below. When you're happy with the schedule, click "Save." To bid more or less during particular time periods, switch to the bid adjustment mode. (You can always switch back.)

Reset to all days and hours   Mode: **Basic** | Bid adjustment   Clock: **12 hour** | 24 hour

Day	Time period	Midnight	4:00 AM	8:00 AM	Noon	4:00 PM	8:00 PM
Monday	Midnight - Noon						
Tuesday	Noon - Midnight						
Wednesday	10:00 PM - Midnight						
Thursday	Running all day						
Friday	Noon - 05:00 PM						
Saturday	Running all day						
Sunday	Running all day						

Save   Cancel

- Note that you may also target your campaign by various other factors, including geographic location, language, network, and device.

All online campaigns >
Campaign: Rolex Watches

● Enabled   Budget: **$100.00/day**   Targeting: **All networks   All devices   English   United States; Canada**

Ad groups Settings Ads Keywords Networks Audiences

Campaign settings

General

Campaign name   **Rolex Watches** Edit

Locations and Languages

Locations ⑦   In what geographical locations do you want your ads to appear?
- Country: **Canada**
- Country: **United States**
Edit

Languages ⑦   **English** Edit

Networks and devices

Networks ⑦   **All** Edit
Devices ⑦   **All** Edit

Extra

Google's targeting features work in a number of different ways to ensure that your location and language-targeted campaigns are delivering ads to the correct user demographic. The first thing Google verifies is the user's *IP address*. An IP address is a unique number assigned to each computer connected to the Internet and usually denotes a general physical location.

Google also has more than 100 country-specific domains such as .com and .fr. A keyword targeted to France appears only on www.google.fr, which is the URL used to access Google in France. This is another way that Google ensures that your ads appear when you specify a geographical location.

Another Google AdWords targeting option is query parsing. For example, if a user searches for the keyword "Philadelphia bookstores" and you have the keyword "bookstores" targeted to the Philadelphia geographical region, your ad appears to that user.

Another variable you can use to target users is through Google's language preference feature. Be careful at the campaign level when you select a language other than English to display ads in English-speaking locations such as the United States, Canada, and the United Kingdom because your language preference applies to all ads within the campaign.

Write Effective Ad Copy

Each of your Google AdWords text ads contains exactly four lines of text. Although text ads have limited space, you can maximize that space with effectively written ad text. The ad consists of a headline, two lines of description, and a display URL that tells users what site they will visit when they click the ad. Specific character limits exist for each line of text. A headline can be up to 25 characters long, and the description lines may contain up to 35 characters. For a complete list of requirements, consult the AdWords Editorial Guidelines at http://adwords.google.com/support/aw/bin/static.py?hl=en&page=guidelines.cs.

The headline of your ad should be as closely related to the keywords within the ad group as possible. If a keyword appears anywhere within a text ad, Google shows that word in bold text, and your ad has a better chance of standing out among competitors.

With regard to the description lines, you should be as specific as possible about the service your Web site offers. Avoid vague calls to action or hyped-up slogans. You want users to know exactly what to expect when they visit your page. Remember, you are paying every time your ad is clicked. Be honest and clear so that customers click your ad only if they are motivated to make a purchase on your site.

The display URL must accurately represent the page the user is being directed to or Google will not show your ad. The display URL does not, however, need to be a real address. For example, if you are targeting users in New York City, you may want your display URL to show as www.Website.com/NYC, even though this is not a real page on your Web site. Your display URL helps target your ad; users may feel your Web site is more relevant to their specific needs and therefore be more likely to click your ad instead of a competitor's ad.

Write Effective Ad Copy

Analyze a Competitor's Ads

1. Navigate to www.google.com.

2. Type a keyword that you are creating an ad for.

- Analyze your competitors' ads to see what types of ads are currently being run.

Create a New Text Ad

1. Log into your AdWords account and click a campaign.

② Click New Ad Group.

③ Name your new ad group.

④ Write a headline for your new ad using keywords that directly relate to the keywords you want the ad to appear for.

⑤ Write a description that is likely to entice someone to click your ad. For example, keywords such as *Official Web site* add credibility and *timeless elegance and distinction* communicate value.

⑥ Scroll to the bottom of the page to complete the required information and then click Save Ad Group.

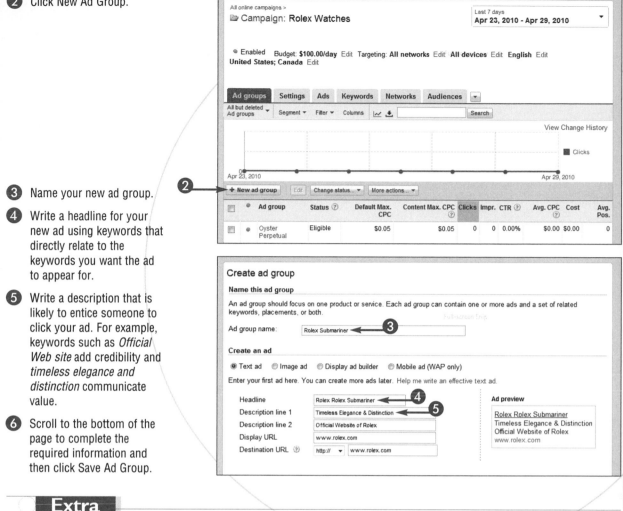

Extra

Google AdWords includes a useful feature called Dynamic Keyword Insertion, which allows ad text to automatically be inserted into your ad based on the specific keyword a user types into the search engine. Using Google's dynamic keyword insertion functionality is a highly effective technique and recommended in most instances. When used correctly, it allows Google to automatically enter the user's search query into the text of your ad.

To use Google's dynamic keyword insertion, you have to add the following phrase into your ad text: {keyword:}. Here is an example of dynamic keyword insertion being used in the headline of a text ad.

> {keyword:Shop For Books Here}
> Used and rare books available.
> Best-sellers available too!
> www.example.com

In this example, if the user were to search for the term "NYC Bookstores," the ad would automatically show the keyword as the headline.

> NYC Bookstores
> Used and rare books available.
> Best-sellers available too!
> www.example.com

If the user searched for a keyword that was too long to appear in its entirety, Google would default to the back-up phrase entered and the headline would appear as "Shop For Books Here."

Experiment with this technique in every line of your ad and see what works best for you. It is an easy way to make sure your ad copy is precisely targeted to the customer's needs, without having to create a specific ad group and ad for every keyword in your account.

Using Keyword Matching Options

An important component of keyword generation on Google AdWords is selecting the correct matching option for each keyword. You can use keyword match options to improve your PPC efforts by making sure that your text ads show when you want them to based on various keyword matching options. There are three main options: broad, phrase, and exact match. Each matching type limits or increases the likelihood that your ad triggers for a given keyword. Broad match is the default setting for every keyword. Therefore, all of your keywords will display on broad match unless you specify otherwise by adding "quotes" around the keyword for phrase match or [brackets] around the keyword for exact match. For example, the syntax for phrase match is "example" and the syntax for exact match is [example].

Broad match keywords trigger your ad whenever an exact keyword or a similar one is typed into a search engine. For example, broad match displays ads for keyword misspellings, plurals, and common synonyms. Broad match also triggers your ad no matter the order in which multiple keywords are entered into the search engine. For example, the broad keyword "buy books online" triggers an ad even when "buy online books" is searched. *Phrase*

match keywords trigger your ad whenever a keyword phrase is entered into a search engine in the same exact sequence. However, a user entering additional words before or after the query will not prevent the ad from triggering. For example, the keyword phrase "books online" triggers an ad if the user searches for "buy books online" but not if the user searches for "buy online books."

The third and most precise match type is called exact match. *Exact match keywords* trigger ads only when the search-engine user's query exactly matches the keyword you have chosen. Unlike the phrase match, if a user enters anything before or after the chosen keyword, your ad is not triggered. For example, the exact keyword "books online" shows only when users enter "books online" exactly as their search query. If a user searches for "buy books online," the ad is not shown.

You should test which match types work best with each specific keyword. Some keywords perform better using broad keyword match, and some perform better as an exact match keyword. Do not be afraid to create a keyword with all three match types; after a week or two, delete the two that do not perform as well as the third.

Using Keyword Matching Options

① Navigate to http://adwords.google.com and sign into your AdWords account.

② Click a campaign.

③ Click the ad group you want to add keywords to.

④ Click the Add Keywords tab.

5 Review the various advanced match type options.

6 Apply advanced match types to your new keywords.

7 Click Save.

- Note the new keywords with advanced match options are in your Google AdWords account.

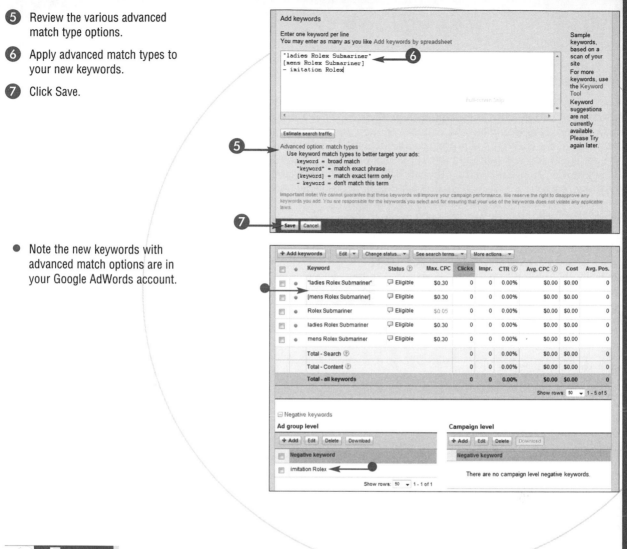

Extra

There is a fourth type of keyword that you can add to your account that is not really a keyword at all. *Negative match keywords* do not trigger ads; rather, they prevent your ads from showing when a certain term is part of the search query. One of the most common negative keywords used is "free." If you sell a product like books, you most likely do not want your ad to appear when a user searches for "free books online" or "free books." Using the negative keyword "free" prevents your ad from showing when "free books online" or "free books" is entered into a search engine.

Negative keywords can also be used with phrase and exact type keywords to prevent ads from showing for more specific terms. Google calls this *embedded match* and it is a more advanced form of keyword matching. If an advertiser sells Harry Potter books but does not want to show for the term "Harry Potter," it can be added as an embedded match. If an advertiser does this, the ads trigger for the term "Harry Potter books" but not the term "Harry Potter."

Set Bidding Strategies

etting bid strategies enables you to maximize your exposure on PPC search engines such as Google and Yahoo. For example, when you set a maximum bid in the AdWords platform, you are telling Google how much you are willing to pay for a click on a specific keyword. You are not setting the amount you automatically pay for each click. Based on what other advertisers are bidding for the same keyword, you may be charged less for each click; the only guarantee is that you will never be charged more than the limit you set.

Your maximum bid is the main factor in determining how high your ad will be shown in the sponsored search results. If you bid higher than other advertisers for the same term, your ad will most likely appear in the top three positions. If you bid too low you may not even show on the first page of results, or sometimes your ad will not appear at all. If your max bid is too low for your

keyword to be shown at all, the keyword is considered inactive for search. Note that just because you are willing to pay more than other advertisers for a particular keyword does not guarantee you will rank in the top few positions for that keyword. Instead, Google takes into consideration other factors, such as the quality and relevancy of your ad text compared to the keyword, as well as the quality and relevance of your landing page.

Bids are something you must monitor on a daily basis. Your competitors will try to edge your ads out of positioning on a regular basis, and you need to be aware of what is happening on the results pages in order to maintain your desired position. In addition, you will want to experiment often by bidding differently based on match type, geographical location, and other factors to maximize your return-on-investment.

Set Bidding Strategies

1 Navigate to http:// adwords.google.com and sign into your AdWords account.

2 Click a campaign.

3 Click the ad group within which you want to edit bids.

4 Select the keywords you want to edit.

5 Click Edit and from the drop-down menu select Edit in Table.

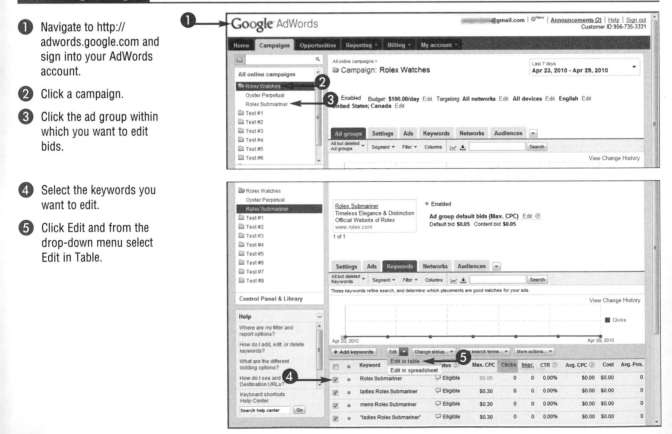

6 Edit one or more of your keyword bids.

7 Click Save.

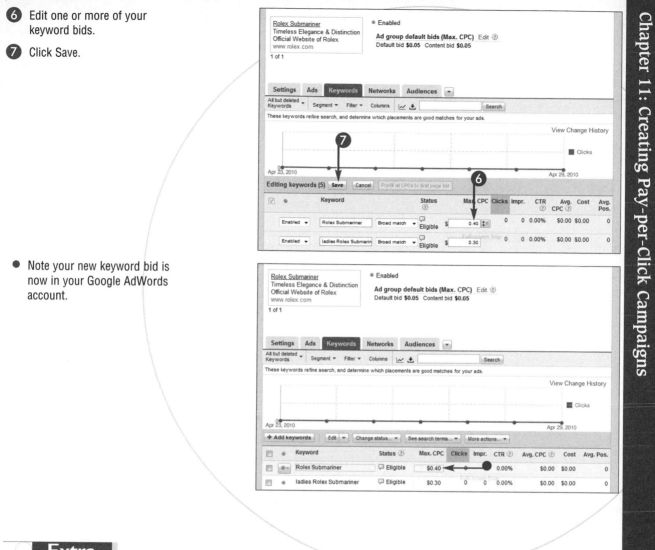

● Note your new keyword bid is now in your Google AdWords account.

Extra

When determining your bidding strategy, ask yourself the following question: How much is this keyword worth to my overall campaign? If you expect a keyword to drive a lot of sales, you want that particular keyword to have a large budget and to be positioned where it will be shown to most users. A high maximum bid with a position strategy of one to three would be a good idea for such a keyword.

On the other hand, if you have a keyword that you suspect may perform poorly but you still want it to appear on Google, you want to set a low max bid. This way, the ad shows lower in the results but still has a chance of being clicked. This could result in an occasional low-cost conversion that you may not have otherwise gotten if you chose not to run the keyword at all.

It takes time to figure out what works for your particular product. Do not be impatient with your bidding strategies. Once you optimize your keyword bids, your account will perform to its full potential, but you will have to actively manage the account to maintain your success.

Run
PPC Reports

The Google AdWords Report Center is a powerful feature of your AdWords account that enables you to create fully customized reports. The Report Center allows you to run reports on the account, campaign, ad group, and keyword levels. Important data about the performance of your Google AdWords account is available to you through the Reporting Center.

The Google AdWords Report Center allows you to pinpoint what is and is not working within your AdWords account. You can run reports on a daily basis at the keyword level to maximize your return-on-investment at a very granular level, and also run detailed historical reports to discover what keywords have performed well in the past.

An account-level report can show you if your account is performing as well as it did last month, and is an effective way to track the progress of your online marketing efforts. In addition to detailed numeric-based reporting, the Google AdWords Report Center allows you to view graphs and charts for a visual representation of your account's overall performance.

Google AdWords allows you to easily export a report in Microsoft Excel. You can use Google's export function to save a copy of the report on your PC, e-mail it to a colleague, and customize the report with your logo. If you are producing a report for a client, you can export it and customize it based on your client's unique needs. Moreover, you can have Google e-mail various reports to anyone you want at any time of the day automatically via report scheduling.

You should spend some time in the Report Center experimenting with different options and features. You may not be aware how helpful a report may be until you run it and see the data it provides.

Run PPC Reports

1. Navigate to http://adwords.google.com and sign into your AdWords account.

2. Click the Reporting tab.

3. Click the Create a New Report link.

4. Choose the report type.

5. Choose the report view.

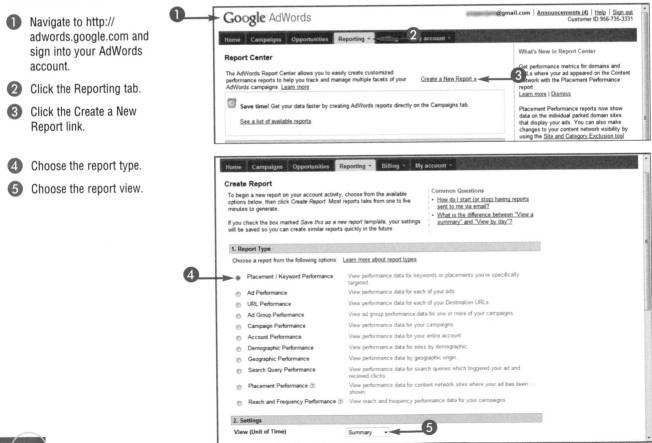

6 Choose the date range.

7 Name your report.

8 Click Create Report.

2. Settings

View (Unit of Time)   Summary

Date Range   ● Last month
                               ○ 5/1/10 - 5/1/10

Campaigns and Ad Groups   ● All campaigns and all their ad groups
                               ○ Manually select from a list

3. Advanced Settings (Optional)

▶ Add or Remove Columns

▶ Filter Your Results

4. Templates, Scheduling, and Email

Name Your Report   Placement / Keyword Report

Template   ☐ Save this as a new report template

Scheduling   ☐ Schedule this report to run automatically: every day

Email   ☐ Whenever the report runs, send email to:

                               For multiple recipients, separate email addresses with commas.
                               ☐ with report attached as: xml

Create Report

9 Click Placement / Keyword Report to view your report.

● Note that you can create a similar report or delete the existing report.

Google AdWords

@gmail.com | Announcements (4) | Help | Sign out
Customer ID:956-735-3331

Home | Campaigns | Opportunities | Reporting ▾ | Billing ▾ | My account ▾

Report Center

The AdWords Report Center allows you to easily create customized performance reports to help you track and manage multiple facets of your AdWords campaigns. Learn more   Create a New Report »

💤 Save time! Get your data faster by creating AdWords reports directly on the Campaigns tab.

See a list of available reports

Last 15 Reports

View your recently created reports here. Your account will save a maximum of 15 reports at any one time.

Report Name	Date Range	Requested ↓	Status	Create Similar	Delete
Placement / Keyword Report	Apr 1, 2010 - Apr 30, 2010	May 1, 2010 8:06:36 AM	Completed	Create Similar	Delete

Show rows: 10 ▾ 1 - 1 of 1 ◀ ▶

What's New in Report Center

Get performance metrics for domains and URLs where your ad appeared on the Content Network with the Placement Performance report.
Learn more | Dismiss

Placement Performance reports now show data on the individual parked domain sites that display your ads. You can also make changes to your content network visibility by using the Site and Category Exclusion tool
Learn more | Dismiss

Common Questions

• What kind of reports will I get?
• In which formats can I download my reports?
• How do I download a report for a specific campaign?

Win customers, not just visitors

Extra

Report scheduling is a great way to stay up-to-date with your account. The AdWords Report Center allows you to schedule automatic reports that are delivered to any e-mail addresses you designate. You can schedule these reports to run daily, every Monday, or on the first of every month. You can also set the report format of your choice. You can also have the report sent to multiple e-mail addresses.

Note that the Report Center delivers the files in a compressed, Zip format. The report must be less than 2MB in order for the report to be sent to an e-mail address. If the file is larger than 2MB, you are notified that you must view the report through the Report Center. You always have the option to download the report directly from the Report Center to your computer if the report is too big to send via e-mail.

You can cancel an automated report any time by going into the Report Center and deleting the report. You can also make any changes to the report if you decide later to include or exclude any information.

Track Conversions

Tracking your Web site conversions enables you to identify and evaluate the success of your advertising and traffic generation efforts. A conversion identifies a specific action performed on your Web site, such as an e-commerce transaction or an e-mail submission.

A key factor in the setup of your Google AdWords account is the installation of conversion tracking code on your Web site. Conversion tracking allows Google to monitor what occurs on your Web site after a potential customer clicks an AdWords advertisement, and to report back to you when a defined conversion occurs. When you enable conversion tracking, Google installs a cookie on the user's browser as soon as one of your ads is clicked. If the click results in a conversion, the Google cookie passes that information back to the AdWords interface and reports the transaction.

Once Google's conversion tracking registers a conversion, the transaction is defined as a *cost-per-action*.

Cost-per-action is the total amount spent divided by the number of conversions and is reported at the campaign level. If you are generating conversions at a cost-per-action at or below your minimum return-on-investment, you are making money.

During the conversion confirmation process, regardless of whether the traction is e-commerce or lead generation, customers are notified that Google is tracking their information with an option to view the AdWords Privacy Policy. This notification appears only if the customer has reached your Web site through the AdWords system. The customer's personal information such as name, address, and credit card is not tracked or recorded.

The Google cookie remains on customers' browsers for up to 30 days to ensure that customers who do not make a purchase immediately are still tracked if they decide to return to the Web site at a later date to complete their order.

Track Conversions

① Navigate to http://adwords.google.com and sign into your AdWords account.

② Click Reporting.

③ From the drop-down menu click Conversions.

④ Click New Conversion.

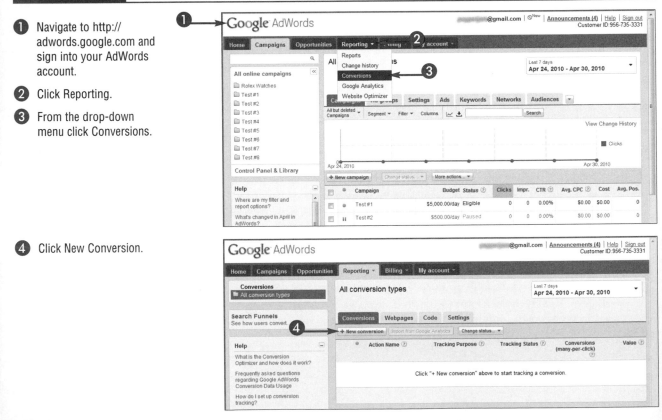

5 Name your action.

6 From the drop-down menu select a tracking purpose, Lead, for example.

7 Click Save and Continue.

8 Provide details about the page where your conversion will be tracked.

9 Click Save and Get Code. Place the code on your site as instructed to begin tracking conversions.

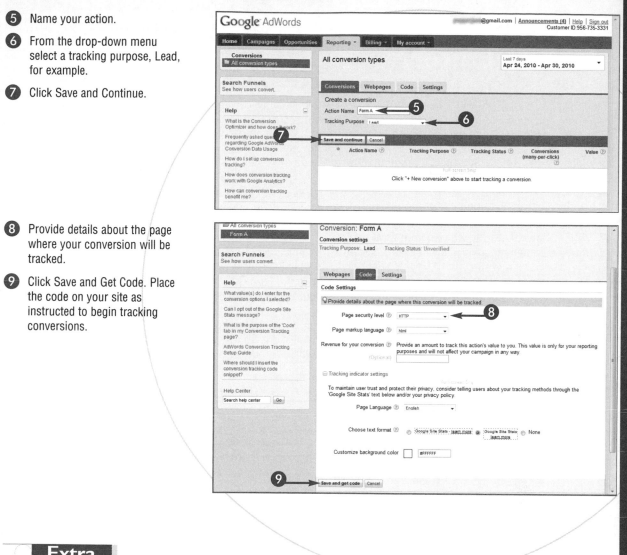

Extra

For advanced conversion tracking, Google offers four primary types of unique conversions you can define. The Purchase/Sale label is used by online commerce sites to track individual customer orders including the revenue that the sale generated. The Lead label allows you to track how many users visited a certain page and entered their contact information. The Lead label may be useful for a Web site whose primary purpose is to drive leads for a business or an e-commerce site that sends catalogs. The Sign-Ups label tracks how many users may have subscribed to a newsletter, downloaded a document, or requested e-mail updates from the site. Finally, the Page Views label can tell you when a visitor browses a valuable page on the site. If your phone number is on the site, you may want to compare how many times it was viewed to how many times it was called.

Google does not limit your ability to define unique conversions. If you want to define your own conversion criteria, you can select the Other label and track whatever data you want. For example, you could track how many people click a specified link such as a "buy it now" button versus how many exit the page with the back button. Also, you could measure newsletter signups on one or more pages of your Web site.

Using Google AdWords Editor

As your AdWords account grows larger, it becomes increasingly more difficult to manage. Google's AdWords Editor helps advertisers manage large accounts and enables you to edit your accounts while offline. AdWords Editor, located at www.google.com/intl/en/adwordseditor, is a free software application that works on both Windows and Apple computers and is continually updated for optimal performance.

AdWords Editor allows you to download your account, make additions and changes at any level of your account, and then post those changes directly to Google when you are done. You can work on your AdWords accounts from any location and then simply post those changes when you are able to connect to the Internet.

However, AdWords Editor is best used for making bulk changes to your account. It can quickly and easily create multiple campaigns, ad groups, text ads, and keywords by allowing you to copy and paste directly from a Microsoft Excel worksheet or text file. There is also a search capability within Editor that allows you to search throughout multiple campaigns and make changes to the individual ads and keywords that meet your criteria.

Another helpful feature of AdWords Editor is the Revert Selected Changes button. If you are working on your account and make any kind of mistake, you can revert that change immediately without uploading it to Google. This can save you time and allows you to see how changes will look in your account without actually implementing them.

Finally, you need not worry about Google's editorial guidelines while utilizing AdWords Editor. If you create a text ad that does not comply with the guidelines, the program alerts you immediately. This ensures that all of your copy is properly formatted when it is sent to the search engine.

Using Google AdWords Editor

① Navigate to www.google.com/intl/en/adwordseditor to download Google AdWords Editor.

② Click Download AdWords Editor.

③ Click Run and follow the steps to download Google AdWords Editor to your computer.

④ Open AdWords Editor and import your AdWords account by clicking File → Open Account.

⑤ Enter the username and password for your Google AdWords account.

● AdWords Editor imports the account.

You can now manage your campaigns, ad groups, ads, keywords, and more within AdWords Editor.

Many useful, advanced options are available with AdWords Editor. For example, with a simple click of a button the program displays duplicate keywords that you are unaware of and provides functionality to easily delete them. Duplicate keywords compete against one another and drive up the cost of your campaigns.

Performance statistics are also available through the AdWords Editor interface. When working on campaigns it is sometimes useful to see how a keyword or text ad has performed in the past. Statistics are available from a customizable date range and are updated any time you request them from Google. Statistics are an integral part of optimizing the performance of your online campaigns and should be utilized on a weekly basis to adjust bids and track performance.

A final, important feature of AdWords Editor is the capability to download complete exports of your AdWords account. This makes it easy to keep backup copies of your account information. If you chose to download your account monthly, you can always import an older version of your campaigns if they were performing better in the past.

Optimize Your Account

To get the most out of your PPC account, you should monitor your account on a daily basis. From keyword bids to ad copy, every aspect of a campaign needs to be monitored and tweaked in order to perform at an optimal level. In addition, you should actively take steps to grow your account as part of your ongoing account optimization strategy.

If your account is not receiving the amount of traffic you think it should, one thing you may need to do is increase your bids in order to get your ads ranked higher. Increasing bids is an easy way to increase the amount of clicks your ads receive. When you click a campaign in your AdWords account, you see a list of your ad groups and the average position of each group. Keep in mind that an ad group that has an average position of 12 or higher does not show on the first page of the search results. This ad group will drive much more traffic if the bids are raised.

The ad copy you are running throughout your account is a very important factor to evaluate when optimizing your campaigns. The text ads triggered when a keyword is searched determine if the customer clicks your link or one of your competitor's. You should always test multiple ad variations at the same time. After a few hundred clicks are accumulated, you can make educated decisions about the ads you chose. If a particular ad is not performing well, delete it. If a different ad is performing exceptionally, improve upon the wording and run similar variations. Also note that Google randomly serves all of the text ads that you have designated to a particular ad group until one ad generates a higher overall click-through rate than the other ads. Google then shows the text ad with the higher click-through rate over the underperforming ads.

Finally, conversion tracking is essential to optimizing your campaign. If a particular keyword is driving clicks but no conversions, or if the keyword is driving unprofitable conversions, the keyword should be deleted. If another keyword is converting well, raise the bids and increase the traffic it drives to your site until you find the perfect balance between generating conversions and return-on-investment.

Optimize Your Account

Review Ad Position

① Navigate to www.google.com/search?adtest=on.

② Enter one of your keywords in the search box.

③ Click Google Search.

● Examine your ad's placement.

Optimize Ad Position

1. Log into your AdWords account.

2. Enter the same keyword in the Search My Campaigns search box.

3. Click the search icon.

4. Find the keyword you are looking for and click it.

5. You can edit the bids, edit or add new ad copy, and change match options as necessary to optimize your ad.

Note: *See the previous task to edit your ad using AdWords Editor.*

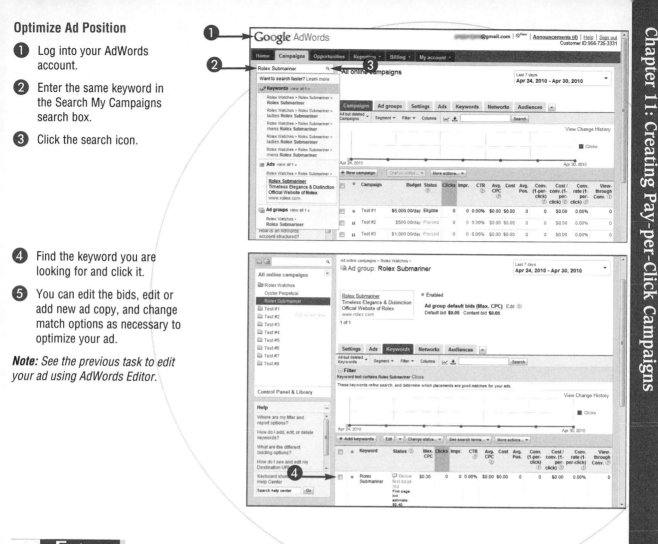

Extra

On-site optimization is one aspect of PPC marketing that is sometimes overlooked. This is where your SEO efforts coincide with your pay-per-click efforts. The more relevant Google determines your site to be for a particular keyword, the less, on average, you are charged per click.

An optimized landing page results not only in lower prices on Google AdWords, but also in a higher conversion rate. When customers are directed to your site through a paid advertisement, you should direct them to the most relevant page to the keyword that was searched. The fewer times potential customers have to click to navigate your site, the more likely they are to make a purchase. Remember, you are charged for a click no matter what, so send the visitor to a targeted landing page.

Finally, remember to always restate the value proposition that drove the customer to the site in the first place. If your text ad includes the phrase "Free Shipping," be sure that the offer is repeated on the Web site. If it is not repeated, customers may think they were led to the site under false pretenses and immediately navigate away from the site rather than explore further.

An Introduction to Quality Score Optimization

In early 2007, Google announced the addition of *quality score* to its AdWords pay-per-click, or *PPC*, platform. Google introduced quality score to ensure that advertisers with the most relevant PPC campaigns rank highest within the Google-sponsored results listings. In the past, advertisers willing to pay more for each click could rank as high as they chose for just about any keyword they wanted. This led to those advertisers with the highest budget and risk tolerance monopolizing the sponsored results; those with limited budgets and less risk tolerance were left behind. Google's introduction of quality score is a sign that Google is interested in serving advertisements that lead to the most relevant search results and overall user satisfaction.

Learn About Quality Score

Recently other leading search engines, including Yahoo Search Marketing and Microsoft's adCenter, have followed Google's lead by introducing quality-based PPC search algorithms. This algorithmic shift within the PPC industry has caused much concern on the part of advertisers who previously were able to gain top placement almost solely based on a willingness to pay more than the competition. Now, in order to succeed, advertisers must approach PPC advertising differently, optimizing the quality score factors that Google and others use when ranking PPC ads.

Quality score-based algorithms take into consideration numerous ranking factors, including the overall quality of your landing page, the structure of your ad groups and campaigns, click-through rate, ad copy, and keyword bid, among other things. One of the major benefits of a high-quality score is a lower overall cost-per-click, which leads to a lower cost-per-conversion across the campaign. In addition, ads with a higher-quality score tend to be ranked higher, on average, regardless of how much an advertiser specifies as a maximum cost-per-click.

Optimize Quality Score

There are some simple and complex methods you can use to optimize your PPC account and generate higher-quality scores. Structuring your account properly is the first, and most important, step of the quality-score-optimization process. Other steps include the quality of the landing pages and the effectiveness of the ad copy.

Test Ad Copy

One of the most important things to do when optimizing an online marketing campaign is to test and retest all your quality-score-optimization strategies. There are limitless tests you can perform on your ad copy, and you can monitor the results using various free tools that Google provides. See Chapter 11 for more information on writing effective ad copy.

Test Keywords Based on Match Type

You can accumulate important information about your keyword performance by testing various match types within your account. You can easily set up and monitor broad, phrase, and exact match ad groups in order to see what is and is not working for you. You should never be hesitant about testing new things. It is the only way to see what kind of traffic is out there and how valuable these keywords are to your PPC campaign.

Test Ad Copy with Advanced Keyword Insertion

By merely inserting your keywords dynamically into your ad copy, you can dramatically increase the clicks your ads receive. There are various options available to you within the AdWords platform, each with different benefits and drawbacks. The only way to decide what works best is to test each one while monitoring the effect each has on your account.

Using Placement-Targeted Campaigns

Placement-targeted campaigns are similar to campaigns on the Google Content Network, but allow you more control over what sites your advertisements are shown on and where on those sites your ad can appear. By learning the differences between networks, you can intelligently decide which method is right for you and your product.

Using Content-Targeted Campaigns

Different types of networks are available to AdWords advertisers as well as different methods of displaying and monetizing ads each network presents. The Google Content Network is one of these channels; it allows you to display your ad on many different Web sites that have something in common with your product. In this chapter you learn how to utilize this avenue and become successful outside the search results.

Test Performance with Dayparting

Some advanced techniques that are used in other forms of marketing translate well to the PPC advertising model. *Dayparting* is a practice widely used by radio and television broadcasters that you may find useful to your online marketing efforts. Just as broadcasters notice different trends across various times of day, online marketers notice similar trends. Learning to have these trends work for you is a very useful skill to possess.

Optimize Your Landing Pages

This chapter shows you how to study the pages you are driving customers to, the *landing pages*, and see how certain aspects of these pages influence customers to make purchases or navigate further into your site. Everything from color to font size comes into play when potential customers visit your site, and understanding how to measure and achieve success is key to improving your quality score and making the most out of every advertising dollar you spend.

After you understand how deep you can dive into your online campaigns, you are armed with the knowledge you need to control the traffic available to your Web site and achieve the greatest return-on-investment possible. The tools to marketing success are completely at your fingertips in the online world, and knowing how to use those tools is a large part of the battle. If you are aware of what is possible, there is nothing holding you back from making the most out of every dollar you spend online to advertise your Web site. As the awareness of your site grows through these paid platforms, free publicity often results from the increased exposure, and you see your search-engine-optimization efforts blossom as a result.

If there is one thing you should take from this chapter, it is this: The best thing you can do for your PPC campaign is to remember your ABTs, that is, **a**lways **b**e **t**esting.

Learn About Quality Score

To build a successful PPC campaign you must optimize the factors that influence quality score such as landing-page relevance and keyword performance. The goals of the major search engines are twofold: Improve end-user experience, and increase shareholder profitability. Although the algorithms search engines use to calculate quality score are not public information, countless advertisers and search-engine marketing professionals have provided data that contribute to a solid understanding of the most important quality score factors.

One factor is landing-page relevance. Bidding on a keyword that is unrelated to the content of your landing page often results in a cost-per-click penalty. Google penalizes you by raising the minimum cost-per-click for nonrelevant keywords to an amount that can make profitability impossible. The same applies to your organic rankings. If your Web page is unrelated to the search query, it does not show in the results. The paid search ranking algorithms are becoming synonymous with the organic ranking algorithms, so be sure that your PPC keywords are relevant to their respective landing pages.

Another important factor is keyword performance. The search engines such as Google, Yahoo, and Bing that provide a pay-per-click advertising service make money when users click the paid ads. Keeping this in mind, you can figure out that certain keyword and ad copy combinations earn the search engines more money than others. These pay-per-click search engines show ads based on an algorithm that determines maximum profitability for the search engines. The driving force behind this algorithm is the *click-through rate*, or the ratio of clicks on an ad to the number of times that ad appears. You can lower your average cost-per-click of a keyword by increasing your click-through rates. Often, you can pay less for a higher position than your competitors if the click-through rates of your keyword and ad combinations are higher.

Google has admitted that more than 100 factors are involved in determining quality score, but you cannot optimize for all those factors because you cannot know what they are. You are best served by optimizing your landing pages for relevancy and optimizing your ad copy for click-through rates.

Learn About Quality Score

Review Your Quality Score

1. Navigate to http://adwords.google.com and sign into your AdWords account.

2. Open your campaign and ad group.

3. Click the Status icon.

Note: See the next task for more information about opening your campaign and ad group.

- The quality score appears here.

Learn about Quality Score

1. Navigate to http://adwords.google.com/support/aw/?hl=en.

2. Click the Ad Position and Quality link.

3. Click the Quality Score link.

4. Click a topic link.

   Review the documentation on a regular basis.

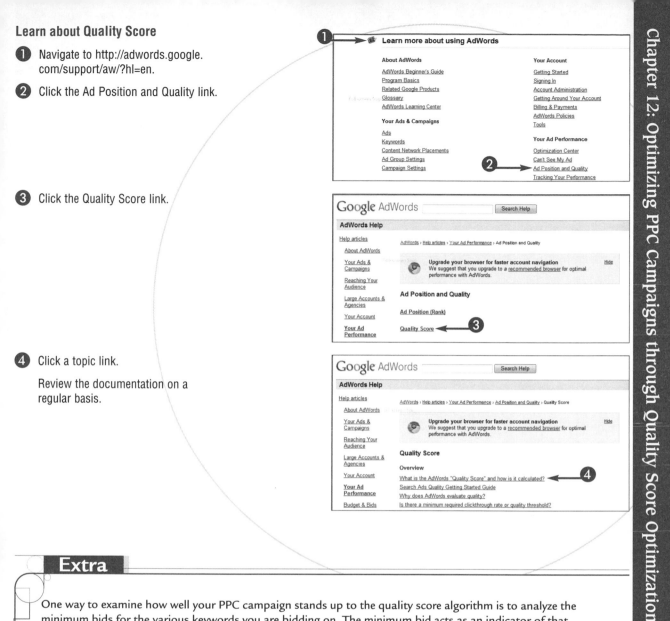

Extra

One way to examine how well your PPC campaign stands up to the quality score algorithm is to analyze the minimum bids for the various keywords you are bidding on. The minimum bid acts as an indicator of that keyword's quality. For example, keywords with a high minimum bid have the lowest quality score, and inversely those with the lowest minimum bid have the highest quality score.

In Google's case, keywords with high-quality scores tend to average about $.05 per click. The search engines flag keywords with minimum bids of $1.00, $5.00, or more as low quality. Sometimes you should just remove these low-quality keywords, especially if they are not relevant to your campaign. Other times, you may want to keep those keywords active. This involves making changes to your landing pages and ad copy to increase relevancy.

Google builds trust in the advertiser over the course of a PPC campaign. Google has an interest in keeping its long-term users happy. Therefore, with greater trust from Google comes lower cost per clicks and higher rankings. In this way, PPC campaigns are becoming more and more like search-engine-optimization campaigns where longevity alone can provide positive results.

Optimize Quality Score

A campaign optimized for quality score can result in a greater return-on-investment from your PPC efforts. To optimize your PPC account, consider the overall campaign and ad group structure, keyword choice, and ad copy.

An optimal campaign and ad group structure does not directly increase quality score, but it does make it easier for you to navigate the PPC account and increase the relevance of your keywords within ad groups. Ad groups contain a group of keywords and ad copy and show when those keywords are searched. The more specific your ad groups, the more specific your ad copy can be for those ad groups. This increases keyword-to-ad copy relevancy and in turn can raise click-through rates. If you sell basketball shoes, create an ad group called Basketball Shoes, and within that ad group you should only have keywords that are directly related to the basketball shoes you sell. You can get even more specific and create ad

groups for every brand of basketball shoes that are sold. The more specific the ad groups, the more specific you can make the ads contained within.

Using the example above, if you are creating ads for your Basketball Shoes ad group, make sure that each ad clearly states that you are selling basketball shoes. Mention basketball shoes as many times as possible in the ad text.

The final step is to make sure you are sending the customer to the most relevant landing page. Again, if your keyword is "basketball shoes" and your ad copy states, "We sell Basketball Shoes!" be sure that when customers click your ad they are taken directly to your basketball shoes page.

The synergy between the keyword, ad copy, and landing page within ad groups is something you can control and optimize to increase quality score.

Optimize Quality Score

① Navigate to http://adwords.google.com.

② Sign into your AdWords account.

③ Click the campaign you want to investigate.

④ Click the ad group you want to investigate.

⑤ Click the status icon to view the quality score.

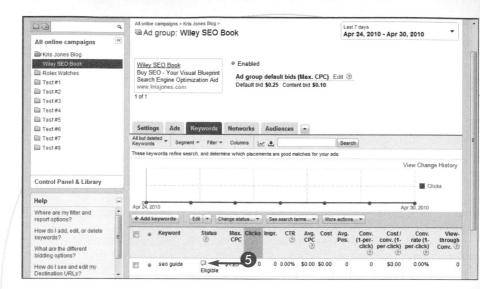

● Notice the quality score shown for your keyword.

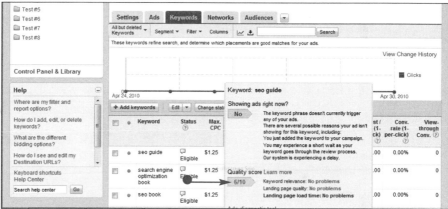

Extra

If a keyword does not seem to be performing well for you, do not necessarily give up on it immediately. Try creating a new, more specific ad group for that keyword and other keywords like it. Write new ad copy with that keyword in the text. You might even want to go as far as creating a new page on your Web site that revolves around that term.

Another easy way to ensure your campaigns are well optimized is to look at the number of specific pages that make up your Web site. A campaign that is correctly quality-score optimized should have at least one ad group for each page within the site. For example, if your Web page is made up of ten separate pages, your PPC campaign should have at least ten different ad groups within it.

Study the structure of your site and create your campaign structure with that in mind. Suppose you have a site dedicated to shoes, and within that site you have a page for tennis shoes, basketball shoes, and running shoes. Consider creating a PPC campaign called Shoes and ad groups within it called Tennis Shoes, Basketball Shoes, and Running Shoes.

Test Ad Copy

A d copy testing is a crucial step in optimizing your PPC account for quality score. Good ad copy causes high click-through rates, and high click-through rates increase keyword performance quality scores. This leads to lower cost-per-clicks and higher ad ranking positions.

Naturally, you should make sure your ad copy is relevant to the keywords located in that ad group. You should try to use the keywords in the ad copy whenever possible. Searchers want to see that the searched keywords are somewhere in the ads they are presented with.

Unfortunately, you are not given much space to work with when creating ads. Google, for example, allows only a 25-character headline, followed by two 35-character description lines, and finally a display URL. Because you have limited space to create an ad, use strong words that influence a searcher's motivation to buy. Words such as

"guaranteed" and strong calls to action like "order now!" motivate searchers to act. Value propositions such as free shipping or price matching are also important to consider when you analyze your marketing competition. The Internet allows shoppers to easily find the best prices and offers online. If your competitors offer perks and values that you do not, you cannot really compete with them.

Try to separate yourself as much as possible from your competition when you write PPC ads. Test numerous ads at the same time, and monitor them closely for differences in click-through and *conversion rates*, the percentage of clicks on your ads that result in a sale. Although increasing click-through rates is important for quality-score optimization, sometimes running ads with lower click-through rates but higher conversion rates is more profitable. Constant testing is the only way to find that perfect ad copy and keyword combination.

Test Ad Copy

① Navigate to http://adwords.google.com and sign into your AdWords account.

Note: *See the previous task for more information about opening your AdWords account.*

② Click the Reporting tab.

③ Click the Create a New Report link.

④ Select the Ad Performance report.

⑤ Choose the data you want the report to include.

⑥ Click the Create Report button.

- You are returned to the Report Center where you can see the recently created reports.

7 Click the name of the report to view the data.

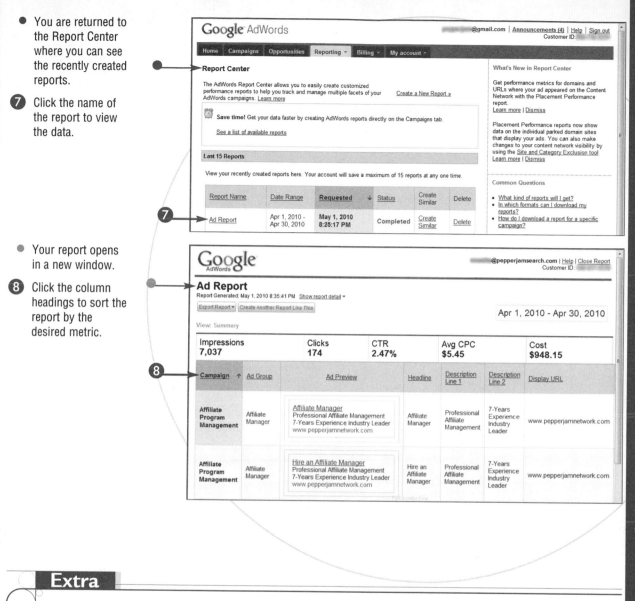

- Your report opens in a new window.

8 Click the column headings to sort the report by the desired metric.

Test Keywords Based on Match Type

As discussed in the previous chapter, Google offers three match types that you can use when you create keyword lists. You can use these match types to show your ad when people search for keywords or phrases that you have not included in your ad groups. These match types are called *broad*, *phrase*, and *exact*.

Broad-matched keywords can generate ads when users search for any variation of that keyword, even synonyms of that keyword. Phrase-matched keywords generate ads as long as the search query contains that phrase. For example, if your ad group contains the phrase-matched keyword "red shoes," your ad may be triggered when someone searches for "size 11 red shoes." Exact-matched keywords can only generate an ad when someone searches for that exact keyword or phrase.

Different match types perform in different ways, and each can have a unique effect on your PPC budget, click-through rates, and conversion rates. You may find that

broad keywords generate too many clicks that never convert. You may also find that exact-matched keywords have a better conversion rate, but that you are just not getting the number of clicks that you expected to see.

An advanced tactic used to optimize based on keyword match types is to separate your keywords based on match type. Take a set of keywords and clone them across three separate ad groups, one for each match type. Monitor these keyword match types, and make adjustments to your bids and ad copy depending on how each perform. Although a broad-matched keyword may not be profitable, that same keyword may be one of your best performers when given a different match type. Other times, a broad-matched keyword can outperform the more specific match types. These differences play an important role in the performance of your campaigns, and it is in your best interest to examine the metrics associated with each match type and make intelligent decisions based upon those metrics.

Test Keywords Based on Match Type

① Navigate to http://adwords.google.com and sign into your AdWords account.

Note: *See the task "Optimize Quality Score" for more information about opening your AdWords account.*

② Click the Reporting tab.

③ Click the Create a New Report link.

④ Select the Ad Group Performance report.

⑤ Choose the data you want the report to include.

⑥ Click Create Report.

- You are returned to the Report Center where you can see the recently created reports.

7 Click the name of the report to view the data.

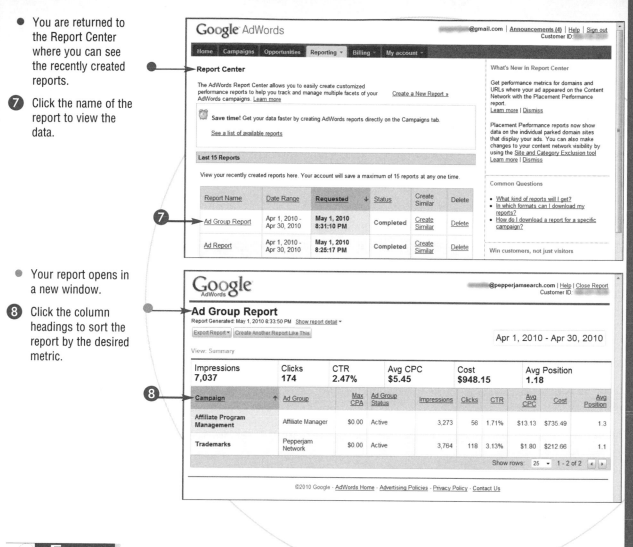

- Your report opens in a new window.

8 Click the column headings to sort the report by the desired metric.

Extra

Remember that when you use broad and phrase match-type keywords, any extra words a searcher enters into the query box along with that particular keyword can still trigger your text ad, even it is something that you do not offer on your site.

For example, if you are running the keyword "shoes" as a broad match type and somebody searches for the phrase "free shoes," your ad appears. In this case, people may visit your site expecting to see a free shoe offer and experience disappointment when they realize no such offer exists. As a matter of fact, Google has expanded the broad match type, and someone searching for "boots" may also see an ad triggered by your keyword "shoes."

Use negative keywords liberally in ad groups that contain broad-matched keywords. Words such as "free" usually do not lead to a sale or lead and should be entered into the ad group as a negative keyword to prevent your ads from showing any time the word "free" is attached to a search query. Adding negative keywords to these ad groups also cuts down on wasted impressions and improves the overall quality score of the ad group by increasing click-through rates.

Test Ad Copy with
Advanced Keyword Insertion

Y ou can use the {keyword} parameter to automatically populate ad copy with the keyword that triggered the display of the ad. This can increase click-through rates and directly influence keyword quality scores. There are advanced methods to format the {keyword} parameter that change the appearance of the dynamically inserted text.

By capitalizing the "K" and the "W" you can have the AdWords platform automatically format your keyword into proper case. For example, the headline {KeyWord:Shop Here} displays the text "Basketball Shoes" when the keyword "basketball shoes" is searched for.

By capitalizing "KEY" the platform automatically formats the entire first word of the keyword phrase in uppercase. The headline {KEYWord:Shop Here} displays the text "BASKETBALL Shoes" as the first line of your text ad. Similarly, using {KEYWORD} displays "BASKETBALL SHOES" as the headline of the ad.

Other variations include {keyword} for all lowercase text and {keyWORD} to capitalize only the second word. Test these various forms of keyword insertion to maximize click-through rates and conversions. You may find that even though an ad is displayed halfway down the page, it still receives sufficient clicks because the uppercase headline grabs the searcher's eye.

Try using different formatting in the different lines of one text ad. You can format the keyword to appear in all capital letters in the headline, but in proper case in the description line. Use these techniques to emphasize keywords and set yourself apart from competitors.

Run an Ad Performance report, discussed in the task "Test Ad Copy," within the AdWords platform to gauge the overall performance of your ad. You can see metrics such as average ad cost-per-click, average ad rank position, and other metrics that are not viewable in the campaign summary.

Test Ad Copy with Advanced Keyword Insertion

1 Navigate to http://adwords. google.com.

2 Sign into your AdWords account.

3 Choose a campaign and ad group to add a text ad to.

4 Click the Ads tab.

⑤ Click New Ad → Text Ad.

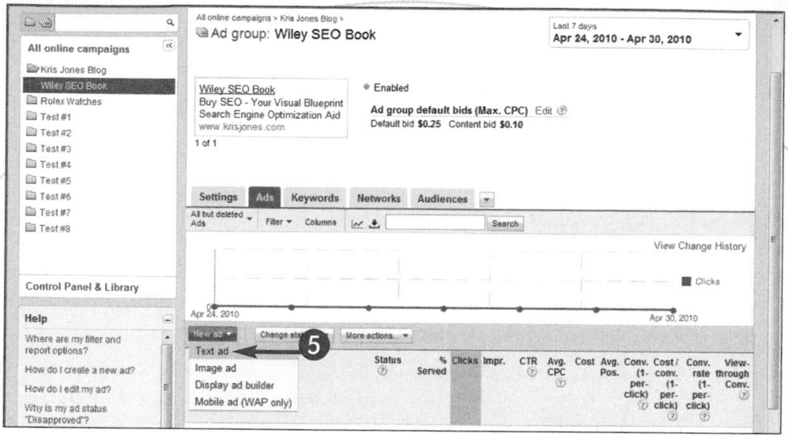

⑥ Enter the {keyword:} parameter into any line of the ad. For example, {keyword: Wiley SEO Book}.

● View the ad preview to ensure you have done this correctly.

⑦ Click Save Ad to save your ad.

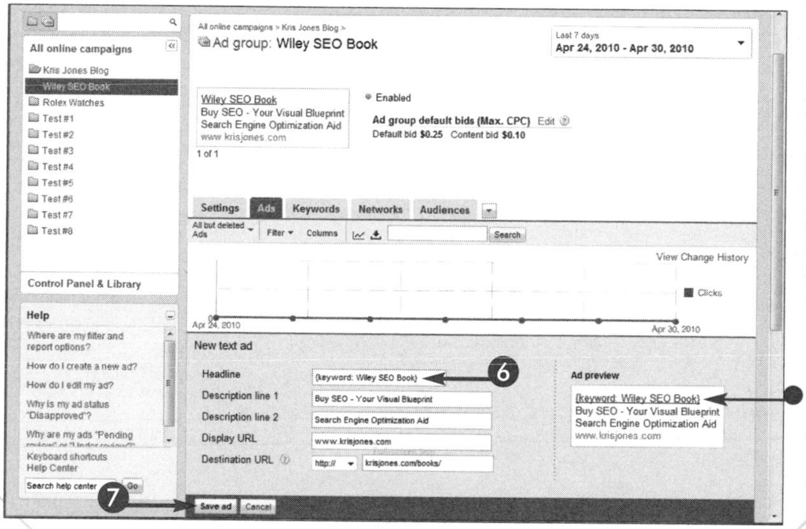

Extra

As mentioned throughout this chapter, one of the major factors affecting quality score at the text ad level is the click-through rate, or *CTR*. Using the keyword insertion techniques discussed in this task can significantly increase the rate at which customers click your ads.

One of the major benefits of a high CTR is that as your quality score increases, keyword and ad combinations become eligible to appear above the organic search results. These top ad positions receive most of the PPC traffic for any given keyword or phrase. These top ad positions can receive a similar amount of traffic to the top organic rankings. If your ad achieves a top position, the CTR is likely to receive a significant boost, again leading to more page views and more conversions.

Advanced dynamic keyword insertion techniques should be practiced with caution. Remember, you are paying for every click, so be careful not to recklessly inflate your CTR. An uppercase headline alone can increase your CTR by a few percent; however, it can also inflate click-through rates by attracting curious searchers who are not necessarily shoppers or buyers.

Using Content-Targeted Campaigns

Within the AdWords platform are various networks to which you can target your campaigns. One of these networks is called the *content network*. Content targeting is basically another word for contextual advertising and is a way in which your ads can reach a wider audience.

When you choose to opt into the content network, Google scans its network of partner sites and determines which are best suited for your ads. This is based on the content that is found on the Web pages within the content network. These pages may be sites about a product that you are advertising, news stories related to your keywords, or blogs about similar products.

Some benefits of contextual advertising include diversified advertising channels and extended reach. Your ads are no longer limited to just the Google search results and may be shown to customers in a different stage of the buying cycle. You also are not limited to only displaying text ads. When you use the content network, you can choose from image, animated, and even video advertisements.

Creating a content-targeted campaign is easy. You can use one of your existing PPC campaigns or you can create a new campaign specifically targeted to the content network. You should create a new campaign with new ad copy if you plan to advertise on the content network. Be sure your keywords are separated into specific ad groups and that your ad copy is directly related to those keywords.

Finally, remember to set different keyword bids for the content network. You may not want to pay as much when you advertise on this particular channel as you do when your ads appear in the search results. Always keep an eye on your budget.

Using Content-Targeted Campaigns

① Navigate to http://adwords.google.com and sign into your AdWords account.

② Click the campaign you want to add to the content network.

③ Click the Targeting: Search Edit tab.

④ Select Content Network and Relevant Pages Across the Entire Network.

⑤ Click Save.

- Note that your campaign is now active on the Google Content Network.

- Examples of content network advertisements.

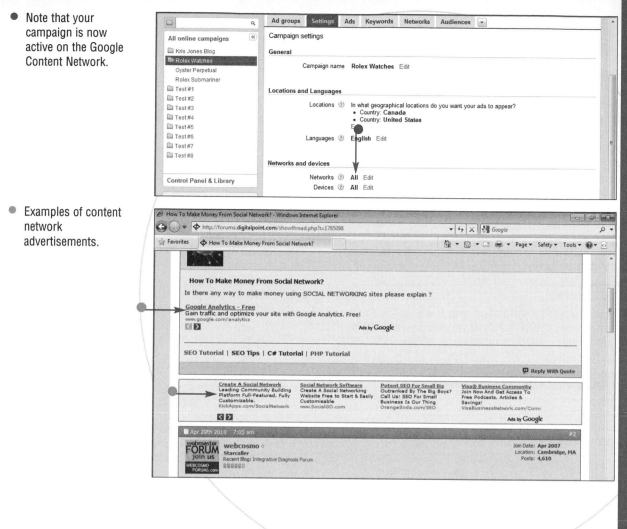

Extra

When you use the content network, remember that the Internet is not a predictable place. Campaigns on the content network run the risk of overspending at a moment's notice. For example, your ad may be displayed on a site that normally receives about 100 unique visitors per day. An ad on this site may only cost you a small amount of money every day; however, if this Web site suddenly generates a large amount of press by being featured on a major news Web site such as Digg.com or in a national magazine or newspaper, the traffic coming into the site could increase dramatically. Suddenly the ad that was costing you very little may start getting more and more clicks. On the content network, a 25 cent daily ad spend can turn into $250 overnight. To avoid this type of overspending, be sure to set strict budgets on your content network campaigns.

You can also restrict your ads from appearing on certain sites. Remember to occasionally run placement reports to see which sites actually drive conversions and which sites drive only nonconverting traffic. Any sites that do not seem to send the right kind of visitors to your site should be excluded from showing your ads in the future.

Using Placement-Targeted Campaigns

Placement-targeted campaigns are similar to content-targeted campaigns in that they allow you to show your ads on any Web site that is a part of the Google Content Network. The difference is that a placement-targeted campaign lets you choose a specific site on which to advertise.

You can choose which sites you want your ads to appear on in two ways. The first way is to name the specific site you want to advertise on. If you are browsing the Web and come across a site that you think your target customers might be viewing, check to see whether the phrase "Ads by Google" appears anywhere on the site. If it does, you can choose this site for your placement-targeted campaign.

The second way you can target your campaign is to give Google a list of keywords or phrases that describe your site. Google then searches through its content network to

find the sites that best match the words you have entered. The platform then returns a list of sites that are related, and you may choose which sites you want to advertise on.

As with all advertising, you are competing with other advertisers for a space on the site. The more popular a site is, the more expensive it can be to show your ad. You are charged on a *CPM* (cost-per-impression) or a *CPC* (cost-per-click) basis. Paying on a CPM basis means a certain amount is charged every time your ad is displayed 1,000 times. Paying on a CPC basis means you pay a certain amount every time your ad is clicked. Each pricing method has its benefits and drawbacks. If your ad has a very high click-through rate, you may pay less per click by choosing CPM pricing. Test the different pricing models with different ad variations to determine which is the most cost-effective method for your campaign.

Using Placement-Targeted Campaigns

1. Navigate to http://adwords. google.com and sign into your AdWords account.

2. Click the campaign and ad group you want to add to the content network.

3. Click the Networks tab.

4. Click the Show Details link under Managed Placements.

5 Click Add Placements.

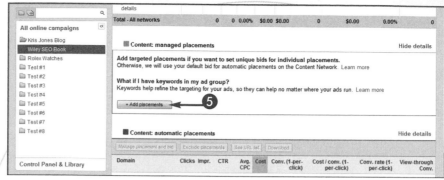

- Note the format for adding placements.

- Note that you can set a default bid for all of your managed placements in this ad group.

6 Click Save.

Extra

Placement-targeted campaigns offer you an option that keyword-targeted campaigns do not: the ability to reach out to a new demographic that you are otherwise unable to target by bidding on keywords. Because of the way the Google Quality Score algorithm works, if you try to bid on a keyword that does not directly relate to the content of your site, you are slapped with a high cost-per-click and risk the chance of your ad not appearing at all. This makes thinking outside the box difficult. Placement-targeting allows you to choose any site that you think might be a worthy platform for your product. This makes placement-targeting an excellent tool for branding campaigns.

For example, perhaps you are marketing a new product for infants. You may have tried bidding on the term "baby shower gifts" on the Google Search Network with limited or no success because your Web site is not focused specifically on baby shower gifts. Using the placement-targeting option you can find sites that offer insight into the baby shower process and choose to display your ad there to successfully target that particular demographic. Keep in mind that your ad has a better chance of showing on Web sites that closely relate to the content of your own Web site.

Test Performance with Dayparting

Dayparting, a technique normally used by broadcasters, is the practice of dividing the day into several parts and airing programs that appeal to a particular demographic known to tune in at that time. In online marketing, dayparting is simply the act of scheduling your ads to run at a particular time that you determine to be more profitable than other times.

Google AdWords gives you two options when it comes to dayparting. You may either stop your ads from showing altogether, or you may have Google reduce your maximum bids by a certain percentage. Both of these settings are sure to save you money and help you spend your budget more efficiently. If you choose to turn your ads off completely, you may miss a chance to get your brand shown at a time when your competitors are not

advertising as strongly. If this is a concern, the best option is to reduce your maximum bids so that your ads still show but at a lower cost.

If you are not sure what times of the day your account is performing the best, you can run a pretty basic test and study the results. The process is simple in principle. Clone your best performing campaign six times and go into the campaign settings for each one. Set each campaign to run for 4-hour intervals throughout the day. Do not yet lower any bids because you want to see the results before you make changes. You should let these dayparted campaigns run for about a month to collect data. When the test is over, use the data you obtained to decide when the best and worst times are to run your campaigns.

Test Performance with Dayparting

① Navigate to http://adwords.google.com.

② Sign into your AdWords account.

③ Select a campaign.

④ Click the Settings tab.

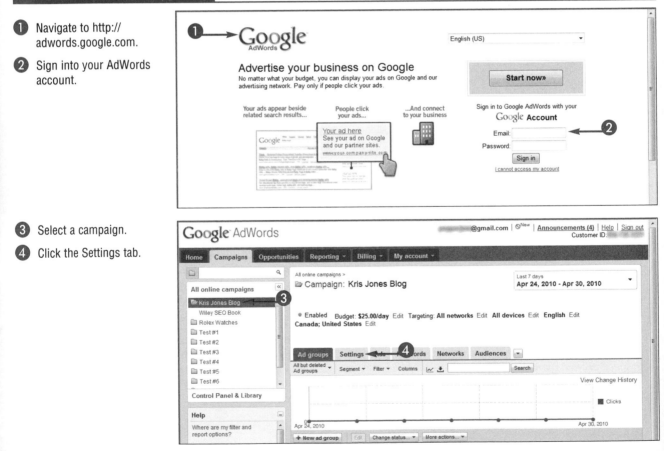

⑤ Click the Edit link to schedule your ads for specific days or hours of the day.

Bidding and budget

Bidding option ⑦ **Focus on clicks, manual maximum CPC bidding** Edit

Budget ⑦ **$25.00/day** Edit

⊞ Position preference, delivery method (advanced)

Ad extensions

Use this option to include relevant business information with your ads. Learn more

Locations ⑦ Business owners - Use addresses from a Google Places account: **None** Edit ⑦

Non-business owners - Use manually entered addresses: **None** Add an address ⑦

Note: addresses that are outside the campaign's target area will not be shown.

Products ⑦ Use product images and information from my Google Merchant Center account: **None** Edit

Phone extensions ⑦ Display click-to-call phone number on iPhones and other mobile devices with full Internet browsers: **None** Edit

Advanced settings

⊟ Schedule: Start date, end date, ad scheduling

Start date **May 1, 2010**

End date **None** Edit

Ad scheduling ⑦ **Show ads all days and hours** Edit ◄──── **⑤**

⊞ Ad delivery: Ad rotation, frequency capping
⊞ Demographic bidding

⑥ Click any time period to select the hours or days that you want your ads to run.

⑦ Click Save.

Your campaign now runs only during the times specified.

Ad schedule

Edit days and times below. When you're happy with the schedule, click "Save." To bid more or less during particular time periods, switch to the bid adjustment mode. (You can always switch back.)

Reset to all days and hours Mode: **Basic** | Bid adjustment ⑦ Clock: **12 hour** | 24 hour

⑥ ►

Day	Time period	Midnight	4:00 AM	8:00 AM	Noon	4:00 PM	8:00 PM
Monday	Running all day						
Tuesday	Running all day						
Wednesday	Running all day						
Thursday	Running all day						
Friday	Running all day						
Saturday	Running all day						
Sunday	Running all day						

⑦ ► Save Cancel

Extra

Keep in mind that customer behavior changes often. There is no such thing as a definitive result for any type of test you may conduct. Your PPC campaigns should always be evolving. Just because something you tried did not work last year does not mean it will not work this year. Perhaps you discovered during the summer months that over the weekends you lost money because nobody seemed to be shopping or even spending time browsing the Internet. If you carry the results of that test into the winter, you are blindly assuming that when the weather gets unfriendly, people will continue practicing the same habits they did when the days were longer and warmer. You could miss out on valuable traffic during the winter months.

You may also discover that the type of product you offer may appeal to a different demographic. If you add anything new to your PPC campaign, be sure to repeat the testing process. Just because the majority of your keywords do not perform at a certain time does not mean that a different product will not perform better at the same time of day.

Optimize Your Landing Pages

The landing page onto which you drop a searcher who has clicked one of your ads is arguably the most important aspect of your PPC efforts. Getting searchers to your site is the easy part compared to getting them to stay and convincing them to either make a purchase or sign up for a service.

The first thing you need to be sure of is that the landing page accurately pertains to the keyword that leads to it. If searchers are dropped on a page that has nothing to do with the term they were looking for, chances are they will feel tricked and navigate away immediately. Google also frowns upon any landing page that is not relevant to what was being advertised.

Next, you need to be sure that the Web page loads in a timely manner. Features such as Flash animation or extremely large images can slow down the loading time of your Web site. This is unfriendly for both SEO and PPC. If searchers click your ad and the landing page takes

a long time to load, chances are good that they may change their mind and navigate away from the site before they see what you have to offer.

Google offers a free landing page optimizer that allows you to customize portions of your landing pages. The optimizer automatically creates different landing page varieties and records conversion statistics about each variation. You can test different content, layouts, image placements, and more. Over time, Google determines which variation converts best and most often displays that version.

Google allows you to test your landing pages by conducting either an A/B experiment or a Multivariate experiment. An A/B experiment compares the performance of entirely different versions of a Web page, whereas a Multivariate experiment compares the performance of content variations in multiple locations on a page. To test one unique landing page versus another you should use an A/B experiment. To test multiple changes to one unique landing page you should use a Multivariate experiment.

Optimize Your Landing Pages

① Navigate to https://www. google.com/analytics/ siteopt/exptlist and sign into your AdWords account.

② Click Create Experiment to get started.

③ Click A/B Experiment.

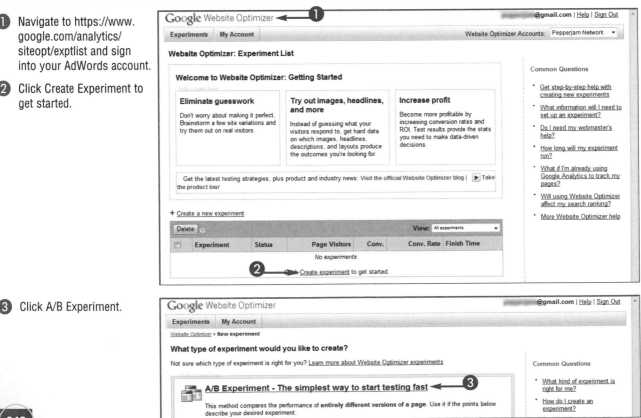

4 Execute each of the steps of the A/B Experiment Checklist.

5 Click the check box once you have completed each of the steps of the A/B Experiment Checklist.

6 Click Create.

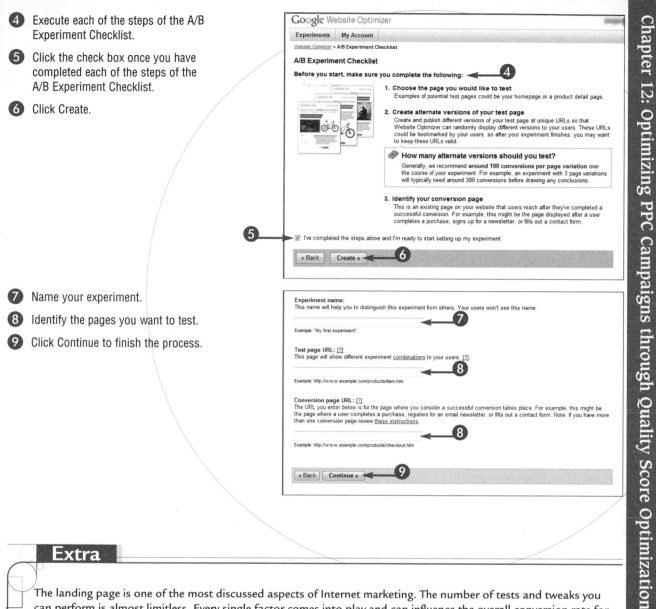

7 Name your experiment.

8 Identify the pages you want to test.

9 Click Continue to finish the process.

Extra

The landing page is one of the most discussed aspects of Internet marketing. The number of tests and tweaks you can perform is almost limitless. Every single factor comes into play and can influence the overall conversion rate for your campaign drastically. You first need to consider if you have chosen the right page. As an alternative to the Google Web Site Optimizer, consider a series of your own simple *A/B landing page tests*. This is a term used to describe sending an equal amount of traffic at equal increments throughout the day to two landing pages. This type of test shows you which page is driving more conversions and which page is causing your potential customer to shop elsewhere.

You can also test various changes within the same landing page. Try tweaking the colors and fonts on your Web site. You may discover that the blue background converts better than the green background. Maybe the image of the smiling customer on your page seems to drive more conversions than the picture of the cute kitten. All these seemingly minor influences play a part in the overall success of your online business, and you would be wise to always test each one.

An Introduction to Optimizing for Other Search Engines

After you have optimized your Web site for the major search engines, you can sit back and catch your breath for a short time, but there are more ways to drive traffic to your Web site other than the three first-tier search engines, Google, Yahoo, and Bing. Many Web sites specialize in organizing very specific types of Web sites rather than trying to index the entire Internet. Getting your site exposure on these more targeted search engines can send extra traffic, or allow you to target a niche that may be too competitive to rank for in the major search engines. As the World Wide Web becomes more and more saturated, the demand is likely to trend toward search engines that specialize in one specific form of media and do it very well.

Specialty search engines cater to specific users by indexing only content within a specific area or niche. For example, some of the most useful specialty search engines allow Web users to search blogs, images, auction sites, social bookmarks, or classified ads. Although you can use Google to search for practically any kind of information, using specialty search engines allows you to minimize nonrelevant search results, as well as become part of the community that is typically associated with niche engines. People who use search engines such as Technorati, eBay, and Shopping.com tend to not only use the engines to search for information, but also to submit their own blogs or products.

Optimize Blog Posts for Technorati

Technorati is an example of one of these specialized search engines. It focuses mainly on blogs and allows users to search only for Web sites that have blogs about the specific topic they are interested in. If you can get your blog to rank highly on Technorati, you can ensure your site's blog will get hundreds of new readers every day and in turn boost the number of links pointing to your Web site.

Unlike leading search engines such as Google and Yahoo that attempt to index the entire World Wide Web, Technorati indexes only blogs. Technorati's primary competitors are Google, Federated Media, and IceRocket. As of June 2008, Technorati indexes more than 100 million blogs.

Optimize Your Web Site for Del.icio.us

Del.icio.us has cornered the market on *social bookmarking*. Social bookmarking is a way for Internet users to store, organize, share, and search *bookmarks* of popular Web pages. A bookmark is used when you want to save a popular Web page to retrieve at a later date. Del.icio.us allows users to share the sites that they visit most frequently and allows other users to gauge which sites on the Internet are the most popular. One of the more useful features of del.icio.us is called *tagging*. A tag is simply a word you use to describe a bookmark. Tagging your bookmarks through del.icio.us allows you to better categorize your favorite Web sites, while also allowing you to share your bookmarks with other users with similar interests.

Social bookmarking is an example of Web 2.0 and appears to be here to stay. Learning how to get your site involved in the social Web is going to continue to be a challenge with many rewards in years to come. At the same time, getting involved on the social Web can draw traffic to your Web site, readers to your blog, and customers to your store.

Optimize Your Images for Google Images

Google Images returns only images when a user enters a search query. This platform allows anyone searching for pictures to quickly browse and download images from all over the Web. Recently, Google began showing select image results as part of its main search results. As a result, getting your images ranked by Google Images can result in significant supplemental Web site traffic outside of traditional search-engine marketing.

You can increase your rankings in Google Images in several ways. For example, make sure that the keyword you want the image to rank for is in the same table cell as the image. Another tip is to put the keyword above or below the image using a `<div>` or floating `<div>` tag. You should also place the keyword in the alt image tag, the image name, and the image meta file summary. Finally, and most importantly, make sure you include the keyword in the same paragraph as the image.

Using Shopping Engines to Drive Traffic

Comparison shopping engines have become one of the most popular places for Web users to compare prices and shop for products online. These engines specialize in giving consumers all the information they need to make thrifty purchases from online merchants. Shopping.com, PriceGrabber, Shopzilla, and BizRate.com are all favorite destinations for Internet shoppers, and if your site offers a product, be sure to get it listed on one or more of the leading comparison engines.

Keep in mind that getting your products listed on the leading comparison shopping engines is not free. You must pay a percentage of any sales referred, or a *cost-per-click*, for every user sent to your Web site by each comparison engine. Although a few comparison engines list products for free, including Become.com and Google Product Search (formerly Froogle.com), the vast majority of comparison engines charge you to list your products.

Increase Exposure on Ask.com

Ask.com was originally known as Ask Jeeves and allowed users to get answers to everyday questions phrased in natural, everyday language. In other words, the phrase "Who is the president of the United States?" would return results that answered that question. The need for this oversimplified search engine diminished as everyday users became more Web savvy and comfortable with the way that search engines like Google and Yahoo worked. In February 2006, the Jeeves character was discontinued and the engine rebranded as Ask.com. Although Ask has faded in popularity over time, it continues to be one of the top five most popular search engines in the United States.

Produce Sales with eBay Auctions

eBay is the number-one name in online auctions. eBay allows users to compete to buy and sell new and used items. Some people have made a full-time job out of this practice. If you know how to get exposure for your products on eBay, you are well on your way to becoming one of those people who count the auction site as a never-ending source of revenue.

Improve Your Ranking on Bing.com

Bing is the search engine of Microsoft Corporation and was released in 2009 to replace Microsoft's predecessor search engines Live Search, Windows Live Search, and MSN Search. Since its launch Bing has captured considerable market share from its primary competitors Google and Yahoo. In addition, Bing announced a partnership with Yahoo to replace Yahoo's existing search technology with Bing, thereby placing its search technology as the second most important next to Google for purposes of search-engine optimization. Ranking well on Bing requires a similar approach to Google; however, unique features of Bing, such as related searches, allow you to tailor your search-engine-optimization efforts to improve your rankings on Bing.

Using Craigslist to Drive Traffic

Craigslist is the ultimate site for advertising your products locally. Whether you are looking for a job, an apartment, or a new family pet, Craigslist has a listing for it. With more than 400 sites dedicated to 400 different cities worldwide, your local Craigslist can deliver highly targeted traffic for free.

Optimize Blog Posts for Technorati

Technorati is an Internet search engine dedicated to searching blogs. Technorati tracks more than 125 million blogs and is arguably the most recognized authority on what is happening on the *World Live Web* at the present time. The Live Web, as Technorati calls it, is the dynamic and ever-changing portion of the Web created by users. User-generated content includes Weblogs, photo sharing sites, and video sharing sites. This type of user-generated media is sometimes referred to as *citizen media*. Although Technorati has expanded its listings to these other types of citizen media, it began with blogs, and that area of the social Web remains its specialty.

Technorati works similarly to the way that other search engines work in that it uses the number of links pointing to a blog to track its popularity, or as Technorati calls it, *authority*. To rank highly on Technorati, you must participate regularly in the blogging community. If you read an article on someone else's blog that you think is well written, post a link to it on your blog; someday that blog's author may return the favor. You should also become a Technorati member and make friends on the site. Users on Technorati can declare your blog a "favorite" and help you rank higher for the key topics you write about.

Another way to ensure that you are appearing in the Technorati results is to tag every blog entry you write with descriptive keywords. Technorati uses descriptive words and phrases to categorize your posts as it searches millions of new blog posts per day. For example, users of Technorati type keywords such as "Steve Jobs" or "iPad" to look for content related to those topics; if your blog post is tagged with these keywords, you increase the odds that your blog is included when these terms are used to perform a search. You should also keep in mind that many items are ranked by the date posted, so be sure to update often.

Optimize Blog Posts for Technorati

1 Navigate to www.technorati.com.

2 Scroll down and click the Technorati Tools link.

3 Click the Blog Widgets tab.

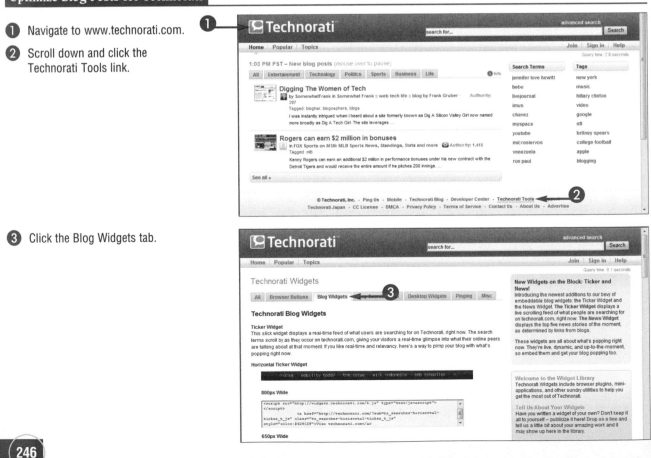

④ Scroll down and copy the Technorati Authority Widget code to your Clipboard.

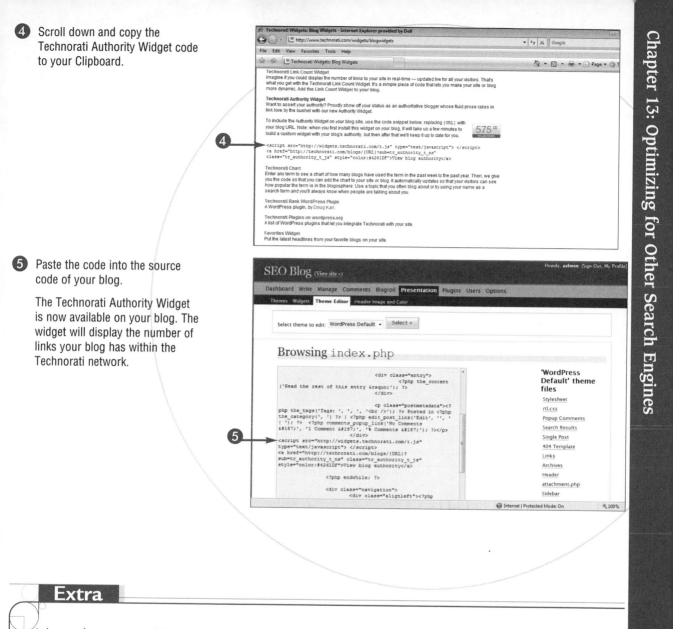

⑤ Paste the code into the source code of your blog.

The Technorati Authority Widget is now available on your blog. The widget will display the number of links your blog has within the Technorati network.

Extra

It is not always easy to think up new and interesting topics to blog about. If you want to get more traffic to your blog and cannot seem to come up with any fresh ideas, navigate to the Technorati "Popular" section and look at the top searches for the day. These topics are a great indicator of what is hot in the blogosphere right now. If any of these popular searches relate in any way to the overall focus of your blog, you should come up with a short, informative article that you can tag with the same keyword. Technorati users frequently check what is popular in their community, and having a recent, interesting, and on-topic blog post related to content and keyword tags from the Popular Searches page is a great way to get your Web site noticed. Targeting what is popular today ensures that your blog is popular tomorrow.

Optimize Your Web Site for Del.icio.us

Del.icio.us is a social bookmarking site. Social bookmarking allows you to store, share, and browse the bookmarked pages that you and others like you have added to their profiles. Just as you can save a page that you plan to visit frequently to your own Internet browser, del.icio.us allows users to save these bookmarks online and access them from any computer at any time. These bookmarks can include links to articles, recipes, blogs, wish lists of favorite products, MP3 podcasts, and other forms of media. Users on del.icio.us share these bookmarks with family, friends, and complete strangers who search the del.icio.us platform for new and interesting sites.

The ranking algorithm on del.icio.us is simple. The more people who save a particular Web site to their profile, the more popular that site is and the higher it ranks on del.icio.us when somebody searches for a related term. However, it is not all about ranking. Many users like to browse the bookmarks of other people with similar tastes, so showing up on these lists is essential to your success. Be sure to build out your own del.icio.us profile and become part of the community. Try trading bookmarks with other users with similar interests to spread the word about your Web site. You can also make bookmarking your Web site easier for other people. Be sure to add the "Save to Del.icio.us" button to your site and to the bottom of every post you create. Giving users a one-click way to save your site is the best way to get bookmarked more often.

Optimize Your Web Site for Del.icio.us

① Navigate to http://delicious.com/help/faq#tools.

② Click the Code link under the question How do I add a "Bookmark on Delicious" button to my website or blog?

③ Copy the code.

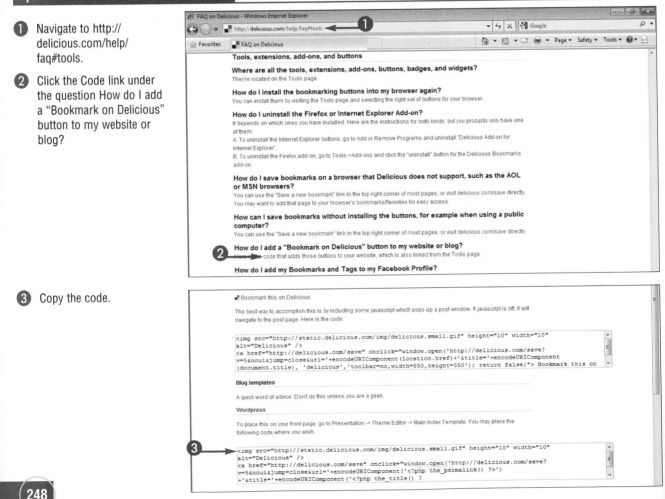

4 Open the source code of the page you are adding the button to.

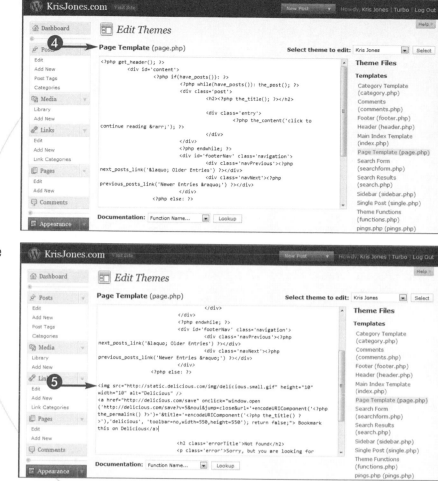

5 Paste the code into the source code of your page.

Your page template now includes the Del.icio.us button.

Extra

Del.icio.us uses tags to make organizing and navigating your bookmarks simple. Tags are one-word descriptors that you can assign to any site you bookmark to your profile. You can add as many tags as you want and go back and edit them at any time. Think of tags as keywords that you choose to describe your bookmarks. If someone else bookmarks another article and uses the same tags that you have, both of your posts are related by this tag and your site becomes more visible. Del.icio.us allows you to search for popular Web sites by keyword tag and also provides an updated list, "tags to watch," which lists five or so popular tags with accompanying Web sites.

You can view all the articles tagged as a certain keyword on one portion of the del.icio.us site, or you may browse the most popular articles tagged with that keyword at a different section of the site. The majority of users who visit del.icio.us go there to find the most popular site related to a specific term. If you can get your site to show in one of these popular searches, you are in a very good position and should see a spike in the traffic to your site as a result.

Optimize Your Images for Google Images

 oogle's Image Search is the most comprehensive image search on the Web. Although the results used to be limited to those who used http://images.google.com, Google now shows image results at the top of and within its regular, organic listings. As search results across the Web become more comprehensive, images have become a highly demanded end result for a search query. As the saying goes, "a picture says a thousand words," and this is true for users who want to know as much about a topic as they can in a short amount of time. For example, if you want to know where Iowa is on a map, would you rather read a 500-word article about it or just see an image of the United States highlighting the location of the state you searched for? Or maybe you are searching for an image for your social media site. Just type what you are looking for into Google Images, and instantly you find a picture you like

and link back to it from your site. The benefits of ranking well in Google Images are significant.

There are a few things you can do to increase your rankings in Google Images. First, be sure your chosen keyword is in the same table cell as the image. Second, make sure that your image's filename is descriptive of the image. Third, put the keyword above or below the image using a <div> or floating <div> tag. Fourth, the keyword should be in the alt image tag, the image name, and the image meta file summary. Finally, and most important, make sure you include the keyword in the same paragraph as the image. This is an example of a well-formatted image:

```
<div style="float:right"><img src="image/
keyword.jpg" /><br>keyword, text, text, text,
keyword, text, text, text, keyword, text,
text, text, keyword.</div><p>text</p>
```

Optimize Your Images for Google Images

1 Open the source of your Web site in Notepad.

2 Locate an image.

```
Padding: 0;
Margin: 0; }
STRONG {
Font-size: 15px;
Font-family: Arial, Verdana, sans-serif;
Color: black; }
-->
</STYLE>
<TITLE>Creating Pages</TITLE>
<META HTTP-EQUIV="Content-Type" CONTENT="text/html; charset=utf-8">
<META NAME="description" CONTENT="Creating search-engine optimized Web pages is the core effort of a succes
marketing campaign.  This page will detail a numer of on-site factors that should be taken into considerati
Web pages.">
<META NAME="keywords" CONTENT="file names,title tags,meta description tag,meta keywords tag,meta robots tag
modifers,creating links,validating HTML">
<META NAME="robots" CONTENT="index,follow">
</HEAD>

<BODY>
```
2 → `<img src="images/header.gif" alt="Chapter 3 Logo" width="500" height="100">`
```
<H1>Introduction </H1>
<P>
Creating search-engine optimized web pages is the core effort of a successful internet marketing campaign.
technical on-site factors such as adding correct file names, title tags, meta description tags, meta keywor
robots tags is crucial to making sure the search-engine spiders can determine the relevance of your Web sit
your content with header tags and other text modifiers allows you to stress the main ideas and topics that
```

3 Using a <div> tag, put the keyword above or below the image.

```
Padding: 0;
Margin: 0; }
STRONG {
Font-size: 15px;
Font-family: Arial, Verdana, sans-serif;
Color: black; }
-->
</STYLE>
<TITLE>Creating Pages</TITLE>
<META HTTP-EQUIV="Content-Type" CONTENT="text/html; charset=utf-8">
<META NAME="description" CONTENT="Creating search-engine optimized Web pages is the core effort of a succes
marketing campaign.  This page will detail a numer of on-site factors that should be taken into considerati
Web pages.">
<META NAME="keywords" CONTENT="file names,title tags,meta description tag,meta keywords tag,meta robots tag
modifers,creating links,validating HTML">
<META NAME="robots" CONTENT="index,follow">
</HEAD>

<BODY>
```
3 → `<div><img src="images/header.gif" alt="Chapter 3 Logo" width="500" height="100"><br />Chapter 3 Logo File</`
```
<H1>Introduction </H1>
<P>
Creating search-engine optimized web pages is the core effort of a successful internet marketing campaign.
technical on-site factors such as adding correct file names, title tags, meta description tags, meta keywor
robots tags is crucial to making sure the search-engine spiders can determine the relevance of your Web sit
your content with header tags and other text modifiers allows you to stress the main ideas and topics that
```

④ Insert the keyword into the alt image tag, image name, and image meta file summary.

```
Padding: 0;
Margin: 0; }
STRONG {
Font-size: 15px;
Font-family: Arial, Verdana, sans-serif;
Color: black; }
-->
</STYLE>
<TITLE>Creating Pages</TITLE>
<META HTTP-EQUIV="Content-Type" CONTENT="text/html; charset=utf-8">
<META NAME="description" CONTENT="Creating search-engine optimized Web pages is the core effort of a successful int
marketing campaign.  This page will detail a numer of on-site factors that should be taken into consideration when
Web pages.">
<META NAME="keywords" CONTENT="file names,title tags,meta description tag,meta keywords tag,meta robots tag,header
modifiers,creating links,validating HTML">
<META NAME="robots" CONTENT="index,follow">
</HEAD>

<BODY>
<div><img src="images/header.gif" alt="Chapter 3 Logo" width="500" height="100"><br />Chapter 3 Logo File</div>
<H1>Introduction </H1>
<P>
Creating search-engine optimized web pages is the core effort of a successful internet marketing campaign.  Taking
technical on-site factors such as adding correct file names, title tags, meta description tags, meta keyword tags,
robots tags is crucial to making sure the search-engine spiders can determine the relevance of your Web site.  Opti
your content with header tags and other text modifiers allows you to stress the main ideas and topics that your con
```

⑤ Save the changes and upload the source to your Web server.

Your image is now optimized for Google Images.

Extra

Another factor to consider when optimizing for Google Images is the size of the images you are displaying. Recommended image sizes are as follows:

- Small: 150 × 150 or smaller
- Medium: Larger than 150 × 150 and smaller than 500 × 500
- Large: 500 × 500 and larger

You should also be sure to keep an eye on the traffic that Google Images sends to your site. If you see that a particular image search is sending the wrong kind of traffic to your site, do not chalk it up as a loss right away. Think of a way to monetize that traffic or redirect it to another page of your site. For example, you can add Google AdSense and an affiliate marketing advertisement related to the image to the page receiving the traffic or to another page on your Web site using a 301 redirect. Similarly, you can build out content around the image and sell advertising through advertising services such as Adbrite or Text-Link-Ads.com. See Chapter 14 for more about monetizing traffic.

You should not optimize images that are unrelated to the content of your site. For example, you may have an image of a monkey on your site just because you think it looks good or fits your theme. Do not worry about optimizing this image; it is not going to send any quality traffic. This also goes for giving attributes to your navigation images.

Increase Exposure on Ask.com

Ask.com was originally known as Ask Jeeves and allowed users to get answers to everyday questions phrased in natural, everyday language. In other words, the phrase "Who is the president of the United States?" would return results that answered that question. The need for this oversimplified search engine diminished as everyday users became more Web savvy and comfortable with the way that search engines like Google and Yahoo worked. In February 2006, the Jeeves character was discontinued and the engine rebranded as Ask.com.

In June 2007, Ask relaunched again with a more simplified interface and a more customized results page depending on the type of search being conducted. Users searching for music are now presented with a listing of tracks by an artist that can be listened to directly from the

Ask results. Similarly, users searching for a particular city are given weather results and maps alongside the standard search-engine results. Although Ask has faded in popularity over time, it continues to be one of the top five most popular search engines in the United States.

A good strategy for optimizing your Ask.com ranking is to try to include as many different forms of content as possible on your site. When a keyword is searched for on Ask.com, the user is presented with multiple forms of media relating to that term. Include an image, video, news article, and blog post along with your regular content and you may be able to appear in multiple sections of the Ask.com results. Going after as much real estate on the Ask.com search engine results page, or *SERP*, as possible is sure to lead to more traffic for your Web site.

Increase Exposure on Ask.com

1 Navigate to www.ask.com.

2 Type a keyword related to your business.

3 Click Search.

● Note the Ask Sponsored Results. Unlike Google, Yahoo, and Bing, Ask incorporates sponsored listings into the actual search results, which provides you with greater control where you appear in Ask search results.

4 Click Images.

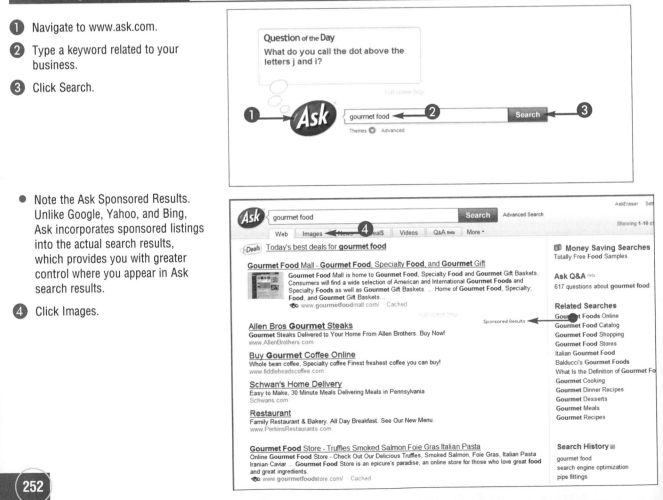

● Note the various images. Incorporating optimized images into your Web site is a good strategy to get ranked on Ask. com and other major search engines.

❺ Click Videos.

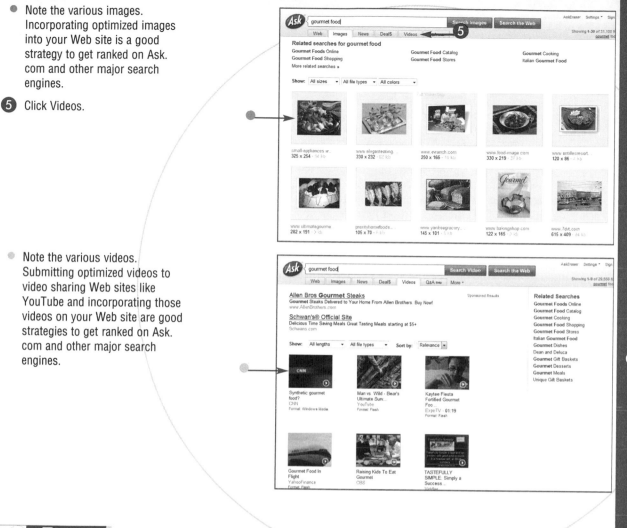

● Note the various videos. Submitting optimized videos to video sharing Web sites like YouTube and incorporating those videos on your Web site are good strategies to get ranked on Ask. com and other major search engines.

Extra

Another area of the Ask.com search engine results page follows the examples of Google, Yahoo, and Bing by displaying sponsored results that are paid for on a cost-per-click basis. These sponsored results appear below the top search listing and above the remaining organic results and allow you to appear in a very high traffic location of the Ask results page. There are several reasons to advertise on Ask.com. Because Ask is trying to break into the market, the cost is significantly lower on average than Google, Yahoo, and Microsoft's adCenter. Moreover, many search marketing experts and experienced PPC advertisers suggest that the quality of traffic on Ask is superior to other leading search engines. However, keep in mind that Ask PPC advertising may not be a good fit for your particular business. Test the service before you reallocate a significant amount of money away from your other search marketing efforts.

Although Ask.com is still part of the Google Search Network and therefore displays AdWords advertising on its site, you should do your advertising directly through the Ask.com platform. As the traffic to Ask.com increases, it is possible that Ask will break its ties with Google. As many advertisers have seen with AdWords, having a history with the platform allows advertisers to be one-up on the competition. Now is the time to get a head start and begin to build that history with Ask.com.

Improve Your Ranking on Bing.com

Bing is the search engine of Microsoft Corporation and was released in 2009 to replace Microsoft's predecessor search engines Live Search, Windows Live Search, and MSN Search. Since its launch Bing has captured considerable market share from its primary competitors Google and Yahoo. In addition, Bing announced a partnership with Yahoo to replace Yahoo's existing search technology with Bing, thereby placing its search technology as the second most important next to Google for purposes of search-engine optimization.

Similar to Google, the most important factor for improving your organic search ranking on Bing is to build your Web site authority through link building (see Chapter 8 for more information on building links). The more quality links that point to your Web site, the more likely it is that you will rank high for your target keywords. Other standard SEO tactics, such as optimizing your title and description meta tags, as well as writing compelling, keyword rich content, lead to better search rankings on Bing.

Unlike Google, Bing provides a section dedicated to related searches as part of its search-engine results page. Related searches provide Bing users with the ability to dive deeper into search results, which means you want to optimize your site accordingly when optimizing for Bing. For example, if you rank well for a broad term such as "gourmet food" on Bing, you also want to optimize your site to rank well on "gourmet food gifts" and "gourmet food store" because Bing offers these related searches as part of the search results provided to a user who types "gourmet food" into the Bing search engine.

Three other areas that are especially important to ranking well on Bing include image, video, and local search. With images and videos make sure you are optimizing images with alt tags and tagging videos with descriptive keywords. With local search make sure your company is listed as part of Bing Maps, located at www.bing.com/maps.

Improve Your Ranking on Bing.com

① Navigate to www.bing.com.

② Type a keyword related to your business.

③ Click the Bing search icon.

● Note the related searches. Related searches provide you with specific keywords for which you will want to optimize your Web site.

● Note that Bing includes Bing Local and Bing Map listings as part of basic search results.

Add Your Business to Bing Maps through the Bing Local Listing Center

④ Navigate to https://ssl.bing.com/listings/BusinessSearch.aspx.

⑤ Fill in the requested information about your business.

⑥ Click Check Your Listing to verify that your company is not already part of Bing Local Listings.

⑦ Type the characters as displayed in the image.

⑧ Click Continue.

● Note that your listing requires that you select categories, review your submission, and submit it before it will become part of Bing Local Listings and Bing Maps.

Extra

An increasingly popular and important part of the Bing search engine is Bing Shopping, located at www.bing.com/shopping. Bing Shopping provides users with the ability to get cash back on all purchases made when shopping through qualified Bing merchants. If you shop online, you want to join Bing Shopping so that you get a percentage of all e-commerce transactions you make through Bing Shopping; if you are an e-commerce merchant, you want to submit your products for inclusion into the Bing Shopping search engine and listing environment.

If you are an advertiser interested in joining Bing Shopping you can do so at http://advertising.microsoft.com/advertising/bing-cashback. Unlike other shopping comparison engines such as Shopping.com and Shopzilla, Bing Shopping works on a cost-per-acquisition model (CPA), not a cost-per-click model (CPC). As a result, click fraud is eliminated and bid management tools are unnecessary, which means you can effectively maximize and manage your return-on-investment.

Keep in mind that in order to qualify for Bing Shopping your Web site must be headquartered in the United States, have e-commerce capabilities, and be able to produce product feeds, among other things.

Using Shopping Engines to Drive Traffic

Comparison shopping engines have been around about as long as the Internet itself. Most of the current comparison shopping engines accept *product feeds* from online retailers and allow users to search and sort these lists by various criteria. A product feed is a file, typically in a CSV or Excel format, that contains information about the products listed on your site. Some of the most popular engines today are Shopping.com, Shopzilla, Bing Shopping, and PriceGrabber. Also, some search engines have added a separate vertical to their engines that allows shoppers to search only products; Google's is named Merchant Center, located at www.google.com/merchants. The pricing structure allows retailers to submit and list products for free and then charge advertisers either by the click or by taking a commission of every sale made through the engine.

The first thing you should do to optimize your product list for comparison engines is to fill in every product attribute that you can. Most shopping engines provide you with these attributes when you download their product feed template. By filling out all the fields provided you increase your click-to-purchase ratio. You should also optimize your product list by removing low inventory items and products with poor sales. Not all comparison engines provide product feed templates. For example, Google Merchant Center provides only a list of attributes to include in your product feed file. Also, note that although you submit your products through Google Merchant Center, shoppers use Google Product Search to view your products.

Be sure to investigate the categories that the comparison engine uses to organize its site, and make an effort to filter your products into these categories. The easier your products are for the engine to organize and the customer to find, the more sales you can achieve.

You should have proper tracking in place so that you can evaluate the success or failure of your comparison shopping campaigns. See Chapter 9 for more information on Web site tracking. Make sure that the information in your product feed is always up to date. Out-of-date product feeds are one of the primary reasons why some merchants fail with comparison shopping. Finally, make sure that you have at least 50 words or more of text to describe each of your products. You can provide both a short and long description of each product in your feed; tailor your descriptions to the unique file specifications of each comparison engine.

Using Shopping Engines to Drive Traffic

① Navigate to www.google.com/merchants and log in using your Google account.

② Click Data Feeds.

③ Click the New Data Feed button.

4. Select a target country.

5. Select a data feed type.

6. Provide a data feed filename.

7. Click Save Changes.

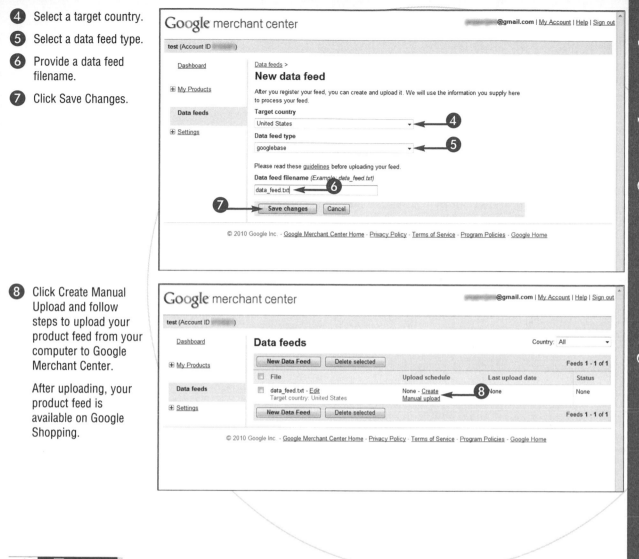

8. Click Create Manual Upload and follow steps to upload your product feed from your computer to Google Merchant Center.

   After uploading, your product feed is available on Google Shopping.

Extra

Comparison shopping engines continue to grow in popularity with both consumers and merchants. These engines are always evolving and adding new, versatile Web 2.0 features. An example of a Web 2.0 engine is ShopWiki (www.shopwiki.com), which combines shopping comparison sites with the popularity of completely user-generated sites like Wikipedia. Buying guides can be written or edited by any user who visits the site. Guides are even created by occasion such as Anniversary Gifts and Gifts for Babies.

Some comparison engines have paid placement pricing models that allow merchants to bid for priority in the search results rather than the product results being sorted exclusively by relevance or price. In this way, you can influence whether your products show up first or third when a user types a keyword that relates to multiple Web sites. Shopping.com uses the bidding model; Google's Product Search uses sorting.

Produce Sales with eBay Auctions

Bay.com is the most popular online auction site on the Web. Online auction sites facilitate the process of listing goods, bidding on items, and paying for them.

The first thing you can do when optimizing your eBay auction is to make the most of your auction's title. Use as many keywords in the title as possible to make your auction relevant to the most user searches possible. eBay allows you to use 55 characters for the title, and you should take advantage of every one.

Next, be sure to keep your description short. Even today, not everyone has a blazing fast Internet connection. Allowing the auction to load in a timely manner increases the number of people who will see what you have to offer.

When you post your auction is also important. Most people use eBay between 8:00 PM and 10:00 PM. Posting your auction at this time ensures that the most people will see what you have to offer. Keep in mind that Sunday is also a high-traffic day for eBay.

Finally, the photos you post of your auction item are probably the most important aspect of your eBay auction. These are what eBay users are looking for when they browse the listings; in fact, most people filter the search results to show only items that include images. Again, make sure the image is the right size. Large, detailed images take too long to load and deter users with slower connection speeds. It is also faster to host your photos off of the eBay site. Web sites like Photobucket allow you to host your photos for free and even provide you with the proper code to cut and paste right into your auction.

Produce Sales with eBay Auctions

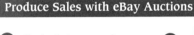

1. Navigate to www.ebay.com and sign into your eBay account.

Note: *Click Register to create an eBay account if you do not already have one.*

2. Click the Sell button.

3. Click Start Selling.

4. Use the search tool or click Browse Categories to find a relevant category to list in.

5. Click Continue.

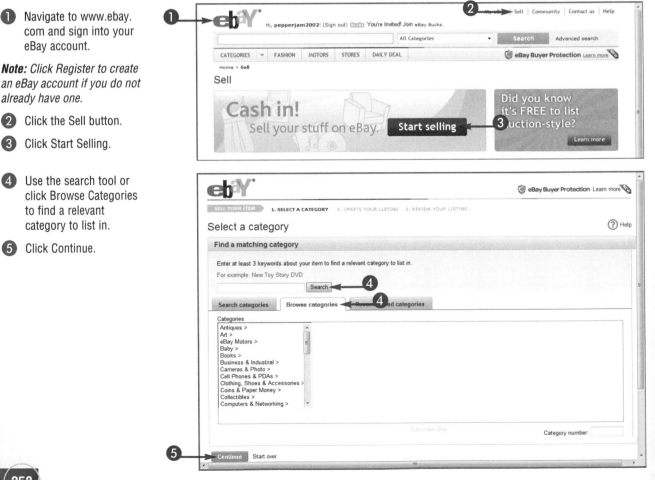

6 Add a title to your listing.

7 Add a subtitle to your listing.

8 Add more information to help buyers find your product in eBay search results.

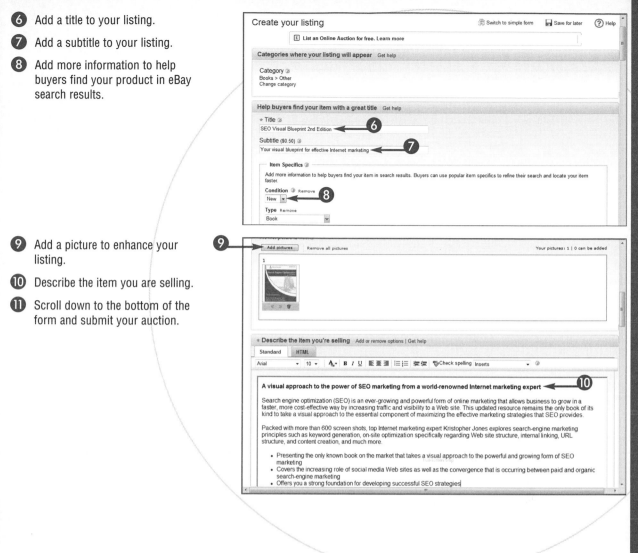

9 Add a picture to enhance your listing.

10 Describe the item you are selling.

11 Scroll down to the bottom of the form and submit your auction.

Extra

One of the easiest things you can do to optimize your eBay auctions along with any other content you post on the Web is to use proper spelling and grammar. People associate poor spelling and grammar with ignorance, and this is the last thing they want to deal with when making purchases on the Internet. Be sure you spell-check everything you post online; you may even want to have someone else proofread your material. Another rule of etiquette is to avoid using CAPS as much as possible. People associate all capital letters with spam and laziness and will likely look elsewhere when blasted with them.

Also, as with everything this chapter has discussed, become part of the community. Create a profile and keep it up-to-date. If you purchase items from other eBayers, be sure to leave them feedback. If customers are happy with the service you have provided, be sure to ask them to post feedback about their experience.

Using Craigslist to Drive Traffic

Posting ads on Craigslist regularly can be a great help in getting your Web site indexed by search engines, which can result in more traffic for your Web site. For example, you can use Craigslist to post listings about new products on your Web site. Keep in mind that whenever you post anything on Craigslist you should include the URL of your Web site.

Craig Newmark founded Craigslist in 1995. Today Craigslist has established itself in around 570 cities in 50 countries and is growing quickly. The site is a centralized network of online communities that offers free classified advertisements. Among the categories that Craigslist encompasses are job listings, internships, housing, dating, and online sales. The site serves more than 20 billion page views per month and has become the leading classifieds service in any medium.

Although Craigslist can be a useful source of traffic to your Web site, you must understand and adhere to the Craigslist terms of service or risk having your Web site

and listings banned from using the service. For example, do not post too many listings at once, and avoid posting multiple times in the same category. In addition, you should place your listings in the most appropriate category related to your product; you should not use multiple aliases attached to the same Web site.

When you make your post, remember to select the option that prevents people from seeing your e-mail address. You do not want Craigslist members e-mailing you directly or automated spambots picking up your address.

For your actual post, the same rules apply that apply to your onsite HTML optimization, as discussed in Chapter 3. Use H1 and H2 headings for the most important keywords. You can also bold anything important within the body text of the post.

Generally Craigslist posts expire after about 45 days, so you should post your ad again so that Google and other search engines continue to index and list it in their search results.

Using Craigslist to Drive Traffic

1 Navigate to your local Craigslist.

2 Click the Post to Classifieds link.

3 Choose the appropriate posting type for your site.

④ Choose the appropriate category.

⑤ Fill in all the required fields using the techniques described in this task.

● Be sure that the OK for Others to Contact You check box is not checked.

Your Craigslist post is now live.

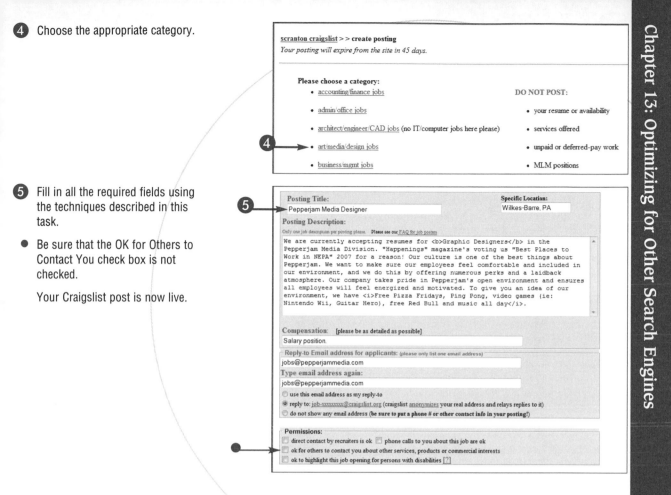

Extra

Local search is becoming more popular as local services such as Yellow Book and Craigslist become more relevant to searchers. Mobile search also targets these local markets, and with smart phone Web browsers on the rise, you should have a presence in the local search results. Local search-engine optimization is easier than regular SEO because the keyword phrases you are targeting are longer and less sought after. Be sure you register your business with Google Maps and Bing Local (see "Improve Your Ranking on Bing.com" for more information) and use platforms such as Craigslist and JudysBook to increase the locally relevant content pointing to your site.

You also need to be sure that you are not just targeting city and state names, but also the ZIP codes and area codes of these places. Include the neighborhood names, local slang words, and landmarks that people use to describe the areas around them.

On the pay-per-click side, the average cost-per-click for a keyword with a city and state tagged onto it is much lower than the keyword by itself. See Chapter 11 for more information about pay-per-click advertising. The search engine automatically displays these ads both to searchers who enter a city name and to those who merely access the site from an IP address in that geographical area.

An Introduction to Monetizing Traffic

This book provides you with a comprehensive strategy for driving organic traffic through effective search-engine optimization, or *SEO*. With improved search-engine rankings, you can maximize the revenue you generate from your Web site. If you are running your Web site as a business, *monetizing* your traffic is likely one of your main interests in improving your SEO efforts. Monetizing your Web site includes implementing one or more revenue-generating activities, such as paid banner placement or affiliate marketing, in order to generate money based on the incoming traffic to your Web site.

If you are running your Web site only as a hobby and simply want to receive more traffic, monetizing your traffic might not be your main priority. However, regardless of your intentions, you should at least possess a fundamental understanding of how Web site traffic is commonly monetized. This chapter provides you with a road map of options to consider and test when you monetize your Web site. From contextual advertising on networks like Google AdSense to affiliate marketing and paid blogging on networks like Pepperjam and ReviewMe, you can find numerous opportunities to monetize your Web site traffic.

Place Google AdSense Ads on Your Web Site

One of the easiest and most common forms of monetizing traffic is through contextual advertising, which requires you to place basic JavaScript code on your Web site. The undisputed leader in this space is Google's contextual ad program, Google AdSense. With the Google AdSense program, you can publish content on virtually any topic and automatically display highly relevant ads that come from the Google AdWords platform. Each time a visitor clicks one of these contextual ads, you receive a percentage of the funds paid to Google for that click. When you have the traffic to deliver thousands of clicks a day, this form of monetization can be incredibly lucrative.

Earn Money with Commission Junction

Unlike contextual advertising with Google AdSense, monetizing your traffic with affiliate marketing programs from Commission Junction requires that a sale be made by a customer who you refer. Whereas Google AdSense pays on a per-click basis, Commission Junction pays a percentage of the total sale made at the merchant Web site. Commission Junction is recognized as one of the leaders in affiliate marketing and offers publishers access to promote some of the top brands in the country.

Earn Money with Chitika Select Ads

Chitika Select Ads for publishers, located at www.chitika.com/publishers.php, is a personalized targeting ad solution that helps you monetize your Web site traffic on a cost-per-click basis by serving highly relevant, search-targeted advertisements. Chitika ad units include both behaviorally targeted text and images, which tends to result in a much higher click-through rate than text or images alone. Chitika is especially well suited for Web sites that receive large amounts of U.S.-based traffic from search engines and can work effectively with any type of content, including automotive, finance, health, electronics, news, sports, travel, and more.

Earn Money with LinkShare

An alternative to Commission Junction is another industry leader, LinkShare. LinkShare offers a variety of affiliate programs, from large brands like Macy's, to small, niche-specific merchants such as Mondera. LinkShare offers advanced reporting features that allow you to carefully track affiliate payments by merchant and analyze the success of your traffic generation strategies. LinkShare also includes many private, invitation-only affiliate programs such as Saks Fifth Avenue and J.Crew that can provide significant value to your Web site if you gain admittance to their programs.

Earn Money with Pepperjam Network

One of the newest affiliate networks to gain momentum and attention is Pepperjam Network, which was founded by the author of this book and acquired by GSI Commerce (NASDAQ: GSIC) in September 2009. Pepperjam Network, located at www.pepperjamnetwork.com, is a next-generation affiliate marketing network with innovative features that the other affiliate networks do not offer, including the ability to chat in real time with existing merchant partners. In addition, the Pepperjam Chat module allows you to approach prospective merchant partners to negotiate commission payouts and to learn more about the program, thereby allowing you to proactively manage your business and build partnerships based on open communication. Leading advertisers on Pepperjam Network include Dick's Sporting Goods, Crutchfield, Bath and Body Works, Mattel, and Speedo.

Sell Reviews with ReviewMe

The topic of paid blogging is a hot debate in today's Webmaster community. The debate centers on whether it is a conflict of interest for bloggers to accept payment for writing reviews about Web sites they know little about. However, many bloggers agree that ReviewMe is a dependable source of income and does not conflict with the integrity of their writing. Once you enter your blog into the ReviewMe system, advertisers can contact you and make an offer for you to blog about their service. If you accept the offer, you write the post and get paid the agreed-upon amount. ReviewMe is owned by MediaWhiz Holdings LLC, which is a large and reputable online company that also owns AuctionAds, Text-Link-Ads, and several other online media properties. ReviewMe has become an important service for advertisers looking to generate buzz and build links, and is a proven system for bloggers to generate income from Web site traffic.

Advertise Cost-per-Action Offers with AZN

Affiliate marketing networks such as LinkShare or Commission Junction pay affiliates on a variable percentage-of-sale basis; newer affiliate marketing networks such as AZN that pay affiliates on a flat cost-per-action, or *CPA*, basis are an increasingly popular alternative. CPA networks pay as little as a few cents to as much as several hundred dollars when a visitor to your Web site is referred to another Web site such as Blockbuster or Match.com and performs an action, such as inputting an e-mail address, signing-up for a free product trial, completing an e-commerce sale, or applying for a credit card. CPA offers are popular because of the fixed payout structure and potentially lucrative compensation model. Moreover, CPA networks tend to take a more hands-on approach to managing top affiliates than traditional affiliate networks, which makes the CPA model extremely attractive to some of the highest producing affiliates on the Internet.

Sell Links with Text-Link-Ads.com

Perhaps more heated than the debate on paid blogging is the debate on the ethics of selling text links. The debate is based upon the belief that advertisers buy links in an effort to manipulate Google's search-engine algorithm that analyzes backlinks to rank Web sites. Despite countless hours of debate, many Web site owners find that selling links is an efficient way to monetize their Web site traffic. Sites like Text-Link-Ads serve as a connection between link buyers or publishers and link sellers or advertisers. Once you become a publisher on Text-Link-Ads, advertisers can purchase a text link on your site; you receive 50 percent of the amount paid by the advertiser on a monthly basis. Text-Link-Ads payouts range from $2.50 to as much as several hundred dollars per link, per month. The more popular your Web site is, the more money you can charge for a text link.

Sell Links through TextLinkBrokers.com

An alternative to Text-Link-Ads is the popular link broker network TextLinkBrokers. TextLinkBrokers offers a link-selling feature that is similar to Text-Link-Ads and other networks. One of the factors that recently set TextLinkBrokers apart from the pack is the addition of *hosted marketing pages*. This is a step up from just buying a link; you actually rent a page on someone else's Web site.

For the purposes of buying links, many search-engine marketing experts suggest that the Hosted Marketing Pages program is incredibly effective. Additionally, hosted marketing pages allow you to monetize your Web site traffic with little effort other than initial placement of code on your Web site.

Place Google AdSense Ads on Your Web Site

Adding contextual advertising to your Web site is one of the fastest and easiest methods to effectively monetize your Web site traffic. Currently, the market leader in contextual advertising is Google AdSense. Launched in 2003, the Google AdSense program allows you to display contextually relevant advertisements on your Web site. The ads are delivered from available ad inventory on Google AdWords. Each time a visitor comes to your site and clicks an AdSense ad, you earn a percentage of the money paid to Google by the advertiser for that click. Although one click is likely to earn a small amount of money, producing thousands of clicks a day can lead to a substantial income.

One of the key reasons that Google AdSense has become the most popular tool for monetizing Web site traffic is because Google consistently provides contextually relevant ads in a fraction of a second. Google displays AdSense ads

on publisher Web sites based on its examination of all keywords on a particular Web page. For example, if the content on your Web page is primarily about renting apartments in Philadelphia, Google analyzes your content and serves advertisements to your visitors related to renting apartments in Philadelphia. Because the ads that Google displays on your Web site are consistently relevant to the content of your Web page, Google AdSense represents an excellent tool to monetize your Web site traffic.

Installing the Google AdSense program on your Web site is easy and requires only a basic understanding of HTML. All you need to do is sign up for an account, create an ad by specifying the size and colors, and then copy and paste a piece of JavaScript into the source code of the Web page you want to display ads. Within 24 hours, Google AdSense analyzes the content of the Web page and begins serving relevant contextual ads.

Place Google AdSense Ads on Your Web Site

① Navigate to www.google.com/adsense.

② Log in using your e-mail address and password.

● You can click Sign Up Now if you do not already have a Google AdSense account.

③ Click the AdSense Setup tab.

④ Select the type of ad you want to create.

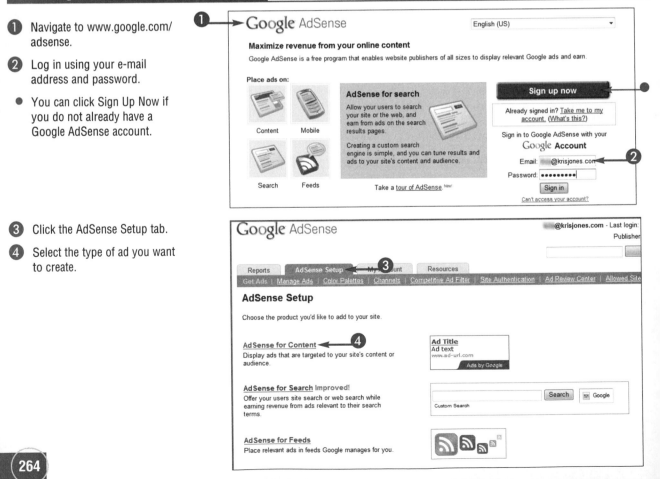

⑤ Follow the steps for customizing the ad type, format, colors, and ad channels.

⑥ After building your ad, copy the provided code and paste it into your Web page.

⑥ ─▶

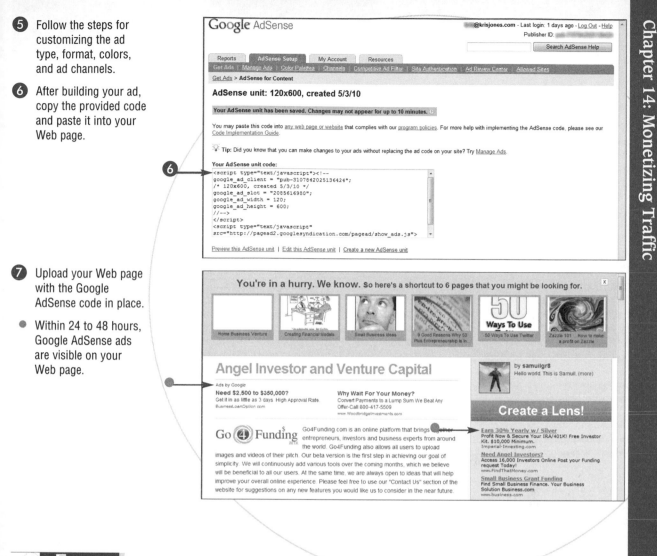

⑦ Upload your Web page with the Google AdSense code in place.

● Within 24 to 48 hours, Google AdSense ads are visible on your Web page.

Extra

Not all Web sites are allowed to join the Google AdSense program and display contextual ads. For example, Web sites that contain content related to adult material are not accepted into the program. Google AdSense also refuses any sites that promote illegal activity, violence, or racism. This also includes the sale of tobacco and alcohol. Nevertheless, Web sites that deal with banned topics attempt to enter the Google AdSense system anyway, but such efforts are typically short-lived. Thus far Google has done an adequate job of enforcing content guidelines within the Google AdSense program.

Google AdSense also gives you the ability to display image, video, and pay-per-action (PPA) ads in addition to the traditional text-based advertisements. Of course, your site can display these additional ad types only if advertisers in your niche create the ads within the Google AdWords system. Currently, most of the high-traffic industries have a substantial number of advertisers purchasing image ads, and the video ads are beginning to gain traction as well; Google's PPA ad network, which may potentially pose serious competition to other related affiliate marketing networks such as Commission Junction, LinkShare, and AZN, appears to be in its infancy.

Earn Money with Chitika Select Ads

C hitika Select Ads for publishers, located at www. chitika.com/publishers.php, is a personalized targeting ad solution that helps you monetize your Web site traffic on a cost-per-click basis by serving highly relevant, search-targeted advertisements. Chitika ad units include both behaviorally targeted text and images, which tends to result in a much higher click-through rate than text or images alone. Chitika is especially well suited for Web sites that receive large amounts of U.S.-based traffic from search engines and can work effectively with any type of content, including automotive, finance, health, electronics, news, sports, travel, and more.

Each Chitika ad unit is customizable and easily integrates with the look and feel of your Web site. Ad units come in more than 20 different sizes, including popular sizes such as skyscrapers and leaderboards. Setting up ads is as easy as selecting your ad size, serving preference, and customizing to the look and feel of your Web site. Note

that with Chitika Select Ads you have the option to display Chitika advertisements only to users who come to your site via a search engine. You may want to select this option when setting up your ad so that regular visitors to your Web site are not burdened with additional advertising that may not be ideally targeted. Alternatively, you can tell Chitika to serve Google AdSense instead.

Chitika Select Ads for publishers allows you to easily track the detailed performance of each individual ad unit you place on your Web site by creating channels. A channel is an individual reporting unit, which Chitika allows you to name so it will be easy to retrieve for reporting purposes. For example, if you create a 486 × 60 ad unit and place it on the top of your homepage, for purposes of tracking results you want to name the channel something like "486x60 Unit / Top of Homepage" — by naming your channel using descriptors you can seamlessly run reports at a later time.

Earn Money with Chitika Select Ads

① Navigate to http://chitika. com/publishers and log-in to your account.

● Note the Chitika Dashboard, which is a quick reference to your earnings and payment history.

② Click Get Started.

③ Select a banner size from the drop-down menu.

④ Click Continue To Next Step.

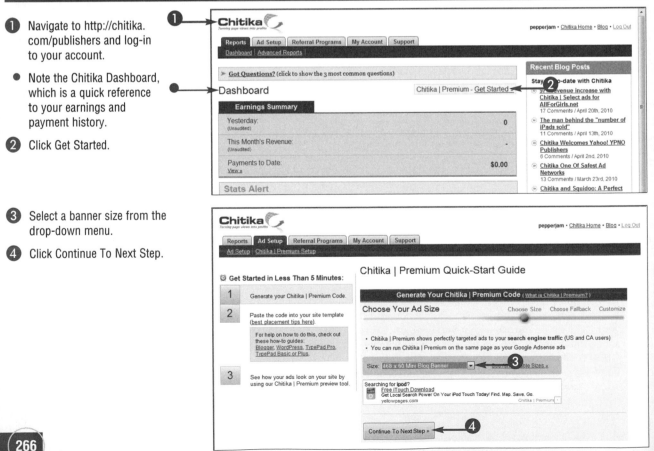

5 Customize your ad by selecting link, text, and background colors, as well as your preferred font.

6 Click Continue To Next Step.

7 Copy the code and follow the instructions to place it into your Web site.

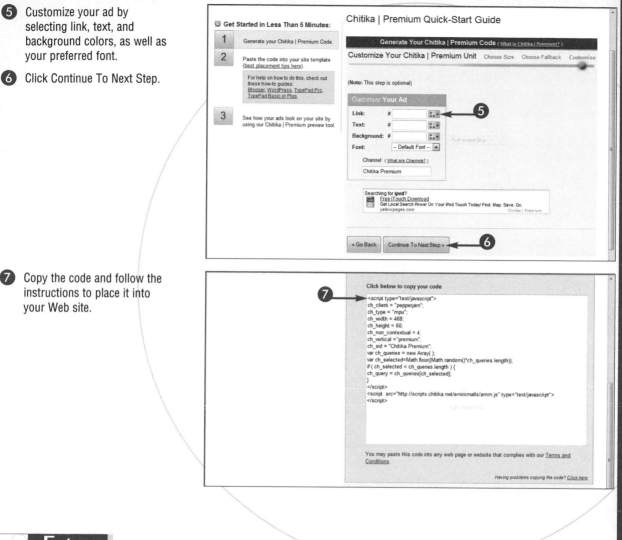

Extra

Another popular ad-serving platform to help you monetize your Web traffic is AdBrite, located at www.adbrite.com. As a publisher on AdBrite you can serve ads from thousands of different advertisers, including large household names, such as Live Nation, General Motors, AT&T, and Verizon.

The AdBrite interface is very easy to use. After signing up for free you can select your advertisers and have your ads up and running in less than 5 minutes. Once you begin publishing advertisements, your publisher dashboard will populate with extensive information about all the different ads that you are running on your site.

In addition to basic text and banner ads, AdBrite offers advanced, interactive types of advertisements to help you monetize your Web traffic. For example, AdBrite Full Page ads are triggered immediately when a visitor arrives at your Web site and appear in the form of a full screen interactive advertisement. Because Full Page ads consume the entire computer screen they tend to have very high payouts compared to other advertisements. Another AdBrite ad format is BritePic ads, which allow you to monetize photos on your site with interactive text ads. Finally, AdBrite Inline ads allow you to display an ad only when a user scrolls over a given word.

Earn Money with Commission Junction

Commission Junction is widely recognized as a leader in affiliate marketing for both advertisers and publishers. The Commission Junction Web site, located at www.cj.com, connects online merchants with online publishers through advanced affiliate tracking and reporting software. Commission Junction provides you with various ways to promote merchant products or services on a pay-for-performance basis. With Commission Junction, you simply add a banner or text link on your Web site and get paid when you refer a sale to one of your merchant partners. Commission Junction has more than 2,000 merchants covering just about every area of e-commerce. Regardless of your Web site topic, there is a good chance that a merchant in the Commission Junction system sells a product relevant to your content.

After you join Commission Junction as a publisher, you can then browse through the list of available affiliate programs. When you find a program that is related to your Web site content, you then need to join that individual program. Depending on the program, your application may need to be individually approved; some programs automatically approve each publisher that attempts to join. After you join an individual affiliate program, you then receive a link code that is specific to your affiliate account. Any traffic that you send to the merchant from this link is tracked, and any sales are credited to your account. The percentage you receive of each transaction varies from merchant to merchant, so be sure to do a lot of testing to see what program makes you the most money.

With a cost-per-sale-based affiliate program, you are directly rewarded for sending high-quality traffic instead of receiving payment on a per-click basis. This makes the commission model very attractive to niche Web site owners with targeted Web traffic.

Earn Money with Commission Junction

① Navigate to www.cj.com.

② Log in using your e-mail address and password and click Go.

● If you do not already have an account, click Publishers ➜ Application to apply for an account.

③ Click the Get Links tab.

④ Type your Web site topic.

⑤ Click Find.

● You can analyze the EPC (earnings per 100 clicks), network earnings, commission percentage, or lead price for each merchant.

6 To apply to a program, select the corresponding check box.

7 Click Apply to Program.

Advertiser Search Results

Results 1 - 6 of 6

	Advertiser	3 Month EPC (USD)	7 Day EPC (USD)	Network Earnings	Sale	Lead	Click	Status	Category
☑	ShoppersChoice	$9.12	$9.28		Sale: 6.00% USD			Active	Virtual Malls
	ShoppersChoice.com » View Links » View Products								
☐	CellPhoneShop	$25.74	$36.75		Sale: 15.00% USD Performance Incentive			Active	Online/Wireless
	Cell Phone Shop » View Links » View Products								
☐	InstrumentPro.com » View Links » View Products	$13.39	$12.54		Sale: 7.00% USD			Active	Music
☐	Best Buy » View Links » View Products	$9.87	$12.38		Sale: 1.00% - 3.00% USD			Declined Application	Consumer Electronics
☐	Creative Labs Affiliate Program » View Links » View Products	$5.87	$7.84		Sale: 3.00% - 6.00% USD			Active	Consumer Electronics
☐	CREATIVE	$0.39	$0.00		Sale: 3.00% GBP			Active	Consumer Electronics
	Creative » View Links								

Results 1 - 6 of 6

Return 25 ▾ results per page

● Depending on the merchant settings and your status as an affiliate, you may be instantly approved, or put into the queue for review by the affiliate managers.

Once approved for a program, you can download banners and links to add to your Web page.

Join Advertiser - Internet Explorer provided by Dell

https://members.cj.com/member/accounts/publisher/affiliations/joinprograms.do?

Join Advertiser

ShoppersChoice.com: Congratulations. Your application has been approved and you are now a member of the advertisers program.

[Close]

CJ ACCOUNT MANAGER   Copyright © 2003-2007. Commission Junction Inc. All rights reserved. | System Time: 8-Jan-2008 11:04 PST

Internet | Protected Mode: On   100%

Extra

One of the more effective strategies for monetizing your Web site with affiliate marketing programs is through *affiliate marketing search arbitrage*. Affiliate marketing search arbitrage is a process where you purchase traffic on a pay-per-click basis and "sell" that traffic to a merchant for a specified commission payout. For example, say you purchase a group of keywords on a pay-per-click basis from Google AdWords related to gourmet food, such as gourmet cheese, Italian olive oil, and Gorgonzola cheese. You can send your PPC traffic to igourmet.com for 12 percent of any sales that occur as a result of the traffic. In essence, you act as a traffic broker, and you profit when the amount of money that you pay for the traffic is less than the amount of commission you get in return.

The two primary affiliate marketing search arbitrage strategies are known as *direct linking* and *landing page driven*. Direct linking is when you purchase traffic from pay-per-click search engines and send the traffic directly to the merchant partner using an affiliate tracking URL. Direct linking does not require that you have a Web site because you send all traffic from the search engine to the merchant. In contrast, the landing-page-driven form of affiliate marketing search arbitrage requires that you purchase traffic from pay-per-click search engines and send the traffic through your Web site prior to the traffic eventually arriving at your merchant partner.

Note that if you use the landing-page-driven form of affiliate marketing search arbitrage, you can enhance the amount of money you make by building search-engine-optimized landing pages. See Chapter 12 for more about landing pages.

Earn Money with LinkShare

Very similar to Commission Junction, LinkShare offers you the opportunity to promote products and earn a percentage of all referred sales. LinkShare, located at www.linkshare.com, was founded in 1996 and has since grown to be a true pioneer in the field of online affiliate marketing. The size and variety of the affiliate programs available within the LinkShare network is one of the most attractive features of the company. This wide scope of programs allows room for publishers in nearly every niche imaginable. Some of the large brands included in the LinkShare network are American Express, Wal-Mart, Lands' End, Radio Shack, and the NFL Shop.

Promoting largely branded items can prove to be a double-edged sword. On one hand, these large brands already have a certain degree of trust built with the consumers. Viewers of your Web site are more likely to apply for an American Express card than apply for a credit card they have never heard of. Branded items also offer a unique opportunity for your SEO efforts. The search volume for highly branded keywords is significant and can result in significant revenue if you can rank within the top ten organic results for a top brand term.

On the other hand, there are some challenges that arise when promoting highly branded products or services. One issue is saturation. For example, you can find NFL Shop products on every major comparison shopping engine, as well as countless other authorized NFL vendor Web sites. Typically, there is far more competition when promoting highly branded products. This same principle applies to SEO and ranking for brand-related keywords. The stronger and more numerous the competitors, the harder it is to rank well in the search-engine results.

Earn Money with LinkShare

① Navigate to www.linkshare.com.

② Click Login, and log in using your username and password.

● If you do not already have an account, click Join and follow the steps to become a new publisher.

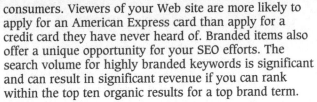

③ Click the Links tab.

④ Select an advertiser from the list.

⑤ Select a link type from the pop-up window.

6 Click Get Link.

7 Copy link code and place it into your Web site.

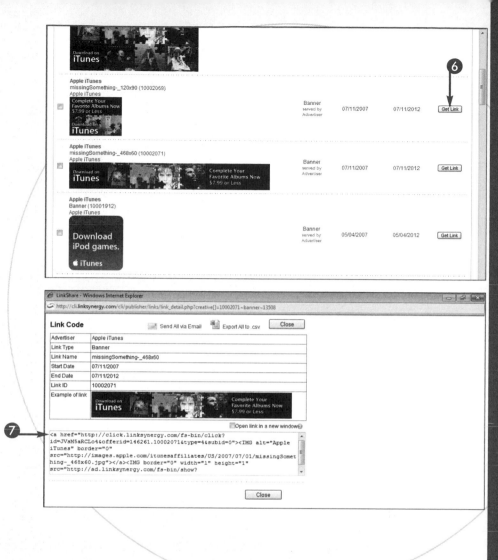

Earn Money with Pepperjam Network

One of the newest affiliate networks to gain attention is Pepperjam Network, which was founded by the author and acquired by GSI Commerce in September 2009. Pepperjam Network (www.pepperjamnetwork.com) is an affiliate marketing network with innovative features including the ability to chat in real time with existing merchant partners. The Pepperjam Chat module also allows you to approach prospective merchant partners to negotiate commission payouts and to learn more about the program, allowing you to proactively manage your business and build partnerships based on open communication. Leading advertisers on Pepperjam Network include Dick's Sporting Goods, Crutchfield, Bath and Body Works, Mattel, and Speedo.

Pepperjam Network was the first affiliate network to offer a measure of affiliate transparency. The Pepperjam Network Transparency System provides advertisers with the disclosure of important information, including reliable contact information, promotional methods, Web site(s), and marketing potential. The system allows advertisers to have more confidence in and more control over the affiliates within their respective affiliate program and also empowers affiliates to build stronger, more profitable advertiser relationships.

Another key feature of Pepperjam Network is pepperjamADS, which is an affiliate marketing widget that you can use to serve customized contextual ads from one or multiple Pepperjam Network advertisers at the same time. The ad units come in various shapes and sizes. You can mix ads from one or multiple merchant partners. For example, you can create a fashion widget with ads from multiple fashion merchants or a specific merchant widget with ads from any one merchant.

Pepperjam Store Builder is Pepperjam's product feed and store builder technology, which features products from hundreds of top Internet retailers and allows you to build dynamic e-commerce storefronts in less than 30 seconds. With Pepperjam Store Builder you can easily select products from one or multiple advertisers and filter results by keyword. In addition, you can easily customize the look and feel of the product feed so that it seamlessly integrates into your Web site.

Earn Money with Pepperjam Network

① Navigate to www.pepperjamnetwork.com.

② Log in using your e-mail address and password and click Login.

● If you do not already have an account and want to become an affiliate on Pepperjam Network, click Join Now under the Affiliates sign-up section.

● If you do not already have an account and want to become a merchant advertiser on Pepperjam Network, click Join Now under the Merchants sign-up section.

③ Once logged into your account, navigate to the Find Partners page located at www.pepperjamnetwork.com/affiliate/managePrograms.php?status=0.

④ Select merchants to join.

● Scroll below for more merchants or use the search functionality to find new merchants to join by category, keyword, or offer type.

⑤ Click the Join button.

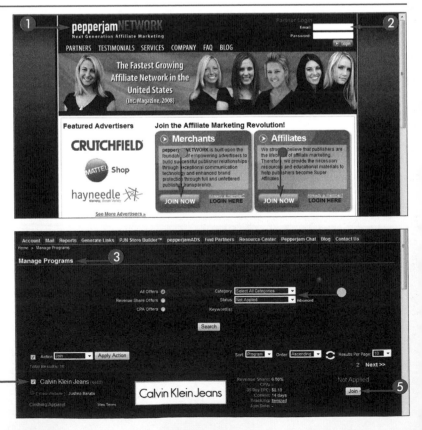

⑥ Navigate to the Generate Links page located at www.pepperjam network.com/affiliate/search joinedprogs.php.

○ Note that you can search for links to specific merchant affiliate programs that you are already joined to or select merchants by category, keywords, or offer type.

● Note that you can scroll further down the page to see more merchants that you are already joined to.

⑦ Click Banners to review available banners and select code to insert into your Web site in order to begin promoting the merchant.

○ Note the various banners available to place on your Web site.

○ Note that you can scroll below for more banners or use the navigation and search functionality located above to pull different types of creatives, including text links, products, and pepperjamADS.

Depending on the merchant settings and your status as an affiliate, you may be instantly approved, or put into the queue for review by the affiliate managers.

Once approved for a program, you can download banners and links to add to your Web page.

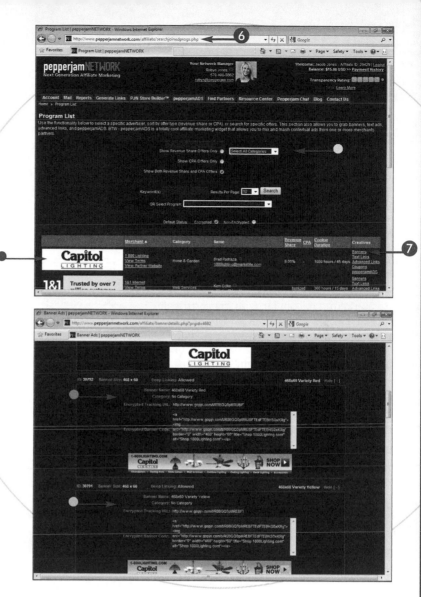

Extra

For advertisers, one of the most challenging aspects of building a successful affiliate program is recruiting new affiliates into the program. To help with affiliate recruitment, Pepperjam Network offers advertisers a recruitment feature called "Recruit Partners" that enables advertisers to easily search for new affiliate recruits by categories, by status (pending or not joined, for example), by transparency ranking, and by method of promotion. Advertisers are given access to the entire Pepperjam Network database of affiliates, which consists of tens of thousands of affiliates and is growing quickly.

For affiliates, one of the most challenging aspects of optimizing an affiliate marketing campaign is gaining access to critical reporting and analytical data. For example, in the case of search marketing affiliates that spend their own money to promote advertiser affiliate programs, having the ability to adequately track and access keyword data is critical. In this respect, Pepperjam Network offers source identification (SID) tracking and reporting, which is beneficial to affiliates that want to track commissions at the keyword level. Affiliates can optimize affiliate campaigns and make more money based on the specific data that is reported through the Pepperjam Network interface or through the Pepperjam Network reporting API.

Advertise Cost-per-Action Offers with AZN

An increasingly popular affiliate network structure and payment method is cost-per-action, or *CPA*. One of the leaders in CPA affiliate marketing is AZN, formerly known as AzoogleAds, located at www.azoogleads.com. CPA advertising allows merchants to specify a flat rate for a defined action such as an e-mail submission or contact form completion. For example, if you send a visitor to a merchant Web site, and that visitor successfully fills out a lead box with his personal information, you receive a predetermined amount of money. A CPA payout removes any fluctuation in payments by the merchant and guarantees you a set dollar amount each time a visitor completes a desired action.

CPA affiliate marketing is popular with many affiliate marketers because of the flat payout structure; often the specified action does not require the referred visitor to spend any money. This usually leads to significantly higher conversion rates than traditional percentage-of-sale-based affiliate marketing.

Although CPA-based offers provide an alternative method for monetizing Web traffic, CPA offers tend to be better if your Web site focuses on specific verticals, such as real estate, music, dating, or financial services. In fact, CPA networks such as AZN tend to have limited monetization potential if your Web site traffic is focused on e-commerce. For example, if your Web site traffic is mostly about topics such as gardening or cosmetics, you are better off promoting a traditional percentage-of-sale-based affiliate offer from a network like Commission Junction. However, if your Web site is about real estate or financial services, you are better off promoting a flat cost-per-action-based affiliate offer such as a micro loan or a credit repair service.

You can join AZN for free and begin promoting CPA offers within minutes. You are required to provide basic information about you and your business, including contact information and a valid tax identification number.

Advertise Cost-per-Action Offers with AZN

① Navigate to www.azoogleads.com.

② Log in using your username and password.

● If you do not have an account, click Become a Publisher.

③ Click Offers.

④ You can narrow the offers by searching for a keyword, selecting a type, or choosing a region and clicking Search.

⑤ Click the title of an offer that fits your Web site topic.

Chapter 14: Monetizing Traffic

6 Copy the tracking URL for the offer.

7 Add the link to your Web site.

Your link is now live and tracks any conversions sent from your Web site.

AZN's popularity and Internet marketing presence is a double-edged sword for new Web publishers. The fact that AZN is a large, reputable company is positive because it can help to settle any uneasiness you as an affiliate may have about actually getting paid for your sales. However, the popularity of AZN also means that the highest CPA offers presented in the network are being used by some of the largest publishers online.

The popularity of AZN can make competing for traffic relevant to high CPA offers extremely difficult. If you plan to use pay-per-click (PPC) traffic to drive conversions to a CPA offer through AZN, be aware that you may go head-to-head with pay-per-click industry pros, and they know what they are doing. If you are not an experienced pay-per-click expert, the SEO techniques learned in this book represent a more realistic and sustainable option for monetizing your Web traffic. If you spend time growing your own Web site and traffic stream, you can always try out different methods of monetization such as the high CPA offers from AZN and other networks.

Sell Reviews with ReviewMe

Despite being a controversial topic, getting paid to do a review on your blog can be profitable. One of the more ethical companies in the realm of paid blogging is ReviewMe. ReviewMe rarely receives as much heat as some of the other pay-for-blogging networks because of its transparency. ReviewMe also does not dictate the content of the blog post. Some networks require that you write a glowing, positive review in order to be paid. Not so with ReviewMe.

Publishing paid reviews is a simple and effective way to monetize a powerful blog. This form of advertising does not require you to have anything on your Web site that actually looks like an ad. So, if standard Web banners and text links are not an avenue you want to pursue, paid blogging with ReviewMe is a very attractive alternative.

ReviewMe is also a very selective network. You must go through an application process to join. Once confirmed, your site is then placed into the ReviewMe marketplace. Advertisers search through the marketplace when they are in need of blogs to publish posts about their products or service. They then select the blogs that they want to commission. This means that you must have a professional blog, or at least a high-traffic and high-page-rank (PR) blog to make a considerable amount of revenue from ReviewMe. If you do not have a powerful blog, you will rarely receive offers from advertisers. That said, you should ensure that your blog is already established and respected before expecting to see significant results from using a network like ReviewMe. See Chapter 10 for more about blogs.

Sell Reviews with ReviewMe

1 Navigate to www.reviewme.com.

2 Click Signup Now.

3 Fill in your personal information in the required fields.

4 Click Create Account.

5 After you view the success page, proceed to your e-mail inbox to validate your account.

6 Log into your account and click Blogger → View Campaigns.

7 Click View to view campaign details.

- Campaign details appear.

8 Click Accept Offer to accept the review offer.

Extra

As with selling text links, which is discussed in the next two tasks, using a network is all about making new connections while saving time and energy. Often, contacting advertisers directly can be a frustrating process when you are first getting started. However, direct sales, which are beyond the scope of this book, typically make you more revenue because there is no middleman.

Using a service like ReviewMe takes the hassle out of the get-paid-to-blog model. There are no more worries about ensuring that an advertiser pays on time, or that a publisher actually writes the promised post. Having a trustworthy company acting as a middleman can prove to be very valuable, despite any fees that may apply.

Once an advertiser makes you an offer, you may either accept or reject it. If you accept, you must then make a post on your blog about the specified product or service. Keep in mind that the advertiser has no control over the tone of the review. If you do not enjoy the product, be honest. However, do ensure that your feedback is constructive. If all you do is bash every advertiser that makes you an offer, you may soon find yourself without any review opportunities.

Sell Links with Text-Link-Ads.com

You can monetize your Web site without ever having to worry about click-through rates, conversion rates, or sale percentages through simply selling text links. Networks like Text-Link-Ads have made selling text links on your site extremely simple. These links are most commonly placed in a Web site's sidebar, which prevents the ads from distracting the user from your page content. This fact alone is extremely attractive to many publishers who are fed up with using the standard-size banner advertisements that many affiliate programs offer.

The motivation for advertisers purchasing these links varies. The most common, however, is to gain link authority and higher positions in the search-engine results. Google's organic ranking algorithm is strongly based on the number and quality of backlinks a Web site

receives. This simple fact has caused the market value of high PageRank links to soar, and networks like Text-Link-Ads act as a middleman to take the hassle out of buying and selling these text links.

You receive a certain amount for each link an advertiser purchases on your Web site, which varies based on several factors, including your Google PageRank, your Alexa traffic rating, the number of pages the link appears on, and also the location in which the link is placed. Generally speaking, the more powerful your site, the more you earn for selling text links.

Selling links through Text-Link-Ads is simple. Just sign up for an account, specify how many links you want to sell, and insert a piece of code into your Web site. As advertisers purchase link spots on your Web site, the ads automatically appear on each page that contains the Text-Link-Ads code snippet.

Sell Links with Text-Link-Ads.com

① Navigate to www.text-link-ads.com.

② Log in using your e-mail address and password.

Note: *If you do not have an account, click Create Publisher Account.*

③ Click Submit Site/Page.

④ Select your categories, title, description, and keywords.

⑤ Choose if you want to sell links on a single page or on your entire Web site.

⑥ Click Continue.

⑦ Select the number of ads you want to show on your Web site.

⑧ Click Submit.

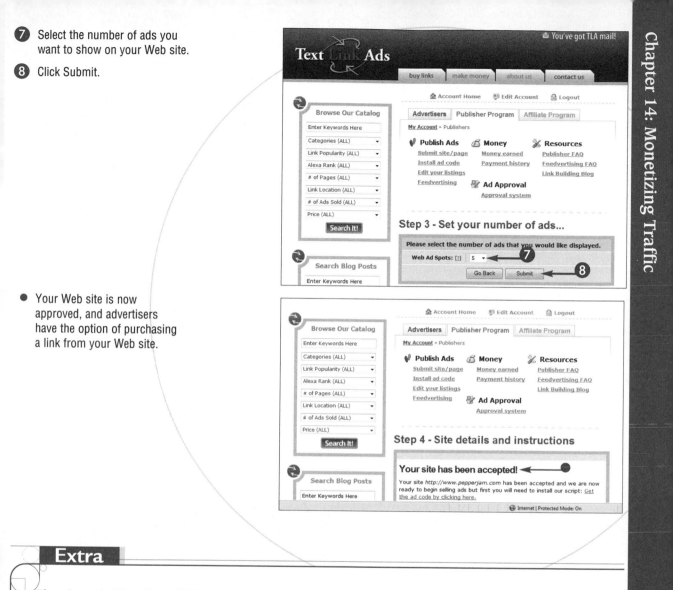

● Your Web site is now approved, and advertisers have the option of purchasing a link from your Web site.

There is much debate in the Webmaster community about selling links. Google discourages the sale of text links because it is commonly used to attempt to "manipulate" the search results at Google.com. Google has responded to this growing trend by filtering the purchased links from PageRank. In theory, this would remove any SEO value from purchasing text links. This is a factor to consider when making the decision to sell links on your page. Many Webmasters have responded negatively to Google's actions, claiming that the search giant is attempting to control the way Web publishers monetize their Web sites outside of Google AdSense. Examine the facts, and make the decision on selling links based on your Web site needs and goals.

Text-Link-Ads acts as a middleman in the link buying/ selling process, connecting publishers to advertisers. As payment for their role in the transaction, Text-Link-Ads currently take 50 percent of all transactions. This means that as a publisher, if a link on your Web site sells for $20, you receive $10. A more profitable method is to find advertisers on your own and negotiate prices; however, that method is much more labor intensive.

Sell Links with TextLinkBrokers.com

Recently, the topic of buying and selling text links has caused a large stir in the Webmaster community. Google has taken a strong stance against buying links, thus making discretion on the part of link-brokering networks a must. One leader in discretely buying and selling links is Text Link Brokers, located at www.textlinkbrokers.com.

Founded in 2003, Text Link Brokers allows you to buy and sell links "under the radar" of the major search engines. The ultimate goal is to allow you to buy and sell links without leaving any visible footprints that identify the link as being paid. Text Link Brokers has taken numerous steps toward making sure that its link services remain footprint free.

Another precaution Text Link Brokers has taken is a careful review of each potential link buyer and seller prior to acceptance into the network. This helps to ensure that your Web site is never penalized for linking to a "bad neighborhood," a low-quality site that the search engines have deemed untrustworthy. Linking to a bad neighborhood or low-quality site is one of the most common worries of publishers thinking about selling links on their Web site. This large level of security acts as a comfort to link buyers. By now, it is widely known that purchasing high-quality links can greatly increase your rank in the search engines. However, the search engines may end up filtering an obviously paid link, thus providing zero SEO benefit for your Web site.

Keep in mind that in addition to algorithmic detection of paid links, major search engines including Google allow anyone (your competitors, for example) to report Web sites that buy or sell paid links. Therefore, you must carefully consider the risks and rewards before buying or selling links from any network, including Text Link Brokers.

Sell Links with TextLinkBrokers.com

1. Navigate to www.textlinkbrokers.com.

2. Click Earn Money, Sell Links under the main menu.

3. Scroll down the Sign Up to Sell page and fill in your personal information in the required fields.

4. Click Submit.

⑤ Your Web site will now be reviewed. You will receive an e-mail with detailing your acceptance and next steps for getting started with Text Link Brokers.

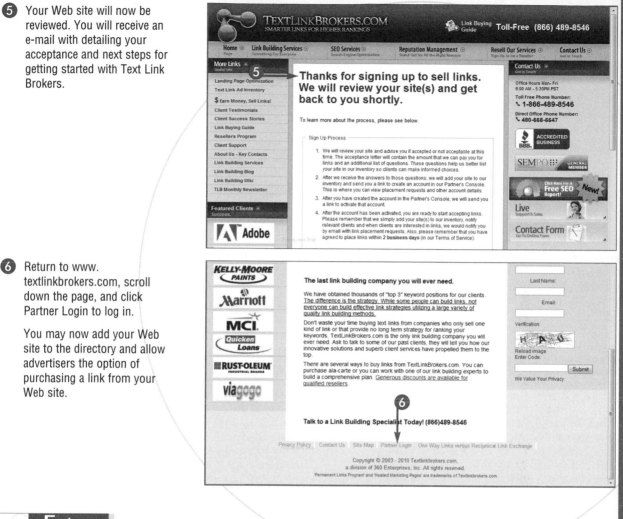

⑥ Return to www. textlinkbrokers.com, scroll down the page, and click Partner Login to log in.

You may now add your Web site to the directory and allow advertisers the option of purchasing a link from your Web site.

Extra

Text Link Brokers currently does not accept any Web site that has a Google PageRank of less than 1. This means that you must wait until your Web site gains a PageRank of 1 or higher before you can even apply to its program to sell text links on your Web pages. This may take some time if your Web site was recently launched, but the wait allows you ample opportunity to grow your Web site content before you monetize it. The earlier chapters of this book provide instruction on how to effectively build Web site content and improve your Web site ranking and reputation.

If your Web site is at least a PR1, there are a few options for monetization with Text Link Brokers. The first is the traditional link inventory. Your site is included in the database and made available to advertisers looking to purchase links.

The second option lies in Text Link Brokers's *hosted marketing pages*. With the Hosted Marketing Pages program, an advertiser pays you, the publisher, to add an additional Web page to your Web site. The additional Web page often contains numerous links that the advertiser specifies. This second method enables you to make far more revenue from your site than just selling links. The fact that hosted marketing pages provide higher-quality links for the advertiser dictates a significantly higher price tag than normal text links.

An Introduction to SEO Plugins

Search-engine optimization (SEO) is often a tedious job and requires you to perform numerous tasks over and over. Fortunately, you can install SEO plugins onto your computer that enable you to save time and more efficiently carry out your SEO efforts.

Browser plugins have become increasingly popular because of the sheer amount of time they save during the search-engine-optimization process. Now, instead of browsing to several different Web sites to research your information, you can view all the data right from one spot in your Web browser. By using SEO plugins, you can quickly access a Web site's PageRank, its age, indexing and backlink information, and even mentions of it in the social media space. Plugins can generate a list of topically

related Web sites that can serve as your gateway to the online community for any given topic.

The SEO plugins commonly used for WordPress have been created out of necessity. The standard installation of WordPress is by far the most popular blogging software; however, it does not support commonly known best practices for on-page search-engine optimization. For this reason, SEO-savvy developers have taken the time to produce powerful plugins that make doing search-engine optimization for your blog far more effective and efficient. From custom title tags to automatic sitemap generation, these plugins are a must for publishers using WordPress to publish content.

Install the Google Toolbar

The Google Toolbar is an add-on for both Microsoft Internet Explorer and Mozilla Firefox. This tool instantly displays the Google PageRank of a Web site, giving you a brief snapshot of Google's opinion of the Web site. The Google Toolbar also highlights any keyword you select whenever it appears on a Web page. This gives you a clear picture of how and where a competitor is using a target keyword or keyword phrase. The Google Toolbar also has a very useful AutoFill feature, which allows you to quickly enter commonly typed strings such as passwords, Web site URLs, e-mail addresses, and more.

Install the Alexa Toolbar

The Alexa Toolbar has been commonly used as the barometer of Web site popularity. The Alexa Toolbar's main function has been to act as a gauge of Web site traffic levels; however, it includes other information that can prove useful. The most important is *related links*, a list of sites that Alexa has grouped together into a community. This grouping is often due to common backlinks being shared across the Web sites. This information is essential when you attempt to break into a community. By making connections with the known Web sites in your market, you stand a far better chance of becoming an authority.

Using the SEO for Firefox Plugin

Aaron Wall has created what has become arguably the most useful and popular SEO plugin to date, SEO for Firefox. This powerful tool displays in one place all the vital technical information you need to assess a Web site's strength. By making use of the search engines and other various application program interfaces, or *APIs*, SEO for Firefox offers a large amount of important data in seconds, saving you from having to go to multiple sources for that same data. This tool can save an immense amount of precious time for any Internet marketer, and is literally a "must have" plugin. This tool lists a Web site's indexing information, backlink information, age, Google PageRank, listings in popular social media sites, as well as listings in large, powerful directories.

Optimize Titles with the WordPress Title Tag Plugin

One of the most important on-page SEO factors is the use of the target keyword in the Web page's title tag. This has proved challenging when running a WordPress blog because the default titles are considerably less than optimal. However, the Title Tag plugin for WordPress solves this problem by allowing you to fully customize the title tag for every page of your WordPress blog. This allows you to write catchy titles for your users and keyword-rich titles for the engines at the same time. Although this process may be time consuming if you already have a large number of pages, it is certainly worth the time and effort in the long run, and goes a long way in aiding your search-engine-optimization efforts.

Optimize Descriptions with the WordPress Description Tag Plugin

Along with Web page title tags, Web page description tags also play a role in the on-page optimization process. Much like the WordPress Title Tag plugin, the WordPress Description Tag plugin allows you to fully customize the meta description tag of each page of your WordPress Web site. This can be used to constantly tweak title tags of Web pages that are already ranking well in an effort to boost organic click-through rates, or *CTRs*. If you already have an immense number of Web pages, you can use this plugin to automatically generate meta description tags for each one. However, you should put the time, thought, and effort into creating your own meta tags if at all possible; see Chapter 3 for more information.

Create Sitemaps with the WordPress Sitemap Generator

Sitemaps are one of the fastest and easiest ways to inform the major search engines about each and every one of your Web site's pages. These powerful files can now be generated automatically by installing the WordPress Sitemap Generator. This generator updates your sitemap every time a new Web page is added to your Web site, and then "pings" the search engines to inform them that you have updated with fresh content. This tool alone can often be enough to complete one of the initial goals of an SEO campaign: getting the search engines to your Web site. By having an accurate and up-to-date sitemap, you help to ensure that all your new content is found and indexed in the major search engines. After all, if your pages are not listed, they can never appear as a search result.

Using the Permalink Redirect Plugin

Long, dynamic URLs are not just unattractive to Web site visitors; they are also more work for the search engines during the crawling and indexing process. The Permalink Redirect plugin addresses this issue by allowing you to create permanent redirects that essentially mask your dynamic URLs, making them appear to be static. These URLs are not only easier for the major search engines to crawl; they are also far easier for your regular Web site visitors to link to from their own Web sites. These new URLs appear static and contain your target keywords, further enhancing your on-page optimization efforts. Effectively using your keywords in your URLs gives you the added bonus of having another section of your Google search result listing highlighted with bold text. If a user performs a Google search using keywords you included in your URL, the keywords appear as bold in the search-engine results pages. This can prove useful by enhancing your click-through rate from the search results page to your Web site.

Install the Google Toolbar

The Google Toolbar is an add-on for both the Microsoft Internet Explorer and Mozilla Firefox Web browsers. The Google Toolbar includes several features that should prove useful during the various stages of SEO. These features include the Google PageRank of a Web page, a tool to highlight a given keyword within a page, and an AutoFill option to cut down on the time spent typing the same information over and over again.

The Google Toolbar displays the Google *PageRank* of any Web site you visit. Google PageRank is a numerical value ranging from 1 to 10 that acts as an indicator of the general importance Google has assigned to the individual Web page. Generally speaking, when you are looking for linking partners, higher PageRank sites are more attractive targets.

The Google Toolbar allows you to highlight any keyword on a Web page. You can insert a keyword into the Google Toolbar to quickly see where and how the keyword is used throughout the Web page. The toolbar highlights the keyword wherever it appears, be it in the headline, subheading, body copy, or internal links.

SEO requires you to perform a number of extremely repetitive and monotonous tasks. These mundane tasks include a range of activities, from signing up for social media accounts to joining affiliate programs. Using the AutoFill feature of the Google Toolbar allows you to substantially shorten the amount of time spent on each of these tasks. AutoFill allows you to enter your information once, and then it automatically fills in the appropriate forms — you do not have to retype the information each time you encounter a new sign-up form.

Install the Google Toolbar

1. Navigate to http://toolbar.google.com.

2. Click Install Google Toolbar.

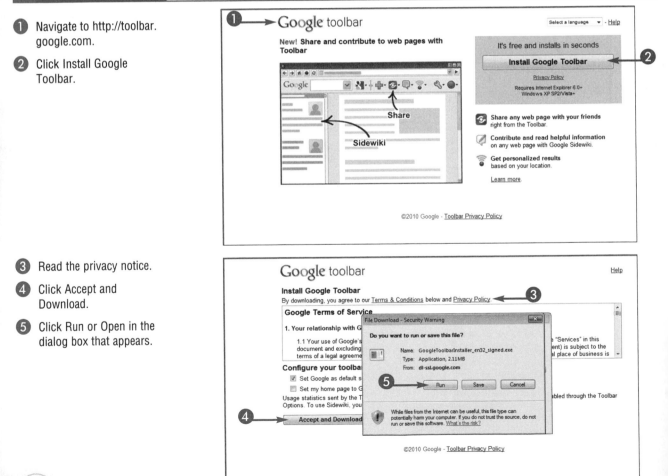

3. Read the privacy notice.

4. Click Accept and Download.

5. Click Run or Open in the dialog box that appears.

6 Follow the prompts to install the Google Toolbar.

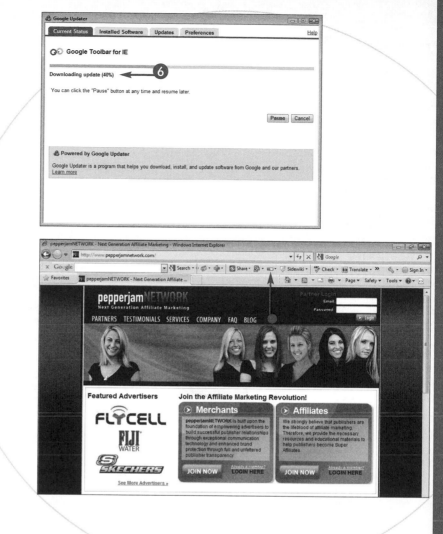

● The Google Toolbar is now installed and displays the Google PageRank of Web sites you visit.

The Google Toolbar offers standard and custom installation options. The custom installation option allows you to add many useful features that do not come as part of the standard installation, including keyword suggestions, comparisons of Google and Yahoo search results, page size lookup, and a view of the code-to-text ratio. These tools are useful shortcuts when you analyze a competitor's Web site, or when you take a step back and review your own work objectively. These tools and many more SEO- and non-SEO-related buttons can be found at http://toolbar.google.com/buttons/gallery.

The Google Toolbar offers an interesting opportunity if you happen to be a Web programmer or developer. For example, you can use a Google application program interface (API) to create your own custom buttons that your users can then add to their Google Toolbar. This is a fantastic way to engage your audience, spread your name, and keep your visitors returning to your site time and again. The work you put into making a custom button can end up paying off considerably, especially given the fact that the Google Toolbar has begun to appear as part of the standard installation of Mozilla Firefox. You can view the developer information for making your own toolbar button at www.google.com/tools/toolbar/buttons/apis.

Install the Alexa Toolbar

The Alexa Toolbar allows you to perform competitive analysis and community research throughout your SEO campaigns. The Alexa Toolbar offers a shortcut to the information that is provided on the www.alexa.com Web site. This information includes an estimate of traffic numbers and patterns, as well as a list of related pages in the same topical community. This information can assist you in spotting seasonal trends, as well as in discovering who is who in a particular industry or niche market.

You can effectively monitor your competitor's Web site and marketing campaigns by carefully evaluating an Alexa traffic graph provided through the Alexa Toolbar. If a Web site shows a spike in traffic, followed by an increased daily average, what happened? Did the Web site get listed on a social media page like www.digg.com? Did the site begin an aggressive PPC campaign? If you want to compete with

other Web sites for top rankings, you need to stay on top of what your competition is doing. You can also use the Alexa Toolbar to help you ask questions about traffic generation strategies that may prove successful for your Web site.

Positioning your site as the authority in your community is important if you want to secure top organic positions. The Alexa Toolbar offers data on *related links*, a list of sites that Alexa has grouped together as being related. Research these related sites and establish relationships with the owners. These relationships are the fast track to picking up valuable citation links. Alexa requires separate downloads of the Alexa Toolbar for Internet Explorer and Firefox browsers. Although the process of installation is the same, you must visit the Alexa Toolbar download page using the specific browser you want to install the toolbar. For example, if you want to install the Alexa Toolbar for Firefox, you must go to www.alexa.com/site/download from your Firefox browser.

Install the Alexa Toolbar

1 Navigate to www.alexa.com/toolbar.

2 Click Install Alexa Toolbar.

3 Review the Alexa Toolbar for Firefox Privacy Policy.

4 Click Accept and Install.

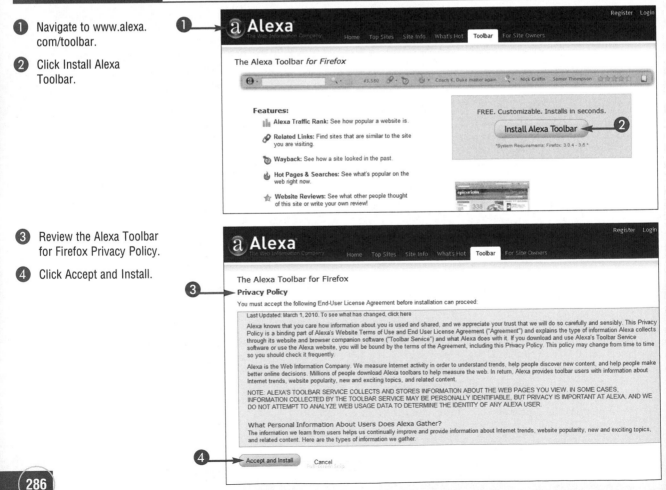

5 Click Install in the window that appears.

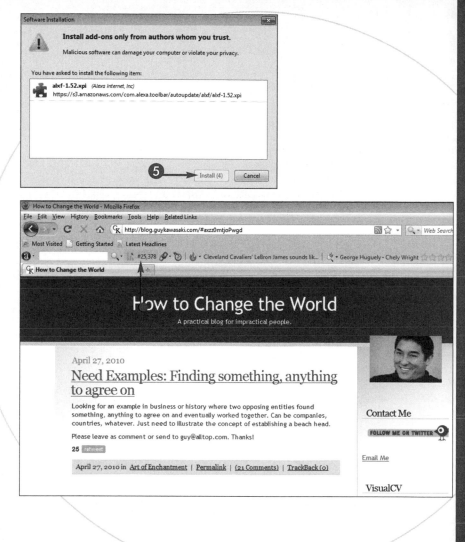

● The Alexa Toolbar is now installed, and displays traffic trends for each Web site that you visit.

Extra

When you install the Alexa Toolbar, you become a member of the Alexa Community. The Web sites you visit are tracked; this tracking helps to increase the relevancy and accuracy of Alexa's data. This information is detached from any personal information regarding your identity and is strictly used for the purpose of accumulating a large sample of data.

With that in mind, Alexa numbers tend to slant in favor of technology or Webmaster-oriented Web sites. Compared to the average Internet user, a larger percentage of technology site readers have the Alexa Toolbar installed, which makes the technology sites look more popular than they actually are. Consider this potential bias when you perform competitive research on Web sites that are technology or Webmaster oriented.

Another competitive research tool that is quickly becoming popular is www.compete.com. Unlike Alexa, Compete. com is not entirely free — you must pay for access to Compete's advanced features. However, Compete.com provides supplemental data to Alexa and is a worthwhile tool to evaluate your competitors' and your own Web site. Using both Alexa and Compete.com allows you to consistently make better decisions regarding your SEO and traffic generation efforts.

Using the SEO for Firefox Plugin

One of the most popular SEO browser extensions is SEO for Firefox, which was created by SEO expert Aaron Wall. SEO for Firefox gathers multiple pieces of marketing data about a Web site and displays that data within your browser alongside the search results from the Google or Yahoo search engine. Because the data is provided to you alongside the actual search results, the SEO for Firefox extension allows you to check the most important statistics of a Web site before you even visit the domain.

Some of the statistics made available by SEO for Firefox for quick view include Google PageRank, Yahoo page and domain links, and number of backlinks. These stats are all valuable pieces of information that, when used together, can give you a clear picture of the relative strength of a Web site.

SEO for Firefox provides a very useful gauge for the number of backlinks a Web page and Web site have, as reported by Yahoo and Bing. The number and topical relevancy of a Web site's backlinks are two of the most critical off-site SEO factors search engines use to determine ranking position in the organic search-engine results. The SEO for Firefox backlinks indicator also provides the number of backlinks that come from a page on an education (.edu) domain, which is usually a primary indicator of the quality of any particular Web site. Links from a page on an .edu domain are generally believed to be more "trusted" because they are more difficult to attain than other domain extensions such as .com or .info.

You can download SEO for Firefox at http://tools. seobook.com/firefox/seo-for-firefox.html.

Using the SEO for Firefox Plugin

1 Navigate to http://tools. seobook.com/firefox/seo-for-firefox.html.

2 Sign up for the SEOBOOK newsletter to receive free tools and gain access to download the SEO for Firefox Plugin.

3 Log into your account and then click the Download Now button.

④ Click Install.

⑤ Click Restart Firefox to restart Firefox and complete the installation.

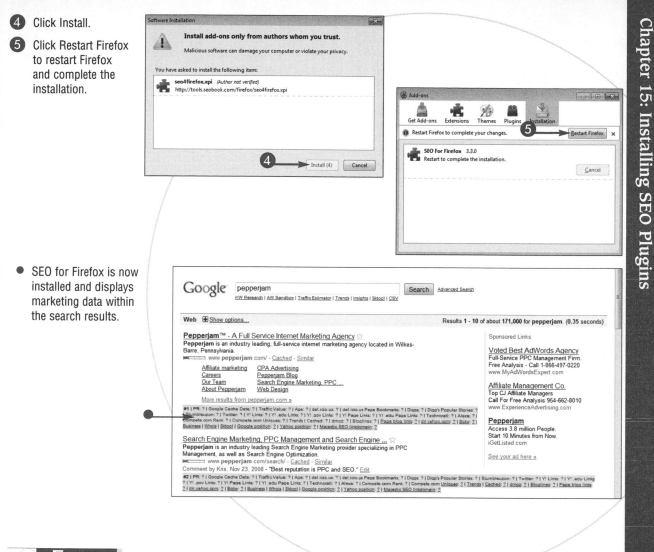

● SEO for Firefox is now installed and displays marketing data within the search results.

Optimize Titles with the WordPress Title Tag Plugin

WordPress has emerged as the most popular blogging content management system available online today. However, the "out of the box" default version of WordPress is limited from an SEO perspective. One of the main faults of the software lies in its handling of the title tags of a page. Given that a Web page's title is one of the more important factors in determining ranking ability, this issue is definitely one that deserves close attention.

The default WordPress setting places the title of the post, or article, as the title tag of the individual post Web page, which is not always ideal. When you write post titles from a copywriting standpoint, you want them to be catchy and draw the reader in. When you create the title tag for a Web page, you want to properly use your target keywords, as well as synonyms and other semantically linked keywords. These two important SEO considerations are often at odds with each other.

The SEO Title Tag plugin solves this problem by allowing you to define a custom title tag for each and every page of your Web site, without making any adjustments to your post titles. Now you can have both a catchy title for your readers and a keyword-rich title for search-engine ranking purposes. This prevents you from having to compromise either aspect of your site and saves you the time it would take to create a title that works fairly well for both. Instead, you can spend your time writing two separate titles that each serves a purpose far better than a hybrid title would.

The SEO Title Tag plugin can be downloaded at www.netconcepts.com/seo-title-tag-plugin.

Optimize Titles with the WordPress Title Tag Plugin

1 Navigate to http://*yourname.com*/wp-admin and log into the administrative section of your WordPress blog.

2 Scroll down the page and under Plugins click Add New.

3 Type **SEO Title Tag 2.3.3** into the search box.

4 Click the Search Plugins button and follow instructions to install SEO Title Tag 2.3.3.

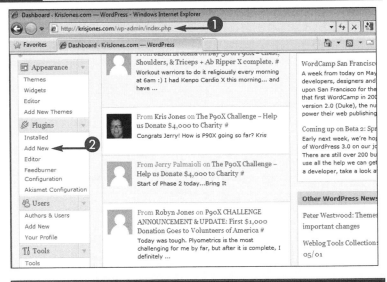

⑤ Activate the plugin within your WordPress admin area from the Plugins page.

⑥ Click Save Changes to save your edits.

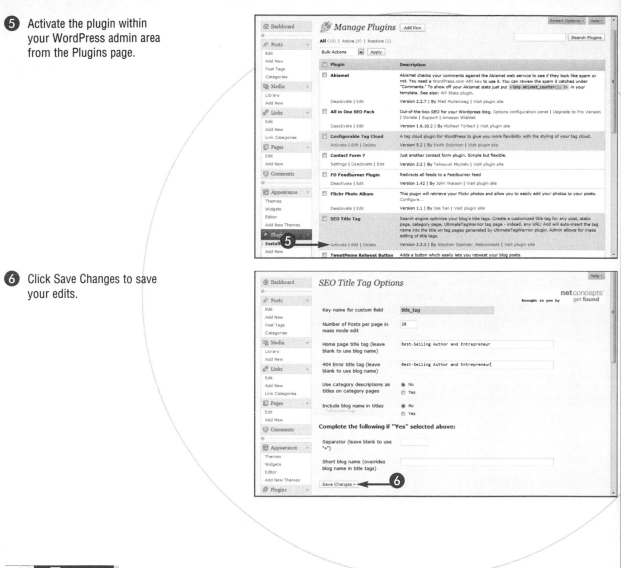

Extra

The SEO Title Tag plugin allows you to set title tags for "secondary" Web pages such as *404 error pages*, or *tag* pages. A 404 error page appears when a visitor tries to access a Web page that does not exist on your site. Of course, you do not want a title that is optimized for ranking your error page, but in this case the plugin would be used to offer a short and concise title instead.

If you decide to use a *tag cloud* on your Web site, each individual tag has its own page. A tag cloud is a visual depiction of user-generated tags. Each Web page lists all the posts that were given that particular tag. The plugin allows you to easily manipulate the title tag for each tag page.

A primary advantage of using the SEO Title Tag plugin is that it allows you to quickly add custom title tags to your Web site's internal search results pages. This can greatly increase the number of Web pages contained in your site, and can prevent a situation from arising where you have several hundred pages indexed with the same exact title.

Optimize Descriptions with the WordPress Description Tag Plugin

The default "out of the box" version of WordPress does not systematically optimize description meta tags. However, WordPress description tag plugins that enable you to easily optimize description meta tags are available. Although keyword and description meta tags are not considered as important as they were in the past, using them is still a good habit to have, and they may eventually be weighed more heavily in the future. Of these tags, the meta description tag has retained the largest value. Often, this tag appears as the short description snippet in the search-engine results for your Web page.

The Add Meta Tags WordPress plugin provides several options for you to optimize your meta tags. The first option is to allow the Add Meta Tags plugin to automatically populate the description tag for you. Although this option automates the description tag, it is not ideal because it

pulls an excerpt of content from the page that may or may not be representative of the page as your description.

If you prefer to have more control, the second option allows you to define a custom description meta tag for every page of your Web site. Although this can be a tedious task if you already have hundreds of pages, it is a rather small addition if you are just starting out and are planning ahead. Adding a custom description to your Web pages should take only a few seconds.

A slightly more advanced use of the Add Meta Tags plugin is to rework the description tags of Web pages that are already ranking well. If the description meta tag is correctly appearing as the two-line description in the search-engine result for your Web page, adjusting the description can have an impact on your click-through rate from that listing. This requires continuous testing, but the testing pays off in the form of more traffic when you find the optimal description.

Optimize Descriptions with the WordPress Description Tag Plugin

① Navigate to http://*yourname*.com/wp-admin and log into the administrative section of your WordPress blog.

② Scroll down the page and under Plugins click Add New.

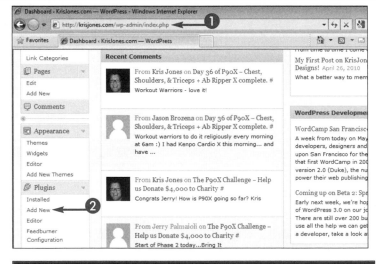

③ Type **add meta tags 1.7** into the search box.

④ Click the Search Plugins button and follow instructions to install Add Meta Tags 1.7.

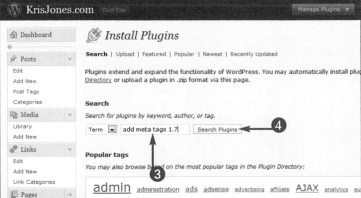

⑤ Activate the plugin within your WordPress admin area from the Plugins page.

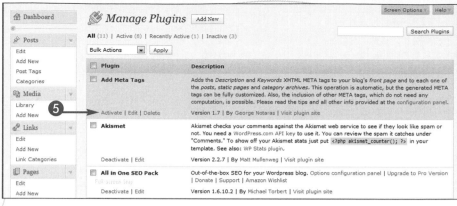

● By default, the plugin uses the post excerpt as the meta description, and the post categories as the meta keywords. No further action is needed to use the default settings.

You can add custom tags to each post or page on the Write Post or Write Page pages.

Your blog meta tags are now optimized.

Create Sitemaps with the WordPress Sitemap Generator

I n 2005, Google introduced the XML sitemap format, and in 2006 it was adopted by Yahoo, Bing, and Ask. This gave publishers a standard format to follow for creating one sitemap that the top search engines could use. You can find specifics about the protocol at www. sitemaps.org.

Because blogs can become very large, a sitemap is often needed to ensure that the major search engines can locate, crawl, and index each individual Web page. However, creating a sitemap by hand every time you make a new blog post gets very boring and redundant. Thankfully, a WordPress plugin called Google (XML) Sitemaps Generator for WordPress takes all the work out of maintaining an up-to-date sitemap.

Once the plugin is correctly installed, your sitemap is automatically rebuilt each time you make a new post. Not only that, the plugin also pings the major search engines to alert them that you have updated your sitemap and added new content. This should bring the search-engine spiders to your site, and then direct them to your newly added Web page or pages.

This plugin makes getting your Web site fully indexed by Google, Yahoo, Bing, and Ask incredibly easy. The more pages you have indexed, the more chances you have of being returned as a search result. This plugin is free, and has consistently been updated to match each update to the WordPress blogging software. However, the developer does accept donations for his time and effort.

Create Sitemaps with the WordPress Sitemap Generator

① Navigate to http://*yourname. com*/wp-admin and log into the administrative section of your WordPress blog.

② Scroll down the page and under Plugins click Add New.

③ Type **XML-Sitemap** into the search box.

④ Click the Search Plugins button and follow instructions to install Google XML-Sitemap.

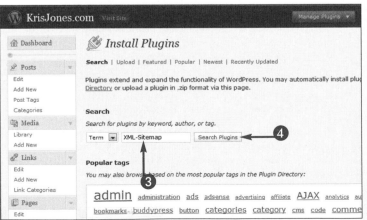

5 Activate the plugin within your WordPress admin area from the Plugins page.

	All in One SEO Pack	Out-of-the-box SEO for your Wordpress blog. Options configuration panel	Upgrade to Pro Version	Donate	Support	Amazon Wishlist
	Deactivate	Edit	Version 1.6.10.2	By Michael Torbert	Visit plugin site
	Configurable Tag Cloud	A tag cloud plugin for WordPress to give you more flexibility with the styling of your tag cloud.
	Activate	Edit	Delete	Version 5.2	By Keith Solomon	Visit plugin site
	Contact Form 7	Just another contact form plugin. Simple but flexible.
	Settings	Deactivate	Edit	Version 2.2	By Takayuki Miyoshi	Visit plugin site
	FD Feedburner Plugin	Redirects all feeds to a Feedburner feed
	Deactivate	Edit	Version 1.42	By John Watson	Visit plugin site
	Flickr Photo Album	This plugin will retrieve your Flickr photos and allow you to easily add your photos to your posts. Configure...
	Deactivate	Edit	Version 1.1	By Joe Tan	Visit plugin site
	Google XML Sitemaps	This plugin will generate a special XML sitemap which will help search engines like Google, Yahoo, Bing and Ask.com to better index your blog.
5	Activate	Edit	Delete	Version 3.2.3	By Arne Brachhold	Visit plugin site
	SEO Title Tag	Search engine optimize your blog's title tags. Create a customized title tag for any post, static page, category page, UltimateTagWarrior tag page - indeed, any URL! And will auto-insert the tag name into the title on tag pages generated by UltimateTagWarrior plugin. Admin allows for mass editing of title tags.
	Activate	Edit	Delete	Version 2.3.3	By Stephan Spencer, Netconcepts	Visit plugin site

6 Click the Click Here link to build your first sitemap. Once built, your sitemap will update automatically each time you write a post.

XML Sitemap Generator for WordPress 3.2.3

The sitemap wasn't generated yet.

6 The sitemap was not built yet. Click here to build it the first time.

If you encounter any problems with the build process you can use the debug function to get more information.

Basic Options

Sitemap files: Learn more
☑ Write a normal XML file (your filename)
☑ Write a gzipped file (your filename + .gz)

Building mode: Learn more
☑ Rebuild sitemap if you change the content of your blog
☐ Enable manual sitemap building via GET Request [?]

Update notification: Learn more
☑ Notify Google about updates of your Blog
No registration required, but you can join the Google Webmaster Tools to check crawling statistics.
☑ Notify Bing (formerly MSN Live Search) about updates of your Blog

Dashboard

Posts
Edit
Add New
Post Tags
Categories

Media
Library
Add New

Links
Edit
Add New
Link Categories

Pages
Edit
Add New

Comments

About this Plugin:
Plugin Homepage
Suggest a Feature
Notify List
Support Forum
Report a Bug
Donate with PayPal
My Amazon Wish List

Sitemap Resources:
Webmaster Tools
Webmaster Blog
Site Explorer
Search Blog
Webmaster Tools
Webmaster Center Blog
Sitemaps Protocol
Official Sitemaps FAQ
My Sitemaps FAQ

Extra

The Google Sitemaps Generator for WordPress provides you an easy way to make sure your WordPress blog includes a Google sitemap. Providing Google with a valid list of all your pages is an incredibly helpful addition to the process of getting your blog fully indexed by Google.

Although certain aspects of search-engine optimization require an attention to detail and interpretation that cannot be done automatically by a script or program, certain tasks can be fully automated. Whenever possible without sacrificing quality, you should make an effort to automate parts of your work. This not only saves you valuable time that could be spent doing more productive work, it also keeps your motivation levels high. Having to perform excessive amounts of mundane grunt work can kill your inspiration to work fairly quickly, so you should automate whenever and wherever you can.

Keep an eye out for updates to the WordPress system. Often, developers of popular extensions and plugins are ahead of the curve, but you do not want to update your copy of WordPress until you know your plugins can handle the switch.

Using the Permalink Redirect Plugin

One of the shortcomings of WordPress from the SEO perspective is the presence of *canonicalization* and *duplicate content* issues. Canonicalization problems (in this sense) refer to the presence of multiple URLs that all return the same Web page. For example

- http://www.example.com
- http://example.com
- http://example.com/
- http://www.example.com/index.html

All the above URLs would commonly refer to the exact same page. However, it is entirely possible for a Web server to return separate files for each request. This is a problem many Webmasters often overlook, but it can be very detrimental to your SEO efforts. If you have 100 links pointing to a Web page, but half the links use the www version, and the other half use the non-www version (example: www.example.com versus example.com), your backlinks are being spread out over two separate URLs, and you are losing out on the weight that each of those links pass to your Web site.

This can also lead to duplicate content issues, or the exact same text appearing on multiple Web pages. If the search engines crawl your site and find the exact same content at six different URLs, which one will they rank for your targeted term? Which version will your visitors link to? There are no certain answers to these questions. Your best bet is to make sure you have all your permalinks and page URLs in order from the beginning to remove any of these issues.

Thankfully these issues with WordPress can be sorted out easily by the addition of the Permalink Redirect plugin. This plugin keeps your link architecture clean and ensures that each page is accessible only through a single URL. It also redirects all variations of a URL to the correct version.

Using the Permalink Redirect Plugin

① Navigate to http://*yourname.com*/wp-admin and log into the administrative section of your WordPress blog.

② Scroll down the page and under Plugins click Add New.

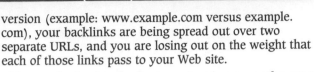
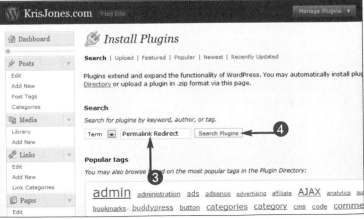

③ Type Permalink Redirect into the search box.

④ Click the Search Plugins button and follow instructions to install Permalink Redirect.

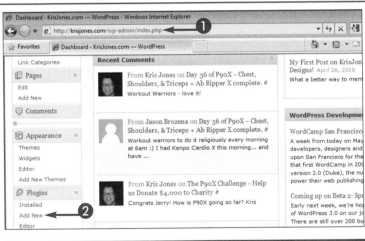

5 Activate the plugin within your WordPress admin area from the Plugins page.

6 When you finish, click Save Changes.

Your redirect settings are saved, and the plugin redirects the specified links.

Extra

Competition for top organic rankings can be fierce. In fact, if you do not ensure that your site is properly protected from these potential canonicalization and duplicate issues, other less-ethical Webmasters may use those flaws against you. By setting up links to the alternate URLs of your content, your competition can potentially create duplicate content problems within your Web site and hinder your ability to rank well on the major search engines.

If you are not using WordPress, visit www.apache.org to learn more about creating your own custom .htaccess file, which can handle your canonicalization issues. By solving your canonicalization issues, you can in effect prevent duplicate content within your own Web site from ever becoming a problem or vulnerability. See Chapter 5 for more about creating an .htaccess file.

Fixes for avoiding duplicate content should ideally be in place before your first piece of content goes online. However, applying these fixes to an existing site, along with a comprehensive sitemap, should be enough to resolve any issues within a few weeks, depending on how often the search engines index your Web site.

INDEX

NUMERICS

C

INDEX

INDEX

INDEX

Read Less–Learn More®

There's a Visual book for every learning level...

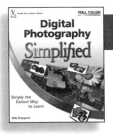

Simplified®

The place to start if you're new to computers. Full color.

- Computers
- Creating Web Pages
- Digital Photography
- Internet
- Mac OS
- Office
- Windows

Teach Yourself VISUALLY™

Get beginning to intermediate-level training in a variety of topics. Full color.

- Access
- Bridge
- Chess
- Computers
- Crocheting
- Digital Photography
- Dog training
- Dreamweaver
- Excel
- Flash
- Golf
- Guitar
- Handspinning
- HTML
- iLife
- iPhoto
- Jewelry Making & Beading
- Knitting
- Mac OS
- Office
- Photoshop
- Photoshop Elements
- Piano
- Poker
- PowerPoint
- Quilting
- Scrapbooking
- Sewing
- Windows
- Wireless Networking
- Word

Top 100 Simplified® Tips & Tricks

Tips and techniques to take your skills beyond the basics. Full color.

- Digital Photography
- eBay
- Excel
- Google
- Internet
- Mac OS
- Office
- Photoshop
- Photoshop Elements
- PowerPoint
- Windows

...all designed for visual learners—just like you!

For more professional instruction in a visual format, try these.

All designed for visual learners—just like you!

Read Less–Learn More®

Visual

Paul McFedries

Excel PivotTables and PivotCharts
2nd Edition

Your visual blueprint™ for creating dynamic spreadsheets

978-0-470-59161-1

Ric Shreves

Ubuntu Linux Desktop

- Get visual instruction on installing and setting up Ubuntu
- See how to use all the powerful, free applications

Your visual blueprint™ to using the Linux operating system

978-0-470-34520-7

Richard Wentk

iPhone OS Development

Companion Web site
Includes sample Xcode projects

Your visual blueprint™ for developing apps for Apple's mobile devices

978-0-470-55651-1

For a complete listing of *Visual Blueprint*™ titles and other Visual books, go to wiley.com/go/visual

Visual

An Imprint of ⊕WILEY

Now you know.